OPERATION MARKET GARDEN.
THE CAMPAIGN FOR THE LOW COUNTRIES,
AUTUMN 1944: SEVENTY YEARS ON

Operation Market Garden

The Campaign for the Low Countries, Autumn 1944:
Seventy Years On

Wolverhampton Military Studies No.20

Edited by John Buckley & Peter Preston-Hough

 Helion & Company Limited

Helion & Company Limited
Unit 8 Amherst Business Centre
Budbrooke Road
Warwick
CV34 5WE
England
Tel. 01926 499 619
Fax 0121 711 4075
Email: info@helion.co.uk
Website: www.helion.co.uk
Twitter: @helionbooks
Visit our blog http://blog.helion.co.uk/

Published by Helion & Company 2018
Designed and typeset by Mach 3 Solutions Ltd (www.mach3solutions.co.uk)
Cover designed by Paul Hewitt, Battlefield Design (www.battlefield-design.co.uk)
Printed by Lightning Source Limited, Milton Keynes, Buckinghamshire

Text © John Buckley, Peter Preston-Hough and contributors 2016
Illustrations © as individually credited
Maps © as individually credited

ISBN 978-1-912390-46-5

British Library Cataloguing-in-Publication Data.
A catalogue record for this book is available from the British Library.

For details of other military history titles published by Helion & Company Limited contact the above address, or visit our website: http://www.helion.co.uk.

We always welcome receiving book proposals from prospective authors.

Contents

List of Illustrations

List of Maps

Notes on Contributors

John Buckley is Professor of Military History in the Department of History, Politics and War Studies at the University of Wolverhampton, UK, and specialises in the Second World War and the interwar era. He is the author of a number of books including *Air Power in the Age of Total War* (1999), *British Armour in the Normandy Campaign 1944* (2004) and *Monty's Men: The British Army and the Liberation of Europe 1944-5* (2013).

Lt. Col. (Retired) Roger Cirillo is the Director of Operational Studies and Book Program Director, for the Association of the United States Army's Institute of Land Warfare. A veteran of twenty three years active service as a commissioned officer in the US Army, he served in armored cavalry assignments in the United States, Korea, and Germany. In addition to staff assignments both at NATO and as the Special Assistant to the Commander-in-Chief, US Army, Europe, he was a military historian, instructor, and combat operations analyst at both the Army's Command and General Staff College and the Center of Military History. He holds a PhD in Military History from Cranfield University, at the Royal Military College of Science, Shrivenham, England. He is currently writing a two volume study on the Allied High Command during the Liberation of Europe in 1944-1945.

Stephen C. Craig is a retired US Army Medical Officer. He taught Military Medicine and Medical History at the Uniformed Services University of the Health Sciences, Bethesda, Maryland from 2004-2015. His published a variety of technical and historical medical papers. His biography of US Army Surgeon General George M. Sternberg, *In the Interest of Truth*, was published in 2014 and *"Some System of the Nature Here Proposed": Joseph Lovell's Remarks on the Sick Report, Northern Department, US Army, 1817 and the Rise of the Modern US Army Medical Department* was released in 2015. Currently, Dr. Craig is pursuing a Ph.D. in Medical History at the University of Glasgow.

Jack Didden was born 1952, the Netherlands, has an MA in English Language and Literature and a PhD in military history. Jack Didden has published sixteen books so far, most of them in Dutch including the standard text about the fighting in the south of the Netherlands between 6 September and 9 November 1944, 'Brabant Bevrijd'. The only three publications in the English language are 'Colin' (1994), a booklet about the 51st Highland Division's part in Operation Pheasant, 'Highlanders in the Low Countries', an article in the After the Battle magazine, issue 120, about the same subject and 'Autumn Gale'(2013) a bulky book about Kampfgruppe Chill and the Allied autumn campaign between 6 September and 9 November 1944. He is currently preparing a book about Kampfgruppe Walther (11 September–13 October 1944).

Matthew Douglass has a Master of Arts degree from the University of New Brunswick with the Milton F. Gregg Centre for the Study of War and Society. He has participated on First and Second World War battlefield tours to Sicily, France, Belgium and Holland with the Gregg Centre as well as the Canadian Battlefields Foundation. He is currently expanding his MA Thesis into a manuscript concerning the New Brunswick Rangers during the Second World War with the New Brunswick Military Heritage Project Series.

Dr John Greenacre spent twenty four years in the British Army as a logistician, reconnaissance helicopter pilot and staff officer before retiring in 2011. He deployed on operations to Iraq and Kuwait, Bosnia and Northern Ireland and also worked in Germany, the Falkland Islands, Canada and Kenya.

In 2009 John graduated from the University of Leeds with a PhD in History with his thesis, 'The Capability Development of British Airborne Forces during the Second World War'. His book on the same subject, 'Churchill's Spearhead', was published in 2010 to coincide with the 70th anniversary of the formation of British Airborne Forces. He has also contributed to several edited publications on the subject of airborne forces during the Second World War. His latest book, 'Ever Glorious' covering the exploits of the Crookenden brothers during the Second World War is due to be published in June 2016.

Russell Hart is a Professor of History and Director of the Diplomacy and Military Studies program at Hawai'i Pacific University in Honolulu, Hawai'i. He is the author of *Clash of Arms: How the Allies Lost in Normandy* (2001) and *Guderian: Panzer Pioneer or Mythmaker?* (2006) and co-author of *The Second World War: A World in Flames* (2004) as well as six additional co-authored works.

Stephen Hart MA FRHistS, is Senior Lecturer with Special Responsibilities in the Department of War Studies at The Royal Military Academy Sandhurst. Prior to Sandhurst, he lectured in the Department of War Studies, King's College London, and in the International Studies Department at the University of Surrey. He has written a number of books and articles on the British and German Armies during the Second World War, including: *Montgomery and "Colossal Cracks": The 21st Army Group in Northwest Europe, 1944-45*, Praeger, 2000, Stackpole, 2007; *The Road to Falaise* (Battle Zone Normandy Series No.13) Stroud, Sutton, 2004; "The Black Day Unrealised: Operation TOTALIZE and the Problems of Translating Tactical Success into a Decisive Breakout" in John Buckley (Ed.), *The Normandy Campaign 1944: Sixty Years On*, Abingdon, Routledge, 2006, 104–117; and "Indoctrinated Nazi Teenaged Warriors: The Fanaticism of the 12th SS Panzer Division *Hitlerjugend* in Normandy, 1944", in M. Hughes and G. Johnson (eds), *Fanaticism and Conflict in the Modern Age*, Manchester University Press, 2004, 81–100. He is currently co-working on a monograph on the defeat of the German Army in North-western Germany during spring 1945.

Dr Tim Jenkins has worked extensively in the field of historic aircraft preservation and restoration and has a primary research interest in the history of science and technology relating to aviation. Tim is a heritage professional with experience of large scale capital conservation and restoration projects in the museums sector. Tim graduated with a Ph.D in History from University of Birmingham and currently holds Visiting Professorship in History & Archaeology at the University of Chester.

Dr Paul Latawski is a Senior Lecturer in the War Studies Department, Royal Military Academy Sandhurst. Before coming to RMAS he lectured at the School of Slavonic and East European Studies (SSEES), University of London where he was also an Honorary Visiting Fellow. He was also an Associate Fellow at the Royal United Services Institute for Defence Studies (RUSI), London. Since 2012 he is a Senior Research Fellow in Modern War Studies with the Humanities Research Institute, University of Buckingham. He completed his Ph.D. at Indiana University USA specialising in Central and Eastern Europe with particular emphasis on modern Poland. His current research interests include: the Second World War with particular reference to the Normandy and Italian campaigns, the Polish Armed Forces in the West, Polish resistance to occupation 1939-45, urban operations, problems of coalition command, post 1945 British contingency operations and the history of British Army doctrine. He is currently writing a history of 1st Polish Armoured Division operations in Normandy.

Nigel de Lee read History, War Studies and International Relations at Leeds, King's London and Cambridge. He taught War Studies at RMA Sandhurst 1973-2001, War and Security Studies at Hull 2004-2007, and is currently teaching Strategy and Military History in the Krigsskolen – the Norwegian Military Academy. He worked 1982-2002 as freelance for Imperial War Museum Sound Archive. He has also held temporary posts at Staff College, US Naval Academy, Annapolis, and the Dutch Military Academy, Breda. He has served as a guide on staff rides and battlefield tours for academic and military clients.

Doug McCabe is Curator of Manuscripts, Mahn Center for Archives and Special Collections, Alden Library, Ohio University, Athens OH 45701 USA. mccabe@ohio.edu

Philip (Phil) McCarty is a PhD student at the University of Wolverhampton, under the supervision of Professor John Buckley. His PhD research is on the British Army of 1940 and the careers of a group of officers after the Battles of France and Norway. A graduate of the University of Manchester and King's College London (MA War Studies, 1984), he worked firstly as a researcher at the Royal United Services Institute and then, from 1986-2012 as an intelligence analyst for the Ministry of Defence. He has been a member of the Council of the Society of Friends of the National Army Museum since 2004, where is the Society's book review editor. He is also a member of the British Commission for Military History, the Army Records Society and the Society for Army Historical Research. Outside military history he is a long-term member of the British Film Institute. He lives in London and the New Forest.

Dr Linda Parker is an independent scholar and author who enjoys attending conferences and writing books, articles and papers. Her main writing and research interests are the military, religious and social history of the twentieth century, but she is also very interested in the history of the Polar Regions. She is a member of the Royal Historical Society and the Western Front Association.

Dr John Peaty FRGS FRHistS holds a PhD and MA in War Studies from King's College London. He is a Fellow of the Royal Historical Society and of the Royal Geographical Society. He is the International Secretary of the British Commission for Military History, the Chair of the Templer Committee of the Society for Army Historical Research, a Founder Member of the Royal Air Force Historical Society, a Life Member of the Institute of Historical Research, a member of the Royal United Services Institute and the Convenor of the Historical Military Mapping Group of the British Cartographic Society. He has published and lectured widely on military history. He is an inveterate battlefield tourer. He works for the Ministry of Defence, where he was formerly with the Army Historical Branch.

Dr Peter Preston-Hough was a visiting lecturer at the University of Wolverhampton and University of Chester. His areas of interest included the Royal Air Force; the Strategic Air Offensive 1940-1945; 617 Squadron in the Second World War; the Air Superiority Campaign in the Far East 1939-1945; airborne warfare and airborne operations, particularly in Normandy and during Operation MARKET GARDEN 1944. He was a member of the British Commission for Military History. Dr Preston-Hough's book, *Commanding Far Eastern Skies*, was published by Helion in May 2015. Sadly Peter died in early 2017.

Sebastian Ritchie is an official historian at the Air Historical Branch (RAF) of the Ministry of Defence. He has a PhD from King's College, London, and he lectured for three years at the University of Manchester before joining the AHB. He is the author of numerous official narratives covering RAF operations in Iraq and the former Yugoslavia, and he has also lectured and published widely on aspects of air power and air operations, as well as airborne operations and special operations in the Second World War. In 2011 he published *Arnhem: Myth and Reality – Airborne Warfare, Air Power and the Failure of Operation Market Garden*.

James Slaughter III holds degrees from West Virginia University, Marshall University, Norwich University, and he is currently a PhD student at the University of Wolverhampton, where is writing his dissertation: *The French Air Force in 1940: A National Failure*. His recent publications include "Military Communication on the Western Front 1914-1918: Similar Experiences, Different Outcomes." In *Information History of the First World War*, and entries in the *Mount Vernon Digital Encyclopaedia*. His interests include military doctrinal development in the interwar period 1919-1939, military theory, and militaries in transition. He works as an analyst for a defense contractor and resides in rural Virginia with his wife Stacy, and his son Logan.

The Wolverhampton Military Studies Series
Series Editor's Preface

As series editor, it is my great pleasure to introduce the *Wolverhampton Military Studies Series* to you. Our intention is that in this series of books you will find military history that is new and innovative, and academically rigorous with a strong basis in fact and in analytical research, but also is the kind of military history that is for all readers, whatever their particular interests, or their level of interest in the subject. To paraphrase an old aphorism: a military history book is not less important just because it is popular, and it is not more scholarly just because it is dull. With every one of our publications we want to bring you the kind of military history that you will want to read simply because it is a good and well-written book, as well as bringing new light, new perspectives, and new factual evidence to its subject.

In devising the *Wolverhampton Military Studies Series*, we gave much thought to the series title: this is a *military* series. We take the view that history is everything except the things that have not happened yet, and even then a good book about the military aspects of the future would find its way into this series. We are not bound to any particular time period or cut-off date. Writing military history often divides quite sharply into eras, from the modern through the early modern to the mediaeval and ancient; and into regions or continents, with a division between western military history and the military history of other countries and cultures being particularly marked. Inevitably, we have had to start somewhere, and the first books of the series deal with British military topics and events of the twentieth century and later nineteenth century. But this series is open to any book that challenges received and accepted ideas about any aspect of military history, and does so in a way that encourages its readers to enjoy the discovery.

In the same way, this series is not limited to being about wars, or about grand strategy, or wider defence matters, or the sociology of armed forces as institutions, or civilian society and culture at war. None of these are specifically excluded, and in some cases they play an important part in the books that comprise our series. But there are already many books in existence, some of them of the highest scholarly standards, which cater to these particular approaches. The main theme of the *Wolverhampton Military Studies Series* is the military aspects of wars, the preparation for wars or their prevention, and their aftermath. This includes some books whose main theme is the technical details of how armed forces have worked, some books on wars and battles, and some books that re-examine the evidence about the existing stories, to show in a different light what everyone thought they already knew and understood.

As series editor, together with my fellow editorial board members, and our publisher Duncan Rogers of Helion, I have found that we have known immediately and almost by instinct the kind of books that fit within this series. They are very much the kind of well-written and challenging books that my students at the University of Wolverhampton would want to read. They are books which enhance knowledge, and offer new perspectives. Also, they are books for anyone with an interest in military history and events, from expert scholars to occasional readers. One of the great benefits of the study of military history is that it includes a large and often committed section of the wider population, who want to read the best military history that they can find; our aim for this series is to provide it.

Stephen Badsey
University of Wolverhampton

Introduction

John Buckley and Peter Preston-Hough

On 17 September 1944 a vast Allied army of airborne troops began landing in southern Netherlands as part of Operation MARKET GARDEN, perhaps the most iconic and dynamic action of its type in history. The attempt by the Allies to lay a carpet of airborne troops across which ground forces of 21st Army Group would thrust over the Rhine and into Germany itself was the brainchild of Field Marshal Bernard Montgomery. For Monty the plan represented an opportunity to deliver the decisive knockout blow to an already reeling Third Reich, and conceivably force a surrender in 1944; for his boss, General Dwight Eisenhower, it offered a real chance of at least getting an Allied bridgehead across the Rhine preparatory to further decisive operations in the autumn.

Yet, just over a week later 1st British Airborne Division had been withdrawn back across the Rhine having suffered crippling losses in the fighting in and around Arnhem, the thrust to link up with them by Second British Army had sputtered to a halt just north of Nijmegen, and the fleeting chance of a victory in 1944 (if it had ever really existed) had been snuffed out. MARKET GARDEN had ended in humiliating failure, far removed from Monty's subsequent and spurious '90% successful' claim.

The consequences of the failure were to prove calamitous both for Allied strategy and for the civilians of the Netherlands. Montgomery's 21st Army Group, and indeed Eisenhower, had gambled on MARKET GARDEN at the expense of focusing on the early opening up the port of Antwerp; the port had been captured intact on 3 September thanks to a lightning quick advance by British troops and the forceful actions of Belgian resistance fighters. But the north bank of the River Scheldt that linked Antwerp to the sea still remained in enemy hands and would continue to be so for many weeks afterwards causing the largest port in Northwest Europe to remain idle until late November. By committing the bulk of 21st Army Group's efforts to MARKET GARDEN and then being forced to defend the corridor created by the abortive thrust to Arnhem, Montgomery was unable to allocate sufficient resources to supporting First Canadian Army's battles in the Walcheren and Beveland campaign that autumn. It was also true, however, that he did not believe it completely necessary to do so until early October. Consequently, the Allies' immense logistical headaches remained for much of the September-November period, with crucial supplies still having to be drawn from Normandy.

The repercussions for the Dutch civilians left outside of Allied held territory in the aftermath of MARKET GARDEN were profound. Those in Arnhem were forced from their homes by the Germans with nothing in the way of provisions, as the remains of the previously sleepy and well-to-do town were firstly looted and then turned into a defensive bastion; Arnhem was to remain in German hands until April 1945. Elsewhere in the Netherlands in retaliation for the efforts of the Dutch underground forces in support of MARKET GARDEN, the German occupiers subjected the civilian population to the privations of the so-called hunger winter.

Operation MARKET GARDEN was undoubtedly therefore a crucial and important aspect of the campaign to liberate Western Europe in 1944-5, whilst subsequently defining the campaign in the Low Countries and Northern France well into 1945. But it was not the only element of the campaign. Indeed, the meeting between Monty and Ike in Brussels on 10 September at which MARKET GARDEN was given the green light, was primarily intended by Montgomery to be a general discussion about Allied strategy in the West, or lack thereof as Monty saw it. Monty wanted to drive Allied efforts in the direction he desired – what became known as the 'single-thrust' strategy – and aimed to force Eisenhower to back him by means of a hectoring lecture. Ike rebuked him but the seeds of their deteriorating relationship were already in place, and in the following months Eisenhower would twice come perilously close to asking the Combined Chiefs of Staff to back him or Monty, a confrontation that would only have resulted in Montgomery's sacking. Blocked by Eisenhower's refusal to bow to his grand strategic vision on 10 September, Monty then produced the MARKET GARDEN plan which Ike enthusiastically backed, a responsibility from which he never shirked, even though it was clearly Monty's concept. Eisenhower though was still agitated about opening up Antwerp and simultaneously maintaining the advance where possible of Patton's Third US Army in the central sector of the western front. The other senior commanders outside of 21st Army Group at SHAEF and 12th US Army Group also saw MARKET GARDEN as just one element of the campaign, even if a startlingly ambitious move on the part of the usually cautious Montgomery. MARKET GARDEN therefore, as far as Eisenhower and indeed Montgomery were concerned, was not the only game in town, though it is now perceived as such.

The emergence of the iconic nature of MARKET GARDEN and its domination of the history of the entire campaign in the west between D-Day and the Battle of the Bulge, and maybe even beyond right to the end of the war, therefore came later. In Britain the film *Theirs is the Glory* (1946) did a good deal for raising awareness of the Battle of Arnhem, but it was the publication of Cornelius Ryan's best seller *A Bridge Too Far* in 1974 and even more the release of the Hollywood blockbuster film of the same name three years later that firmly established the place of MARKET GARDEN at the heart of the history of the 1944-5 campaign to the detriment of many other more brutal and bloody battles fought by the Allies and Germans in the autumn and winter of 1944-5.

The film in particular has forged many myths and misconceptions about the campaign, as well as about a number of the personalities involved, most obviously

Lieutenant General Frederick 'Boy' Browning, and although there have been many, many books about MARKET GARDEN, or more often in the United Kingdom just Arnhem, in the years since, the influence of Ryan's bestseller remains strong, and offers us an insight into how populist military history both works and shapes our understanding of key events. When examining Ryan's research materials and correspondence for *A Bridge Too Far* it is evident who the primary players were in shaping Ryan's interpretation – Jim Gavin was in constant touch with Ryan throughout the process, Lewis Brereton to a degree, and Brian Horrocks and Allan Adair hardly at all, whilst there was no contact with Miles Dempsey (who died in 1969 but research for the book had begun two years before) or Viscount Montgomery himself. Equally tellingly, as Sebastian Ritchie has pointed out, no senior air force officers were interviewed. Consequently, in correspondence a few months before his death in 1974, Ryan noted that the British and the Allied air forces did not come out of his book well, whilst US 82nd Airborne Division generally did. When Richard Attenborough and William Goldman came to frame the perspective of their film shortly after Ryan's death, they added a further layer of questionable interpretation, the near character assassination of Browning (who had died even before the book had been researched and written) being the most obvious example, a representation not nearly so substantially supported by the book.

One of the most pervasive elements of the film and indeed the book has been the idea that intelligence about German armour and the II SS Panzer Corps was deliberately distorted and withheld in the days leading up to beginning of the operation. The key piece of testimony was that of Major Brian Urquhart, whose interview for *A Bridge Too Far* in the late 1960s greatly animated Ryan who thought he had found his 'smoking gun'. In truth Urquhart never stated quite as clearly as Ryan later wrote that the flow of events was as depicted in the book and more obviously still in the film. Other interviews carried out with British intelligence officers seemed to contradict Urquhart's assessment (though they were either not so prominent in the book or not included at all) and Urquhart himself later wrote in much less specific terms about the timing and nature of his concerns of September 1944. Yet, the image of a conscientious intelligence officer trying to make an arrogant and condescending Browning rethink MARKET GARDEN is one of the most enduring aspects of the film and has probably done more than anything else to shape the popular view of the crucial factors in the final failure of the operation.

The emphasis on the vital role of the SS in defeating the Allies during MARKET GARDEN, which therefore underscores still further the pivotal nature of Browning's egregious decision to 'ignore' the intelligence about their presence in and around Arnhem, is also one that is now firmly established in much of the literature. Yet, the majority of the Axis troops who thwarted the Allies, particularly in the first few vital hours of MARKET GARDEN, and paid a heavy price for so doing, were scratch forces, not the elite troops of the SS. Their efforts in the Anglophone world have gone rather unacknowledged. Many other elements of the operation have also been overshadowed by the focus on certain key actions, particularly in Nijmegen and Arnhem, whilst the wider campaign in the Low Countries has been virtually obscured by the MARKET GARDEN action.

After the passage of seventy years, and with a number of new interpretations and perspectives having now emerged on the above issues and indeed many other aspects both on MARKET GARDEN and the campaign in the Low Countries in the autumn of 1944 more generally, it seemed an ideal time to re-evaluate this iconic part of the war, this infamous operation and the wider campaign to liberate Western Europe in the autumn of 1944.

Thus, we decided to bring together many leading historians, interested parties and indeed veterans, to look again at the campaign in a conference held by the Centre for Historical Research at the University of Wolverhampton in September 2014. This collection represents many of the papers delivered and indeed some that could not be due to particular circumstances, and covers this period of the war from many different perspectives and angles. Though the central focus is undoubtedly MARKET GARDEN, we have consciously attempted to place the operation into the wider context of the war at the time and thus a number of chapters examine key issues and elements of the campaign beyond though broadly tangential to the attempt to reach over the Rhine in September 1944. The collection is not intended to offer an exhaustive account of the fighting, but to offer deeper insights into particular areas of the battle and the campaign that will prompt us to re-evaluate and reinterpret MARKET GARDEN, which after some seven decades and forty years since *A Bridge Too Far* is perhaps overdue.

1

Learning to Lose?
Airborne Lessons and the Failure of Operation Market Garden

Sebastian Ritchie

On 10 September 1944, the commander of 21st Army Group, Field Marshal Bernard Montgomery, convened a meeting at his tactical headquarters in Belgium to finalise Second (British) Army's plans to cross the River Rhine, the last major natural barrier protecting the western frontier of Hitler's Germany. In attendance was the Second Army Commander, Lieutenant General Sir Miles Dempsey, and the Deputy Commander of First Allied Airborne Army, Lieutenant General Frederick 'Boy' Browning. Operation Comet, envisaging a crossing via the Neder Rhine Bridge at Arnhem by XXX Corps with the support of the British First Airborne Division and the Polish Parachute Brigade, had been halted the previous day because of intelligence suggesting that German forces in the Arnhem and Nijmegen area were being significantly strengthened. On this basis, Dempsey believed there was a strong case for redirecting the operation against a more southerly Rhine crossing point – Wesel.

Nevertheless, Montgomery continued to favour the northern axis of advance, and received crucial support from the British Chiefs of Staff in the form of a signal urging him to strike north to cut the supply lines bringing V2 missiles from Germany to their launch sites along the Dutch coast. And so Arnhem was retained as the objective. To deal with the enlarged German presence in the area, the airborne component within the plan was expanded by a further two divisions, the American 101st and 82nd Airborne Divisions.[1] Within hours, the Supreme Allied Commander, General Dwight D. Eisenhower, had approved the plan. Such was the genesis of Operation Market Garden.

There are many differing assessments of the decision to launch Market Garden; praised as a bold gamble in some quarters, the operation has been dismissed as

---

1   The National Archives TNA: WO 285/9: Dempsey diary, 9 and 10 September 1944; Nigel Hamilton, *Monty: The Battles of Field Marshal Bernard Montgomery* (London: Hodder & Staughton, 1981), p. 438.

reckless folly in others. Much depends on the criteria employed. But there is one potential basis of assessment that has not yet received much attention from historians. By the summer of 1944, the airborne medium was no longer the novelty it had been when Germany invaded France and the Low Countries; the Allies had staged several landings in the European and North African theatres. How far, then, did the Arnhem plan exploit this past experience? It is curious that this elementary issue should have been ignored for so long, given the scale of the literature on Market Garden and the fact that the earlier operations gave rise to numerous lessons documents, after-action reports and doctrine papers.

Yet the question is surely worth asking, for the lessons process is a key component within the broader field of information exploitation, which is fundamental to the success of all military undertakings.[2] Indeed, it has long been accepted that learning is vital not only to avoid past mistakes, but also to increase the likelihood that success will be repeated. This is why military organisations attach so much importance to the operational recording and reporting functions. This study will therefore seek to identify the principal lessons drawn from the development of airborne warfare between 1942 and 1944, and assess the extent to which they influenced the Market Garden plan. Additionally, to provide a further valuable insight into the more prominent themes, the exploitation of airborne lessons between Market Garden and Operation Varsity, in March 1945, will be considered.

While the end result is primarily an essay in military history, the issues addressed here might well offer some food for thought to the modern defence community. There is, to this day, an awareness that the military lessons process does not always function as it should. Significant efforts are consistently assigned to lessons gathering, but the mere identification of a lesson does not always mean that it will subsequently be exploited. Moreover, there is a marked variation in this regard at the different levels of warfare; broadly speaking, it appears easier to exploit tactical lessons than operational ones.[3] The following analysis primarily focuses on the operational level, with the aim of providing at least some insight into why this should be so.

Early in the Second World War, the Germans led the way in the development of the airborne medium. The Allied airborne forces were created in response at very short notice, and in great haste. At every level, the task was rendered all the more difficult by a near-total lack of experience, expertise and doctrine. The Allies sought to study and learn from German experience, but their new airborne forces were ultimately designed for a very different purpose. They were created to support the opening

---

2   Eliot Cohen and John Gooch, *Military Misfortunes: The Anatomy of Failure in War* (New York: Free Press, 2006), pp. 26, 233.

3   For an interesting recent discussion of this problem, see Joel Lawton, 'How the Limited Use of Lessons Learned Failed to Form a Cohesive Strategy in Operation Enduring Freedom', *Small Wars Journal*, 10: 1 (November 2014), http://smallwarsjournal.com/jrnl/art/how-the-limited-use-of-lessons-learned-failed-to-form-a-cohesive-strategy-in-operation-endu (accessed 22 June 2015).

of the Second Front – effectively, to facilitate amphibious landings. The basic principle was spelled out by the Chief of the Imperial General Staff in 1942:

> We are all agreed that for the defeat of Germany it will sooner or later be necessary for our armies to invade the Continent. To do this we shall first be confronted with the attack of strongly defended beaches. The employment of the Airborne Division in the rear may offer the only means of obtaining a footing on these beaches.[4]

This approach had direct tactical implications. British amphibious doctrine was based on the principle of surprise, with landing forces being moved under cover of darkness and put ashore just after daybreak. If airborne troops were to support dawn amphibious landings, they would have to be infiltrated some hours earlier, to give them sufficient time for assembly and deployment. In short, they would have to land during the night. This was in stark contrast to German doctrine, which had ruled out night airborne operations at an early stage.[5]

From this, it will be noted that Market Garden did not align with the original Allied airborne concept. It was launched after the amphibious phase of Operation Overlord and in broad daylight; effectively, it was an operation that emerged out of a search for a very different type of airborne mission. And yet this was not, in fact, a new situation. The Allies had been confronted by a similar scenario at the end of 1942, albeit on a far smaller scale. In Operation Torch, in Tunisia, airborne troops had been employed at the time of the initial landings, and the Allies had then been compelled to find alternative uses for them. The result was a series of short-notice battalion-scale deployments in support of the ground offensive, in a forward reconnaissance role, targeting airfields like Bone and Youks les Bains.

As these missions were mounted almost without warning, they were preceded by only minimal planning and preparation, with all the risks that this entailed. Fortunately, for the first three, this was of little consequence as they were unopposed.[6] The fourth mission, targeting enemy airfields at Depienne and Oudna, went catastrophically wrong, the battalion concerned suffering very heavy casualties during a protracted fighting withdrawal across 50 miles of desert. That battalion was none

4   Air Historical Branch (AHB): Air Publication (AP) 3231 (1951), *The Second World War 1939-1945, Royal Air Force, Airborne Forces*, p. 48.
5   Systematic experiments in night jumping did not even begin in Germany until 1942; see AHB: US Foreign Military Studies publication MS P-051 (1950), *Airborne Operations: A German Appraisal*, p. 86.
6   John Warren, *Airborne Missions in the Mediterranean 1942-1945* (United States Air Force Historical Division Research Studies Institute, Air University, 1955), pp. 5-13.

other than 2 PARA, under its new commanding officer, Lieutenant-Colonel John Frost.[7]

The post-operation lessons process was not, at this stage, especially searching. However, the subsequent reports correctly identified the key issue, which was the lack of integrated command and control – the absence of airborne and air transport expertise and input at higher command levels. From this had stemmed a number of planning errors, the worst being the cancellation of the ground offensive that was supposed to link up with 2 PARA after they had dropped at Depienne. Problems had also resulted directly from the launch of consecutive missions at very short notice. Adequate mapping and intelligence briefing material had rarely been made available; at Depienne, many 2 PARA troops had been so poorly prepared that they did not even know where they were going to drop. The other subject that received close attention in the post-operation reports was the airlift, but it was difficult at this stage to draw meaningful conclusions due to the prevailing lack of experience and doctrine.[8]

These four issues – command and control, the link-up with ground forces, the need for sufficient lead time and the airlift – would become recurring airborne learning themes throughout the Second World War, and had already surfaced in German airborne lessons documents, based on their experiences in the Low Countries and Crete. There was, however, one important difference between the Allied and German perspectives at this stage. After sustaining very heavy losses in the assault on Crete, the Germans had acquired a far greater respect for their adversaries and were more prepared to accept that airborne planners must factor the enemy into their calculations realistically.[9] Ultimately, to employ modern military parlance, the enemy has a vote. By contrast, despite 2 PARA's misfortunes, the Allies were as yet less inclined to moderate their confidence in the notion of airborne invincibility. Browning complained that a great opportunity had been missed to use airborne troops in an assault on Tunis, acting 'in a semi-independent role', although, in all probability, the result would have been another costly failure.[10]

It was one thing to identify lessons; it would prove far more difficult to ensure that they were exploited. In their next operation – Operation Husky, in Sicily in July 1943 – the Allies reverted to concept and employed airborne troops to support a dawn amphibious landing; subsequent lifts were also scheduled at night because of the perceived threat posed by enemy air defences in daylight. The airborne missions

7   For a first-hand account, see Major-General John Frost, *A Drop Too Many* (London: Cassell, 1980), pp. 74-100.
8   Frost, *A Drop Too Many*, pp. 74-100, 103; AHB: War Office official monograph (1951) Lieutenant-Colonel TBH Otway, *Airborne Forces*, pp. 78-82.
9   Sebastian Ritchie, 'Learning the Hard Way: A Comparative Perspective on Airborne Operations in the Second World War,' *Air Power Review*, 14:3 (Autumn/Winter 2011), pp. 13-16.
10   TNA, WO 106/2707: Report on Visit to North Africa, 19-30 December 1942, by Major General F.A.M. Browning, 7 January 1943.

were enlarged to brigade scale, the operation was planned as a set-piece affair, and it involved the first large-scale use of assault gliders.

From an airborne perspective, Husky went disastrously wrong because the Allies completely failed to grasp the difficulties involved in mounting night airlifts at brigade scale, at long range, with an extended approach over water, in live operational conditions. Only a small minority of airborne personnel were delivered accurately to their objectives; the landings were otherwise widely dispersed, and many gliders came down in the sea.[11] The operation was followed by the most extensive and rigorous airborne lessons exercise of the Second World War, involving the British and the Americans, separately and jointly, and also the different armed services and the government departments responsible for them – the War Office and Air Ministry in the British case. Prominent issues again included command and control, on broadly the same grounds as in North Africa, and the need for more planning and preparation time. The critical importance of the link-up between airborne and ground forces was also stressed, and it was acknowledged that, when the airborne had prevailed, they had faced only limited opposition. Future operations in the Northern European theatre were likely to be confronted by far stronger enemy forces. But the major focus, predictably, was the air, and the key lesson identified was the need for better air preparation and, especially, aircrew training.[12]

It is easy to see why the Allies reached this conclusion but, ultimately, it was the wrong lesson. The fundamental problem was only partly related to the standard of aircrew. More important was the basic Allied airborne concept itself. In truth, there was not an air force in the world that could have executed the Husky lifts successfully in the summer of 1943, which is not so very different from saying that, judged by the standards of the time, they were impossible. Mission success would have required a level of aircrew proficiency far beyond anything that could be reconciled with the parallel requirement to deliver the airborne forces en masse. Given the prevailing time and resource constraints, and the fact that aircrew took far longer to train than airborne soldiers, greater mass was always likely to translate into a lower average aircrew training standard, and hence difficulties executing anything more than a simple lift plan.

11   AHB: 38 Wing RAF Report on Training and Operations in North Africa and Sicily, May/July 1943; AP 3231, *Airborne Forces*, p. 90; Otway, *Airborne Forces*, pp. 120-127. See also Warren, *Airborne Missions in the Mediterranean*, pp. 33-52; Maurice Tugwell, *Airborne to Battle: A History of Airborne Warfare* (London: William Kimber, 1971), pp. 164-166.

12   AHB: Notes on the Planning and Preparation of the Allied Expeditionary Air Force for the Invasion of North West France in June 1944, Appendices, Joint War Office/Air Ministry Report on the Employment of Airborne Forces; U.S. War Department Training Circular 113, 9 October 1943; un-numbered SHAEF memorandum dated 19 January 1944; Combined Chiefs of Staff Paper 496. See also AHB: US Army Air Forces Board Project (T) 27, Long Range Study of Airborne Operations, 29 April 1944.

The real lesson of Husky was that the airlift plan must be matched to the average ability of the aircrew available. Indeed, in many ways, this was the critical path in any airborne operation, and the fundamental basis of success or failure. Yet any such conclusion would have been at odds with the elementary Allied concept of using the airborne in support of amphibious operations – something that was always likely to involve complex night lift plans that had to be moulded and shaped around the seaborne mission. To complicate matters further, Allied planning was based on a further rapid expansion of the airborne forces, which was virtually certain to be accompanied by more dilution of aircrew training standards. Without any change of concept or a reduction in the rate of airborne expansion, there would always be a very strong chance that the difficulties experienced during Husky would be replicated in subsequent airlifts.

The post-Husky lessons exercises had an important impact on planning and preparation for Normandy in 1944, which they were, in large part, designed to assist. There were significant improvements in the area of command and control, air and airborne forces securing considerably more influence within the planning process, and there were sustained efforts to raise the standard of aircrew training, especially in the key area of night navigation.[13]

But the basic Allied failure to identify the cause of the Husky airlift debacle ensured that, in many respects, the Sicilian experience was repeated. The elementary point at issue was exposed with absolute clarity by a dispute that erupted over the American glider landings, which had to be made in the close *bocage* country inland from Utah Beach. The American troop carrier commander, Major-General Paul Williams, protested that his aircrew could not land in this area in darkness. Montgomery's response was that they should be *ordered* to land there, as if a simple order would be enough to enable safe and accurate glider landings in terrain that was obviously unsuitable for the purpose.[14] Nothing could better illustrate the ignorance of airborne matters that persisted at senior Allied command levels, even at this relatively late stage of the war.

The preparations for Normandy witnessed an almost continuous tension between the goal of mass delivery and the need to execute what would again be an extremely difficult airlift. Where mass was concerned, the Allies now moved in just a few months from brigade to divisional scales, with all that this implied in terms of expanding the airlift available and, of course, the throughput of qualified aircrew. The Americans raised the required number of aircrew but only by fielding many undertrained and inexperienced personnel on D-Day, and basing their night air navigation on the follow-my-leader principle; in other words, only the formation leader was actually

13   Ritchie, 'Learning the Hard Way,' pp. 21-22.
14   AHB: Notes on the Planning and Preparation of the Allied Expeditionary Air Force for the Invasion of North West France in June 1944, Appendices, Appendix V/46, Minutes of a Meeting between the Air C-in-C and C-in-C 21st Army Group, 28 May 1944.

proficient in night navigation.[15] The British similarly achieved sufficient lift for two brigades, but this was by allocating one drop to 46 Group, RAF, which had only recently formed and was far less experienced than 38 Group. Despite this, it was 46 Group that ended up with the more difficult delivery task to the north of the British airborne lodgement area.[16]

In the British sector, around Ranville, the landings were very successful. Nevertheless, on the ground, assembly in darkness was a drawn out process, and most units went into action substantially under strength.[17] But the lifts to the more outlying British drop zones and virtually all the American zones were inaccurate and widely dispersed, with all that this implied in terms of reduced force cohesion and combat power for the airborne divisions. In this context, the impact of enemy intervention was all the more serious, many airborne tactical missions were not completed and airborne mission success came to depend heavily on the speed of reinforcement from the beaches, and on artillery support from the beach landing forces. The areas brought under airborne control were far smaller than originally planned.[18] The perception of airborne mission fulfilment in Normandy is largely founded on the broader success of the amphibious landing operation, and on the most high-profile tactical actions, such as the Pegasus Bridge coup de main.

The airborne landings in Normandy were not followed by lessons studies comparable in depth to those undertaken after Husky, and some of the main reports did not appear until the end of the campaign. However, the inquest on the airlift began almost immediately after D-Day. The Americans were hugely frustrated by the failure of their lift and their senior troop carrier commanders now became convinced that future operations should, if at all possible, be mounted in daylight.[19] This conclusion was underpinned by the successful British lift on the evening of D-Day, Operation Mallard, which achieved an unprecedented level of accuracy.[20] By contrast, the RAF was not prepared to abandon night operations entirely, believing that they might still be possible with sufficient training and navigational aids.[21] The American view was unquestionably the more realistic, given the operational context and continuing pressure to increase troop carrier and glider capacity still further.

In other respects, however, there was more unanimity where lessons identification was concerned. Both the British and American airborne agreed on the immense value

---

15   John Warren, *Airborne Operations in World War II, European Theatre* (United States Air Force Historical Division Research Studies Institute, Air University, 1956), pp. 7-9, 20, 23, 24.

16   AHB: AP 3231, *Airborne Forces*, p. 108.

17   AHB: AP 3231, *Airborne Forces*, pp. 129, 132; Otway, *Airborne Forces*, pp. 178-179.

18   AHB: AP 3231, *Airborne Forces*, pp. 125-128; Warren, *Airborne Operations*, pp. 39, 42, 47-48, 52, 57-58, 61-69.

19   Warren, *Airborne Operations*, p. 61.

20   AHB: AP 3231, *Airborne* Forces, p. 134.

21   AHB: Otway, *Airborne Forces*, p. 199.

of the preparations that had, over several months, preceded the operation. They also now acknowledged that, in the Northwest European theatre, it would be necessary for airborne plans to take far more account of the potential enemy reaction, and they accepted that their fortunes in Normandy had been heavily dependent on rapid reinforcement from the beaches. 6 Airborne Division noted that ammunition expenditure for airborne mortars and artillery had far exceeded rates that could be sustained by air and stressed the importance of the most intimate collaboration between airborne and ground forces to secure effective artillery support and other capabilities that the airborne lacked.[22] 101st Airborne echoed these sentiments.

> The airborne troops must receive prompt support from formed ground units. In Operation NEPTUNE, the 101st Airborne Division could not have maintained itself much over 24 hours without support … The timely arrival of the 4th Division relieved the airborne troops of concern for their front to the North and East and allowed the elements to reform around Hiesville. The previous conception that an Airborne Division can maintain itself independently for two or three days should be revised downward for action in FORTRESS EUROPE.[23]

Reviewing airborne lessons at the operational level in the aftermath of the Normandy landings, the following major themes may be identified: first, the need for sufficient notice, for planning and preparation; second, the importance of integrated command and control, from the beginning of the planning process; third, the necessity for prompt relief by conventional ground forces; fourth, the requirement for a realistic assessment of the likely enemy response. Then, finally, there was the airlift, something that had so far proved exceptionally difficult to match with the Allies' basic airborne operational concept.

But now, once again, that concept was to change. With the amphibious phase of Overlord complete, the Allies were confronted by the situation they had faced after Torch in 1942. They now envisaged a ground offensive extending from Normandy to Germany, with a succession of short-notice airborne missions being mounted in support. Potentially, Allied ground forces might be blocked by a river line, or some other defensive position. Vertical envelopment could then be exploited to unhinge the enemy defences, allowing the advance to resume. 21st Army Group cited a possible requirement for approximately five airborne divisional operations between D-Day and D+90 and, after D+90, four divisional operations every sixty days.[24]

---

22   AHB: 6th Airborne Division Report on Operations in Normandy, 6 June – 27 August 1944, Conclusions.

23   AHB: Notes on the Planning and Preparation of the Allied Expeditionary Air Force for the Invasion of North West France in June 1944, by PS to Air C-in-C, AEAF, p. 316.

24   AHB: AP 3231, *Airborne Forces*, p. 146.

Such an approach, viewed in the context of past airborne lessons, raises one imme-diate question. Since those early operations in North Africa, almost every post-oper-ation and lessons report had noted the importance of allowing sufficient lead time before airborne missions were launched. How, then, could this assessment have been so readily revised in the summer of 1944? The surviving records offer no clear answer, but the Allies were very soon to be reminded of the difficulties inherent in short-notice planning.

June, July and August witnessed successive proposals for employing the airborne, but no operation materialised. As time passed, pressure grew to find a use for the newly created First Allied Airborne Army, and proposals for their employment became increasingly divorced from reality. During the first ten days of September, five possible missions were under consideration at different times. Two of these, Linnet 1 and 2 were quite pointless airborne job creation schemes,[25] and the third, Comet, was an exceptionally high-risk venture that envisaged accomplishing the Market Garden mission with just one airborne division – 1st Airborne.[26] The fourth envisaged an airborne assault on Walcheren Island, a location not reached by Allied ground forces until the beginning of November.[27] It is to be suspected that any airborne troops landed there in the interim might have found themselves at something of a disadvantage.

The fifth proposal was for Market Garden itself, combining XXX Corps' advance across Holland to Arnhem with an airborne assault of unprecedented scale, first considered on the morning of 10 September and approved by Eisenhower only hours later, for launch within a period of just five days, subsequently extended to seven.[28] The consequences, in terms of planning and preparation, were many and varied and were, overwhelmingly, adverse. Most obviously, there was no opportunity to evaluate and test the plan via close scrutiny of its component parts, and Market Garden was unique among the larger Allied airborne operations in that it was not preceded by any rehearsals or exercises.[29] Less well known, perhaps, is the fact that the commanding general of First Allied Airborne Army, Lewis Brereton, felt strongly that no operation so far east should be attempted from UK air bases; he believed his forces should first deploy to the continent.[30] On this point, he was undoubtedly correct, but there was no opportunity to implement his recommendations before Market Garden was mounted.

That Market Garden could have been authorised despite his misgivings illus-trates how a second recurring airborne lesson was also ignored in September 1944. The importance of integrated command and control had, as we have seen, featured

---

25   Warren, *Airborne Operations*, p. 27.
26   Major-General R.É. Urquhart, *Arnhem* (London: Pan, 1958), pp. 28-29.
27   TNA: WO 205/197: Brereton to Montgomery, 9 September 1944.
28   TNA: WO 285/9: Dempsey diary, 10 September 1944; WO 219/4998: Operation Sixteen Outline Plan, 10 September 1944; Hamilton, *Monty*, p. 451.
29   Warren, *Airborne Operations*, p. 99.
30   TNA: WO 219/2186: Brereton to Eisenhower, 1 September 1944; WO 219/2121: memorandum by SHAEF planning staff, 4 September 1944.

in lessons reports after North Africa and Sicily, and pronounced efforts had been made to improve airborne command processes before Normandy. And yet, Market Garden must rank as one of the very worst Second World War examples of planning in isolation. Airborne Headquarters was kept in the dark until Browning – the *deputy* airborne commander – returned to England from Belgium, announced that Montgomery was intending to mount the operation, and then added that the Supreme Commander had already approved it.[31]

Market Garden required the lift of 35,000 troops and colossal quantities of equipment over a distance of around 300 miles, 100 of which were in enemy-occupied territory still protected by a functional integrated air defence system. The concept was critically dependent on employing the airlift plan devised two weeks earlier for Operation Linnet,[32] but Linnet's objectives had been closer to the UK, further from Germany, and in an area from which German air defences had largely been withdrawn. Nevertheless, before Market Garden was submitted to Eisenhower, there was no prior consultation with the Allied air forces concerning either the general outline of the plan or the specific issue of whether, in fact, it would be possible to recycle the Linnet airlift. Equally, although Market Garden was no less dependent on two American airborne divisions, 82nd and 101st, they were not consulted either. It was merely assumed that they would happily embrace the tasks assigned to them. Subsequently, at the very first planning meeting called to discuss the operation, Browning's concept began to fall apart. Nothing could illustrate more clearly the importance of bringing all the key stakeholders into the planning process at the earliest possible stage. It was Williams, of 9th Troop Carrier Command, who pointed out that the Linnet airlift plan could not be used in the manner that Browning was suggesting. The Linnet plan had been based on double-towing the American gliders, but the additional range to the Market Garden objectives meant that there was no alternative to the conventional one glider per tug configuration. In short, the American glider deployment rate would now be halved.[33]

Worse was to follow within hours, when Williams' staff rejected the entire Linnet timetable due to the increased range, reduced hours of daylight, anticipated turn-around problems between lifts and concerns about the weather.[34] Consequently, whereas the first two Linnet lifts would theoretically have been completed within about 12 hours, the first two Market Garden lifts were scheduled over a period of about 20 hours, weather permitting. Moreover, due to the absence of double tow,

---

31   AHB: Report by First Allied Airborne Army, *Operations in Holland, September–November* 1944, p. 9; Hamilton, *Monty*, p. 451.
32   TNA: WO 219/4998: Operation Sixteen Outline Plan, 10 September 1944.
33   For the initial briefing and subsequent discussion, see TNA: WO 219/4998: minutes of a meeting called by Commanding General, First Allied Airborne Army, 10 September 1944.
34   TNA: WO 219/4998: memorandum by Lieutenant Colonel Thomas Bartley, 10 September 1944.

these two lifts would bring in far fewer gliders for the American divisions; the third Market lift had now to deliver nearly half of the American glider force.[35] Then, to add insult to injury, the commander of 101st Airborne flatly rejected the tasking assigned to his division. This was not unreasonable, as it envisaged their dispersal across a 30-mile area served by seven separate landing zones. Brereton fully supported his objections, leaving no alternative but to change the plan.[36] The revised tasking concentrated 101st Airborne within a more limited area, but cancelled a proposed landing south of Eindhoven, where a very small German force halted XXX Corps' advance for much of the day on 18 September.[37]

The third lesson, concerning the link-up between the airborne and ground forces, was not very much more influential, in spite of the emphasis attached to this issue by the British and American airborne in Normandy, only months before. They had based their conclusions on landings that were only a few miles from the Normandy beaches, but 1st Airborne Division would be deployed 64 miles behind the front line; for 82nd Airborne, the distance would be 50 miles; both divisional areas lay close to the German frontier. Relief would depend on XXX Corps' ability to advance rapidly up a single, narrow, road that would have been very vulnerable to blocking action even if it had not been intersected by multiple waterways as well as the Eindhoven and Nijmegen conurbations. This axis of advance had, in fact, been specifically rejected by 21st Army Group planners at the beginning of September because of the number of water obstacles involved.[38] Potentially, if 101st or 82nd Airborne failed to capture just one of these barriers, the British advance might be halted, leaving 1st Airborne Division in a desperately isolated and exposed position on the far side of the Neder Rhine. Effectively, the all-important link-up required the Americans to deliver absolute tactical mission success – an aspiration that lay far beyond anything they had previously achieved.

Then, finally, there is the question of the German response. The Arnhem operation, from its original inception under the auspices of Operation Comet, was a particularly high-risk venture. Indeed, Comet not only incorporated Market Garden's multiplicity of interlinked and interdependent features and its challenging axis of advance; it also relied too heavily upon a single airborne division, dispersed over a huge area, and it did not provide for any airborne support to capture the more southerly bridges in the proposed battle area. XXX Corps' capacity to seize successive crossings between the Albert Canal and Grave was simply taken for granted. It was a plan that could only have succeeded against weak and disorganised opposition. However, it soon became

35   Warren, *Airborne Operations*, pp. 89, 226; TNA: Air 37/509: No 11 Group Operation Instruction No. 39/1944, 2 September 1944.
36   TNA: WO 219/4997: memorandum by Brereton, 11 September 1944.
37   Warren, *Airborne Operations*, p. 89; Karel Margry (ed), *Market Garden Then and Now* (London: Battle of Britain International, 2002), p. 254; TNA: WO 171/1256: War Diary, 2nd Irish Guards (Armoured Battalion), 18 September 1944.
38   Hamilton, *Monty*, p. 429.

clear that German forces in Holland were being strengthened, and specific intelligence was received that *II SS Panzer Corps* (*9* and *10 SS Panzer Division*) had been sent to the Arnhem-Nijmegen area to rest and refit.[39] It was, primarily, in response to this unwelcome news that Comet was enlarged into Market Garden. Hence the Allied plan certainly did not ignore the German threat.

And yet the proposed solution was, in fact, based on two assumptions that proved to be unsound. One problem, as we have already seen, was that the enlarged airlift could not be completed as rapidly as Browning initially expected; the other lay in the interpretation of the intelligence. While ULTRA and other sources confirmed that *II SS Panzer Corps* had been sent to the Arnhem area, little was known of their operational readiness beyond their need to 'rest and refit'. The enemy battle state had therefore to be assessed by Montgomery's intelligence staff, which was headed up by Brigadier Edgar 'Bill' Williams. Williams was an Oxford history Don, who had entered the Army through the reserves in 1939. He was in no sense a professional intelligence officer, and his apparently senior rank was entirely nominal. He did not even hold an intelligence post until 1942. He was doubtless a very clever and gifted analyst, but we may legitimately question whether he was the right man to lead what was, by that time, a large multi-division intelligence organisation.[40]

The assessment, as both he and Montgomery subsequently admitted, was a substantial underestimate.[41] Moreover, although Williams later claimed to have opposed the launch of Market Garden, his documented analysis always appears to play down the threat posed by *2 SS Panzer Corps*. A 21st Army Group intelligence summary dated 12 September noted that '9 SS and 10 SS were last identified in the great retreat on First US Army Front. There cannot be much left of them.'[42] Even after *9 SS Panzer* was actually encountered in the Market Garden corridor on 17 September, Williams insisted that 'the division cannot be in a very formidable state.'[43]

Furthermore, Williams' staff, along with their counterparts in Second Army and XXX Corps Intelligence, actually reported something of an improvement in the situation at Arnhem after Market Garden was approved. First Allied Airborne Army's intelligence chief was told that previously identified threats had miraculously receded and the only German reinforcements to have appeared in the Low Countries 'had been put in to thicken up the line' they were attempting to form on the Albert Canal. There was 'no direct evidence that the area Arnhem-Nijmegen is manned by much

39   TNA: DEFE 3/221: Signal XL 9188, 5 September 1944.
40   *Daily Telegraph* obituary, June 1995, http://oldedwardians.org.uk/obits/etwilliams.html (accessed 22 January 2015).
41   Field Marshal the Viscount Montgomery of Alamein, *Memoirs* (London: Collins, 1958), p. 297; Richard Lamb, *Montgomery in Europe 1943-45: Success or Failure?* (London: Buchan & Enright, 1983), p. 225.
42   TNA: WO 171/133: 21st Army Group intelligence summary 159, 12 September 1944.
43   TNA: WO 171/133: 21st Army Group intelligence summary 160, 18 September 1944.

more than the considerable flak defences already known to exist.[44] This assessment was duly passed on to the airborne divisions. 1st Airborne Division's head of intelligence wrote on 14 September, 'a more optimistic estimate can be made of enemy forces actually in the Divisional area.'

> The main factor, on which all sources agree, is that every able-bodied man in uniform who can be armed is in the battle – the Germans are desperately short of men and it is improbable that any formations capable of fighting will be found in an L[ine] of C[ommunication] area, however important it may be ... Identifications in the Albert Canal area satisfactorily prove that practically all the enemy troops which could have been in Northern Holland are now actually engaged.[45]

The British intelligence staffs were also caught off-guard by the Germans' ability to muster, at minimal notice, additional ad hoc battle groups and other formations – albeit with lower-grade troops – to counter-attack the airborne around the Rhine crossings.[46] Interviewed many years later, Williams remained blissfully unaware of their role in the Allied defeat, which he (and many others) blamed entirely on *II SS Panzer Corps*.[47]

At the operational level, therefore, the Market Garden story raises important questions about the Allies' capacity to exploit past experience. And yet, after Browning's initial briefing to First Allied Airborne Army on 10 September, one component within the tactical plan would ironically be shaped almost entirely by past lessons, and this was the air plan. For the Allied air forces now did their utmost to ensure that past lessons were observed, their focus being on the areas that had proved so problematic in the past – accuracy and safety. All other issues were deemed to be of lesser importance.

To achieve this goal, it was essential, first and foremost, to match the airlift task to the capabilities of the available aircrew. It is true that moon conditions would have prevented a night lift at the time Market Garden was launched, but it is most unlikely that the USAAF would have accepted anything other than a daytime lift under any circumstances. Given the depth of the operation and the overflight of enemy-occupied territory, the daylight transit might well have been very vulnerable to enemy

---

44 TNA: AIR 37/1217: Information from Northern Group of Armies, Second Army and XXX Corps, as at 1100 hrs, 12 September 1944, by Lieutenant Colonel A. Tasker, G-2, FAAA, 12 September 1944.

45 TNA: AIR 37/1217: Operation Market, 1st Airborne Division Planning Intelligence Summary No. 2 dated 14 September 1944, prepared by G2 (I), 1st Airborne Division, 14 September 1944.

46 Robert Kershaw, *It Never Snows in September: The German View of Market-Garden and The Battle of Arnhem, September 1944* (Hersham: Ian Allen, 2004), pp. 108-112, 119-120.

47 Lamb, *Montgomery in Europe*, p. 225.

interference, but this problem was addressed via large-scale fighter escort and patrol-ling operations, deliberate flak suppression, and evasive routing – steering the troop carrier and glider streams around known flak concentrations and major routes along which mobile flak might have been deployed. Drop zone and landing zone selection was based on a small number of large, easily visible areas, where gliders could land safely en masse; the lifts were also timed to exploit the best visibility conditions, and two separate air routes were identified to provide greater tactical flexibility.[48]

Since the Second World War, historians have consistently argued that the air plan was deeply flawed.[49] And yet the results represented a spectacular advance over past operations. Casualties in transit were kept to the minimum and the landings effected on 17 and 18 September were the most accurate and concentrated divisional-scale airborne insertions of World War Two. The contrast with Normandy and Sicily could not have been more pronounced, but the Allied achievement also improved signifi-cantly on anything previously accomplished by the Luftwaffe.[50]

The accuracy of the lift and the fact that it was executed in daylight allowed the airborne troops to unload, assemble and deploy at nearly full strength in a fraction of the time taken in Normandy.[51] This, in turn, gave them a far better chance of fulfilling their tactical objectives; the proportion of airborne tactical missions completed during Market Garden substantially exceeded the proportion fulfilled in the earlier opera-tion.[52] Moreover, this tasking was largely executed by the airborne alone – unsupported – whereas many airborne missions in Normandy would not have been accomplished without the support of the beach landing forces, as we have seen. The Allies only came close to victory in Operation Market Garden because the airlift was so successful.

It should have been possible, on the basis of Market Garden and of earlier experi-ence, to ensure that the final airborne operation launched in the European theatre, Varsity, was a resounding success. After Arnhem, there was another major airborne lessons collection exercise and, once again, senior planners sought to ensure that this paid dividends. Far more time was allowed for planning, command and control was

---

48   Warren, *Airborne Operations*, pp. 89-93; TNA: WO 219/4998: memorandum by
     Lieutenant Colonel Thomas Bartley, 10 September 1944.
49   William Buckingham, *Arnhem 1944* (Stroud: Tempus, 2004), p. 231; Martin Middlebrook,
     Arnhem 1944: The Airborne Battle, 17–26 September (London: Penguin, 1995), p. 443.
50   For the most comprehensive account of the airlifts, covering the whole operation, see
     Warren, *Airborne Operations*, Chapter 4.
51   Warren, *Airborne Operations*, pp. 102, 112-114.
52   Out of the multiplicity of crossings, only the bridges at Son and Nijmegen were not
     secured. By contrast, the British airborne lodgment area in Normandy was far smaller
     than originally planned. Of the various American missions, only one of the four causeways
     from Utah Beach was captured outright by 101st Airborne and they also failed to establish
     a firm northern perimeter line linking with 82nd Airborne, or to seal off southern flank
     of the Utah beachhead. Similarly, 82nd Airborne failed to establish adequate protection
     on their northern flank and were unable to capture the La Fière, Chef-du-Pont and Pont
     l'Abbé bridges.

more effectively integrated, and no risks were taken with the link-up between ground and airborne forces. Second Army were to cross the Rhine before the airborne landings began, only a few miles to the east.[53]

And yet, measured by the standard set in Market Garden, the relatively low-risk Varsity airlift was by no means an unqualified triumph, the British glider landings being particularly problematic. This was because the tactical requirements of both Second Army and the airborne forces were given priority over the basic air delivery task. Effectively, the cart was placed before the horse. To that extent, there was a failure both to identify and exploit one of the key lessons bequeathed by the Arnhem venture.

There were two important planning failures. The first was the failure to co-ordinate 2nd Army's Rhine crossing plan with the all-important airlift. Covering the crossing was possibly the largest smoke screen ever generated, maintained for more than a week over a 50-mile front. And yet, incredibly, no one identified this as a potential hazard from the air perspective. The airborne DZs and LZs lay well within the area that would be covered by the smoke screen during the river crossing, and there was no scientific basis for predicting how rapidly the smoke would disperse.[54]

To this mistake was added another – the employment of a so-called tactical glider landing scheme, whereby gliders would land in small groups immediately adjacent to the objectives of the troops on board, rather than using the large, concentrated landing patterns employed in Market Garden.[55] This would have been hard enough for the glider pilots who landed so successfully in the British sector in Normandy, and at Arnhem. But so many of those pilots had been lost during Market Garden that it had been necessary to rebuild the Glider Pilot Regiment at short notice using RAF personnel transferred from the aircrew reserve pool. They received only the most limited training before Varsity was launched.[56]

The tactical landing scheme was the brainchild of the Glider Pilot Regiment commander, Brigadier George Chatterton, himself a highly experienced pilot.[57] He should easily have understood the limitations of the new aircrew under his command and tailored the landing plan accordingly, matching aircrew competence and aircrew task by employing that most elementary of planning principles – *keep it simple*. Instead, in a misguided attempt to demonstrate the assault glider's tactical flexibility, he needlessly complicated an already difficult task.

And so, on 24 March 1945, around 400 British gliders cast off just beyond the Rhine, after a largely successful transit from East Anglia. They then descended into Second Army's smoke screen, the effects of which were magnified by the ongoing

53 AHB: 38 Group RAF Report on Operation 'Varsity', 20 May 1945, para 110; Warren, *Airborne Operations*, p. 161.
54 Warren, *Airborne Operations*, p. 174.
55 AHB: 38 Group RAF Report on Operation 'Varsity', 20 May 1945, para 24-26.
56 AHB: AP 3231, *Airborne Forces*, p. 185.
57 AHB: Otway, *Airborne Forces*, p. 301.

battle on the ground, and began to circle, haplessly seeking their assigned tactical landing areas in conditions of minimal visibility, and in the face of a formidable barrage of German flak. The tactical plan disintegrated almost immediately, and the landings were spread over a large area. Many gliders were damaged or destroyed, or came under fire as soon as they touched down.[58] The casualty rate sustained by 6 Air Landing Brigade in Operation Varsity totalled approximately 40 per cent, most of the losses being incurred during the landing phase;[59] the 2nd Oxfordshire and Buckinghamshire Light Infantry lost half their strength in a period of about twenty minutes.[60] Huge quantities of glider-born stores and equipment were either permanently written off or could not be deployed in battle on Varsity's first day.[61]

The after-action reports clearly sought to play down the extent of the British glider debacle, and this post-operation whitewash continues to influence historical perspectives in a very misleading sense. The sanitised version of the airlift story is employed to support the argument that the Arnhem air plan failed: in Varsity, it is implied, all the mistakes of Arnhem were rectified, and this was a major factor in the operation's success. The selection of landing areas close to the airborne objectives is typically cited in support of this contention.[62]

Yet the reality is very different. In fact, the British glider lift in Varsity turned into a shambles due to the neglect of lessons that had been painstakingly observed during Market Garden. Had such heavy losses been sustained in the first Arnhem landings, 1st Airborne Division's prospects of capturing the bridge or holding out for an appreciable length of time would have been substantially reduced. As it was, in Varsity, the consequences were far less significant as the Rhine crossing operation was, in many ways, a sledgehammer to crack a nut. Varsity did not succeed because the airlift addressed the many and varied air planning blunders allegedly committed at Arnhem. It succeeded because the airborne forces were assigned far less ambitious objectives, and were very promptly reinforced by 2nd Army.

58   Warren, *Airborne Operations*, p. 174; Otway, *Airborne Forces*, p. 308.
59   Howard N. Cole, *On Wings of Healing: The Story of the Airborne Medical Services, 1940–1960* (Edinburgh: William Blackwood, 1963), p. 166.
60   TNA: WO 171/4320: 6 Air Landing Brigade Headquarters War Diary, 24 March 1944.
61   AHB: Otway, *Airborne Forces*, pp. 318. After a recovery effort extending over several days, the final equipment losses included 46 per cent of 6th Airborne Division's jeeps, 44 per cent of their trailers, 44 per cent of their carriers, half their light tanks, 29 per cent of their 75 mm Howitzers, half their 25 pdrs, 56 per cent of their 17 pdr anti-tank guns, 29 per cent of their 6 pdr anti-tank guns and 56 per cent of their Dodge 3/4 ton weapon carriers.
62   Lloyd Clark, *Arnhem: Jumping the Rhine 1944 and 1945: The Greatest Airborne Battle in History* (London: Headline Review, 2008), pp. 281, 301.

Conclusion

So much has been written about Market Garden over time that the inevitable question often arises: what else is there to say? In fact, recent years have witnessed a variety of new approaches to the study of this famous operation, ranging from the German perspective to the air dimension, and now even including a biography of Browning.[63] This paper offers another new line of enquiry, by viewing Market Garden in the context of airborne lessons exploitation. It was an approach that appeared all the more profitable after initial investigation suggested that there had, in fact, been a remarkable consistency across German and Allied airborne experience where the key operational lessons were concerned.

By the summer of 1944, the Allies knew that the prospects of airborne mission success were significantly improved by lead time, they had fully acknowledged the need to bring all major stake-holders into the airborne planning process from the earliest stage, they appreciated that rapid relief or reinforcement of the airborne was essential, that realistic allowances had to be made for the enemy response, and that the airlift could make or break the entire enterprise. Nevertheless, they took serious risks under all five headings when Market Garden was planned. The operation was launched at exceptionally short-notice; the formal airborne command chain was deliberately bypassed; the plan assigned an immensely challenging and risky link-up task to XXX Corps, and, while it sought to factor in the enemy vote, its approach to doing so was founded on flawed assumptions about enemy capability and about the Allied reinforcement rate. Browning's solution to the threat posed by *2 SS Panzer Corps* was, in particular, based substantially on recycling an airlift plan prepared for an entirely different operation; too late, it transpired that this lay beyond the realms of practical achievement.

There can only be one conclusion: in a very real sense, a failure to exploit past operational lessons contributed significantly to the Allied defeat. More than this, it is clear that the remarkably high airborne achievement rate at the tactical level owed much to more effective lessons exploitation by the Allied air forces. Market Garden was the only large-scale airborne operation mounted by the Allies in the European theatre in which airlift task and aircrew ability were properly aligned, and it was via this means that the RAF and the USAAF finally accomplished the accurate and concentrated airlifts that had eluded them in the past. This, in turn, offered enormous advantages to the airborne forces.

---

63   On the German perspective, see Kershaw, *It Never Snows in September*; for the air
      dimension, see Sebastian Ritchie: *Arnhem Myth and Reality – Airborne Warfare, Air Power
      and the Failure of Operation Market Garden* (London: Robert Hale, 2011); on Browning,
      see Richard Mead, *General 'Boy': The Life of Lieutenant General Sir Frederick Browning*
      (Barnsley: Pen & Sword, 2010).

These gains were particularly important in Market Garden, given the depth of the objectives and the fact that the airborne had to operate independently for a considerable period of time. In Normandy, the Allies were less dependent on the airborne, and tactical failure by multiple airborne units could be accommodated within the broader Allied plan; similarly, in Varsity, the costly and shambolic British glider landings ultimately did not matter. In Market Garden, without the successful airlift, any prospect that the airborne might independently have fulfilled the formidable array of tasking assigned to them would have been limited in the extreme. The contest would not have been decided after several days; it would have been settled within the first 24 hours.

Why, throughout history, have military organisations so often failed to exploit past lessons? There are many potential answers. Personalities, politics, institutional and cultural factors all play their part. But the evidence of Market Garden strongly suggests a tension between longer-term lessons exploitation and short-term prioritisation; at the operational level, the short-term factors proved far more influential. In this case, the critical element was the push from the top of 21st Army Group, which led to the operation being devised in isolation and swept aside such objections as were subsequently raised. The outcome illustrates perfectly why there is a formal military lessons process, but there is still no fail-safe means of ensuring that past lessons are integrated into operational planning. The tension between lessons exploitation and short-term agendas remains with us to this day.

2

Market Garden and the Strategy of the Northwest Europe Campaign

Lt-Colonel Roger Cirillo, PhD, USA (Ret)

Airborne forces were a prime asset for the invasion of Europe. The Normandy plan (NEPTUNE) employed airborne troops to the flanks and rear of the American and British landing beaches giving both depth and security to the wide lodgment. An additional division remained as a contingency attack force within the battle area or in any one of the dozen operations plans that percolated to support the fluid Normandy battles. No opportunities for its use, however, ever developed.[1]

In August 1944, Eisenhower centralized airborne planning and control under SHAEF (Supreme Headquarters, Allied Expeditionary Force), while placating the airmen by creating an Airborne Forces Headquarters, to train the units jointly, plan, and mount airborne operations. The tactical planning and actual command of the airborne divisions involved would be transferred to the employing Army Groups for operations. The commander for the Airborne Force, a U.S. Airman, Lt. Gen. Lewis H. Brereton, renamed his command First Allied Airborne Army (FAAA). Brereton's appointment didn't improve coalition operations. He appointed no British officers in operations positions and made his headquarters into a mirror image of a US Air headquarters noting that the air operation was primary over ground operations. He was not popular with the British, nor did he get on with his British deputy, Lt. Gen. F.A.M. Browning. Brereton's lack of organizational focus didn't help. Brave, and a bold, wide-ranging thinker, he didn't take pains with following up on details.[2] FAAA assumed control of the British 1 Airborne Corps, the U.S. XVIII Corps (Airborne),

1   Roger Cirillo, *The Market Garden Campaign: Allied Operational Command in Northwest Europe, 1944.* Department of Defence Management and Security Analysis, Cranfield University, 2002, PhD Thesis, Chapters 1-3, passim.
2   US Army Military History Research Collection. *Diary of Major General Floyd L. Parks.,* passim, NARA RG 331. *FAAA Organizational Files,* 322 FAAA; interviews, LTG Elwood R. "Pete" Quesada, USAF (Ret), 1984 by author.

IX Troop Carrier Command, and 38 Group RAF. 46 Group remained subject to Air Ministry control.[3]

During this time, Air Chief Marshal Sir Trafford Leigh-Mallory and his Allied Expeditionary Air Force (AEAF) headquarters asserted its brief as the final arbiter of tactical air plans, including airborne drops, their escort, and air support for airborne operations. While AEAF was soon to be inactivated, in the interim, it retained this authority and exerted it, even after Airborne Forces Headquarters were organized into a separate command. SHAEF reinforced Leigh Mallory's approval authority over FAAA plans and the requirement for his headquarters to coordinate escorts.[4]

Eisenhower's headquarters published planning guidance for future airborne plans on 16 August, following the general outline of its own Broad Front concept. Some guidance covered the ten plans already on the boards.[5] Brereton complained that airborne operations could not be mounted on short notice to meet opportunities, rather that they should be cast to create strategic situations. Eisenhower agreed in principle, but still pressed for a workable plan. He worried about the approaching fall weather. Ike wanted to commit the airborne into SHAEF's campaign to exert control over the ground war.[6]

On 19 August Eisenhower informed Montgomery by letter that he would assume complete ground command on 1 September, and informed the Combined Chiefs of Staff (CCS) on 22 August of his restructured command set-up. Having already put Bradley in the picture, Montgomery unveiled a bold concept inspired by the perceived destruction of the German Army in the West.[7] Later, Montgomery described his concept as "the Schlieffen Plan in reverse." He sent his Chief of Staff, the affable Maj. Gen. "Freddie" de Guingand to brief Eisenhower and gain his confidence in the idea.

3   FAAA 322 op. cit; History of the First Allied Airborne Army. Berlin: Headquarters, FAAA, 1945.

4   Air Ministry: Royal Air Force in the Second World War Series, *Airborne Forces 1951*, Chapter 8.

5   Lewis H. Brereton. *The Brereton Diaries: The War in the Air in the Pacific, Middle East, and Europe. 3 October 1941-8 May 1945*. New York: William Morrow and Company, 1946. August 1944. US Army Military History Institute. Diary of MG Floyd L. Parks. August, 1944, passim. Existent planning had been done by 1 Airborne Corps and 21 Army Group and referred to SHAEF. See also Air Ministry: Airborne Forces, Chapter 8 and War Office: The World War 1939-1945 Army: Airborne Forces, Lt. Col. T.B.H. Otway, 1951, Chapter XVI.

6   Cirillo, discussion of plans and creation of the Airborne Army. See also correspondence with AEAF cited concerning roles and responsibilities Air Ministry, *Airborne Operations*, and Papers of Air Marshal Sir Leslie Hollinghurst [Imperial War Museum]; Tedder to Eisenhower, 16 August, Rawson; Eyes Only: Top Secret Correspondence Between Marshall and Eisenhower. Eisenhower lost control of Strategic bombers on 14 September 1944.

7   He had been informed by SHAEF correspondence, 19 August. Eisenhower Papers, Vol. IV, item 1901.

Montgomery's military plan relied on the time honored military principle of maximum concentration against the primary objective designated by the CCS, the Ruhr, while picking up coastal ports, airfields, and the major northern ports along the way in a self-sustaining offensive whose deep flank could be covered by air and ground elements moving from the DRAGOON invasion force operating out of the Marseilles ports, and entering the Theater to serve as SHAEF's southern Army Group. From an overall command perspective, Eisenhower would have two wings, a northern wing of two Army Groups of three plus armies and two tactical air forces directed by Monty/Bradley and a Southern Army Group and Tactical Air Force of two or three armies directed by Lt. Gen. Jacob L. Devers. Depending upon resupply, elements, or the entire Third Army (Patton), could be attached to either wing.[8]

He described his "master plan" [concept of the operation] in writing for his Chief of Staff, but discussed it the next day with Eisenhower alone. Bradley had informed Monty only that morning that he intended to attack east, and a surprised Montgomery felt that Bradley had "been gotten at." His only recourse was to sell Eisenhower. Montgomery's notes in brief said:

1. The quickest way to win this war is for the mass of the Allied armies to advance northwards, clear the coast as far as ANTWERP, establish a powerful air force in Belgium, and advance into the RUHR.
2. The force must operate as one whole, with great cohesion and so strong that it can do the job quickly.
3. Single control and direction of the land operations is vital for success. This is a whole time job for one man.

He clinched his argument, guaranteeing its failure, with his belief that "To change the system of command now, after having won a great victory, would be to prolong the war."[9] None of this was militarily unsound, but politically a catastrophe in a coalition whose senior partner had decided to shear itself of any foreign influence, especially in an election year, and by a general, whose name came to represent everything

---

8   Field Marshal Montgomery, *Memoirs*. New York: World Publishing, 1958, p. 239. Despite Eisenhower's claims, SHAEF, never in its early plans, expected to cross deeply into Germany or reach the Ruhr prior to victory. See NARA, RG 331 Post Overlord Plans Vol. 1; Eisenhower, *Crusade In Europe*. Garden City, New York; Doubleday and Company, 1949, pp. 228-229. See also WAR Department Historical Division Special Staff MS Planning For Continental Operations, 2 Volumes, files, US Army Center of Military History. These files detail logistical estimates and deployment and have early plans charts. SHAEF deliberately excluded 21 Army Group from campaign planning while in England and on the continent. Note, it was known then that 6th Army Group would become part of Eisenhower's command in September but not at the time of the plan's inception.

9   Msg. Montgomery to de Guingand, for Eisenhower, 21 August 1944, Montgomery Papers, {Imperial War Museum}.

American generals hated about the British and who had been ordered to assume ground command over Montgomery.[10]

Eisenhower signaled Montgomery after his meeting that Bradley's Army Group will thrust forward on its left, its principal mission initially to be support Montgomery's mission of clearing the northern coast, but its eventual mission to turn east towards the Ruhr. Montgomery was given authority to coordinate the left wing of this army. Eisenhower gave Bradley the priority of clearing Brittany and building up in front of Paris before moving eastward, with the move of the First Army on Montgomery's flank getting priority. Bradley ignored this. There would be no great single thrust.[11]

The same day that Antwerp fell to advanced elements of 2 Army, 3 September, Montgomery approved COMET, a one and a half division drop of airborne elements on bridges across the Waal and Neder Rijn designed to outflank the Siegfried Line, cut off northern Holland, and put 21 Army Group onto the flank of the Ruhr. Airlift would be by the RAF 38 and 46 Groups with the bridges seized by glider coup de main before dawn and followed by brigade-sized airborne drops several hours later.[12]

Designed to follow a broken, running enemy, COMET relied upon the full pressure of Lt. Gen. Courtney Hodges's First US Army in the Aachen Cologne corridor, the main avenue into Germany by all of Hodges' eight divisions including most of his thousand plus tanks. A similar number of British armored vehicles would trickle up Holland's roads and onto the flank of the North German plain using the rail and road bridges over the Neder Rijn. Montgomery believed First Army would support his attack, as "he could coordinate the left of Hodges's army." Weather delayed the airborne operation, and the enemy grew stronger. Bradley meanwhile developed his own operations further away from 21 Army Group, ignoring the intent of Eisenhower's earlier campaign guidance.[13]

COMET was a combined operation, employing both RAF 38 and 46 Troop Carrier Groups, plus the American 50th and 52nd Troop Carrier Wings, both veteran units. A U.S. Troop Carrier Wing would tow gliders on D+1. These used many of the same LZ/DZs used later in MARKET. The bridges at Grave, Nijmegen, and

10   Marshall to Eisenhower, Eyes Only, W-82265, 17 August 1944, pp. 128, 129.

11   Message, 24 August, Eisenhower to Montgomery, EP, iv 1910; See also Eisenhower, FWD-13765, 4 September which limits Patton to bridgeheads on the Moselle until after 21 Army Group and First Army seized Rhine bridgeheads. EP, IV. Items 1933/1946 SHAEF War Diary G-3, 13 September 1944.

12   This assumed release of aircraft for 46 Group. Williams and Brereton had confined COMET to British divisions only, leaving the airborne force perilously small. Maj. Gen. M.B. Ridgway consistently attempted to create the belief as did Lt. Gen. Bradley, that the US XVIII Corps was a US, not an Allied airborne asset, and that the Army Groups, essentially had their own dedicated airborne corps. It was not, and they did not.

13   TNA, WO 171 See Daily intelligence assessments, 2 Army. Also, Operations Plan COMET, RG 331, FAAA Files. EP, IV, Eisenhower to commanders, 29 August, 1944 ; item 1920; Eisenhower to Montgomery, 24 August, 1944. See also Omar Bradley. *A Soldier's Story:* New York: Henry Holt, and Company, 1951, passim.

Arnhem were each to be seized by coup de main parties of six Horsa Gliders before daylight (0430) while the first lifts would drop at 0800. A second lift would bring in the balance of the 1st Airborne Division and the `1 Airborne Corps Headquarters at approximately 1800 (or early the next morning) and the Polish Airborne Brigade. A third lift would follow the next morning. This plan assumed minimal ground resistance and full support from U.S. First Army in the Aachen corridor directed at the Ruhr. The attack was planned for 8 September.[14]

The order was signed by Major General Paul Williams, IX Troop Carrier Commander and Combined Task Force Commander. Remarkably, Air Marshal Leslie Hollinghurst, was not invited by AEAF to the original planning conference for COMET due to a staff error. Brereton named Williams as air commander due to the larger number of U.S. aircraft being used. More importantly, Browning, who had drafted the order, noted the lifts should be as in LINNET, but Williams cut out the American division, making the drop for one and a half divisions, a decision approved by Brereton who apparently unilaterally overrode SHAEF guidance that all of FAAA was for 21 Army Group use.[15]

Bradley resented 21 Army Group's airborne priority and claimed a great logistical cost lay in the repeated stand downs of transports being readied for canceled air drops. LINNET and then COMET both cost supply sorties, Bradley estimated as much as a million gallons of fuel per day might have been carried for each day lost. While this seems excessive, perhaps 5 million gallons might have been carried using this calculation with indeterminate results on the battlefield.[16]

Holding Patton on a loose leash to cross the Moselle with available fuel, on 4 September, Bradley modified his plan, to send Third Army (minus a corps in Brittany) and First Army (minus a corps to support Montgomery) to attack east and link with forces from the south. SHAEF rationalized that the full four divisions of the Airborne Army plus the reinforcing support of First Army equalized the strength of the front, thus maintaining the Northern Front's "priority." The fact remained, that Bradley had 20 divisions with four enroute, and Devers a further 8. Four more American divisions arrived monthly from the United States. Montgomery had 15 divisions plus 3 airborne, plus a Brigade, if the airborne was committed. Another division was available for fly-in. This spread Eisenhower's eventual Allied Force (assumed for mid-September) over more than 400 miles of front, and concentrated

---

14   Plan COMET, op. cit.
15   OPERATION COMET FILE, RG 331, NARA, also US Army War College Files, Military History Institute, Major General Floyd Parks Papers, Diary. See also, Air 37/776 correspondence 6, 7, 10 September, 26 August. Leigh Mallory. Hollinghurst, Brereton re: Airborne Planning regarding COMET and LINNET. Staff notes, 11 September, Parks Diary regarding Brereton recommendation on divisions for MARKET.
16   Bradley, *Soldiers Story*, pp. 401-406, 414.

them nowhere. Moreover, Hodges's left-hand corps had been halted in place. Bradley weakened, rather than strengthened his left north of Aachen.[17]

Montgomery's signaled on 4 September, "I consider that the time has come where one really powerful and full-blooded thrust towards Berlin is likely to get there and thus end the war. He noted, "There are only two possible thrusts: one by the Ruhr and the other via Metz and the Saar."[18] Eisenhower's disagreement set the tone for his strategy for the rest of the war. "While agreeing with your conception of a powerful and full blooded thrust towards Berlin, I do not, repeat not, agree that it should be initiated at this moment at the exclusion of all other maneuvers ... My intention is initially to occupy the Saar and the Ruhr, and by the time we have done this, Havre and Antwerp should be available to maintain one or part of the thrusts you mention."[19] Frustrating to Montgomery, was his statement, "In this connection, I have always given, and still give, priority to the Ruhr and the northern route of advance ..."[20]

While waiting for COMET to be mounted, Dempsey reported stronger German elements to his front, including some SS tanks. With 8 corps still grounded in Normandy to provide its transport to support Second Army's other corps, and 12 corps pushing to support the Canadians clearing Channel ports, Dempsey's 30 Corps held up, waiting for the airborne drop, appreciating that a 60 mile armor dash would cause the Germans to blow the bridges halting the drive through the heavily compart-mented and soon to be waterlogged Dutch countryside. Operations therefore halted short of Belgian-Dutch border. Lt. Gen. Brian Horrocks, the 30 Corps Commanding General, estimated about 100 miles more running for his tanks in his fuel stores.[21]

Montgomery asked to see Eisenhower intending to get one last grab at a full blooded push in the north with Hodges's army accompanying Dempsey towards the Ruhr before German defenses solidified into a firm line. Before seeing Eisenhower, Montgomery canceled COMET and ordered a strengthened plan using the entire First Allied Airborne Army in a drop, penciled in as plan 16 and by dark, named MARKET. The full blooded attack, not a new airborne plan, however, was the purpose for seeing Ike. First Allied Airborne had already been committed for 21 Army Group's use.[22]

17   The Aachen Corridor was the major avenue of approach into Germany and arguably, the dividing line for a Northern Approach. This corps was also shorn a division, and halted for lack of fuel until Montgomery complained.
18   Montgomery, M 160, 4 Sep 1944 cited in Cirillo, op. cit., p. 323.
19   Eyes Only, Eisenhower to Montgomery 5 September.
20   Eisenhower to Montgomery, 5 September 1944, SHAEF FWD-13889, EP, IV,
21   TNA WO 285 *Diary of Miles Dempsey*, September 1944, passim. Cab 106, Horrocks, *Corps Commander.*
22   Dempsey took responsibility for MARKET GARDEN, as indeed the planning was approved by him save the drop zones, though Browning appeared to have designed the drop concept. See comments cited, Cirillo, and CAB 106;

2 Army had studied airborne operations since before D-day, and Lt. Gen. Sir Miles Dempsey, its commander, had achieved linkages with airborne coup de main bridge-seizing forces both in Sicily and Normandy. Holland offered similar choices as did the Rhine crossings between Arnhem and the Ruhr that Montgomery had designated for 2 Army to study.[23] This had led to the tactics behind COMET, and MARKET which was to be a "Super COMET" with the airborne seizing bridges and passing an armored division through cleared enemy areas.[24]

Dempsey conferred with Browning on 10 September, and with Montgomery and Brereton approving, a far strengthened airborne plan overlaid the COMET concept. The ground thrust was extended from the Dutch border which would have been captured up through Eindhoven under the original COMET plan. This required the addition of another airborne division to gap the distance including several small bridges and one large canal bridge. Divisions filled the former brigade drop areas.[25]

MARKET added the U.S. 101st and 82d Airborne Divisions to the 1 Airborne Corps, which had planned COMET for Dempsey, detaching them from Ridgway's XVIII Corps which retained some logistical responsibilities.[26] During their meeting, a sometimes sharp discussion took place between Monty and Eisenhower who refused Montgomery priority for a northern thrust or control of Bradley's First Army which was essential he felt to coordinate the attack on the Ruhr. As always, Eisenhower refused to impose a synchronization of offensives among his Army Groups, nor did he ever attempt to personally direct operations of two Army Groups along their boundaries.[27]

While some argued Monty believed he could still have a northern thrust alone, MARKET fit Eisenhower's plan as an enabling piece to clear Antwerp and reach the Rhine. It also cut off the Germans in Holland which could be rounded up during the winter months. Monty had already predicted no river assaults would be possible

---

23   COMET objectives, Dempsey Diary discussion of priorities, September 1-10.

24   Cirillo, op. cit., Rhine Delta map. Planning maps for COMET and MARKET. GARDEN makes operational sense, only in the light of Montgomery's M525, dated 13 September, which outlines his campaign plan and details First Canadian Army to clear the ports, and Second Army to seize a bridgehead prior to outflanking the Ruhr in coordination with U.S. First Army. This follows Eisenhower's earlier FWD 13765, 9 September, and his 13 September FWD 14758 both in EP, Vol. IV.

25   Brereton told Arnold that he was told by Dempsey [on the 12th] that the capture of Eindhoven would be an easy affair. The German line was still thickening and drops were then assumed south of the Son Bridge. Dempsey permitted Brereton to eliminate the airborne drop zones between Eindhoven and Zon to seize both the town and the bridges within the town and the Zon canal bridge by coup de main. See file Brereton-Arnold Correspondence. In the event Eindhoven was taken easily, but the Zon bridge was lost. Lewie had lost the plot. The bridges were key. The failure to seize all the bridges simultaneously was the prime cause of MARKET's failure.

26   These are outlined in the XVIII Corps After Action report which also notes it was ready to assume operational command.

27   Cornelius Ryan. *A Bridge Too Far*. New York: Simon and Schuster, 1974.

during ice season as pontoon bridges couldn't be placed on the Rhine. Montgomery wanted to risk ending the war on a concentrated push as large as possible. Eisenhower saw a looming strategic pause due to logistics, and the inevitable spring campaign. If a bridgehead was seized at Arnhem, little doubt could have been in Montgomery's mind that First Army would have had to been thrown in both to protect his southern flank on the west side of the Rhine and eventually across the Rhine for 21 Army Group to have any operational effect. Antwerp or Rotterdam would have to have been brought on line quickly to manage the 25 or so divisions Montgomery's planners estimated were essential for his concept to work. 30 Corps alone would not have gone into the Ruhr. 2d Army relied on the Channel ports coming on line before Antwerp to provide their logistical support with Dieppe already being assaulted and cleared before MARKET began.[28]

MARKET was designed to seize no less than six bridges along a major route from the Belgian-Netherlands frontier to the city of Arnhem and then to pass an armored corps along the main route to continue northwards to the Zuider Zee, a total of 99 miles. It was seen as a pursuit, the column march-ordered so, following a breakthrough of a thin crust defense and a rapid transit through scattered, reforming remnants of units.[29]

Deep within Holland, several destroyed Panzer Division headquarters were known to be forming units, and straggler lines were gathering up survivors from the great eastern exodus from the destruction of the Wehrmacht in the west. Defense pockets at the water lines were the only defenses expected. MARKET assumed not only confusion and weakness still reigned, it intended to preempt the formation of a solid defense with a reformed army on the northern flank of the Siegfried Line. MARKET would exploit the gap perceived as open, and outflank the Siegfried Defenses before they could be manned by the survivors of the Western divisions from the Normandy battles, known to be forming by the newly arrived First Parachute Army Headquarters. On 15 September, 1 Airborne Corps assessed the armor threat at 50-100 tanks in Holland, with most near the front line, an accurate assessment. Unit strengths and exact locations were not available. Enemy tanks did not appear in the Arnhem fight until D+2, though a larger number of survivors from allegedly destroyed SS units

---

28   See comments by Simonds in Ms, Strategy, Montgomery Papers, IWM. The complex and contradictory logistical argument is covered by Roland Ruppenthal in Logistical support of the Armies, Volume II: Washington: Office of the Chief of Military History, 1958, Chapter 1; and "Liberation Campaign" 4 volumes, National Archives of Canada, RG 24 files; see also 21 Army Group; *Administrative History of the 21 Army Group.* Stacey, The Victory Campaign and RG Crerar Diary, September notations. See also Roland Ruppenthal. "Logistics and the Broad Front Strategy." In *Command Decisions.* (ed.) Robert Kent Greenfield, Washington: Office of the Chief of Military History, 1960, pp. 419-427.

29   See Cirillo, p. 408. Montgomery M525, 14-9-1944 Directive.

existed, the strengths, nor exact locations, not being reported accurately by ULTRA. Armored units move![30]

The added strength given to MARKET reflected not only the reaction to the buildup of the German defenses and arrangement of broken units in depth in the enemy rear, but the days of delay, that also permitted a strengthening of the accompanying ground attack designated GARDEN consisting of all of 2 Army's corps, with 8 Corps' piecemeal movement from Normandy. It would attack from the march on 30 Corps' southern flank. Simultaneously, Canadian First Army continued clearing ports on the long coastal belt in turn. Montgomery from 12 September onwards told Crerar that the Scheldt must receive priority at the earliest possible moment ensuring that First Canadian Army adapt their operations to support this. But one last port needed clearing, Calais.[31]

Air operations were coordinated by AEAF on 12 September at Stanmore. Close air support, however, considered the responsibility of the Tactical Air Forces, was not covered for the operation, though escort missions for transports, counter air, airfield attacks, resupply and diversions were coordinated. The AEAF report notes, "… the air forces continued to lend support to ground operations during the whole period that the intense phase the operation lasted."[32] This appears to have shifted air support onto Broadhurst's back while his superior, Air Vice Marshal Sir Arthur Coningham, remained concerned with operations over the Scheldt. Remarkably, the usually truculent Coningham said nothing.[33]

MARKET was an air force plan. It followed the Army's request but not the commander's intent. The air plan was finalized on 13 September by Major General Paul Williams of IX Troop Carrier Command, the designated air commander. It was never planned at 21 Army Group or 2 Army and delivered complete to those headquarters with changes on the 15th. Williams's decisions restructured the ground battle, dividing the battlefield in space and time by delivering forces at distances and in phases that violated the original intent of the ground commanders as they had designed and understood the plan. They had assumed rapid captures of the major

30   Cirillo, pp. 397-400, discussion of 21 Army Group Intelligence summaries, 2d Army Intelligence, and 1 Airborne corps estimate; Situation Maps, Kershaw, *It Never Snows In September*. See comments, Cirillo, op. cit; and Kershaw, *It Never Snows*, as well as Hinsley, vol. 3, Part II. Passim.

31   Dempsey Diary, Estimates, Montgomery Diary C.P. Stacey. *The Victory Campaign: The Operations in Northwest Europe 1944-1945*. Ottawa: The Queen's Printer and Controller of Stationery, 1960, Chapter XIV and XV passim, and p. 358-360; NAC, RG 24, Crerar Papers, First Canadian Army War Diary Orders, September, 1944.

32   AEAF Dispatch, para. 377. He notes 7800 sorties were flown in support mostly against flak but also as counter-air missions accounting for 159 enemy aircraft claimed destroyed.

33   AEAF Report, Vincent Orange. *Coningham: A Biography of Air Marshal Sir Arthur Coningham*, Washington: Center for Air Force History, 1992, Chapter, 16, pp. 214-216.

bridges and several days of good weather for reinforcing drops.[34] Dempsey and Browning were clear as to what they believed would work.[35] Their only choice was cancellation *after* shutting down air supplies along the front for nearly two weeks, virtually an admission that the Airborne Army couldn't handle a strategic mission. There was no competing airborne concept.

Williams was designated air commander due to the number of aircraft he commanded, as he had been for COMET. Leigh Mallory recommended Air Marshal Hollinghurst who had planned all previous operations with Browning. Hollinghurst's familiarity with British coup de main operations and airborne commanders, and whose offers to help the British Airborne were ignored, despite his command of the air task force for the British airborne sector. Williams, was inflexible in regard to the Army's concept as opposed to his own Troop Carrier plans. Air Marshal Hollinghurst was willing to risk planes, Williams was not. The COMET plan was noncommittal about authorizing two drops in a day though, it did have glider coup de main operations. Williams proved intransigent to British recommendations before, especially when 38 Group had been left out of LINNET and COMET planning by FAAA and IX TCC, making it an American planned show with a British Airborne Corps. Separate tactics for each sector were never considered. Brereton or his chief of staff were apparently never approached on this.[36]

Leaving the bridges for later capture was a fatal idea. Besides abandoning surprise, it left the bridges open for enemy movement. The enemy use of the then unobstructed Arnhem road bridge to pass reinforcements south into Nijmegen proved fatal to the Arnhem phase of the operation for the advancing British columns. Despite American claims of seizing bridges and accomplishing their missions, the timing of these events proved fatal. The loss of the Zon bridge, the delay in capturing the Nijmegen bridge by the American divisions, and failure to block the Arnhem bridge and road eliminated the advantage of surprise and control of the road that the armor column needed and the airborne required to survive. What may have been done is problematic, what is clear is that Williams refused to hear any British proposals from the RAF or Army concerning solutions that would have aided 1 Airborne Division. Considering that he had begun as an attack aviation officer, Williams' lack of imagination in combining

---

34   see Brereton, Short Estimate of the Airborne Operation Market, 11 September 1944, Hq FAAA, RG 331; Cirillo, Taylor, Swords. Williams concurred in single drop zones for divisions as easiest to find, cover, and manage air flow simultaneously. In the event, the 101 had two, the 82d had two, the 1 Airborne had two, all in close proximity within their zones, *Parks' Diaries*, Conference Notes, 10-15 September, individual days.

35   *Floyd Parks Papers, Diaries, September 10, 1944.* A careful reading of Browning's original notes, Brereton's famous "Thunderclap Surprise" speech in the 10 September Conference notes, and the 15 September IX Troop Carrier Drop Plan reveals a dichotomy in thinking. See letter, 10 September, Brereton to Leigh Mallory, Air 37/776.

36   Air Ministry, *Airborne Forces*, has the most detailed analysis of the air and ground operations. Dr. John Warren, *Airborne Operations in the European Theater*, Air Historical branch, is the best American analysis.

flak suppression and a coup de main or using multiple drop zones north and south of the river simultaneously seems remarkable in hindsight. His insistence on keeping the air clear of air support while failing to communicate with the continent kept 30 Corps from having a dedicated CABRANK cover over its column attempting to move northward.[37]

The daylight drops following the counter-flak preparation was a problem. The turn-around for fighter escorts wasted most of a day. No attempt to phase the two together relying on the suppression of the flak attacks to get the troop carriers in, and might have permitted the before daylight coups de main if the suppression missions were flown early or if they followed strafing fighters. A second late day drop, and all day ground attacks would have changed the odds. With no single commander for MARKET GARDEN, the airmen and ground soldiers deadlocked. This was the price of Eisenhower's fragmented command, if not Ike as in Normandy, logically Montgomery and Leigh Mallory should have called the shots together, yet the organization chart had been eliminated putting FAAA under SHAEF, whose airman did nothing. SHAEF's own bad siting and incompletely established communications made the Supreme Commander impossible to be the single mind controlling the front. Second Army ran GARDEN. Dempsey had no authority to say no. Montgomery seeing no gain in arguing further, accepted a bad deal, a rarity for a man who prided himself on having the stuff to have a battle "teed up" before starting it. Coningham and Tedder had endlessly poisoned the air with "Monty's caution," this time, he showed none and neither of those Air Marshals did anything in their substantial arenas to alleviate the risks and of course, neither Tedder nor Coningham helped. Williams' belief that the airborne could hold drop zones for subsequent days' drops showed an ignorance of airborne fighting that was historic. He ignored Hollinghurst's pleas to remedy this, by doubling the drops on each day. No one at First Allied Airborne bothered to ask if air support was guaranteed for the divisions prior to ground link up.[38]

Montgomery had accepted the risk Dempsey and Browning had outlined to him on September 10 and based his northern thrust upon it, and had asked for the theater's full backing as the Allied main effort. Not only did the crucial fuel he needed for his flank corps not materialize for Dempsey as promised, but the full cooperation of Hodges to attack in the Aachen corridor simultaneously to break through and fix

---

37 Browning biography, passim. Hollinghurst had been willing to fly COMET. For MARKET, he was willing to execute coup de main glider missions, and double lifts on the first day for the British operation. Americans did not favor Glider operations for assaults, nor airborne drops for "assaults." British commanders believed that losses of 40% were possible and acceptable if this mission was successful. Ian Gooderson. *Air Power at the Battlefront: Allied Close Air Support in Europe 1943-1945*. London: Frank Cass, 1998, pp. 87-91.

38 One of the senior British officers, who asked not to be identified, told me in the early 1980's that an American corps would have reached them (he was there) at Arnhem.

enemy reserves as part of one big attack never happened. Horrocks' corps would bear the brunt of the enemy defense on three sides of its penetration.[39]

Typically, Monty got half of what he wanted, and then Eisenhower went off and released Bradley from any restrictions placed on his attacks. Thus Ike negated his own directive of 13 September, nor did he ever understand his responsibility in coordinating the attacks of his Army Groups especially when a key avenue was along the Army Group boundary![40]

The Air Plan reflected the fractional authority cherished by the airmen who refused to work for each other. It did not solve all the air problems, only those relating to the delivery of the airborne divisions and their resupply. The air "support" left out fire support provided by interdiction or close support missions. Williams had once crossed swords with Leigh Mallory in Normandy and overlooked and overrode Hollinghurst. Brereton seemed remote from real command. The American airmen had the full backing of both Generals Marshall and Arnold in Washington who had decided that 1944 would be the end of British domination of the war and that no U.S. aircraft would be commanded by the RAF. Coningham did not seem to view any of this as his problem, as if the British army was of no consequence to his mission. In essence, the airmen's attitude assured no seamless air support of the ground operation would be provided, a contradiction to the reason which was why the airborne operation was mounted by airmen in the first place.[41]

As Eisenhower, Leigh Mallory and Brereton had approved MARKET and Tedder was present went it was discussed, Coningham's 'cooperation' with GARDEN was never questioned.[42]

Regular daily operations coordinated with groups dealing directly with their Army counterparts. His headquarters and 21 Army Group Main were close by and they coordinated daily. The Airborne elements were part of Airborne Army and hence had to be coordinated through their planners – also airmen known to Coningham from Normandy. 21 Army Group's Coordination Meeting on 15 September at their Main with their Brigadier Ops (Air) noted, "It was agreed that ground attacks for the airborne forces should be provided by 83 GROUP RAF in accordance with the normal procedure. The army air support communications would centre on HQ

---

39   Horrocks, *Corps Commander*.
40   Eisenhower Directive, 13 September 1944, FWD 13765 op. cit.
41   See discussions Cirillo, Chapter 9, pp. 387-428. This details the complexity and mechanics of the air plan and the relationship of the drop zones and objectives on GARDEN and Second Army's plan. Enemy intelligence as known is cited.
42   MARKET was an air plan whose final authority was the Supreme Commander.

SECOND ARMY."[43] 2 TAF shared a Joint Army-Air Operations room, making it impossible for them not to be read in on any MARKET information.[44]

The Supreme Commander designated Air Support for airborne operations as the responsibility of Leigh Mallory. As Tedder and Coningham had openly and successfully conspired to have him fired, and finally to have his headquarters removed, it was no wonder that neither cooperated willingly with him. Unfortunately, Eisenhower failed to ensure Tedder, his "air advisor," check on air plans, even though he had just committed the theater reserve, "the Airborne Army." Tactical Air responsibility on the continent reverted to Coningham due to communications as they unilaterally agreed, but not when IX TCC flew in the MARKET corridor. Coningham never bothered to see Brereton about this. Neither airman sought the other out, and Broadhurst and the Army were left in the lurch.[45]

83 Group's taskings for MARKET came not from 2 Army but from AEAF, and included covering 30 Corps's first days advance. These are reflected in the G-3 conference notes.[46] Column cover, recce, and close support were standard missions. Support of the airborne perimeter could have been requested either through Airborne HQ channels or technically through 2 Army channels, who assumed command of the divisions upon their arrival in Holland. Coningham somehow decided he needed special requests from either Brereton or Leigh Mallory or Montgomery to provide support for these within 1 Airborne's area which lay outside of Broadhurst's sector.[47]

The fact that 1 Airborne Corps had no fully functioning "tentacle", and that 1 Airborne division had its American forward air liaison element withdrawn by the RAF, further assured that the key battles for the river crossing of the Waal, Elst, the Arnhem bridge, and the defense of the Oosterbeek perimeter had no close support and intermittent air coverage in general. U.S. forward air control teams were also provided by Ninth Air Force. 101st Airborne Division, did, however, have an air liaison element, which arrived by glider on D+ 1, and noting it, obtained air support through it. Certainly, the British Airborne's failure to secure a proper ASSU link with the RAF is one of the war's more shameful episodes of lack of Air Ministry-War Office lack of cooperation. The fact that the Corps Commander seemed to believe he had adequate communications also says volumes for the lack of training and the hastiness that FAAA and 1 Airborne Corps were put together with. 1 Airborne Division, however, had seen combat in the Mediterranean, and had been on operational standby

43   See Cirillo for discussion on Coningham, Quesada, Broadhurst. See Cirillo, pp. 178, pp. 180-182 on responsibilities of FAAA versus AEAF. Air Force Historical Research Agency: Stearley Files, FAAA, AFRHC, Reel, B5049.
44   *Administrative History 2 TAF. 1947.* This describes general operations of the Tactical Air Force and its operations room.
45   NARA, RG331 MARKET IX TCC Plan; Cirillo, AEAF Report.
46   Stearley notes. G3, FAAA. Op. cit.
47   Broadhurst, correspondence with author, 1990.

since before NEPTUNE. Its communications failures, due to equipment and training were unjustifiable.[48]

Brereton, who had commanded the Ninth Tactical Air Force, never inquired apparently through American or RAF channels to increase fighter bomber support to the columns or to the flanks and forward of 30 Corps. Considering the much acclaimed river crossing of the Waal, and much maligned attack north of the Nijmegen bridge were done nearly bereft of air support, certainly no close air support, or *RAF* presence against visible panzers and enemy troops, the AIR-LAND nature of airborne battle was totally absent and excused by Coningham who claimed, "no one asked" when Broadhurst begged to intercede with fighter bombers based on Phantom intelligence concerning 1 Airborne's plight.[49] 2d Army's RAF ground contact car and its liaison team remain an undocumented feature in this fiasco.[50]

The air's major mission was to be there and participate. While medium and heavy bombers had been used in the Mediterranean by Tedder and Coningham, neither suggested any aerial intervention by any type aircraft of emergency reinforcement, using the 17th Airborne Division (recently operational) or even elements of the 6th Airborne Division or Gliderborne elements of the 52d Lowland Division which had been offered. No emergency planning was called for despite the unraveling of events from the beginning. Maj. Gen. Hakewill-Smith did offer to commit a brigade of his division early by glider if reinforcements were needed.[51] FAAA continued resupply schedules adjusting for weather and ignoring the ground situation that clearly required air support.[52]

---

48   38 Group's Operations Order designates U.S. Ninth Air Force as the Air Support for ground troops on D-Day, but does not clarify if this relationship would continue throughout the operation. It apparently was changed, anyway, as the U.S. FAC Teams assigned were withdrawn by the Americans from 1 Airborne Division, but one flew the mission anyway, but gained notoriety by destroying its radio voluntarily due to misreading the battlefield and thus cutting off the division from any hope of connecting directly with air elements.(see Airborne Invasion of Holland, US Army Air Forces Pamphlet.) See *Communications Annex, Corps Order. Market Garden Report, 21 Army Group.* Browning's biographer claims RAF personnel landed with the corps headquarters were untrained, leaving his tentacle useless. Dempsey, likewise, seemed unconcerned about the air support of 30 Corps attack northward (Broadhurst to Cirillo, 1990 letter). Richard Mead, *General 'Boy': The Life of Lieutenant General Sir Frederick Browning.* Barnsley: Pen and Sword, 2010, Chapter 21, passim. See also Geoffrey Powell. *The Devil's Birthday: The Bridges to Arnhem 1944.* London: Buchan and Enright, Publishers, 1984, p. 191.

49   Broadhurst, ibid. Parks Diary, 20-26 September 1944, passim.

50   Gooderson accounts for the contact car earlier, but not north of the Waal River; Shelford Bidwell & Dominick Graham. *Fire-Power: British Army Weapons and Theories of War 1904-1945.* London: George Allen and Unwin, 1982, pp. 273-274.

51   52nd Lowland Division.

52   Broadhurst Letter. Sebastian Ritchie argues that air support had nothing to do with failure which demonstrates a remarkable ignorance of the battles along Hell's Highway, the Waal Crossing, at Elst, and the swarming of the Oosterbeek Perimeter, all of which would have

Tedder, Brereton, Coningham, Williams, Hollinghurst, Broadhurst were airmen; only Broadhurst seemed to be leaning forward as part of a fighting team. Tedder and Coningham were absent. Montgomery's continuing telegraphic fight with Eisenhower and telephonic prodding of Crerar continued, as well as being physically cut off from the fight prevented his presence from affecting operations directly. He and Coningham might then have sorted things out, though he would have had to go rearward to find Coningham.[53]

Considering the broken nature of the ground, and the lack of fuel or fixing forces provided by allies to the flanks, only the airmen could intervene at short notice. Instead, weather, and transport schedules overrode any semblance of tactical reality.[54] Leigh Mallory, who had flown ground support at Amiens in 1918 and had commanded Army Cooperation Command understood the problem, was marginalized by his boss and Tedder, who assumed his duties but without the title on 15 October. Leigh Mallory, in fact, had departed on 22 September at the height of the MARKET crisis, and his rear operations room continued coordinating air missions but not functioning as an air command post. It became part of the SHAEF air section using former AEAF personnel.[55]

Brereton spoke for the airmen when he wrote General Arnold immediately after the operation and said, "MARKET" was a great success. Arnold correctly perceived the army's feelings when he answered that Washington did not view it that way, and that a tight drop and losing few aircraft, the airmen's goal, had no purpose if the objectives were not gained. Brereton was thrilled at the low air losses, the compact drops, the wonderful supply tonnages delivered. The Army had failed, not the airmen. They just didn't link up.[56]

The airmen like Coningham had claimed the air was equal TO the ground force. This is a bureaucratic not an operational argument for a particular situation. Airborne warfare is about seizing or taking ground objectives. The airmen commanding MARKET, NEVER tried to support, neutralize or directly support or reinforce troops on an objective, and had no insurance of a constant umbrella over the endangered columns or airheads. They established a safe transport route, a safe air space management schedule, and expected the huge resources spent on Troop Carriers and fighter bombers to play by the rules of air planners with no experience in air ground

benefited from close air support. MARKET would have benefited had Broadhurst, not Coningham, been at 2 TAF.

53   Montgomery's plans officer was cut off on the ground attempting to go forward, and Dempsey's chief of plans was shot down in a light aircraft though unhurt, both advised him to remain at the command post. Nigel Hamilton. *Monty: The Field Marshal. 1944-1976*. London: Hamish Hamilton, 1986, p. 87.

54   RAF Vol IV, OTWAY, AIR MINISTRY, Montgomery. FAAA Report.

55   Pogue, op. cit., pp. 274-275.

56   Letter, Lt. General Lewis H. Brereton To Gen. H.H. Arnold, cited in Cirillo, op. cit. p. 505.

operations. Coningham and Tedder, hid behind personality 'flaws' of Leigh Mallory and Montgomery as their excuse for not supporting their operations as if war was a popularity contest. The refused to recognize it was THE allied airborne attempt to jump the Rhine. Their own considerable narcissism was unhelpful and it should be recognized that their making noncooperation a "personal vendetta" was costly in Allied lives.

Air Marshal Broadhurst summarized the situation for the author: "I was completely flabbergasted at the time to find than an operation of that magnitude was laid on without any proper communications between the Airborne drop and the local Army/Air Headquarters."[57] First Allied Airborne Army whose sole job was to facilitate the employment of both airborne and air elements in the ground campaign failed dramatically to understand that communications at every level had to be continuous beyond the drop itself. This was the price of having a team of airmen who believed air had primacy over ground operations. There was no "air-land" battle.

Brereton, conceptually, understood, the potential for an airborne army. He outlined its possible use to Eisenhower while trying to increase his own command by gaining XVIII Airborne Corps attachment to his own Ninth (Tactical) Air Force. He foresaw a seamless air-ground battle under a single commander, a flash of brilliance that never materialized in the organization later created.[58] He was not the man to command it no doubt, and Eisenhower not the visionary to create it, Ike tried for the bureaucratic solution, keeping both AEAF and FAAA while failing to monitor both during MARKET GARDEN.[59]

Brereton's concept theoretically might have worked in an all-American system. The Americans had long range fighter bombers, forward air control parties, cooperative air commanders, and a lack of mutual hatred that were demonstrated all too often in Airborne Corps and RAF meetings. Eisenhower's goal of an Allied Airborne team could not be achieved in six weeks, even if personalities and prejudices could somehow be frozen for the duration of the war.

Two things had worked against this. The 1 Airborne Corps and XVIII Airborne Corps had not equipped its divisions permanently with air-ground liaison teams and radios, nor long range communications to deal directly with FAAA in the UK or its supporting aircraft. Neither was up to the challenge.[60]

Secondly, the egos of the air leaders, and command systems insisted upon by AEAF, 2 TAF and FAAA all commanded by airmen, had ignored that the primary reason for the operation was to put soldiers on an objective and to link formations with them rapidly. With this objective, the first objective should have been, to support this

---

57   Letter Air Marshal Broadhurst to author, 28 March 1991.
58   Cirillo, Chapter 4: "Creating The Prince's Greatest Fear." See Memorandum 4 August 1944, Brereton to Eisenhower.
59   Ibid.
60   Browning admitted his selection of Walch as Chief of Staff was a disaster for a combat role which further complicated his own Headquarters training.

aim. No cost, no effort, no risk should have been considered too high for the airmen, yet they safe-sided their part of the operation. Hollinghurst and his British airmen figured casualties as high as 40% would be justified by success.[61]

While training has been blamed, the British army also took the back pew to the other services in equipment and personnel. It is remarkable that Eisenhower created an "Army" without authorization for headquarters, equipment, people, and expected it to launch operations immediately. 1 Airborne Corps had a legitimate reason to exist and was fought by the War Office who refused it equipment and personnel over pettiness and war office authorizations by bureaucrats. Likewise the Royal Air Force failed to staff it with trained air-ground liaison personnel.[62]

Upon these thin reeds, 35,000 men left the skies in the hopes of changing the course of the war. FAAA was only six weeks old as an organization.

MARKET GARDEN was the logical and bold use of the Airborne Army. Eisenhower's commitment of the Airborne Army was more complex than simply the employment of an unused asset, and has been used as part of larger debates on the overall strategy and command of the war, and of the competence of Eisenhower, Montgomery, Brereton, Browning, and the value of airborne forces. The assessment of Strategy by the U.S. Theater Board held on the lessons of the war, repeated the basic four avenues assessment made by the SHAEF staff and held the correctness of attacking all along the line.[63]

The report stressed that the original logistical estimates counted on the Brittany ports to supply and stage U.S. divisions arriving from the states. Eisenhower justified backing both avenues with an equal sized attack by arguing that the logistical support for the southern attack was no more difficult than the northern blow.[64] Additionally, the assessment infers that Antwerp's availability was not an original assumption in the Broad Front plan which was based on German assumed surrender on D+360 not far within Germany and only a month after Antwerp's capture. The primary ports basis for OVERLORD were the Brittany Ports, the Marseilles Group, and the Channel Ports. Central to the maintenance of the American armies would be the Brittany ports, and the Commonwealth armies the Channel ports.[65]

Beyond the D+270 line forecast in SHAEF's original planning, lay Antwerp, with the expected end of the war occurring by D+360. An attack towards the Ruhr would

61   Mead, op. cit., Chapter 21 passim; Hollinghurst Papers, Hollinghurst-Browning correspondence. Ibid.
62   Browning's critics felt it was grandstanding on his part. Corps organization was logical and copied by the Americans. See Mead, op. cit., pp. 156-158.
63   *Headquarters, US Army Forces European Theater. THE GENERAL BOARD: Strategy in Western Europe 1944-1945. Report No. 1.* Passim.
64   Theater Board Report, p. 49, 52. This assessment also does not discuss 6th Army Group, the Marseilles Ports, and uses his 9 Sept assessment to the CCS as a basis.
65   See NARA, COSSAC OUTLINE OVERLORD, RG 331, SGS SHAEF 381 OVERLORD.

be mounted at this time while a secondary attack south of the Ardennes would be mounted by U.S. forces.[66] Eisenhower's decision to try for a Rhine bridgehead as well as maintain a southern push to the Rhine was estimated after MARKET GARDEN to shift his campaign forecast to an attack against the Ruhr and along the Rhine commencing after January 1, 1945.[67] SHAEF had not sufficiently thought through the ramifications of both doing MARKET and a 12th Army Group attack. As a logistical pause of up to ninety days had been forecast before a full offensive could be made, planners also theorized that movement could be maintained along the northern coast, while the southern front built up, thus moving towards needed Channel ports and Antwerp, which had figured in planning as early as 1941. Eisenhower had seen such a concept in the early ROUNDUP plans in 1942.[68]

How this "street knowledge" of plans played amongst generals who had planned for over half a year is impossible to say, but such considerations should have been raised by their staffs in their estimates. Montgomery's plan relied upon active support by First Army to draw enemy strength before and during MARKET GARDEN, a force he calculated as 8 or 9 divisions in early September. His planner, Lt. Col. Charles Richardson, estimated a 15 division push for the Aachen Corridor as needed to reach the Rhine and turn north. This estimate was made before the 40 division plan was proposed. Given the location of the Panzer Reserves that interfered with MARKET, and the primary German intelligence estimates for the threat of airborne drops (near Wesel), the probability of their deployment to fight a strong attack in the Aachen corridor is high. Additionally, both SHAEF's staff, and Eisenhower looked to FAAA for using a portion of its troops to speed the opening of the Scheldt. This was opposed personally by Brereton and Ridgway. Later, this further made MARKET look like a bad deal.[69]

Eisenhower was easily convinced by Bradley and Patton to diminish any support to a northern attack. Hodges stopped XIX Corps to move his V Corps across the Meuse on Patton's flank, then obeyed orders and eventually moved the corps but only after transferring a division laterally to Patton on the other end of the Army Group front. Patton was permitted to move two corps past his defensive line, and Bradley equalized his fuel allotments for his armies despite Eisenhower's claim that the main effort on the primary approach, Aachen, would be supported. Both armies halted for

---

66   RG 331, SHAEF 381 POST-NEPTUNE PLANNING FORECAST NO. 1, p. 3, map sketch.
67   SHAEF POST-NEPTUNE FORECAST, SHAEF G-3, FORECAST OF OPERATIONS, GCT 370-32/PLANS, 26 October 1944, p. 2.
68   TNA, CAB 44/242 Invasion of Europe, Planning Period, 1940-1944; *Administrative and Logistical History of the ETO MS, Vol. 1, Planning for Continental Operations, 2 Volumes*. See Cirillo, Ibid, Chapter 5, "Campaign Plan," for a discussion of planning and logistics as well as estimates of enemy resistance.
69   COMET outline plan. Parks file. Army War College.

two weeks about the time of MARKET due to fuel and ammunition shortages.[70] Ammunition shortages later plagued the opening of the Scheldt Estuary though SHAEF and others criticized the Canadians for their large allotment of artillery in preparations despite their crisis in manpower shortages which never seemed to be a strategic consideration by SHAEF planners.[71]

MARKET received virtually no assistance in ground attacks on the front or by extensive interdiction along the front due to the strategic bomber missions flown simultaneously. RAF bombers supported clearing the Channel ports. Rather, daylight strategic bombing continued. MARKET which was the largest airborne mission of the war, yet didn't get a D-Day type priority. This was Eisenhower's fragmented view of war.[72]

By granting no overarching priority to any attack, all sectors failed to develop their potential due to logistical shortages. This included the critical missions of opening the Scheldt and the missions to gain a bridgehead across the Neder Rijn. With no priorities, all failed at some point, as Montgomery predicted. Half successes turned into grinding battles, some of which such as the Siegfried Line battles continued until interrupted by the major German counteroffensives in December and January. While Montgomery struggled with his campaign on September 22, Eisenhower polled his American Army Group and Army Commanders all of whom publicly state in front of SHAEF's staff that they still had fuel and ammo to drive through to the Rhine. No such capability existed. The Brittany ports plan was cancelled, and Antwerp was designated the short term answer while the Marseille ports waited for shipping to be rerouted to the ports there as no priority had been established by SHAEF for its use. It is interesting, that Eisenhower's meeting was held on future planning, and never addressed what elements could be used to recover the faltering situation at Arnhem or in the Aachen corridor.[73]

Eisenhower held to his announced objectives, the Ruhr and the Saar, but first, he believed it necessary for all armies to close on the Rhine all along the front. MARKET GARDEN was a logical extension of that objective set. Had Eisenhower given priority to one, then the other with the object of opening one set of ports to support each drive, both might have been achieved with less cost and fewer accusations among his generals.

Eisenhower's post campaign assessment of destroying the enemy forward of the Rhine matches Haig's assessment that the battles prior to August, 1918 were necessary

---

70   See Siegfried Line Campaign.
71   Both Commonwealth Armies suffered chronic replacement issues as did the French. Tedder claimed that they were drugged by the use of bombers
72   MARKET's support was its troop carrier and supply lift, not supporting maneuvers. The closest US corps, XIX, was essentially grounded, during the crucial period. British 8 Corps likewise lacked fuel for a simultaneous attack with 30 Corps.
73   See post conference correspondence.

attrition battles that guaranteed the victory of the 100 days.[74]There was enough truth in the statement to use in his final despatch. He claimed, in Crusade in Europe, his plan, to close on the Rhine, destroy the German army west of the Rhine, and follow up with thrusts through Germany to "Clean out the remainder of Germany... was ...carefully outlined at staff meetings before D-Day, was never abandoned, even momentarily, throughout the campaign."[75] Eisenhower's strategy benefited from the attrition caused by the Red Army, the Strategic Bombing Campaign, and a one for one trade of soldiers in a slugging match that will forever be criticized for lost opportunities and a total lack of imagination in the use of airpower, mobility, sea power, and possibly airborne forces, though the latter were too brittle a force to survive on their own, and used most of a theater's air resources to mount a significant operation.

In another flurry of increasingly sharper correspondence in October, Eisenhower directed most strongly that the problem was Antwerp not command of the First Army, while Montgomery underscored the two issues he had harped on since 4 September. The issue was taking the Ruhr and the issue of time. Then and in his last plea, Monty noted that one effort totally supported concentrated attack of the largest supportable force might still take the Ruhr. He also noted that effort could be Bradley, but only one could be made and all others must give everything in support. Eisenhower was clear this was not what he wanted. Antwerp was necessary for a final attack across the Rhine, the main effort of which would be in the north. In the end, Dempsey and Hodges gave divisions in support to achieve this objective.[76]

This clarifies the divided view of MARKET GARDEN in the strategy of the war. To Eisenhower, it was an expedient bridgehead needed later. It used the airborne. It cut off the Germans in Holland. It bypassed the Siegfried Line. It was bold. To Montgomery, it was the belief that a major offensive could win the war, or at least set up the conditions for imminent collapse, following a pause, regrouping, and a final major offensive.[77] In defining the objective of Berlin, he used the Ruhr as the enabling objective knowing that its destruction would end Germany's ability to wage war. Given his sensitivity to logistics, it is assumed he understood that there would be operational pauses. Montgomery also noted that the Allies retained a sea power advantage using the German north coast for supplies as well as airpower. He understood that the massive German war machine covered millions of square miles of continent, but was fixed by the Red Army, the Allies in the Mediterranean, the allied armies on the western front, and the Allied strategic bombing forces. He did not expect the rest of Allied forces to sit and wait for his force to end the fighting. He asked for a priority of means sufficient for his aim.[78]

---

74   See Report to the Combined Chiefs July, 1945. Washington. Government Printing Office, 1946, p. 121.
75   Eisenhower, *Crusade in Europe*, pp. 228-229.
76   Pogue. Rawson, *Eyes Only*, pp. 147-151.
77   Major-General David Belchem. *All in A Day's March.*London: Collins, 1978, pp. 230-239.
78   Montgomery to Eisenhower. Chapter Memoirs.

MARKET GARDEN was merely an operation of war to Eisenhower, a salaam to the airmen to use their Airborne Army. MARKET GARDEN was Montgomery's attempt to shift the balance in the west toward the Allies before their advance culminated in logistical overstretch. It was a Napoleonic conception that needed an overall commander with Napoleonic energy and authority. Eisenhower had that authority, but he did not have that fire so the decision that Montgomery believed should have been made in August and certainly no later than the first of September, was never made, and MARKET proceeded with the inevitability that Overlord did when a brief weather respite appeared. The risk of failure seemed less than the cost of cancelling another major effort. The inevitability of a halt had to be dealt with despite the gamble. Eisenhower, Brereton, Montgomery, Dempsey, Leigh Mallory and Tedder all had enough knowledge of the risks to demand a halt, yet none did. The fact that Eisenhower's communications did not fully become operational till late September shows the extent of the political nature of SHAEF's assumption of command, and not control of the ground battle.[79]

The question of putting off Antwerp became important later, as Montgomery drew his sustenance from the Channel ports, and regardless of the state of the occupied approaches, the estuary had already been mined and was unusable for a period. Eisenhower had given Montgomery too large a sector for the forces in hand, and Monty had overestimated the capability of the Canadians to clear the coast themselves. Everyone wanted to keep pushing forward, the same reason that Patton had failed to seize the Brittany ports.[80]

MARKET failed for technical reasons, and these will be argued by airborne advocates to the end of days. The fact that ground forces reached within sight of the airborne perimeter indicates that the vagaries of weather, and bad luck made it a close run thing. GARDEN succeeded to the Waal in spite of the lack of American support, it moved 63 miles, and had Eisenhower showed closer interest, it might have held all of its gains which were key to the major Rhine crossings in PLUNDER/VARSITY in March 1945.[81]

79 Montgomery, Memoirs, Chapter 15. EP, Volume IV, Stephen Ambrose. *Supreme Commander: The War Years of General Dwight D. Eisenhower.* Garden City: Doubleday & Company, Inc., 1969, Chapters 12, 13 passim; Pogue, op. cit., pp.261-265, 275-278, p. 278 fn. 40.

80 Major L.F. Ellis. *Victory In the West: Volume II: The Defeat of Germany.* With Lieut. Col. A.E. Warhurst. London: Her Majesty's Stationery Office, 1968, p. 350. The official historian criticizes Eisenhower and Montgomery for this.

81 21 Army Group, 2 Army, XVIII Corps (Airborne), 2 TAF, FAAA. Ninth US Army Reports PLUNDER/VARSITY. Various.

3

Operation MARKET GARDEN: The Manpower Factor

John Peaty

Introduction

Both at the time and subsequently, British Army formations involved in OP MARKET GARDEN have been heavily criticised: the Guards and Infantry Divisions for caution and slowness, the Airborne Division for incaution and haste.

This paper will argue that no proper analysis of British military operations in the autumn of 1944 can afford to ignore an important factor: manpower. Over the years many factors have been put forward to explain the failure of MARKET GARDEN. There can be no doubting the great importance of some of these factors, such as intelligence. However, unlike manpower, such factors are well known and have been repeatedly examined. This paper will argue that an appreciation of the manpower factor is essential for a full understanding of the British Army and MARKET GARDEN.

The aim of this paper is to contextualise British Army operations in NW Europe during the autumn of 1944, specifically MARKET GARDEN. It is still not widely appreciated that the operations of 21st Army Group took place in the context of a severe manpower crisis, namely much depleted infantry formations and units and an acute shortage of reinforcements to replenish them. It will be argued that the Guards and Airborne Divisions bore some responsibility for causing this situation. It will be further argued that their actions in relation to MARKET GARDEN were influenced to some extent by this situation.

I will first outline the background and then look in turn at Guards Armoured Division and 1st Airborne Division.

Background

The manpower crisis was predictable and had been predicted before a single man set foot in Normandy. The Army had not been allocated the quantity and quality of manpower it required, the other Services having been given priority. It had not received enough good men. In any Army only a certain number of men have the physical fitness, youth, mental robustness and motivation necessary for combat. On the eve of D-Day only 70.7% of British ORs were both A1 and under 41.[1]

Best use had not been made of the manpower possessed by the Army. The Army's manpower inevitably had to be distributed between the operational theatres, a global empire and the home base as well as between the "teeth" and the "tail". However, both the home base and the "tail" had grown massively during the war.

Those men suitable for combat had of course to be spread among the "teeth" arms. That in the British Army during the war the armour, the artillery, the engineers, the signals and the infantry had to compete for those men suitable for combat was inevitable. What was new however was the diversion of many men suitable for combat away from the RAC, the RA, the RE, the R Signals and especially the Infantry and into Elite Forces like the Guards and Special Forces like the ABF.

Although in the autumn of 1944 only 2.11% of the British Army's manpower was devoted to the AAC and the Guards, appearances can be very deceptive. Two points need to be appreciated. A considerable quantity of manpower in the other arms, the infantry especially, was in fact devoted to the ABF over and above the AAC. The quality of manpower devoted to the ABF and the Guards was out of all proportion to the quantity of manpower devoted.

It is therefore unsurprising that in the autumn of 1944 the British Army experienced a manpower crisis. Because of the crisis, drastic measures were taken to boost the supply of, and reduce the demand for, infantry reinforcements. Large numbers of RAF and RN personnel were transferred to the Army; within the Army, large numbers of RA personnel were retrained as infantrymen; and many infantry formations and units were broken up. Although a drastic step, breaking up infantry formations and units would both reduce demand and produce a number of infantrymen for immediate use as reinforcements.

Well before D-Day the War Office had forecast that, at the end of September 1944, the Army in the field would have an infantry deficit of 35,300 and that 5 infantry divisions would have to be broken up by the end of the year. With regard to NW Europe, the War Office forecast that the deficit would be 14,500 by the end of October, 18,040 by the end of November and 22,300 by the end of the year and that 2 divisions would have to be broken up by the end of the year.[2]

Contrary to what one often reads or hears, the War Office forecast proved accurate. At the end of September 21st Army Group had an infantry shortage of 10,000: infantry battalions under-strength by 2,000 plus an empty reinforcement pool which needed refilling to the tune of 8,000.[3] The shortage did indeed grow to 14,500 during October.[4] After Normandy an infantry division (the 59th) and an infantry brigade

1   Adams papers, LHCMA: AG's lecture of 29th May 1944, AG Stats branch memo.
2   TNA: Directorate of Staff Duties: manpower: WO32/10899.
3   Major LF Ellis, *Victory in the West*, Vol. II, p.141.
4   TNA: Home Forces file: Provision of drafts for "Overlord": WO199/1335.

were broken up; another infantry division (the 50th) was broken up by the end of the year.

Yet during the crisis there was a large number of men in NW Europe and a huge number in the UK. However, one must not be misled by gross figures. One needs to focus on the number of infantry in the field and the number "draftable" i.e. suitable and available to be reinforcements for the infantry in the field. Contrary to D'Este's often-quoted figure, there were not in the UK at the end of June more than 115,000 "draftable" infantry.[5] There were less than 15,000[6] – an extremely low figure only 3.5 weeks into the NW Europe campaign.

At the end of September the British Army had 16 infantry divisions in or available for the field, of which half were in 21st Army Group.[7] Of these 8, one was in process of disbandment because of the manpower crisis (59th), shortly to be replaced by Britain's last uncommitted infantry division (52nd). In round figures, each had a War Establishment i.e. authorised strength of 18,400, of which only 7,600 (40%) was in the division's nine rifle infantry battalions. Therefore, at the end of September the authorised strength of Montgomery's infantry divisions were about 147,200 and the authorised strength of their rifle infantry battalions – which was understrength and for which reinforcements could not be provided – was about 60,800. However, while the WE of an infantry battalion was about 850, only about 400 were riflemen.[8] Therefore, there were only 3,600 riflemen in an infantry division, making a total of only 28,800 riflemen in Montgomery's infantry divisions. There were of course many more infantry battalions in the field besides those in the infantry divisions: in armoured divisions, in non-divisional infantry brigades and on their own. However, this figure of 28,800 is key. It is essential to appreciate that the spear wielded by Montgomery had an extremely small point.

It is also essential to appreciate that it was this point which suffered the most casualties. Between D-Day and the end of August, 21st Army Group sustained 70,000 battle casualties, of which 39,000 (56%) were rifle infantry.[9] By October, as Montgomery informed Brooke, his infantry divisions had sustained an average of 7,500 casualties each, approaching 40% of divisional strength. The situation was of course a lot worse than this figure indicates as most of the casualties had been sustained by the infantry battalions and within the battalions by the rifle companies and platoons. Some battalions were down to only 18 officers.[10] As Lindsay recalled in his superb memoir of the campaign, in his battalion of 51st Division the rifle companies had only 2 instead of

5   Lieut-Col Carlo D'Este, *Decision in Normandy*, p.268.
6   TNA: Home Forces file: Provision of drafts for "Overlord": WO199/1335.
7   TNA: General Return of the Strength of the British Army for the quarter ending 30th September 1944, AG Stats: WO73/162.
8   Directorate of Selection of Personnel, SP3, 'The Infantry', Job Analysis (Field), April 1945, App. III.
9   TNA: AG Stats file: casualty returns: WO32/11172.
10   IWM: Montgomery papers, LMD63/60, Montgomery to Brooke, 19 October 1944.

5 officers and he feared a debacle if one of the surviving officers was hit and then men refused to advance or even retreated.[11]

Wigram, who revolutionised infantry training in Britain and who fought and died in Italy, pointed to the qualitative differences within the infantry. In "whatever regiment – whether good or bad", he assessed that of a typical under-strength platoon of 22 men, 6 will be "gutful... go anywhere and do anything", 12 will be "sheep" who will follow if well led and 4 to 6 will be "cowards", who will be ineffectual or will run away.[12] It cannot be denied that the burden of the fighting undertaken and the casualties suffered by infantry units, whether in Italy or NW Europe, fell heaviest on those in the first of Wigram's groups, thereby rendering those units less effective, slower and more cautious over time.

It cannot be emphasised enough that the one armoured and two infantry divisions spearheading the advance of 30 Corps on Arnhem were all under-strength and tired as the result of their exertions in the Normandy campaign and the pursuit across France and Belgium. Guards Armoured Division, 43rd Division and 50th Division had all seen fierce fighting and sustained heavy losses in Normandy, not least among key leaders such as battalion, company and platoon commanders. Landing on D-Day, by Arnhem 50th Division had endured more than 3 months almost continuous fighting. It was tired and depleted. By the end of August it had suffered 6,630 casualties, the second highest loss of any British division. Jary's superb memoir of platoon command in 43rd Division is eloquent about that Division's manpower problems during the campaign.

Guards Armoured Division

As their name implies, the Guards were the bodyguards of the Sovereign and, as such, a "corps d'elite". They comprised two regiments of Horse Guards (the Household Cavalry) and five Regiments of Foot Guards (the Grenadier, Coldstream, Scots, Irish and Welsh Guards).

Importantly, the Guards were semi-autonomous. They were responsible for their own recruitment, training and reinforcement. Alone of the Army, they did not participate in the General Service Corps and continued to recruit and train "in house". They were extremely choosy about their intake: recruits had to be perfect physical specimens. In particular, they had to be tall and strong. Recruits not up to their stringent standards were rejected. Recruits accepted by the Foot Guards and Household Cavalry were naturally denied to Line Infantry and Cavalry units. Moreover, Foot Guards and Household Cavalry personnel were never cross-posted i.e. they were never used to reinforce Line Infantry and Cavalry units.

---

11   Col Sir Martin Lindsay, *So Few Got Through*, pp.122-3.
12   TNA: Lionel Wigram, Report on Sicily ops, 16 August 1943, P2: WO231/14.

For the duration of the war, should the Household Cavalry and Foot Guards have been allowed to remain semi-autonomous or should they have been obliged to participate fully in the Army's recruitment, assessment, training and reinforcement machine? If they had been so obliged, there would have been a more equitable distribution of high quality manpower within the Army and the Army would not have had to run and staff two machines in parallel.

The Household Cavalry was expanded during the war but not greatly. One of its 2 regiments provided deep recce for Guards Armoured Division during the NW Europe campaign. The Foot Guards were greatly expanded during the war however. In mid 1944 there were 6 brigades of Foot Guards: 1 armoured division (with 1 armoured brigade and 1 infantry brigade) and 1 tank brigade in NW Europe; 2 infantry brigades in Italy; and 1 infantry brigade in the UK (201st, which had been disbanded in Italy and resurrected in the training role at home). There were 26 battalions either in these 6 brigades or unbrigaded. Of these 26 battalions: 12 were rifle; 1 was garrison; 5 were training; 1 was motor; 3 were armoured; 3 were tank; and 1 was armoured recce. It is noteworthy that, of these 26 battalions, only 17 were serving overseas and of these only 9 were rifle.[13] Should the Foot Guards have been expanded to 26 battalions? Should 8 battalions have been converted from rifle to armoured, tank, armoured recce and motor in order to form an armoured division and tank brigade? In light of the shortage of infantry and the abundance of armoured and tank formations (there were 3 other armoured divisions and 6 other armoured or tank brigades in Normandy),[14] would it not have been better for them all (with the exception of a necessary number of training and garrison battalions) to have remained rifle? In mid 1944 there were 36,911 Foot Guards (excluding POWs, trainees etc.) Of these, 10,922 were in NW Europe: 3,437 Rifle (3 battalions); 6,560 Armoured (3 battalions), Tank (3 battalions) and Armoured Recce (1 battalion); and 925 Motor (1 battalion).[15] Note that only 40% were employed in the rifle or motor role.

The Guards made a significant contribution to the NW Europe campaign. Guards Armoured Division comprised: 5th Guards Armoured Brigade with 3 armoured battalions and 1 motor battalion; 32nd Guards Brigade with 3 rifle battalions; and 1 armoured recce battalion. After the Normandy campaign, the unwieldy Brigade structure was dispensed with and the Division was reconfigured into four battle groups, each consisting of an armoured or armoured recce battalion and a rifle or motor battalion of the same Regiment. This enabled the armour and infantry to work closely together, the operations in Normandy having clearly demonstrated the necessity for a combined arms approach to overcome German defences. Each battle group

---

13   TNA: General Return of the Strength of the British Army for the quarter ending 30th
      June 1944, AG Stats: WO73/161.
14   Major LF Ellis, *Victory in the West*, Vol. I, App. IV, Pt. I, pp.521-30.
15   TNA: General Return of the Strength of the British Army for the quarter ending 30th
      June 1944, AG Stats: WO73/161.

was allocated a squadron of the Household Cavalry for probing. 6th Guards Tank Brigade comprised 3 tank battalions. Its role was the direct support of infantry in the assault.

Only a handful of individuals and no units of the Guards served east of Suez. This had been the tradition down the centuries, like the control exercised by the Guards over their own recruitment and training. In a global conflict this opt-out from deployment to the East was a hindrance to the War Office and should have been set aside, as should the opt-out from the GSC. That they were not tells us a great deal about the influence of the Guards.

The Guards had enormous influence in political and social circles. Guards Armoured Division was commanded by Major-General Allan Adair: the one man who, because of the semi-autonomous position and the influence of the Guards, Montgomery said he could never sack. Considerable exertions, at the behest of Churchill, were made to maintain the great strength of the Guards, at the expense of the rest of the Army – the Infantry of the Line especially – and of the RAF.

On 18th March 1944 Weeks (DCIGS) warned Montgomery of a looming shortage of infantry reinforcements.[16] He wrote: "Within the general infantry position the Guards present a special problem. As things are at the moment we are very short against Guards infantry requirements and have recently had to disband 201 Guards Brigade in Italy. Even after this step it seems quite possible, on present casualty forecasts, that we shall not be able to keep up the 2 brigades out there". There was at the moment a pool of Guards armoured reinforcements which had been built up for "Overlord". However: "As soon as your 32 Guards Brigade starts to get casualties the infantry position will become worse than ever, and in fact quite out of hand". A possible solution would be to remove 6th Guards Tank Brigade from 21st Army Group and replace it with 28th Armoured Brigade from the UK. 6th Guards Tank Brigade could then be broken up and its men, together with some of the Guards armoured reinforcements, retrained as infantry. This should provide an extra 1,200 Guards infantry reinforcements reasonably early because all were basically trained as infantry, and would materially improve the reinforcement position for Italy and 32nd Guards Brigade. An alternative would be to withdraw 5th Guards Armoured Brigade from Guards Armoured Division, but this was full of snags as all its battalions were regular.

In his reply to Weeks of 19th March, Montgomery wrote: "I consider that 6 Gds Tk Bde should be broken up at once and the men be retrained as infantry. I hope that this will improve the reinforcement position for the Inf Bde in the Gds Armd Div (32 Gds Bde)". 28th Armoured Brigade should be given to 21st Army Group in place of 6th Guards Tank Brigade.[17] The break up of the Guards Tank Brigade and the conversion of its personnel back to riflemen would not have been popular with those concerned or

16   TNA: Cabinet Office: military narrative file: CAB106/313.
17   Ibid.

easy to accomplish. However, given the exclusivity of the Guards, it seemed the only way to overcome the looming shortage of riflemen.

Shortly after this exchange of letters, Churchill learned of the proposed break up of 6th Guards Tank Brigade, apparently from Montgomery. In his minute of 4th April to Montgomery,[18] Churchill told Montgomery that after a good deal of thought he was prepared to discuss the matter with the War Office. Meanwhile he had ordered that no action to destroy the brigade was to be taken. In his minute of the same day to Grigg (Secretary of State for War) and Brooke (CIGS),[19] Churchill said that the disbandment of the 6th Guards Tank Brigade would be "disastrous". He proposed that it should serve with the Guards Armoured Division in NW Europe until it could no longer be sustained.

On 7th April, as Brooke recorded in his diary that night, after the presentation of the D-Day plans at Montgomery's HQ, "PJ Grigg, Monty and I had an interview with the PM to get him to face the reduction of formations in the Guards Division, as they can no longer find reinforcements. We had the usual difficulty. He has been got at by MPs and produced every sort of argument against what is an inevitable necessity".[20]

In his minute of 9th April to Grigg and Brooke (copied to Montgomery),[21] Churchill said that he had carefully considered the points they had put to him. He implored them not to melt down the Guards but instead keep up the Guards at the expense of the Line. This was what the Russians and the Germans did. He wrote: "...special terms raise "esprit de corps". No one doubts that the performances of the Guards fully justify the prestige which attaches to them. Therefore, I wish that the Guards should draw upon the Line and that the existing Guards formation shall be maintained, not only from Guards recruits, but where necessary from Line recruits". He had already given approval for the pooling of the two Guards Brigades in Italy. But he did not agree to the abolition of the 6th Guards Tank Brigade. At least 25,000 men should be transferred from the RAF Regiment to the infantry including the Guards.

In his minute of 18th April to Grigg and Sinclair (Secretary of State for Air),[22] Churchill said that it was necessary to transfer at least 25,000 men from the RAF Regiment to the infantry. In a forthright minute of 20th May to Sinclair,[23] Churchill repeated his request that 25,000 RAF Regiment men be transferred to the infantry, including "two thousand good men for the upkeep of the Guards" who were required urgently. On 30th May a special Cabinet meeting was held at 10 Downing Street under Attlee (Deputy PM) with the sole purpose of pressurizing the RAF into

18   Sir Winston Churchill, *History of the Second World War: Closing the Ring*, p.704.
19   Ibid, pp.704-5.
20   Sir Arthur Bryant, *Triumph in the West*, p.180.
21   Churchill, p.705.
22   Ibid, pp.705-6.
23   Ibid, pp.710-11.

transferring men to the infantry, especially the Guards.[24] At the meeting Sinclair agreed to transfer 1,500 from the RAF Regiment to the Guards and get another 500 RAF personnel to volunteer for the Guards. A far cry from the 25,000 RAF Regiment men requested, but better than nothing.

In his minute of 6th June to Grigg and Brooke, as the Army waded ashore in Normandy, Churchill assured them that he appreciated the Army's manpower problems and promised them that he would not relax his pressure on the RAF and RN to transfer men.[25] Thanks to Churchill's intervention, the Guards Armoured Division and Tank Brigade survived to the end of the war – which is more than can be said for many Line Infantry formations and units. It is believed that Montgomery never forgave Churchill or the Guards.

The considerable resources absorbed by – and strong preference given to – the Guards during the war could be justified if their performance in the field was impressive, more impressive than that of ordinary formations and units. However, contrary to their own and Churchill's claim, it was not. No one denies their smartness and precision on the parade ground. However, their combat effectiveness has frequently been questioned. A lack of drive and imagination on the battlefield has often been alleged. Critics have repeatedly said that the Guards did not always live up to their superior status and exalted reputation.

Critics have pointed in particular to the failed attempt by Guards Armoured Division to relieve the besieged 1st Airborne Division at Arnhem. Granted that the Division was required to advance along a single axis and over many water obstacles against heavy opposition. Nevertheless, American veterans of MARKET have criticised the "by the book" approach of the Guards: stopping when they had outrun their support, leaguering for the night and resuming the advance in the morning rather than forging on ahead.[26] Actually, a good case can be made for the Guards. The men were tired, tanks are vulnerable at night and leaguering was sensible.

The critics also ignore the manpower context: the Division was short of infantry to work with and protect the armour (as forecast by Weeks) and several of its personnel were recent transfers from the RAF (as arranged by Churchill). The spearhead of the Division's advance on Arnhem was the Irish Guards battle group with an armoured and an infantry battalion. However, the infantry battalion (3rd Irish Guards) was seriously understrength, having lost 105 men killed and many times that number wounded in Normandy. As the battalion war diary records, on the day before the operation was launched: "It was decided as result of casualties and lack of reinforcements to re-organise the Bn temporarily on a three coy basis".[27] In other words, the battalion was a company or 25% understrength.

24 TNA: War Cabinet committee papers: CAB78/21.
25 Sir Winston Churchill, *History of the Second World War: Triumph and Tragedy*, pp.685-6.
26 General James Gavin, *On to Berlin*, pp.181-2.
27 TNA: 3 Irish Guards, Battalion War Diary, 16 September 1944: WO171/1257.

The Guards have been criticised from within their own ranks, by distinguished wartime veterans. Howard, who served with the Guards in Italy, believes that the creation of Guards Armoured Division was both unnecessary and a mistake. It was unnecessary because by then there was no shortage of armoured formations. It was a mistake because armoured warfare did not suit the Guards or play to their strengths. Guardsmen were big men and unsuited to tanks. The Guards were rightly admired for their discipline and steadiness. Yet armoured warfare called for dash and initiative. Guards Armoured Division displayed neither at Arnhem.[28] Farrell, who commanded a squadron in the Guards Tank Brigade in NW Europe, wrote in a letter to me: "I agree, as do many of my war-time colleagues, that it was a mistake to form a Guards Armoured Division. It would have been better to have left the five Guards Brigades as Infantry to strengthen up five infantry Divisions, or possibly to form out of them a Guards Infantry Division as in the first war".[29]

Following the creation of a Guards division in the First World War, the creation of a Guards division in the Second was perhaps inevitable. Surprisingly, it appears that in neither war was the creation the result of detailed discussion. Yet, surely, certain questions should have been asked and satisfactorily answered before the creation was sanctioned. Would not the training and discipline of the Guards be put to better use by distributing the Guards (either as brigades or battalions) throughout the Army? Could the strength and quality of the division be maintained? Would the creation of an elite division cause ill-feeling in the Army? What would be the effect on morale throughout the Army if the division failed?[30] And if the creation of a Guards division had been decided upon after a careful weighing of the pros and cons, surely the same procedure should have been followed to decide whether it was to be an armoured division.

Some inescapable questions are prompted by this examination of the Guards. Should they have been allowed to continue to recruit, train and reinforce "in house"? Should they have been greatly expanded? Should a substantial proportion have been converted from rifle into armoured, tank, armoured recce and motor? Should they have fielded an armoured, a tank and an infantry brigade in NW Europe rather than three infantry brigades? Was the creation of an armoured division and a tank brigade and their maintenance until the end of the war sensible? Given the critical shortage of Line Infantry (which was to a certain extent both caused and exacerbated by the Guards) and given the great number of armoured and tank formations available, I would have to answer all these questions in the negative. Was the performance of the Guards during the war exemplary, particularly at Arnhem? I would

28   Professor Sir Michael Howard, BCMH conference on the Guards, RHQ Household Cavalry, 15th November 1997.
29   Major Charles Farrell: letter to the author of 29th Oct. 1998.
30   Christopher McCarthy, BCMH Conference on the Guards, RHQ Household Cavalry, 15th November 1997.

again have to say no but I would argue that at Arnhem there were extenuating circumstances, not least that the Guards were hamstrung by a lack of infantry to support the armour.

1st Airborne Division

During the war the British Army created many Special Forces, the largest of which were the ABF. They were forces trained and equipped to perform a special task: enter the battlefield from the air, either dropping by parachute or landing by glider, a task believed to be beyond the capability of ordinary forces.

Within the British Army during the war there were many legitimate demands on manpower besides the infantry. What was "not legitimate, or even sensible", in the view of Terraine, was "the creaming off" of good men "into various "private armies" by means of which, it was naively supposed, set-piece battle with its heavy loss could be avoided". These "private armies" included the ABF: "Worst of all the "offenders", it must be said".[31]

Britain's ABF had their origin in Churchill's reaction to the German's spectacular use of ABF in the Low Countries in 1940. Churchill called for the "Deployment of parachute troops on a scale equal to five thousand".[32] The result was the birth of the Parachute Regiment. Following the German's spectacular use of ABF to conquer Crete in 1941, he ordered Britain's ABF to be greatly expanded.

In mid-1944 there were 16,623 personnel on the strength of the AAC: paratroopers, glider-borne infantry and glider pilots.[33] This figure does not convey the full extent of the manpower belonging to ABF as it only covers those in the AAC. In mid-1944 ABF comprised 1st Airborne Division (in the UK), 6th Airborne Division (in Normandy) – each with a WE of 12,148 personnel[34] – and 2nd Independent Parachute Brigade (in the Mediterranean): a total of 7 brigades comprising 14 parachute and 6 airlanding battalions. This means that to the AAC figure must be added almost 15,000 personnel under command of ABF but belonging to corps other than the AAC – making a total of over 30,000.[35] A substantial number but one which was to be greatly increased prior to Arnhem. All the above figures exclude the Canadian parachute battalion and Polish parachute brigade which were integral parts of Britain's ABF and saw action in Normandy and at Arnhem respectively.

---

31   John Terraine, *The Right of the Line*, p.642.
32   Churchill minute to Ismay, 6th June 1940: Churchill, *History of the Second World War: Their Finest Hour*, pp.246-7.
33   General Return of the Strength of the British Army for the quarter ending 30th September 1944, AG Stats: WO73/162.
34   Ellis, *Victory in the West*, Vol. I, App. IV, p.535.
35   General Return of the Strength of the British Army for the quarter ending 30th September 1944, AG Stats: WO73/162.

Britain's ABF were created before the infantry shortage. However, given that in war the infantry always bear the brunt of the casualties and that an Army always run short of infantry first, certain questions are inescapable. Was it wise to have created 14 Parachute battalions (each of 29 officers and 584 other ranks) and 6 Airlanding battalions (each of 47 officers and 817 other ranks)? Half of the Parachute battalions were formed out of volunteers from other units, mostly infantry; the other half were formed by the conversion of ordinary infantry battalions – as were the Airlanding battalions. Was it wise to have converted 13 ordinary infantry battalions into Parachute or Airlanding battalions? Was it wise to have encouraged volunteers for 7 Parachute battalions away from their original (mostly infantry) units? It would be possible to answer these questions in the affirmative if it could be demonstrated that the infantry's burden was lessened by the creation and continuing existence of the ABF. However, it cannot. The ABF neither obviated the need for lots of good infantry nor saved the infantry from having to do a lot of hard fighting and sustaining heavy casualties.

In addition to the significant numbers who were lost to the infantry by either volunteering or being re-roled as Airborne, we must consider the qualitative impact of the loss of these men on the infantry. Qualitative factors are of course harder to assess than quantitative ones. However, we may examine the standards set for paratroopers. It was laid down that volunteers to the newly formed 1st Parachute Brigade "must be first class fighting soldiers and show keenness, intelligence and initiative and must be men of first class character only".[36] It should be noted that all recruits to the Parachute Regiment had to be volunteers, even when their unit was converted. When an infantry battalion was converted into a parachute battalion, a large proportion of men were posted out, either on conversion or subsequently. For example, when 8th Parachute Battalion was formed by conversion, 175 men were posted out even before parachute training had begun because they refused to volunteer to be a paratrooper or failed the parachute medical.[37] Whether volunteering individually or when their unit was converted, there can be no doubt that the ABF attracted from the infantry a large slice of the most aggressive, enterprising and fittest men. It cannot be denied that many of those men drawn into the ABF from the infantry belonged to the first of Wigram's groups, those "Ready for Anything".

During the war ABF spent remarkably little time in action and even less time in action in their designed role. To the dismay of their promoters and supporters, during the liberation of Europe there was little scope for using ABF in the role for which they had been intensively trained and expensively equipped. Britain mounted only five major airborne operations during the liberation: Sicily; Normandy; Southern France; Holland; and the Rhine. There was however a great need to use ABF in the ground

---

36   TNA: Airborne Policy. Memo regarding the formation of 2 additional battalions, 26th August 1941: WO32/9778.
37   TNA: 8th Parachute Battalion, Battalion War Diary, 18th-22nd December 1942: WO166/8559.

role because of the shortage of infantry – a role for which their Parachute (unlike Airlanding) battalions had neither the weapons nor the numbers and in which they did not excel.

2nd Parachute Brigade remained in the Mediterranean and was made an Independent Brigade when the ABF were withdrawn to the UK to prepare for D-Day. In the period 1943 to 1945, usually in the ground role, it was almost continuously in action and therefore indisputably earned its keep.

6th Airborne Division was used in the Airborne role on D-Day and kept in Normandy fighting on the eastern flank in the infantry role throughout the campaign. It was withdrawn to the UK shortly before Arnhem. It was shipped out to Belgium because of the German breakthrough in the Ardennes. Withdrawn to the UK again, it was used, for the second and last time in the Airborne role, in the crossing of the Rhine and then took part in the advance to the Baltic. It therefore spent almost two-thirds of the NW campaign in theatre though only on D-Day can it said to have been a game changer.

1st Airborne Division, operating as a division and in the airborne role, saw action only twice during the war, spending a total of 17 days in contact with the enemy: in Sicily for 8 days and at Arnhem for 9. It saw no action for an entire year: September 1943 to September 1944. It spent 10 boring and frustrating months (November 1943 to September 1944) in the UK training and preparing for operations in support of 21st Army Group which were repeatedly cancelled. Hence its eagerness to go into action at Arnhem, over-eagerness in fact. Too readily it agreed – unlike Sicily and Normandy – to forgoing a coup de main, to landing and drop zones miles from the target, to being deployed by day and to being transported in more than one lift.[38]

Apart from boredom and frustration, there was another powerful consideration behind the Division's eagerness to deploy, one which has rarely been mentioned. As Carver (who commanded an armoured brigade during the operation) later wrote: "If they were not employed now, they foresaw disbandment and the use of their troops as normal infantry, if the war went on much longer".[39] As a 50th anniversary piece in the "British Army Review" noted: "Had 1st Airborne Division not been committed to MARKET GARDEN (or something like it) pressure to bring it into battle as an infantry division, or worse, to break it up, would have become acute".[40]

The Division's eagerness to get into action come what may had disastrous consequences. At Arnhem it suffered 7,167 casualties.[41] It was hors de combat for the remainder of the war, though it was not disbanded (which would have been sensible) but rebuilt with new personnel.[42] To create a Division with a WE of 12,148 men; to

38   Col Terence Otway, *Airborne Forces*, pp.263-4.
39   Field Marshal Lord Michael Carver, *The Seven Ages of the British Army*, p.277.
40   "Carbuncle", 'On an Excess of Bridges', *British Army Review*, No. 108, p.89.
41   Otway, p.283.
42   Ibid, p.324.

have it spend a whole year out of action training and planning; to have it engage the enemy for a mere 9 days; and to have it effectively destroyed in those 9 days, is not the most cost-effective use of 12,148 men, manpower shortage or not.

It is often forgotten by historians of MARKET GARDEN and of ABF that in September 1944 ABF included a fully manned and completely fresh infantry division. In fact the Division was over-manned, far exceeding its WE. In mid-1944 52nd Division contained 22,500 men of whom 8,140 were rifle infantry. After spending years in Scotland training for warfare in Arctic climate and mountain terrain for deployment in Norway, on 3rd August 1944 it was re-roled as Airportable as part of ABF – taking the number of men under command of ABF to well in excess of 50,000. During MARKET GARDEN it: "Was to be flown in NORTH of ARNHEM as soon as airstrips were available and were to concentrate in reserve nearby in accordance with orders to be issued on landing".[43] Of course the airstrips were never captured and so it was never deployed. We will therefore never know what effect the deployment of its 9 airportable battalions would have had on MARKET GARDEN. Re-roled as an ordinary infantry division, it arrived in Europe by sea in October.[44] Replacing the disbanding 50th Division, it first saw action in the polders of Holland – an ironic fate for a Division which had spent most of the war trained and equipped to fight in mountains.

In September 1944, for many and various reasons, everyone – SHAEF, 21st Army Group, ABF, 1st Airborne Division and 52nd Airportable Division – wanted to launch MARKET GARDEN and get these two divisions into theatre as quickly as possible.[45] Of course the primary reason was to get across the Rhine and end the war quickly while the Germans were unbalanced, a laudable though unrealistic aim. But there were other reasons why it was desired to deploy these long idle, intensively trained, expensively equipped, fully manned and fresh divisions – including I would argue the need to show a return on a substantial investment and the need to address the problem of tired and depleted infantry divisions and lack of infantry reinforcements in theatre. It was simply not sensible or justifiable for ABF – totalling more than 50,000 men, many of them "first class", as we have seen – to be unengaged in the autumn of 1944 (save for a brigade in the Mediterranean). I believe it probable that without MARKET GARDEN, 1st Airborne Division would, at the very least, have been put into the line as infantry, just like 52nd Division. I further believe that the eagerness of 1st Airborne Division to participate in MARKET GARDEN was due in part to an awareness of this probability.

Referring to the proliferation of Special Forces like ABF in Britain during the war, Perry comments: "Certainly a considerable amount of effort was expended in

---

43   TNA: Notes on the Operations of 21st Army Group, 1st September 1945: WO106/4472.
44   Lieut-Col HF Joslen, *Orders of Battle*.
45   Charles B Macdonald, 'The Decision to Launch Operation Market Garden', *Command Decisions*, pp.429-442.

developing such forces and in the eyes of some military authorities they did not give a worthwhile return for the resources they absorbed".[46] One of those military authorities, Slim, was extremely critical of Special Forces. He wrote that: "Private armies – and for that matter private air forces – are expensive, wasteful, and unnecessary". Slim held that Special Forces had three drawbacks. Special Forces: reduce the quality of the rest of the army (especially the infantry) by skimming off the best soldiers; encourage the belief that certain operations can only be carried out by specially trained men; can only be employed for limited periods before they have to be withdrawn for recuperation.[47] Perry endorses Slim's list and adds a fourth drawback: "Special Forces, because of the exigencies of the moment, will often be called on to carry out tasks allocated to more regularly constituted units, when they prove to be untrained and ill-equipped for those tasks".[48] The British Army's experience of Special Forces in general and of ABF in particular during the war provides overwhelming evidence to support the views of Slim, one of the greatest commanders in the history of the British Army, and of Perry, an authority on the manpower of the Commonwealth Armies in the World Wars.

On any rational assessment, the inflated and under-employed Special Forces which the British Army possessed during the war – and of which ABF were the largest and the least used – were not cost-effective. They specialised in performing a particular role and were trained and equipped accordingly. Large numbers of picked troops, highly trained and specially equipped, were kept waiting for long periods to be used for short periods. They were very reluctant to be employed as infantry and when they were they did not shine. Special Forces attracted the very fittest (both mentally and physically) and most enterprising men to the detriment of the rest of the Army, the infantry especially. Recruits were attracted by better conditions; better pay (e.g. parachute pay); glamour; danger and excitement; propaganda; escape from the frustrations of drill, sentry duty and fatigues.[49] Even when ordinary infantry units were converted into the parachute role, "undesirables" i.e. the unwilling, the unfit, the elderly, the difficult etc. were ruthlessly weeded out and posted elsewhere in the Army.

It is significant that the three most formidable Armies during the war – the German, Russian and Japanese – did not create and maintain ABF on the same scale as the British Army. The German Army employed a small number of ABF to capture Norway, Holland and Belgium and a larger number to capture Crete. The British Army, mesmerised by the success of German ABF, created its own ABF in response to Norway, Holland and Belgium and then in response to Crete increased them to a size which dwarfed German ABF. Ironically, the German Army, painfully aware of the narrowness of its victories in Norway, Holland, Belgium and Crete and of the

---

46   FW Perry, *The Commonwealth Armies: Manpower and Organisation in two World Wars*, p.59.
47   Field Marshal Lord Slim, *Defeat into Victory*, pp.546-9.
48   Perry, p.221.
49   Carver, p.274.

heavy losses that its ABF had suffered, decided to employ its ABF in the ground role thereafter, as the British Army found to its cost in Italy and in Holland.

The great investment which Britain put into ABF during the war has been criticized by distinguished soldiers and reputable historians. In the estimation of Carver, during the war ABF did not have a "general effect on the conduct of operations. Occasions suited to their employment occurred only rarely, and their use did not prove as decisive as had been hoped". Carver regards only the German use of ABF Forces in Crete and the British and American use of ABF in Normandy as crucial.[50] I find it hard to disagree with the verdict of MacDonald: "The conclusion appears inescapable that airborne forces as employed in the Second World War were a luxury – spectacular, impressive, and often highly useful, as many a luxury can be, but a luxury nevertheless. The expense of training specialised airborne troops, the diversion of resources from other programmes, the leadership denied regular units by the diversion of highly qualified and motivated men into elite units, and the cost of providing special equipment such as planes, gliders, parachutes – all these would have to be weighed against the results. Even the oft-expressed contention that by their very existence airborne troops forced the enemy to disperse his resources and his reserves to protect vital installations cannot be supported".[51]

Conclusion

It is undeniable that the Guards and ABF, both having a high profile and glamorous reputation coupled with control over their own recruitment, were able to attract large numbers of volunteers and to pick those men they wanted and reject those they did not. There is no doubt that the Guards and ABF thereby creamed off much good material from the infantry and thus helped to cause and exacerbate the critical shortage of infantry which afflicted the British Army during the last year of the war.

During the war the Guards were greatly expanded. Extraordinary measures were taken to maintain the inflated and unsupportable strength of the Guards during the last year of the war, such as the transfer of RAF men. The number of Guardsmen greatly increased during the war but Guardsmen were never cross-posted, never used to reinforce non-Guards units. Yet, because of the infantry crisis, during the last year of the war cross-posting was common among Line Infantry units. The Russians had Guards, as Churchill said. However, they were not the same as Britain's Guards. They were troops who had earned the title of Guards in battle and who could be deprived of that title if they failed.

It is both ironic and paradoxical that Churchill, who constantly criticised the Army's declining infantry strength during the war, should be the man primarily responsible

---

50   Ibid, p.287.
51   Charles B MacDonald, 'Airborne Armies', *History of the Second World War*, Vol. 7, p.2962.

for the dramatic expansion of the Guards and the creation and continuance until the end of the war of the Guards Armoured Division and the Guards Tank Brigade.

Inevitably, the main loser from the creation and dramatic growth of Special Forces like ABF during the war was the infantry. During the last year of the war, with the British Army critically short of infantry, many Special Forces formations had to be employed as infantry, including those belonging to the ABF. Seen against the background of a global shortage of infantry, this can only be considered as entirely justified. That there was a need during the war for a small, specially trained and equipped force to raid behind enemy lines, few would deny – least of all Slim or the present writer. It is clear however that the creation and maintenance of Special Forces of the great number, variety and size possessed by the British Army during the war – not least the Airborne Divisions, the Independent Parachute Brigade and the Airportable Division – was indeed expensive, wasteful and unnecessary.

The creation and dramatic expansion of Britain's Special Forces during the war – most especially the ABF – were primarily due to the interest, support and determination of Churchill, who was a sucker for any "cloak and dagger" enterprise. It is both ironic and paradoxical that Churchill, who continually bemoaned the Army's declining infantry strength during the war, should be the man most responsible for depriving the infantry of large numbers of suitable personnel through his support for Special Forces in general and ABF in particular.

I believe that the evidence presented in this piece clearly demonstrates three things. Firstly, that the diversion of a large quantity of high quality manpower away from the infantry and into the Guards and ABF took place during the war. Secondly, that, measured by damage inflicted on the enemy or by time spent in contact with the enemy, neither the Guards nor ABF fully repaid the special treatment given to them or the heavy manpower investment made in them during the war. Thirdly, that the diversion of manpower away from the infantry and into the Guards and ABF helped both to cause and to exacerbate the infantry shortage which afflicted the British Army during the last year of the war.

To assess MARKET GARDEN properly, I believe it is essential to appreciate that it took place in the context of an acute manpower shortage, a shortage which was to some extent caused and exacerbated by the creation and continuance of Guards Armoured Division and 1st Airborne Division. If 50th Division, 43rd Division and Guards Armoured Division were cautious and slow, as has been alleged, I suggest that one explanation is that they did not have enough infantry to prevail. If 1st Airborne Division was incautious and hasty, as has been alleged, I suggest that one explanation is that it did not want to be deployed as infantry or broken up and used to reinforce the infantry.

4

A Week Too Late?

Jack Didden

In popular mythology Market Garden is synonymous with the heroic stand and ultimate defeat of the British 1st Airborne Division at Arnhem. However, the outcome had already been decided before the operation was even launched. Additionally, the fighting south of the river Maas was a major factor, to the ultimate failure something which was recognized by Lieutenant-General Sir Miles C. Dempsey (Second Army).[1] One of the units that played a key role in all of this was Kampfgruppe Chill.[2] This is part of its story, which begins at the end of August 1944.

The Allied Strategy until 4 September 1944

The end of the fighting in Normandy and the catastrophic losses suffered by the German *Westheer*, meant that the Allies needed to rethink their strategy.[3] After weighing the various proposals, on 22 August Eisenhower told his subordinate commanders that Montgomery's Twenty-First Army Group was to proceed north of the Ardennes while Bradley's Twelfth Army Group was to strike south of there.[4] To aid the British army group he assigned the First Allied Airborne Army (Lieutenant-General Lewis H. Brereton) to Montgomery. Also the bulk of the petrol for Bradley's army group would go to the First US Army which supported Montgomery's drive. Bradley and Patton were, understandably, annoyed, but Montgomery had problems to take into account which the Americans did not have. One aspect he needed to

---

1   Letter to Major L.F. Ellis, 18th June 1962, The National Archives, Kew, (TNA) WO 285/29.

2   This article is a reworking of part of my Ph D study, Jack Didden, *Fighting Spirit*, Drunen 2012.

3   This section, unless otherwise specified: Forrest C. Pogue, *The Supreme Command*, OCMH 1954, pp.244-260, and John Ehrman, *Grand Strategy Volume V*, London 1956, pp.379-382.

4   In line with the guidelines issued by SHAEF (TNA WO 160-4338, 22.08.44).

consider in particular was the civilian population back in England suffering from attacks by V-1 flying bombs launched from northwest France.[5]

Although Eisenhower had warned of the growing logistical problems a day earlier, Montgomery still believed that 'one really powerful and full-blooded thrust (...) is likely to get there and thus end the German war.'[6] Montgomery's directive M523, dated 3 September, radiated this optimism.[7] In this short document he described two bold aims: 'To advance eastwards and destroy all enemy forces encountered.' and 'To occupy the RUHR [capitals in original], and get astride the communications leading from it into Germany and the sea ports.' Montgomery instructed Second Army to advance eastwards, starting on 6 September, towards the Rhine anywhere between Arnhem and Wesel, meanwhile threatening the area around Düsseldorf south of there. This may sound overly optimistic in hindsight, but the idea that an advance as far as the capital of The Netherlands was likely at that time was shared by his opponents. They also believed that their troops would be unable to halt the Allies and therefore *General der Flieger* Friedrich Christiansen, *Wehrmachtbefehlshaber in der Niederlanden,* asked *Oberbefehlshaber West* for urgent permission to destroy the Amsterdam (and Rotterdam) docks because he did not have enough troops to turn them into fortresses.[8] Clearly the expectations at the highest Allied level were that the next few days would be a piece of cake, even after a twenty-four hour period of rest and refitting before continuing on Wednesday 6 September. To assist the ground forces and secure bridgeheads Montgomery asked First Allied Airborne Army (Lieutenant-General Lewis H. Brereton) to set up an operation in which the 1st Airborne Division and the Polish Parachute Brigade were employed. The operation proposed on 3 September was called Comet. The idea was to secure crossings of the Waal at Nijmegen and the Rhine at Arnhem using the 1st Airborne, the Polish Brigade and the 52nd (Lowland) Division. The operation was to take place on 6 or 7 September. The plans took longer to draw up than envisaged and they were not ready until the 7th. A storm warning then postponed its execution until the following day. Meanwhile a great deal had happened on the ground.

The German Strategy until 4 September 1944

At the highest levels German commanders had no idea how to deal with the Allied advance since the collapse in Normandy. All that the *Oberkommando der Wehrmacht (OKW)* could tell its generals was 'auf Zeitgewinn abstellen. (...) Daher Forderung

---

5   Soon, 8 September, joined by the V-2 rockets (Unternehemen Pinguin); Fritz Hahn, *Waffen und Geheimwaffen des deutschen Heeres 1933-1945,* Dörfler n.d., pp.174-5.
6   Pogue, *The Supreme Command,* p.253.
7   Details: M 523, 03.09.44.
8   Kriegstagebuch (KTB) Heeresgruppe B 06.09.44, 23.50 hours.

Kämpfen, Verteidigen, Halten, Truppe und Führung seelisch stärken.'[9] This directive, desperate in tone, was of little use to the commanders on the ground. While Montgomery oversaw his troops conquer France and Belgium, *Generalfeldmarschall* Model, commanding *Heeresgruppe B*, was trying to think of a way in which to stem the tide.[10] In his *Lagebeurteilung* on 24 August, the first since being appointed as *Oberbefehlshaber (Ob) West* a week earlier, Model simply reported to the *OKW* that his own troops were 'burnt up' and that there was no prospect of receiving any reinforcements before the end of the month. By and large Hitler accepted Model's analysis, admitting for once that the forces required to hold the present line were simply not there. A few hours later he ordered the fortifications of the *Westwall* to be reoccupied and extended.

On 31 August Model concluded that he was at the end of his tether as he no longer had any forces to put against what the Germans called the 'örtlich-operativen' or local operational breakthrough of the Allies which had smashed the centre of *Heeresgruppe B*.[11] This crisis began on 25 August and lasted until 4 September.[12] While Von Zangen's *15. Armee* was rushing back along the Channel coast as fast as it could, to maintain its integrity, the remnants of *5. Panzerarmee* were being overtaken left right and centre by speeding Allied armoured units. In view of this the only option Model saw for *Heeresgruppe B* was to try and reach the *Westwall* before it was utterly destroyed. Once more Model urged the *OKW* to occupy the *Weststellung*, as it was also referred to, without further delay. The next day, 1 September, the situation reached crisis point for the German High Command. A wedge had been driven between *15. Armee* and *5. Panzerarmee* by the British troops who were in the outskirts of Lille.[13] The celerity of the advance surprised the Germans and Hitler in impotent fury described it as 'eine Frechheit.'[14] Model intended to close this gap and he ordered *7. Armee* to set up a security line between Louvain and Namur. But it was too late. Near Mons the remnants of six German divisions were encircled and after a brief battle 25,000 soldiers were taken prisoner. This was the end of *5. Panzerarmee* as a fighting force. There was no longer a cohesive frontline between Lille and Charleroi. Full panic now set in among the troops. At last, the *OKW* and Hitler realized that the situation had fundamentally altered. On 2 September the *OKW* issued new instructions for the fighting in the West. The idea of trying to stem the Allied advance by successive lines of defence was finally abandoned, instead *Heeresgruppe B* was to fight a delaying action from now

9   Lagebeurteilung OKW/WFSt (Jodl), 05.07.44, in Andreas Kunz, *Wehrmacht und Niederlage*, R. Oldenbourg Verlag 2007, p.61.
10   This section, unless otherwise specified, Joachim Ludewig, *Der deutsche Rückzug aus Frankreich 1944*, Verlag Rombach 1994, pp.175-7.
11   Office of the Chief of Military History (OCMH) MS D-327, p.1.
12   Ibid, pp.1-2.
13   This section, unless otherwise specified, Ludewig, *Der deutsche Rückzug*, pp.219-240.
14   Helmut Heiber, *Lagebesprechungen im Führerhauptquartier*, DVA 1962, p.648.

on.[15] As the directives for the future strategy were issued, there was still a yawning gap between *15.* and *7. Armee* and through it the Guards rushed, capturing Brussels. Meanwhile remnants of German divisions continued to flood back to the *Heimat* among them the *85. Infanterie-Division* commanded by *Generalleutnant* Kurt Chill.

Chill and the 85. Infanterie-Division until 4 September 1944

The origins of the unit which was to play a pivotal role in the autumn fighting could not have been less auspicious.[16] The *85. Infanterie-Division* was one of six divisions raised in the *25. Welle* (wave or mobilisation drive) on 10 February 1944.[17] From October 1943 these divisions were organized along new guidelines with only six rifle battalions instead of nine.[18] The so-called 1944 type infantry divisions compensated for this by getting a *Füsilier-Bataillon* instead of the old reconnaissance unit and by increasing the number of automatic weapons.[19] The new divisions also had two regiments instead of three. Total strength, in theory, was 8,725 all ranks.[20] The new division was commanded by *Generalleutnant* Kurt Erich Chill who was born in West Prussia in the Prussian town of Thorn (today Torun in Poland) on 1 May 1895.[21] Chill fought in the First World War, initially in *Infanterie-Regiment 61* at the Somme, and from 1916 as an observer in the *Fliegertruppe* (Flying Corps) in Flanders. He ended the war with the *Eisernes Kreuz II. Klasse* and the *deutsches Ordenschild*. After the war Chill, by then a *Leutnant*, left the army and joined the police in 1919. He rose through the ranks, becoming a *Hauptmann* in 1924 and a *Major* with the *Landespolizei* in Merseburg in 1935. The same year he was trained at the *Offizier Schule* where he

---

15   Percy Schramm, *Kriegstagebuch des Oberkommandos der Wehrmacht*, Bernard & Graefe Verlag 1982, 7/I, p.365.

16   Unless otherwise specified, this section, Schuster MS B-846, pp.4-32.

17   II Cdn Corps, IS 54, 16.09.44. The others were the 77., 84., 89., 91. and 92. ID.

18   There is considerable confusion as to the size of an average German rifle battalion at that time. Based on the average company strength in 85. I.D. which was 80-90 (II Cdn Corps IS 33, 13.08.44 and First Cdn Army K 208-11, 16.08.44) it should number about 350-400 men (four rifle companies plus the staff company). This estimate is confirmed by KTB 88 AK, 08.09.44, B 262, which describes a 'mittelstarkes' Btl as 300-400. But then there is another strength figure, 689, given in II Cdn Corps IS 52 Part II, 07.09.44, based on unspecified captured German documents; also the official German company strength is given as 142 all ranks (Kriegsstärkenachweisungen, Band 2, Infanterie, 1943/44 (NARA RG 242, T 87, Roll 391, 168-170) which would add up to a battalion strength of 600-700. An explanation for the difference could be that the latter two documents give the theoretical number (Sollstärke), whereas the others are based on the actual figure (Iststärke).

19   Kriegsstärkenachweisungen, Band 2a, Infanterie, 1944 (NARA RG 242, T 87, Roll 391).

20   Brian A. Reid, *No Holding Back, Operation Totalize, Normandy, August 1944*, Stackpole 2005, p.392.

21   This section, Personalakten Chill (National Archives and Records Administration, Washington (NARA) RG 242, unless otherwise specified.

received the qualification 'voll befriedigend'. He then decided to re-join the army. On 1 July 1935 Chill once more found himself back in army uniform.

Chill first served as a *Major* with *Infanterie-Regiment 65* and in 1937 was put in charge of *1. Bataillon* of *Infanterie-Regiment 1 (1. Infanterie-Divison)*. It was in this role that he entered the war as an *Oberstleutnant*. The *1. I.D.* under *Generalleutnant* Joachim von Kortzfleisch, took part in the attack on Poland in the northern attack group (*3. Armee*). Rather surprisingly, considering what was to come, Chill did not do particularly well as a battalion commander. In the first assessment, dated 18 February 1941, Kortzfleisch said that Chill was very diligent, an excellent comrade and a good instructor, but that his leadership in Poland had been neither skilful nor successful. Clearly he had not made much of an impression on his superiors. Maybe that is one of the reasons Chill was sent to Halle in February 1940 where he served as a tactics teacher. In December he found himself in charge of a regiment, *Infanterie-Regiment 45 (21. Infanterie-Division)*. He was promoted to *Oberst*, but even so his divisional commander, *Generalmajor* Otto Sponheimer, felt that Chill was not yet ready for the next step in his career. That was to change dramatically over the next two years.

Just one year later Sponheimer, by then a *Generalleutnant*, was full of praise for Chill. The *21. Infanterie-Division* fought as part of *Heeresgruppe Nord* and advanced as far as the town of Volkhov.[22] Then the tables were gradually turned on the Germans and the division eventually ended up southeast of Leningrad.[23] There it was engaged in extremely fierce fighting as part of *I. Armeekorps* (*General der Kavallerie* Phillip Kleffel) which the Russians were trying to cut off. Instead, the Russian Second Shock Army (*General Leytenant* Andrei Vlassov) was surrounded and eventually destroyed after some hard and bloody fighting.[24] Apparently the experiences in Russia had changed Chill for the better as a soldier as he was now increasingly praised for his performance. Sponheimer wrote, 'Charaktervolle, klare Persönlichkeit, seine Einsatzbereitschaft in schwierigen Lagen verdient Hervorhebung. Durch sein persönliches Beispiel reisst er mit. (...) Taktisch gut beanlagt, sicher im Entschluss, gründlich in der Befehlsgebung. (...) Zum Div. Kommandeur voll geeignet.'[25] Nevertheless, Chill would still have to wait another six months before finally being assigned his own division.

Chill was originally supposed to command the *126. Infanterie-Division* because its commanding officer, *Generalleutnant* Laux, was taking over as commander of an improvised Corps. However, before setting off Laux persuaded his superiors to nominate *Oberst* Harrie Hoppe (the hero of Schlüsselburg) who had been with the division from its inception.[26] So Chill was assigned the *122. Infanterie-Division* instead. In December

---

22   Victor Madej, *Russo-German War No. 27, Autumn 1942: Defeat of Barbarossa*, Allentown 1988, pp.14-5.
23   *Das Deutsche Reich und der Zweite Weltkrieg, Band 4, Beiheft, Skizze 1*, DVA 1983, pp.18, 19, 25.
24   Earl F. Ziemke and Magna E. Bauer, *Moscow to Stalingrad*, OCMH 1987, pp.190-8.
25   Assessment 08.04.42 in Personalakten.
26   Lose, 126. ID, 113.

1942 he was promoted to *Generalmajor*. Chill did not rest on his laurels, and half a year later, on 1 June 1943, he was promoted to *Generalleutnant*. On 15 October 1943 he was awarded the coveted *Ritterkreuz*, further proof that in Russia he had really honed his skills. His division was part of the successful effort to block the expansion of a Russian breakthrough at Nevel which had surprised the Germans.[27] He performed so well that he was mentioned in the *Wehrmachtsbericht*, the daily broadcast by the German armed forces.[28] The battle at Nevel dragged on for another three months. By then Chill had left his division. In March 1944 he was ordered to set up the new *85. Infanterie-Division*.

The personnel of the *85. I.D.* were generally new call-ups from *Wehrkreis XII*, but additional replacements later came from *Oberbefehlshaber West* and even included Russians (so-called *Hilfswillige* or *Hiwi's*), Poles and Czechs.[29] In view of the impending Allied invasion the division was not

Generalleutnant Kurt Erich Chill (1895-1976), commanding officer of the eponymous *Kampfgruppe*. (Didden/Swarts collection)

to be trained in Germany, but in the Crecy area in northwest France where it was subordinated first to *LXXXII. Armeekorps* and then *LXVII. Armeekorps*. The officers were mostly veterans. The division had only a very limited number of vehicles, but since it was to be part of the strategic reserve some kind of mobility was essential. This was resolved by procuring large numbers of bicycles. The deadline for equipping the *85. I.D.* was 15 May, but this was not met and the division had a thirty per cent deficiency in equipment. This issue was not resolved until the end of July. Following the invasion of Normandy on 6 June 1944 the *85. I.D.* was ordered to assemble north of the Somme in the Abbeville area, ready to march within twelve hours. Nearly two

---

27 Madej, *Russo-German War No. 31, Summer-Autumn 1943*, Allentown 1987, pp.13-5.
28 *Die Wehrmachtsberichte 1939-1945*, Band 2, Köln 1989, p.629.
29 The divisional staff consisted of *Oberstleutnant i.G.* Kurt Schuster, Ia (Operations), *Major i.G.* Weber, Ib (Supply and Administration) and *Oberleutnant* Zörkler, Ic (Intelligence). The two infantry regiments were commanded by *Major* (from 1 September *Oberstleutnant*) Georg Heinrich Dreyer (*GR 1053*) and *Oberst* De La Chaux (*GR 1054*).

months passed before the *15. Armee* was finally sent to Normandy.[30] On 31 July Chill received orders from the army that his division was to assemble north of the Seine at Rouen ready to cross the river at a moment's notice. The *85. I.D.* was finally to receive its baptism of fire.

Baptism of fire

The division set up three march groups centred around *Grenadier-Regiment 1053, 1054* and *Artillerie-Regiment 185* respectively.[31] Progress was slow and the Seine was not crossed until 7 August when Chill learned that his division was to come under *I. SS. Panzerkorps* (*SS Brigadeführer* Fritz Krämer).[32] There the division was to take over from the *12. SS. Panzer-Division Hitlerjugend* (*SS-Oberführer* Kurt Meyer) which was being bled white fighting the Canadians. Just one week later First Canadian Army launched Operation Tractable. The goal was to envelop Falaise and seal the 'bag' around the German troops in Normandy from the north. To assist the ground troops saturation bombing was asked for. The results were devastating for the German troops facing the onslaught and the *85. Infanterie-Division* together with its sister division, the *89. Infanterie-Division*, took the brunt of the bombing.[33] The number of those killed or wounded is unknown, but the Intelligence officers of II Canadian Corps noted drily that 'casualties were heavy' and that '85 has probably not more than two battalions left.'[34] The commanding officer of the SS-division put it more graphically when he bluntly stated about the effects of the Allied bombing, 'verwandeln die Stellungen der 85. Infanteriedivision in einen Friedhof.'[35] In fact Chill himself reported the following day that he had only a battalion and a half of infantry and two guns left.[36] In addition 1,010 of Chill's men were taken prisoner.[37] As yet *Füsilier-Bataillon 185* and the divisional artillery, south of the Laison river were unaffected.[38] However, during the second stage 171 prisoners were taken from *Füsilier-Bataillon 185* meaning that, adding the wounded and killed, the battalion basically ceased to exist as a fighting force.[39] In total, during the week that followed, 1,527 men were captured

30   Pogue, *The Supreme Command*, pp.193-4.
31   This section, unless otherwise noted, Schuster, pp.11-33.
32   Not as Schuster (13) erroneously states II. SS. Panzerkorps (Cf. Ellis, *Victory Volume 1*, map p.432) and Martin Blumenson, *Breakout and Pursuit*, OCMH 1984, Map IX.
33   John Man, *The Penguin Atlas of D-Day and the Normandy Campaign*, Viking 1994, p.124.
34   II Cdn Corps, Intelligence Summary (IS) 34, 15.08.44.
35   Panzermeyer, *Grenadiere*, Schild Verlag GmbH 1965, p.299.
36   Blumenson, *Breakout and Pursuit*, p.531.
37   P.C. Stacey, *Official History of the Canadian Army in the Second World War, the Victory Campaign Volume III, The Operations in North-west Europe 1944-1945*, Ottawa 1960, p.248. The First Canadian Army as a whole captured 1,299 Germans that day.
38   Ibid.
39   Ibid.

by the Canadians, a number which had increased to 1,834 by early September.[40] The divisional losses were so huge that by the time it arrived in Belgium it was reduced to just 1,534 all ranks.[41] Chill's division was no longer a fighting force in any sense of the word.

Hitler purportedly said that 15 August was the worst day of his life.[42] That day marked the beginning of the end for the German army in Normandy. Two days later the remnants of the *85. Infanterie-Division* were no longer holding a cohesive front and they were barely capable of offering determined resistance.[43] The division was by then reduced to just one regiment, *Grenadier-Regiment 1053*, in which all the infantry was gathered, together with some artillery and smaller divisional troops.[44] It had been a gruelling three days for Chill and he complained that he 'had never known such tiredness. It caused hallucinations and a complete sense of non-being. (…) We craved for sleep and slept like the dead; we could have slept for days.'[45] Still, the division did not disintegrate it had performed as best it could under the circumstances.[46] Luckily for Chill and his men they had been pushed eastwards and northwards, in effect, out of the pocket which was slowly forming.[47]

One of the major problem for Chill was trying to maintain cohesion while pulling back. To make matters worse, for the time being Dreyer's *Kampfgruppe* was subordinated to the *21. Panzer-Division* (*Generalleutnant* Edgar Feuchtinger), south of the Seine where it was the last unit to cross at Rouen. One thing Chill managed to do, was to keep officers who had become superfluous for the moment in a so-called divisional reserve, so that he could make use of their services whenever and wherever this was needed.[48] This measure would soon stand him in good stead. On 29 August the

---

40 First figure: Terry Copp, *Fields of Fire, The Canadians in Normandy*, Toronto 2008, p.280; quoted in Lieb, *Konventioneller Krieg*, p.441. Second figure: II Cdn Corps, IS 50, 07.09.44. The sister division of the 85., the 89. (Generalleutnant Conrad-Oskar Heinrichs) suffered equally badly losing 1,566 men as POWs to the Canadians.

41 KTB 88 AK, 14.09.44, A 265. This is completely at odds with Zetterling (*Normandy 1944, German Military Organization, Combat Power and Organizational Effectiveness*, Manitoba 2000, pp.235-6) who claims that the 85. ID 'only' lost 3,000 men and still had 5,000 men left at the end of August. The evidence for this is a document by the OKH Org. Abt. from 16.10.44 about the situation on 1 September. Oddly enough this document shows a loss of at least 5,000 men, but this is dismissed by Zetterling as 'overly pessimistic' without providing any proof of why this would be the case.

42 Ellis, *Victory I*, p.431.

43 James Lucas and James Barker, *The Killing Ground, The Battle of the Falaise Gap, August 1944*, London 1978, p.123.

44 Kurt Schuster, OCMH MS B-846, organisational table.

45 Lucas and Barker, *The Killing Ground*, p.122. Unfortunately they do not give the source of this quote.

46 Ibid, p.24.

47 Meyer (304) somewhat scathingly notes that the 85. ID was being pulled out 'um Verkehrsaufgaben zu lösen.' There is no evidence for this derogatory remark.

48 Kurt Schuster, OCMH MS B-424, p.24.

non-fighting elements of the division were back in the area where they had originally trained, around Abbeville on the river Somme. Here it received reinforcements in the form of an 880-men strong so-called *Marschbataillon*[49] which had only one rifle for every five men and three machine-guns in total. The same day Chill was ordered by *7. Armee* to form a *Kampfgruppe* together with the remnants of the *84.* and *89. Infanterie-Division* to guard the Somme crossings on both sides of Péronne.[50]

However, the seed would not germinate yet for a number of reasons: the division had no troops fit for combat, it could not reach the designated area before 1 September, the connection with the *89. I.D.* had been lost since 18 August and the *84. I.D.* consisted only of a regimental staff.[51] The order was moot anyway since the Allied pursuit caught up with the retreating Germans before they could reach the Somme. The division was therefore allowed to pull back to Brussels to be reorganized there on 1 September. The following day it was ordered to reform inside the *Reich*. In the meantime *Kampfgruppe Dreyer* was told to re-join its parent unit.[52] On 3 September the divisional staff reached Turnhout in Belgium, ready to move on. Dreyer and what was left of his battle group – about a hundred men – arrived the following day. Then things took an unexpected turn.

Antwerp

Monday 4 September marked the day that the crisis for the retreating *Wehrmacht* came to a head as Antwerp was liberated and the door to Germany was wide open. The Allies had reached what Clausewitz called the 'culmination point' where the defenders might finally halt the attackers provided they had enough troops left.[53] It was a day that would turn out to be of crucial importance for the rest of the war. On the same day that Antwerp was captured by the 11th Armoured Division the gap between the *15. Armee* and the *7. Armee* had widened to no less than one hundred kilometres (see map 1). Desperate times call for desperate measures and Hitler decided to recall an old warhorse, 69-year old *Generalfeldmarschall* Gerd von Rundstedt, to take over as *OB West*, correctly judging that holding two jobs (*OB West* as well commanding *Heeresgruppe B*) was too much even for Model, who could now concentrate on the latter. Von Rundstedt was to take over on the following day. The fall of Antwerp on 4 September was a real shock to German commanders. It meant that the *15. Armee* was now cut off and might be lost for good. Model sent a cry for help to Hitler's headquar-

---

49   Orginally set up by the Wehrkreise to conduct draftees to the zone of operations, later they became replacement pools for the Feldersatzbataillone, the first line reinforcement battalions (*German Order of Battle*, B9-10).

50   Order 7. Armee, quoted in full in II Cdn Corps, IS 48, 05.09.44.

51   Kurt Schuster, OCMH MS B-244, pp.28, 29 and 31.

52   Schuster, B-244, (27) states that it was temporarily attached to the 33. ID. That is impossible since that division was disbanded in 1940.

53   General Carl von Clausewitz, *Vom Kriege*, Vier Falken Verlag n.d., p.517.

ters at Rastenburg.[54] His telegram jolted the German High Command into action. Both *OKW* and Hitler realised that *LXXXVIII. Armeekorps* (*General der Infanterie* Hans Wolfgang Reinhard) with its single division plus a few battalions could never plug the gap on its own. They would have to put in more troops, in fact a whole new army. But where to find one?

That afternoon a phone call went out to *Generaloberst* Kurt Student, *Oberbefehlshaber der Fallschirmtruppen* in Berlin-Wannsee.[55] He was ordered to form a defence behind the Albert Canal from Antwerp in Belgium to Maastricht in the Netherlands with a new army, to be called *1. Fallschirmarmee*. The new army was to come under *Heeresgruppe B*. *Flak* support was to be provided by the *18. Flakbrigade* which was on the run from France plus thirty heavy and ten mixed *Flak* batteries from *Luftgaue VI* and *XI*.[56] The idea was an extension of the *Weststellung* from Aachen along the Albert Canal to Antwerp.[57] This stretch was called the *Brabantstellung*.[58] This now became Student's responsibility. What mattered to Hitler and Goering was that while Student was not a military genius, he was known to be a '*Steher*', a tough commander in defence, which was what they needed at this stage of the war.[59] In addition to *LXXXVIII. Armeekorps*, Student was assigned an impressive array of troops, at least on paper. Still, one of the divisions was a static one (the *719. Infanterie-Division*), one was composed of convalescents (the *176. Division zur besonderen Verwendung*) and the paratroop units were spread all over Germany and would need a few days to reach the battlefield. Time was not on his side. But he was in for a pleasant surprise.

Early on 5 September Reinhard drove to his new advanced headquarters in Moergestel (near Tilburg) where he arrived around eight a.m. While his staff was settling in, he travelled on to the Albert Canal some forty kilometres further south. There was only one question on his mind: would his troops arrive in time or would the Allies win the race? As he neared the front-line Reinhard came across small groups of soldiers aimlessly hanging about. Angrily he told officers to assemble them into ad-hoc units. By accident he also stopped a *Hauptmann* who turned out to be the signals officer of the *85. Infanterie-Division*. The officer had totally unexpected, but wonderful news for Reinhard.[60] He told Reinhard that Chill had already set up blocking positions behind the Albert Canal, roughly between Herenthals and Hasselt. Chill had just arrived in Turnhout when he learned of the fall of Brussels. As he had

54 KTB H Gr B, 04.09.44, I a 6944/44.
55 Details this section Student, article in *Der deutsche Fallschirmjäger*, issue 9, 1964, pp.3-4.
56 KTB 88 AK, 05.09.44, C 210, and KTB H Gr B, 05.09.44, Ia 7006/44.
57 Walther Hubatsch, *Hitlers Weisungen*, Bernard & Graefe Verlag 1983, pp.272-4.
58 Christ Klep and Ben Schoenmaker (ed.), *De Bevrijding van Nederland 1944-1945, oorlog op de flank*, 's-Gravenhage 1995, p.87. The name refers to the old dukedom of Brabant on the western edge of the Holy Roman Empire, covering the current Dutch province of Noord Brabant and much of central Belgium.
59 Ibid.
60 Story of Chill's actions, Kurt Schuster, OCMH MS B-846, pp.40-2.

found both in Russia and in France that orders from higher up were often slow, he decided on his own initiative, to collect groups of stragglers and set up an improvised defence. His officers assembled the men in Turnhout, assessed their fighting ability and then divided them into groups which were sent either to the Albert Canal or kept in reserve.[61] At noon on 5 September the newly formed battle group was mentioned for the first time.[62]

There are no official documents stating the exact composition of Chill's unit that first day, but various sources make it clear that the following units were included at the beginning: *Fallschirmjäger-Artillerie Regiment 2, Marine Ersatz Abteilung Wilhemshaven, 6., 16.,* and *21. Schiffstamm-Abteilung, Marine Artillerie Versuchskommando, Marine Flak Schule (Hauptmann Jahn), Landesschützenbataillon (Bahn) 484, Wachbataillon 737, Sicherungsbataillon 772, Marschbataillon z.bV. 301.*[63] Many of them were put under *Hauptmann* Oswald Pohl (*Füsilier-Bataillon 85*). In addition there were five *Fliegerhorst Kommandature* (airfield security detachments) in France and Belgium.[64] No figures exist about the strength, but we know that Dreyer (*Grenadier Regiment 1053*) had only about a hundred men left, that Pohl was in charge of a small *Kampfgruppe* of 330 men, that *Oberst* Buchholz (*Sicherungs-Regiment 35*) commanded 1,100 soldiers, while the airfield security detachments totalled 900 men. All in all Chill could muster about 2,400 men to hold the new line, roughly equivalent to six line battalions of medium strength. However, there were hardly any machine-guns and some of the men had been issued Italian rifles. Moreover, Chill had no artillery, no anti-tank weapons and no *Flak*. And then there was the dubious quality of the men, none of whom had been properly trained as infantry. Chill and his staff set up three *Kampfgruppen*, named Buchholz, Seidel and Dreyer after their respective commanding officers.[65] Reinhard was delighted with these unexpected reinforcements and told Chill that from now on his group was subordinate to *LXXXVIII. Armeekorps*. The first test would be battle for the Albert Canal line.

61   Schuster, B-424, p.42.
62   KTB 88 AK, 05.09.44, A 106, and KTB H Gr B, 05.09.44, 12:00 hours.
63   KTB 88 AK, map 07.09.44 (NARA T 314/Roll 1625), and War Diary 50 (N) Division, IS 64 (09.09.44) and First Cdn Army, SIR 17.09.44.
64   The Fliegerhorst Kommandanture were: Montdidier, Conneilles, Amy, Rosieres and St.Denis (KTB 88 AK, B 265, 09.09.44 and B 271, 13.09.44).
65   Oberst Buchholz commanded Sicherungs-Regiment 35 (map 88 AK NARA file T 314 R1626 63289/5) but his background is unknown, Oberstltnt Georg Dreyer commanded GR 1053, Oberst Paul Seidel commanded a Sperrgruppe in 352. ID. near Paris, Kampfabschnitt Versailles (2nd Army IS 102, 14.09.44 and Ziegelmann, 10). Oberst Stein (Fl. Rgt. 51) took over from Seidel on 14 September in all likelihood because Seidel was called back to Germany where 352. ID was being reconstituted as 352. VGD in Flensburg starting on 21.09.44 (Andris J. Kursietis, *The Wehrmacht at War 1939-1945, The Units and Commanders of the German Ground Forces during World War II*, Aspekt 1999, p.192, Ziegelmann, p.16).

Bloody Triangle

On Tuesday 6 September, after having halted for 24 hours, XXX Corps resumed its advance. The situation had now changed dramatically as the leading troops were soon to find out. The fighting over the next ten days would take place in an area between two major canals, the Albert Canal and the Maas-Scheldt Canal. This area forms a kind of convoluted triangle between Herentals, Lanaken and Neerpelt. Here the British would face the first serious resistance since the end of the fighting in Normandy in what would become a 'bloody triangle'. Instructed by Field-Marshal Montgomery (Twenty-First Army Group) to push ahead in the perceived gap in the German front, Major-General A.H.S. Adair (Guards Armoured Division) sent his division northeast towards the Netherlands on 6 September.[66] The first stop was to be at the Albert Canal where crossing were to be seized. These were to be the start line (SL) for the advance to the river Rhine that was planned for the following day.[67] Starting from Brussels, Adair ordered 32 Guards Brigade to go to Beringen, while on the left 5 Guards Armoured Brigade would advance to Geel. Only at Beringen did the Guards manage to cross the Albert Canal. Chill was ordered to counterattack and did so immediately.

Although he was unable to annihilate the British bridgehead, the *Kampfgruppe*, assisted by *schwere Heeres Panzerjäger-Abteilung 559*, did manage to block the advance towards Leopoldsburg, forcing the Guards to take the only other route north which ran via Hechtel where they ran into the newly arrived *Fallschirmjäger* of *Fallschirmjäger Regiment (FJR) 20* (see map 2). So how did this affect the Allied and German plans? Montgomery's operational plans as laid down in directive M523 were frustrated completely. In their plans Montgomery and Dempsey had envisaged XXX Corps as starting their advance towards the Ruhr, anywhere between Arnhem and Wesel, on 7 September. Because of the fierce German defence, that day the leading Guards units were still stuck at Beringen and Hechtel instead. Things then took a turn for the worse for the British and the advance crawled almost to a standstill. A request from the War Office to Montgomery on the 9th asking him how soon he could 'rope off the coastal area contained by ANTWERP – UTRECHT – ROTTERDAM [capitals in original]' in connection with the danger of the V-1 and V-2s must have rankled in his mind even though he answered, somewhat laconically, that he expected to be able to do this 'in about a fortnight's time.'[68] Eisenhower, reporting on the same date, was more cautious and reported that German resistance was 'stiffening somewhat' now

---

66   Roden Orde, *The Household Cavalry at War: Second Household Cavalry Regiment*, Gale & Polden 1953, pp.276-282; D.J.L. Fitzgerald M.C., *History of the Irish Guards in the Second World War*, Gale & Polden 1949, pp.461-2.

67   War Diary 1st Gren Gds, 05.09.44.

68   Message VCIGS and answer Montgomery, 09.09.44, TNA WO106/4338, 29A.

that Allied troops were closing in on the German border.[69] Nevertheless, he felt that it was 'doubtful' that the Germans would be able to block the Allied advance effectively.

But he was wrong and it was not until 11 September, when the Irish Guards captured the Neerpelt bridge that the first German line of defence had been cracked. Finally Montgomery began to feel less sanguine about the pace of the operations and he informed Lieutenant-General A.E. Nye, the Vice-Chief of the Imperial General Staff, that he was 'meeting with more opposition than he had expected.'[70] Chill was largely responsible for this opposition. But there was no time for him to rest on his laurels. While successfully halting the Allied advance in the area of Leopoldsburg and Beringen, he also had another crossing to contend with on his right flank, south of Geel. There the other half of Chill's battle group, *Kampfgruppe Dreyer*, was to face its first real test in battle.

Geel

Another of those battles lost in the mists of military history, like the one at Beringen which took place almost simultaneously, is the battle for Geel (see map 3). Nevertheless both deserve closer study as they mark the end of the Allied 1944 summer campaign or, to put it the other way round, the beginning of the slugging match that character-ized the fighting on the Western Front for the next few months. While the battles were still raging north of Beringen and at Hechtel, British Second Army had established two more bridgeheads across the Albert Canal, south of the town of Geel. These were to be the next focal points of some extremely intense fighting for *Kampfgruppe Chill* and one in which *schwere Heeres Panzerjäger-Abteilung 559* inflicted, but also incurred, very heavy losses in the second big clash of armour against armour.

On 7 September Demspey instructed the 50th (Northumbrian) Division to cross the Albert Canal south of Geel as soon as possible. As darkness feel units of 69 Brigade began to cross near Het Punt. The responsibility for this stretch of the Albert Canal was *Kampfgruppe Dreyer's*, named after *Oberstleutnant* Georg Dreyer, *Kommandeur* of *Grenadier Regiment 1053*. This was one of the three regiments of Chill's original divi-sion and the only one more or less intact although it now had the size of a battalion.[71] In addition Dreyer commanded *III/Grenadier Regiment 723* plus *Flieger Regiment 51* and *53*, altogether about 3,500 men.[72] Forty-one year old Dreyer was the stereotypical Germanic warrior with his pointed face, blonde hair and blue eyes.[73] He looked young for his age, was energetic and he was one of the senior officers who had helped Chill set up the blocking position behind the Albert Canal four days earlier.[74] He was to

69   SCAF 78, 09.09.44, TNA WO106/4338, 31B.
70   Letter VCIGS to CIGS, 11.09.44, TNA WO106/4338, 33 A.
71   Schuster B-424, Appendix 10.
72   KTB 88 AK, 09.09.44, B 265.
73   1st Cdn Army, IR POW 85 ID, 08.11.44.
74   Schuster B-424, p.41.

Soldiers of *II./Grenadier-Regiment 723* in the market square in Beringen early on 6 September. The 7.5 cm *Pak 40* gun on the left points in the direction of the Albert canal which the Welsh Guards will cross that afternoon. (Didden/Swarts collection)

play a key role in the autumn campaign.[75] However, that night his men along the Albert Canal were at first caught napping and a bridgehead was quickly established by the 6th Green Howards. As dawn broke this would all rapidly change and confused fighting soon broke out. Despite numerous counterattacks the bridgehead remained in British hands. But it was clear to the 50th Division that more troops were needed to capture Geel. During the afternoon of 8 September the divisional commander, Major-General D.A.H. Graham, ordered 151 Brigade to leave Brussels and as soon as possible establish a bridgehead at Steelen further east. The following day the two bridgeheads had become one big one and thanks to a Class 40 bridge the first tanks of the Nottinghamshire Yeomanry (the Sherwood Rangers) began to cross.

---

75 This was no accident since in his last assessment he was described as 'zuverlässiche, gereifte Persönlichkeit, passionierter Soldat, energisch. Besitzt Tatkraft und Schwung, Führernatur.'

Dawn patrols sent out on 10 September by all three battalions of the Durham Light Infantry met with mixed responses from their opponents.[76] It was to be a set-piece battle after all. As a result of the artillery barrage some houses were set alight, a number of civilians lost their lives and, supported by the Sherwood Rangers, the 6th Durham Light Infantry captured Geel. The German response was not long in coming. Reinhard at one p.m. decided to order the *Jagdpanther Kompanie* of *559* to Geel to help restore the situation. It was a fortuitous decision even though the unit could only muster half of their strength.[77] What followed was a confused battle in which Dreyer's men penetrated the bridgehead, but then fell victim to their own audacity because they lost three *Jagdpanther* although they managed to knock out seven British tanks in return. The next day, 11 September, Geel itself was retaken, a minor triumph for Dreyer.[78] The following morning he proudly reported that the old front-line had been restored.[79] Both the British infantry and the tanks had taken a terrific beating. All in all the 50th (Northumbrian) Division had suffered severe casualties. The Sherwood Rangers during their two days in Geel had seen eleven tanks knocked out and two damaged, the highest number since fighting in the desert.[80]

Chill's rag tag band of thrown together *Luftwaffe* men had performed much better than Reinhard had expected. It was a tremendous achievement for *Kampfgruppe Chill*, especially considering the poor supply situation; most of the men had not had a full food ration in weeks.[81] The outstanding achievement of *Kampfgruppe Chill*, aided by the *Jagdpanther Kompanie* of *559*, was the result of tactical insight and skilful manoeu-vring. Temporarily blocking the advance of the 50th Division also meant that Model could now concentrate his meagre resources against the bridgehead near Neerpelt (Joe's Bridge). The effective defence in the 'Bloody Triangle' and subsequent delay forced Montgomery to revise his operational plans. The result was directive M525 (Market Garden).

Ten Aard

If Geel and Beringen are all but forgotten battles, this applies even more to the battle for Aart or Ten Aard as it is known these days. Here is a battle which has indeed been completely gone from the annals of military history it seems, and when it is referred

---

76   This section based on the war diaries of 50 Division, 69th, 151st Brigade and Nottinghamshire Yeomanry.
77   KTB 88 AK, 10.09.44, A 207 gives seven, B 268 gives six, 50th (N) Division, Intel Sum 66 (based on interrogation of a PoW of 53. Fl.Rgt.) mentions seven, while Second Army Intel Sum 1202 again gives six.
78   http://www.ritterkreuztraeger-1939-45.de/
79   KTB 88 AK, 12.09.44, 10.29 hours.
80   T.M. Lindsay, *Sherwood Rangers*, Burrup, Mathiesen & Co, 1952, p.131.
81   War Diary Guards Division, IS 67 (PoW interview).

Testimony to the intense fighting in Geel. This Sherman of the Sherwood Rangers was knocked out along the Stelensebaan. It is one of the thirteen that were lost to the unit, the highest number since fighting in North Africa. (Didden/Swarts collection)

to it is sometimes erroneously called the battle for Geel.[82] The reasons for its neglect are probably twofold, it was a genuine defeat during a period that the Allies were generally winning, and it was largely fought while Market Garden was taking place. Still, the fighting at Ten Aard had a serious impact on Market Garden. Once again *Kampfgruppe Chill*, supported by part of *schwere Heeres Panzerjäger-Abteilung 559* was the key player (see map 4).

It all began on Tuesday 12 September, the day that the 15th (Scottish) Division took over from the 50th (Northumbrian) Division south of Geel. Dawn patrols on 13 September discovered that the enemy had pulled back. After learning that the Germans had cleared the area south of the Maas-Scheldt Canal Major-General C.M. Barber decided to repeat the tactics that had paid so well in crossing the Seine barely a fortnight earlier. He wanted once more to dispense with a set-piece battle, but rather operate by stealth.[83] This meant that he would do without an extensive reconnaissance,

---

82   E.g. H.G. Martin, *Fifteenth Scottish Division*, Blackwood 1948, p.129, and Patrick Delaforce, *The Black Bull*, Allan Sutton 1993, p.148, who call it the Gheel bridgehead, which is patently wrong as that battle was the struggle that took place the preceding week.

83   Cf. Stephen Ashley Hart, *Colossal Cracks, Montgomery's 21st Army Group in Northwest Europe, 1944-45*, Mechanicsburg 2007, pp.174-8.

build-up of ammunition and all the other ingredients that normally preceded a river crossing. By doing so he was taking a calculated risk. Both 44 and 227 Brigades were ordered to push on to the canal and see if they could get across.

Following the withdrawal behind the Maas-Scheldt Canal *Kampfgruppe Chill* had had to give up its best formations, the bulk of *Fallschirmjäger-Regiment 6* and *2. and 3./ schwere Heeres Panzerjäger-Abteilung 559*. But Chill was still in command of a sizeable force. Besides his own divisional staff, he still had *Grenadier-Regiment 723, I./FJR 2, II./FJR 6* and *Kampfgruppe Dreyer* (although since Geel *Flieger-Regimente 51* and *53* were mere shadows of their former selves, having lost over half their complement). On top of that *II./SS-Grenadier Regiment Landstorm Nederland* was now transferred to him. *I.* and *III./Fallschirm Panzer Ersatz und Ausbildungs-Regiment Hermann Göring*.

The first assault, on the right, by 6th King's Own Scottish Borderers failed miserably, the second one, by the 8th Royal Scots, took place around the time the 6th KOSB sank down exhausted. Since all the bridges at Ten Aard had been completely destroyed, this crossing was made using assault-boats. Throughout the afternoon of 14 September *Kampfgruppe Dreyer* put pressure on the 8th Royal Scots and the probing attacks became bolder as time wore on. Two SPs from *1./schwere Heeres Panzerjäger-Abteilung 559* taunted the battalion's positions from a copse northwest of the village. They parked themselves just a hundred and fifty metres away and fired at any movement until British artillery fire eventually drove them away.[84] The real counterattack started at ten p.m. when *I./Fallschirm Panzer Ersatz und Ausbildungs-Regiment Hermann Göring* under *Hauptmann* Johann Wimmer was flung straight into the cauldron at Ten Aard.[85] In a kind of modern day Trojan horses Wimmer's were transported in buses which drove up to a point about two hundred metres north of the road and the by-pass junction. Before the startled Royal Scots could call down artillery fire the *Fallschirmjäger* had jumped out and were running towards them, killing or capturing most of the Royal Scots forward platoon.[86] The attack was so fierce that it was only halted about a hundred metres from the canal bank.

As dawn broke on 15 September the Royal Scots were hanging on to their territory for dear life. The situation was confusing in the extreme as the German troops held positions in the bridgehead intermingled with those of the Royal Scots. However, at ten a.m. Wimmer's *Fallschirmjäger* disengaged so that their own artillery could bombard the tiny bridgehead. At least it would be easier now for Brigadier Cockburn to send in reinforcements. However, as a result of flooding the 6th Royal Scots Fusiliers under Lieutenant-Colonel I. Mackenzie, who were supposed to have crossed on 14 September had to wait a full twenty-four hours, until they could go over to

---

84   The SPs can only have been Jagdpanther as the vehicles from the Hermann Göring-Regiment had not yet arrived.

85   III./ *Fallschirm Panzer Ersatz und Ausbildungs-Regiment Hermann Göring* under Major Werner Krahmer was the Flak and artillery battalion in support, this stayed back at Retie.

86   Eyewitness interviewed by Chris van Kerckhoven.

the north bank in assault boats. Finally, at noon the Royal Scots Fusiliers started to go across and the village was once again in Allied hands. Wimmer's *Fallschirmjäger* counterattacked once more. They suffered appalling losses, but managed to push the Scots back for the second time. The bridgehead had, once again, shrunk to almost nothing. The Scots only managed to hold on because all of the divisional artillery now mercilessly pounded the German lines.

Saturday 16 September saw little action at Ten Aard. Artillery now played a key role. The only thing preventing the Scots from breaking out was the German artillery. The only reason the Scottish battalions inside the bridgehead survived were the defensive fire (DF) tasks from the divisional artillery around Geel. A diversionary attack by 227 Brigade further east failed miserably and at the end of the day the situation in Ten Aard was back to where it was on the first day, a stalemate. The following day was spent planning. Barber realised that he needed to come up with something to break the deadlock. The new solution he came up with was Operation Flood.[87] The idea was to enlarge the bridgehead by ordering 227 Brigade to make new crossings immediately to the right and left of Ten Aard early the following day. However, XII Corps (Lieutenant-General Neil Ritchie), decided differently. Ritchie's Corps was supposed to protect the left flank of XXX Corps after its breakout from the Neerpelt bridgehead. But because of the fierce resistance at Ten Aard the 15th Division was clearly getting nowhere and Ritchie decided to develop the main axis of advance the following day from a new bridgehead further east, north of Lommel. This task was assigned to the 53rd (Welsh) Division. As a result Operation Flood was cancelled and the 15th Division was merely told to maintain pressure at Ten Aard and hold the canal line from Geel eastwards.[88] The stalemate therefore was an important tactical and operational victory for *Kampfgruppe Chill*. Just holding on to the bridgehead for the Scots was pointless and on 20 September it was abandoned.

That still leaves the question: what was the point of all the suffering? Lieutenant-General Ritchie (XII Corps) thought it had been useful. On 19 September he sent a letter to Barber.[89] In this he wrote that Horrocks (XXX Corps) thought capturing Ten Aard had greatly helped Market Garden. Horrocks contributed the rapidity with which his troops had broken out of their bridgehead at De Kolonie to the fact that "a very great proportion of the German's available resources had been drawn against the 15th (Scottish) Division front." That seems typical wishful thinking, since it was basically just one battalion supported by artillery that prevented the Scots from expanding the bridgehead. Also, the deadlock continued even after the start of Operation Market Garden when Chill had been forced to send two battalions of *Grenadier-Regiment 723* east to counter the new threat. There is a case for putting it the other way round. Because the iron corset around Ten Aard could not be

---

87   War Diary 15th Scottish Div, 17.09.44, Appx C.
88   Martin, *Fifteenth Scottish Division*, p.143.
89   Martin, *Fifteenth Scottish Division*, p.146.

broken open, the 15th (Scottish) Division was unable to break out of the bridgehead (Operation Flood), capture Turnhout and advance on Tilburg, rolling up the whole of *LXXXVIII. Armeekorps* right wing covering Antwerp. Consequently the Scots could not block the escape route of *15. Armee* just as its divisions were entering the mainland, or prevent them from becoming involved in the Brabant (western) side of Operation Market Garden. Even worse, XII Corps was slow in securing the left flank of XXX Corps during Market Garden in effect preventing more Allied troops from reaching Nijmegen. This, in very a real way, contributed to the failure of Market Garden.

Once again Chill and Dreyer had triumphed over their opponents, this time even more dramatically than at Geel. The circumstances, terrain and weather, had been working in their favour. On the other hand, they had less artillery, no tanks (and only two *Jagdpanther*), little ammunition and a hodgepodge of troops. This success was also quite an achievement since the strength of *Kampfgruppe Chill* was far below what it had been just a week earlier. On 17 September Chill commanded just four battalions of which one was strong, four were average and two were in tatters, giving him about 1,500 men.[90] Admittedly this time the sector covered by the *Kampfgruppe* was just thirty-five kilometres (Herentals to Lommel), but that still came out to one man every twenty-three metres, a far from comfortable situation. By continually counterattacking Chill had kept the Scots off balance all the time. Ten Aard was a major tactical victory for the Germans with operational consequences for the Allies.

A few days later Chill and his subordinate commanders would once more need their professional skills in the battles to come. Even as they were pulling back behind the Antwerp-Turnhout Canal on the night of 22/23 September they had been anxiously watching their left flank for five days. Here Market Garden had been unfolding since 17 September.

Hell's Highway

On Sunday 24 September Operation Market Garden was like a ship dead in the water, only the captain still hoping to make port. As Lieutenant-General Brian Horrocks (XXX Corps) climbed to the top of Valburg church, it promised to be another typically Dutch autumn day, sunny and not too cold (14° C) but with the occasional shower.[91] Horrocks took a look across the river Neder Rijn (as the Rhine is known here) to the shrinking bridgehead still occupied by the 1st Airborne Division.[92] He was determined to make one final effort to get across the Rhine. He felt that it should be possible to put at least one battalion of the 43rd (Wessex) Division across and possibly, if things went well, even cross further west to carry out a left hook and attack the German forces from the rear. The outcome of Market Garden was hanging

90   KTB 88 AK, 17.09.44, B 292.
91   KNMI jaaroverzicht 1944.
92   This section, Sir Brian Horrocks, *Corps Commander*, Sidgwick & Jackson 1977, pp.121-3.

in the balance.[93] After having issued orders he drove back to St.-Oedenrode (still firmly in Allied hands) to meet Dempsey. Horrocks' optimism was as unrealistic as the pessimism that prevailed on the German side.[94] *Generalfeldmarschall* Model, *OB Heeresgruppe B*, went so far as to suggest a gradual withdrawal behind the Maas and Waal. Hitler disagreed and instead ordered the two armies to hold their present positions and plug the gap at Veghel through a concentric attack.[95] That was exactly what *Kampfgruppe Chill* was trying to do that day.

The attack was to begin as early as possible.[96] At eight a.m. Reinhard joined Chill in his new headquarters in Schijndel.[97] He also saw Dreyer and Von der Heydte. The plan was for Dreyer to make a wide hook via Eerde, his left flank attacking north of the Zuid Willemsvaart, while Von der Heydte's group would advance in a parallel direction further west. *Fallschirm-Bataillon Jungwirth* would follow closely on their heels to cover the right flank. Although *Fallschirm-Bataillon Jungwirth* had only been assigned a limited mission, the American successful defence of Eerde, meant that the centre of gravity began to shift during the day. The lead party, about forty *Fallschirmjäger* and two *Jagdpanther*, crossed the road.[98] Soon more groups followed, a third *Jagdpanther* among them. As soon as it was really dark, more and more *Fallschirmjäger*, most of them from 9. and 10./*FJR 6*, crossed the road and joined the group around Logtenburg.[99] Altogether around two hundred men established themselves in the woods astride and south of the Allied Centre Line. It is also clear that at least one, but probably more *Panzerjäger* from *Panzerjäger-Kompanie 304* joined in as well.[100] Finally two or three 8.8 cm *Flak* guns reinforced the *Kampfgruppe* under *Major* Huber.[101] Once again, the Allied lifeline had been severed.

The German success in blocking the artery to Nijmegen and beyond was the final straw that broke the camel's back for Operation Market Garden. On Monday 25 September General Dempsey (Second Army) decided to withdraw the 1st Airborne

93 Which were Demsey's sentiments also (Cf. Demspey, The Second 100 Days, TNA WO 285-10, 24.09.44).
94 This section, Percey E. Schramm (Her.), *Kriegstagebuch des Oberkommando der Wehrmacht 7/I*, Bernard & Graefe 1982, p.396.
95 Heeresgruppe B, 25.09.44, Ops 839/44.
96 This section, War Diary 44th Royal Tank Regiment, Leonard Rapport and Arthur Northwood Jr., *Rendezvous with Destiny, a History of the 101st Airborne Division*, 101st Airborne Division Association 1948, pp.362-371, Jack Didden en Maarten Swarts, *Einddoel Maas*, De Gooise Uitgeverij 1984, pp.90-3.
97 KTB 88 AK, 24.09.44, 08.10 hours.
98 War Diary 50th (N) Division, 24.09.44, 17.46 hours.
99 Volker Griesser, *Die Löwen von Carentan*, VS-Books 2007, p.195.
100 Second Army, Intel Log, 25.09.44, serial 18 mentions six 'tanks', ibid, serial 46 mentions four 'tanks', War Diary 44th RTR, 26.09.44, morning report (see also below).
101 Allied sources (Second Army Intel Log 25.09.44, serial 46 and 7th Armoured Div. Intel Sum 106) mention 200 men and two 8,8 cm Flak, KTB 88 AK, 25.09.44, A 464, mentions 2½ companies which comes roughly to 200-250 men, plus three 8,8 cm Flak.

Division from the bridgehead that night. Their position was no longer tenable. Montgomery agreed and at 09.30 hours he confirmed Dempsey's decision. Finally Horrocks was told. He had spent the night at 50th Division headquarters. Early in the morning, with the help of a carrier platoon from the 9th Durham Light Infantry he made a wide detour of the German blocking position.[102] Later that morning he was back at his headquarters north of Nijmegen. The atmosphere was gloomy. The 4th Dorsets who had crossed the Rhine the previous night had suffered such casualties that they were unable to reinforce the bridgehead. There was nothing left to do for Horrocks but oversee the withdrawal. Meanwhile the road was still blocked.

While it was still dark both sides prepared for battle. There was no need for fancy plans. Huber's mission was simple: block the road and take Veghel bridge by attacking through Eerde, while Poppe's *59. I.D.* covered the right flank by attacking St.-Oedenrode. For the Allies the task was not very complicated either, it was 'to get the road open again'.[103] From the southwest units of the 7th Armoured Division with two companies from the 502nd Parachute Infantry Regiment would proceed north. At the same time the 506th, supported by the Shermans of 44th Royal Tank Regiment would advance from the northeast. This force of five battalions plus should have been enough to remove the blockade by a few German companies. But the nut proved to be a tough one to crack and the *Kampfgruppe* held out all day. It was not until the early hours of 26 September that Huber's group finally began to withdraw towards Wijbosch, a tricky manoeuvre, surrounded as it was on all sides by enemy units. But Huber's men successfully extricated themselves. The *88* guns were towed back by the three *Jagdpanther* of *559*.[104] Around ten a.m. all the German troops were back at the assembly area in Wijbosch, southeast of Schijndel. By first seeking the weak spot in the Allied defences and then quickly setting up an all-round defence in a location ideally suited for that, Chill's men had managed to keep the Allies occupied for nearly two days before slipping away and pulling back to safety.

Conclusion

Monday 4 September was one of the turning points of the war. It was the day of desperate German measures to plug the gap and man the Albert Canal line, the day that Antwerp was captured, the apogee of operation Overlord, and also the day that one of the major opportunities of the war was lost. By postponing the operation for twenty-four hours Montgomery and Dempsey squandered a unique opportunity. In an analysis three years after the events, almost to the day, *Generalleutnant* Bodo Zimmermann, reflecting on the Allies breaking through towards the Ruhr while simultaneously cutting off *15. Armee*, wrote that 'in my opinion, which is shared by

102 War Diary 50th (N) Division, 25.09.44, 11.25 hours.
103 Rapport and Northwood, *Rendezvous with Destiny, p.*371.
104 KTB 88 AK, 26.09.44, A 473.

the then Chief of the General Staff, OB West (Gen. Blumentritt), both moments (...) together would have caused the final German military collapse as early as the fall of 1944.'[105] But Von Zangen's army was ignored and only the Ruhr was considered.

However, it was never a mistake, but rather a calculated gamble on their part. Montgomery and his staff were aware that, 'The Albert Canal and the 15th Army are our immediate concern.'[106] Three days later the intelligence staff unequivocally stated that, 'Meantime 15th Army continues to extricate itself over the Scheldt to provide reinforcements for other parts of the front.'[107] In other words, they knew the risk they were taking. The vehicles of XXX Corps still had about a hundred litres of petrol each and could easily have advanced for another day. In all likelihood the 11th Armoured Division could have crossed the Albert Canal (especially as most of the bridges had not been mined yet and some had even been seized by the Belgian resistance). From Antwerp one straight road leads to Woensdrecht and Bergen op Zoom. Possession of those towns meant that there would be no way out for *15. Armee*. If the Allies had acted exactly as the Germans feared they would cut off the Beveland isthmus and Von Zangen's army would have been completely trapped against the coast.[108] If Horrocks had ordered Roberts to bypass Antwerp instead of telling him to take the town this manoeuvre could have been executed the day before.[109] But even as things stood, the operation might still have succeeded on 5 September. Von Rundstedt's Chief-of-staff, Westphal, wrote in his memoirs, 'Die Trümmer der Heeresgruppe B reichten nicht mehr aus, eine zusammenhängende Widerstandslinie aufzubauen.'[110] The results of continued Allied pressure would have been devastating. Afterwards Montgomery and Dempsey used the logistics situation as an excuse to explain the reversal.[111] However, it should be borne in mind that no armies had ever been more amply supplied than the Allied ones in World War Two. In fact, both General Marshall and Churchill criticised the lavish rear services and supply tables. When questioned by the latter, staff officers answered that their troops simply required a higher standard of comfort and welfare than the Germans.[112]

The Allied commanders continued to ignore *15. Armee* and instead hoped to continue 'swanning' as far as Germany. But the advance became stuck in the bloody triangle Herentals – Lanaken – Neerpelt, largely as a result of the skilled defence put

105 Letter dated 10 September 1947, OCMH MS D-0327, p.3. At the time Zimmermann was Ia to OB West.
106 Second Army, IS 94, 06.09.44.
107 Second Army, IS 97, 09.09.44.
108 Or be evacuated by sea, not an option, in view of the strength of the Royal Navy.
109 As Horrocks himself admitted afterwards (Horrocks, *Corps Commander*, p.81).
110 Siegfried Westphal, *Heer in Fesseln*, Athenäum Verlag 1950, p.261.
111 Martin Van Creveld, *Supplying War, Logistics from Wallenstein to Patton*, Cambridge University Press 1977, p.227.
112 Walter Scott Dunn Jr., *Second Front Now – 1943*, The University of Alabama Press 1980, p.177.

up by *Kampfgruppe Chill*. The consequences were far-reaching and, 'The Allies never fully regained their momentum (…) until March 1945.'[113] In subsequent engagements at Geel and Ten Aard, Chill's battle group thwarted all British attempts to outflank the German defences north of Antwerp (and at the same time secure the left flank of XXX Corps after the start of Market Garden). The final blow was dealt by the *Kampfgruppe* when it successfully cut the Corridor near Schijndel, effectively putting an end to any chance there may still have been of salvaging the operation.

The successful defence put up by *Kampfgruppe Chill* from 6 September forced Montgomery and Dempsey to rethink their operational plans and turn Operation Comet into Market Garden. As a result the airborne operation was not only expanded but, more crucially, delayed until a date where German defences were stronger than they had been a week before, particularly along the flanks of the main advance. Although Montgomery afterwards felt that the operation had been 'ninety per cent successful',[114] he conceded that the operation had at least partly failed. He saw two principal reasons for this, one was the weather, the other was the *'surprising'* concentration of forces the Germans had managed to put together.[115] This concentration should not have been surprising as *Kampfgruppe Chill* had stalled Second Army's advance from the day it was resumed.

The author of a recent book about Market Garden has a strong case when he claims that during World War Two airborne operations on the whole were not very successful.[116] The reasons for this: they were expensive, they were often characterized by high casualties and mission failure, or only partial success, and successive airlifts proved to be very problematic to set up.[117] Hence, Market Garden had only a slim chance of succeeding, but only if 'the airborne could be promptly relieved by conventional ground forces'.[118] The problem was that the ground troops had to rely on a single road initially. A widening of the flanks by VIII and XII Corps would have alleviated the situation, but XII Corps in particular failed in this objective and the first week one road was all that led to Nijmegen and beyond. The attacks on this one artery, starting on the second day when the *59. Infanterie-Division* and the *107. Panzerbrigade* tried to make contact at Son, were crucial to the failure of the operation.[119] The attack was unsuccessful, but forced the Allies to divert considerable resources to deal with it. After two days the attacks moved further north, to the bridge at Veghel, but again the two attacking German groups failed to make contact. It was then that Reinhard

113 Ian Kershaw, *The End*, Allen Lane 2011, p.388.
114 Field-Marshal the Viscount Montgomery of Alamein, *Normandy to the Baltic*, Hutchinson & Co Ltd. n.d., p.149.
115 Ibid.
116 Sebastian Ritchie, *Arnhem, Myth and Reality, Airborne Warfare, Air Power and the Failure of Operation Market Garden*, London 2011, pp.1-2.
117 Ibid, pp.83-4.
118 Ibid, p.259.
119 An idea shared e.g. by C.P.M. Klep in Klep and Schoenmaker, *De Bevrijding*, p.156.

turned to *Kampfgruppe Chill*. This attack was more successful and for forty-four hours all contact between the base and the head of the operation was severed. Operation Market Garden was already dead in the water by that time, but this counterattack dashed any hope either Horrocks or Montgomery may still have harboured and effectively helped finish off the operation. Chill and his battlegroup had put a spoke in Second Army's wheels from 6 September up to the end of Market Garden. In essence, it was never 'a bridge too far', but always 'a week too late'.

Bibliography

Martin Blumenson, *Breakout and Pursuit*, OCMH 1984.

General Carl von Clausewitz, *Vom Kriege*, Vier Falken Verlag n.d.

Terry Copp, *Fields of Fire, The Canadians in Normandy*, University of Toronto Press 2008.

Martin Van Creveld, *Supplying War, Logistics from Wallenstein to Patton*, Cambridge University Press 1977.

Das Deutsche Reich und der Zweite Weltkrieg, Band 4, Beiheft, Skizze 1, DVA 1983.

Patrick Delaforce, *The Black Bull*, Allan Sutton, 1993.

Jack Didden, *Fighting Spirit*, De Zwaardvisch 2012.

Jack Didden en Maarten Swarts, *Einddoel Maas*, De Gooise Uitgeverij 1984.

Die Wehrmachtsberichte 1939-1945, Band 2, Köln 1989.

Walter Scott Dunn Jr., *Second Front Now–1943*, The University of Alabama Press, 1980.

John Ehrman, *Grand Strategy Volume V*, HMSO 1956.

D.J.L. Fitzgerald M.C., *History of the Irish Guards in the Second World War*, Gale & Polden 1949.

Volker Griesser, *Die Löwen von Carentan*, VS-Books 2007.

Fritz Hahn, *Waffen und Geheimwaffen des deutschen Heeres 1933-1945*, Dörfler n.d.

Stephen Ashley Hart, *Colossal Cracks, Montgomery's 21st Army Group in Northwest Europe, 1944-45*, Stackpole 2007.

Helmut Heiber, *Lagebesprechungen im Führerhauptquartier*, DVA 1962.

Sir Brian Horrocks, *Corps Commander*, Sidgwick & Jackson 1977.

Walther Hubatsch, *Hitlers Weisungen*, Bernard & Graefe Verlag 1983.

Ian Kershaw, *The End*, Allan Lane 2011.

Christ Klep en Ben Schoenmaker (ed.), *De Bevrijding van Nederland 1944-1945, oorlog op de flank*, Sdu 1995.

Andreas Kunz, *Wehrmacht und Niederlage*, R. Oldenbourg Verlag 2007.

Andris J. Kursietis, *The Wehrmacht at War 1939-1945, The Units and Commanders of the German Ground Forces during World War II*, Aspekt 1999.

T.M. Lindsay, *Sherwood Rangers*, Burrup, Mathiesen & Co, 1952.

James Lucas and James Barker, *The Killing Ground, The Battle of the Falaise Gap, August 1944*, London 1978.

Joachim Ludewig, *Der deutsche Rückzug aus Frankreich 1944*, Verlag Rombach 1994.

Victor Madej, *Russo-German War No. 27, Autumn 1942: Defeat of Barbarossa*, Allentown 1988.

John Man, *The Penguin Atlas of D-Day and the Normandy Campaign*, Viking 1994.

Karel Margry, *Market Garden*, After the Battle 2002.

H.G. Martin, *Fifteenth Scottish Division*, Blackwood 1948.

Field-Marshal the Viscount Montgomery of Alamein, *Normandy to the Baltic*, Hutchinson & Co Ltd. n.d.

Roden Orde, *The Household Cavalry at War: Second Household Cavalry Regiment*, Gale & Polden 1953.

Forrest C. Pogue, *The Supreme Command*, OCMH 1954.

Leonard Rapport and Arthur Northwood Jr., *Rendezvous with Destiny, a History of the 101st Airborne Division*, 101st Airborne Division Association 1948.

Brian A. Reid, *No Holding Back, Operation Totalize, Normandy, August 1944*, Stackpole 2005.

Sebastian Ritchie, *Arnhem, Myth and Reality, Airborne Warfare, Air Power and the Failure of Operation Market Garden*, Hale 2011.

Panzermeyer, *Grenadiere*, Schild Verlag GmbH 1965.

Percy Schramm, *Kriegstagebuch des Oberkommandos der Wehrmacht 7/I*, Bernard & Graefe Verlag 1982.

Schuster, Oberstleutnant i.G. Kurt-Arthur, Aufstellung und Einsatz der 85. Inf. Division im Westen, Februar bis November 1944, OCMH MS B-244.

Schuster, Oberstleutnant i.G. Kurt-Arthur, Fortsetzung zu Aufstellung und Einsatz der 85. Inf. Division im Westen, Februar bis November 1944, B: Einsatz der Division, OCMH MS B-424.

Schuster, Oberstleutnant i.G. Kurt-Arthur, The 85th Infantery Division (Feb-Nov 1944), OCMH MS B-846.

P.C. Stacey, *Official History of the Canadian Army in the Second World War, the Victory Campaign Volume III, The Operations in North-west Europe 1944-1945*, Roger Duhamel 1960.

Siegfried Westphal, *Heer in Fesseln*, Athenäum Verlag 1950.

Zetterling (*Normandy 1944, German Military Organization, Combat Power and Organizational Effectiveness*, Manitoba 2000.

Earl F. Ziemke and Magna E. Bauer, *Moscow to Stalingrad*, OCMH 1987.

5

Allied Close Air Support during Operation Market Garden: A Lesson in Planning

Jamie Slaughter

Close Air Support (CAS) played a key role in Field Marshal (then General) Bernard Montgomery's successful campaign against Field Marshal Rommel in North Africa. A CAS system was in place but, but not best utilized, before Montgomery's arrival.[1] In fact, it was Montgomery, with his skilled planning and penchant for training, who first successfully integrated CAS into Allied ground operations in the Mediterranean, and Europe.[2] By Operation Overlord, CAS had evolved into a powerful and potent instrument, and it played an important role in subsequent operations until September 1944. 'The lesson seems to be', Monty had written, 'that full advantage must be taken of the flexibility of air forces to direct every ounce of power when the decisive moment arrives on to what is then the decisive target.'[3]

Close Air Support during Operation Market Garden encountered a number of difficulties. Due to the number of units involved with the operation, its short duration, and the restricted terrain, the most efficient way to digest the role of CAS in Operation Market Garden is to break it down into three sections: planning and the pre-battle, operations, and conclusions. Compared to previous operations, planning was rushed and concerning CAS, terribly incomplete. Marginal pre-operation strikes and preparations in light of the supposed concerns were inexplicable. During the operation, CAS ran the gamut from very, to marginally, to ineffective due to a number of direct and indirect influences. What had been a smoothly functioning and indeed improving machine, temporarily devolved during Operation Market Garden.

1   Ian Gooderson, *Air Power at the Battlefront*. London : Frank Cass, 1998, p.26.
2   Jonathan R. House. *Combined Arms Warfare in the 20th Century*. Lawrence : University Press of Kansas, 2001, p.127.
3   Nigel Hamilton, *Monty: The Battles of Field Marshal Bernard Montgomery*. NY: Random House, 1994, p.71.

Planning and Pre-Battle Strikes

The 'miracle' of Operation Market Garden was the logistics involved in dropping three divisions (The US 82nd and 101st Airborne, the British 1st Airborne, and the Polish Brigade) in about one week. This was a daunting and impressive effort. Poor and questionable planning concerning CAS in particular offset this feat.

Anybody familiar with the fundamental facts concerning Operation Market Garden has doubtlessly read of the great concern German flak was to the planners.[4] The 82nd Airborne and the 1st Airborne were provided very poor drop zones to assuage air planners' fear of the quality and quantity of flak believed to be in the battle zone.[5] Remarkably, however, little was done to directly target the suspected flak positions prior to the battle.

In the area between the US 82nd and 101st and encompassing the 1st Airborne, the RAF targeted three German airfields and one Flak position the night before the drops.[6] In the American sector, immediately preceding the drops, medium and heavy bombers struck suspected armor and flak positions immediately before the drops.[7] These were conducted from at least 20,000 feet, and in the process, they encountered little flak.[8]

While enemy defenses were somewhat suppressed prior to operations, the amount of overall preparation seems light compared to previous attempts. A partial explanation for this is the so called "...Victory Virus..." a genuine belief that the Germans were essentially defeated and on the verge of collapse.[9] This 'illness' was so widespread, administrators were preparing to take over German civil operations by November, 1944.[10] To paraphrase another leader, the Allies were betting they could just kick in the door and the whole thing would collapse. The over-optimism and under-planning during operation reflected this. Unfortunately, poor planning also combined with a "...lamentable lack of security..." and the Wehrmacht in the Netherlands was alert and ready for the Allied attack.[11] "Model's intelligence officer issued daily warnings of an imminent British offensive, probably to be launched in the direction of Nijmegen, Arnhem, and Wesel. The Objective was the Ruhr. Intelligence was further

---

4   Martin Middlebrook, *Arnhem: The Airborne Battle*. Mechanicsburg: Stackpole, 2009, p.388.

5   Ibid., p.388.

6   Ibid., p.74.

7   Ibid., p.74.

8   John C. McManus, *September Hope : The American Side of a Bridge Too Far*. NY : NAL Caliber, 2014, pp.72-75.

9   Alistair Horne and David Montgomery, *Montgomery: The Lonely Leader, 1944-1945*. New York: Harper Collins, 1994, p.273.

10   Nigel Hamilton, *Monty : The Field Marshal 1944-1976*. London : Hamish Hamilton, 1986, p.3.

11   Alistair Horne and David Montgomery, *Montgomery*, p.285.

convinced that airborne troops would be used, as they had in Sicily and the invasion of Normandy."[12]

The Allies developed a rather effective, if sometimes dangerous method of dealing with enemy battlefield flak. They utilized a method familiar to any Wild Weasel pilot today: fly over the battlefield, and shoot back at what shoots at you.[13] This was accomplished by sending in CAS aircraft to draw the flak into the fight then neutralize it. The methodology may seem counter-intuitive, but it was effective for the nimble, fast moving fighters and fighter-bombers, that were able to use speed and maneuver to help evade flak.

The most inexplicable part of all the planning of Operation Market Garden was the orders given to the escort and CAS aircraft operating in the British (1st Airborne) sector. First, no CAS aircraft could operate while drops or resupplies were underway.[14] Second, it was strictly forbidden for the fighter aircraft escorting the transports and bombers conducting the drops to break off from patrol and engage ground targets.[15] The losses to German aircraft were generally light with the exception of the instance where the escort did not manage to rendezvous with the transports. However, the slow lumbering transports and bombers flying in the British sector, along easily predictable routes, with no flak suppression from designated CAS or escorting fighter aircraft made fat, easy targets for enemy flak.

Considering the concerns over flak that caused the 82nd and 1st Airborne Divisions to disperse well away from optimal drop zones, this seems quite strange. Other than the rather light and frankly optimistic suppression/destruction of enemy flak by the bombers the night before, the transports were ordered into a suspected nest of flak with no real means to defend themselves. These fundamental planning flaws are indicative of the continued conflicts between leadership and the air staffs during the brief planning for Operation Market Garden.[16]

The bizarre non-strategy for dealing with flak in the most vulnerable sector of Operation Market Garden in the run up to the operation is best explained by little coordination with CAS planners. In the XXX Corps sector, this may partially explain the pause for the planning, it was 'business as usual'. XXX Corps was essentially moving out of their extant battle positions into the American and eventually the British zone. The preparation for CAS operations in the area of the 1st Airborne was, however, very questionable.

The 2nd Tactical Air Force (TAF) was responsible for CAS in the 1st Airborne (British) zone of operations.[17] Amazing as it seems now, the commander of the 2nd

---

12   Robert Kershaw, *It Never Snows in September: The German View of Market-Garden and the Battle of Arnhem, September 1944.* Croydon: Ian Allan, 2013, p.31.
13   John C. McManus. *September Hope*, pp.86-87.
14   Martin Middlebrook, *Arnhem: The Airborne Battle*, p.388.
15   Ibid., p.388.
16   Alistair Horne and David Montgomery, *Mongomery*, p.287.
17   Martin Middlebrook. *Arnhem : The Airborne Battle*, p.68.

TAF, Air Marshal Sir Arthur Conginham, was left out of all the planning meetings for Operation Market Garden save one, on 16 September, the day before operations began.[18] Regardless, the weather in Belgium where the 2nd TAF HQ was located was so poor, he could not make it to England.[19] While it is difficult to attribute any one element as the principle failure, the fact that the commander of CAS units meant to support the most extended and vulnerable aspect of Operation Market Garden was invited as an afterthought is incredulous. Furthermore, his absence from the majority of meetings whereby his presence and critical input concerning the mission's success or failure failed to dissuade anyone in command from launching Operation Market Garden is even more condemning.

Interestingly, Lieutenant General Lewis Brereton, the commander of the First Allied Airborne Army, had only recently moved to his new position from commanding the US Ninth Air Force.[20] No evidence has surfaced indicating Brereton objected to the CAS plan. This seems very strange considering his previously held positions. Brereton, like many of the Allied airborne commanders might have been wondering whether his command would ever see action again during the war. Overconfidence combined with a desire to get his command into action overrode what should have been a clarion voice questioning the air plans in the least, if not the operation as a whole.

There is one final interesting facet regarding planning for CAS during Operation Market Garden. The Garden element, the airborne units, utilized a different method for coordinating CAS than their non-airborne comrades.[21] The best reason given for this is the status of the airborne units that existed outside the parameters of the 'regular' army, and trained and operated separately.[22] This included not only how the airborne units communicated with CAS, but the equipment that communicated with as well.

Finally, the infamous 'radio' issue must be addressed concerning the 1st Airborne. Unbeknownst to most, especially those who tend to turn to cinema for history, the radios meant to help coordinate CAS for the 1st Airborne, were American, not British, and they were manned by American airborne troops.[23] Although those in power recognized the fact that communications equipment given to airborne troops was delicate considered the way it was delivered, and to an extent underpowered, there was no apparent attempt to improvise or improve this system until the lessons of Operation Market Garden were learned the hard way.[24] (For a fascinating analysis of the overall Airborne communications problem refer to Major John Greenacre's

18   Ibid., p.68.
19   Ibid., p.68.
20   Middlebrook, *Arnhem 1944*, p.16.
21   Ian Gooderson. *Air Power at the Battle Front*, p.96.
22   Ibid., p.97.
23   Middlebrook, *Arnhem: The Airborne Battle*, p.105.
24   Ian Gooderson, *Air Power at the Battle Front*, p.98.

article 'Assessing the Reasons for Failure: 1st British Airborne Division Signal Communications during Operation Market Garden'[25]). Overall, the failure of the operation, including the CAS plan was the result of the "...cascading consequences of shoddy planning..."[26]

CAS in Action during Operation Market Garden

Largely, CAS was 'business as usual' in the American sector and as far as XXX Corps was concerned. CAS was active from the moment the 82nd and 101st landed, and XXX Corps crossed its line of departure. In this sector, CAS did effectively support the transport aircraft and suppress the flak arrayed against them.[27] While any loss of transport aircraft was critical considering the need to continually support especially the 1st Airborne, and the demands outside the Operation Market Garden area of operations which the transport had to address once the operation was theoretically over in 'three days', the four percent losses initially incurred in this zone were considered acceptable, if not a success, in light of flak being able to operate against slow, straight flying aircraft dropping paratroops in daylight.[28] Additionally, communications were generally good in these sectors, and CAS was fulfilling all of its traditional roles, including flak suppression as weather and time permitted.

Some CAS procedures showed improvement from Normandy to the Netherlands where XXX Corps was concerned.[29] The fact that CAS units only had to follow one road to find XXX Corps was the unseen benefit in the monumentally poor decision to try to push an armored column up a single road against a grossly underestimated enemy. Unlike Normandy or Falaise where finding the general location of the target was occasionally difficult, CAS could generally find the road in friendly territory and follow it right up to the advance limit of XXX Corps. There was another side to this, however: the Germans repeatedly cut the road behind XXX Corps during the advance, which muddled an otherwise simple targeting scheme and increased the likelihood of friendly fire. Additionally, it made placing anti-aircraft defenses easier for the Germans as the Allied route of advance was predictable.

If navigation was easy by following the one road up country, Operation Market Garden's terrain could hardly have been worse for CAS. The many small cities and towns made CAS operations difficult. Targeting enemy troops in urban areas with

25   Major John Greenacre, 'Operation Market Garden: Assessing the Reasons for Failure: 1st British Airborne Division SignalCommunications during Operation'Market Garden'. *Defence Studies* 4, no. 3, pp.283-308.
26   Williamson Murray and Allen R. Millet. *A War to be Won: Fighting the Second World War.* Cambridge: Harvard University Press, 2001, p.441.
27   John C. McManus, *September Hope*, pp.86-89.
28   Ibid., p.100.
29   Ian Gooderson. *Air Power at the Battle Front*, pp.85-88.

precise fire was very difficult, especially when they were in close contact with friendly troops.

CAS operations in the British sector were not as successful. The requirements to resupply the 1st Airborne kept transport and bomber aircraft in the air for well beyond the planned three day period. Further, CAS continued to operate under the same restrictions keeping them at bay from aiding in suppressing enemy flak when low level supply, troop drops, or bombing runs were made by Allied transports and bombers.[30] The flak concern was legitimate. Continued efforts to succor the 1st Airborne in Arnhem were hampered by the fact that very little was done to suppress German flak having a field day with the lumbering, fat, low altitude bombers and transports operating in daylight. The losses were exacerbated by the fact the transports were unable to communicate via radio with the troops in Arnhem and most of the supplies meant for the entrapped paras went to the Germans or were isolated in No-Man's-Land.

The radios delivered to Arnhem with the wrong operating equipment, were, in fact, American, and designed to facilitate ground to air communication and cooperation.[31] These teams actually arrived on the first drop, earlier than previously scheduled.[32] Unfortunately, during the entire course of the battle, they were out of action. German fire damaged the sets in the final stages of the battle, even though it seems various individuals tried desperately through the course of the battle to operate them.

Unfortunately, due to operating orders (a bomb line was in place to theoretically protect Allied troops on the ground in Arnhem), no communication, and the timetable for the operation completely unraveled upon first contact, the first Allied CAS did not strike German units fighting directly against the embattled paratrooper until 24 September, when the battle for the Arnhem sector was essentially lost.[33] This was achieved not through direct air to ground communications as it should have been, but by a tedious process of sending requests back through XXX Corps, that was eventually reached by radio, and then up the communications chain to the 2nd TAF.[34] Unsurprisingly, due to the amount of time required, and the tight urban terrain in Arnhem, few enemy targets were actually spotted and fewer likely hit in the very strikes against German forces in the area before the subsequent surrender and escape of the 1st Airborne.

The flak suppression scheme had almost predictable results. In the American zone, where CAS operated actively against flak at most times, the loss and damage to the transports was kept relatively low in the American sector, whereas in the British sector, of the Dakotas which managed to return to their bases, "... sixty-six percent exhibited flak damage."[35] Clearly, the relatively light amount of high altitude bombing

30   John Terraine, *A Time for Courage*, p.670.
31   Martin Middlebrook, *Arnhem : The Airborne Battle*, p.69.
32   Ibid., pp.69-70.
33   Ibid., p.375.
34   Ibid., p.375.
35   Ibid., p.391.

directed at suspected flak positions was not terribly effective. Restrictions placed upon escort aircraft and CAS aircraft only added to Allied losses in the British sector by allowing German flak units to operate mostly unhindered by counter fire. As the operation developed loses in aircraft and aircrew became graver as German defenses became better organized.[36]

One further thing hindered CAS during Operation Market Garden: the weather. The weather turned bad almost immediately.[37] During the entire operation after the initial drop, the weather was generally rainy and very poor for air operations and CAS. The result was that even when calls did come in for support from one group, squadron, etc., it was frequently impossible to fly the mission. Out of ninety-five requests for CAS the RAF received during Operation Market Garden, fifty were unfulfilled due to weather.[38]

Conclusions

Operation Market Garden was a very rushed undertaking. Ironically, Field Marshal Montgomery had beaten his German adversaries across North Africa, Sicily, Italy, and France by not rushing his planning or operations.[39] He was, to use an American analogy, a trainer and organizer like McClellan, but a fighter like Grant. The successful operations he undertook against his German and Italian adversaries were not rapier thrusts designed to prick the heart of the enemy and end the fighting in a swift, sudden thrust, but blows designed to crush and maul; Monty was excellent at wielding a hammer. "Monty clearly overrode the advice not only of his staff but also of the army commander responsible for the operation."[40] Montgomery certainly failed to concentrate the flexibility of Allied combat air power on the decisive spots during Operation Market Garden.

It is beyond the scope of this paper to analyze the personal reasons behind Montgomery's insistence upon Operation Market Garden and its rushed planning. It is enough to state that the consummate planning for which Monty was known was almost completely absent from Operation Market Garden. Inexplicable orders and rules of engagement, a scant attempt at enemy air defense suppression in light of a tremendous concern for same, bad weather, overwhelming communications problems, and an unreasonable assumption that the Wehrmacht was finished, and bad terrain for combined arms operations combined to create a disaster for the British 1st Airborne, and a nightmare for CAS which up to September 17, 1944 had seen its operations

36   Martin Bowman, *Operation Market Garden: Air War Market Garden: The Build Up to the Beginning*. Barnsley: Pen and Sword, 2012, p.51.
37   John Terraine, *A Time for Courage*. NY: MacMillan, 1985, p.670.
38   Ibid., p.670.
39   Jonathan House, *Combined Arms Operations in the 20th Century*, p.127.
40   Stephen Ashley Hart, *Colossal Cracks: Montgomery's 21st Army Group in Northwest Europe, 1944-45*. Mechanicsburg: Stackpole, 2007, p.130.

continually improving. This lack of planning, and poor planning otherwise, kept CAS from being the decisive force it could have been during Operation Market Garden. It also permanently damaged the relationship between the British and the Americans for the remainder of the war in the ETO, alienating those who up to that time had tried to accommodate the rough personality, but admittedly effective leadership of Field Marshal Montgomery.[41] If not outwardly appreciative of Montgomery, Eisenhower and Bradley in particular did at least try to understand his need to try and conduct a British effort meant to bolster Britain's post war position in a war effort in the West now dominated by the United States. Operation Market Garden destroyed most of that good will. Later, Montgomery's boast that he saved the Americans during the Battle of the Bulge, eliminated what good will remained.[42] Montgomery himself and postwar biographers, who were generally supportive, tended to gloss over Operation Market Garden as an anomaly in an otherwise very successful record, which it was. It was a very expensive anomaly.

Operation Market Garden revealed to an extent what CAS could and could not do, and it disclosed weaknesses. The most important lesson for CAS was the value of planning. Arguably, better planning, which would have included CAS planners form the start, would have made a major difference in CAS, especially in the 1st Airborne sector. While the XXX Corps drive was to an extent 'business as usual', the airborne landings clearly were not. The concern over flak especially during daylight operations and the subsequent lack of active suppression which could have been provided by CAS during drop and resupply operations is inexplicable unless one accepts that the 'victory virus' theory.

Further, Operation Market Garden proved that CAS does not operate in a vacuum. CAS was not and never will be a 'fix-all' for bad planning or operations gone awry. Following the Normandy breakout, the sweep across France revealed what CAS could do under the proper circumstances, especially at Falaise.[43] However, this was when CAS was operation with fast-moving mobile forces, which had unhinged enemy defenses and could strike almost at will against on enemy on its heels. While CAS performed admirably in XXX Corps drive, it was clearly no solution for operating on poor or restricted terrain, determinedly defended by an experienced enemy, which was clearly not on the 'verge of collapse.'

The weather also hindered CAS operations. Forecasts were a benchmark of Allied operational planning and in this case, the Allies virtually ignored them. Allied CAS was undoubtedly one of the most potent forces available, but it could only operate when the pilots and planes were able to fly.

41   Rick Atkinson, *The Guns at Last Light : The War in Northwest Europe, 1944-1945*. NY : Henry Holt, 2013, pp.288-289.
42   Ibid., pp.483-484.
43   Ian Gooderson. *Air Power at the Battle Front*, pp.117-119.

One final lesson learned, which was acted upon, was that using multiple systems for coordinating CAS was counterproductive. By Operation Varsity, airborne elements were communicating with CAS in the same manner as conventional ground forces. Troops expected to operate together, especially under very adverse circumstances, needed to speak a common operational language even if their respective jobs and philosophies were quite different.

In short, CAS operations analyzed as a part of Operation Market Garden are perhaps best summarized by the criticism, that taken as a whole, the Allies were unable to grasp the concept of operational warfare in Northwest Europe during from 1944-45.[44]

44   Williamson Murray and Allen R. Millet, *A War to be Won*, p.443.

6

Mission Impossible?
The Mobilization of the German Replacement Army and its Role in the Thwarting of Operation 'Market Garden', 17-18 September 1944

Russell A. Hart

Scholars have paid relatively little attention to the role that the mobilization of the German Replacement Army (*Ersatzheer*) played in the thwarting of the Allied attempt to bounce the Rhine in Operation Market Garden. In response to the landing of the 82nd US Airborne Division southeast of Nijmegen and astride the Reich frontier, the Sixth German Military District (*Wehrkreis VI*) in Westphalia and the northern Rhineland mobilized instructors, recruits, convalescents, leave personnel and garrison troops and threw them against the U.S. airborne forces as they tried to first consolidate their drop zones and then take the two vital Waal bridges at Nijmegen, the vital stepping stone to Arnhem. These countermeasures delayed the fall of Nijmegen and therefore contributed to the thwarting of Market Garden.[1]

Studies of German countermeasures have largely focused on the commitment of the *10th SS Panzer Division "Frundsberg"* in delaying the capture of the Nijmegen bridges for four days, thereby directly contributing to the failure to relieve the beleaguered 1st British Airborne Division at Arnhem. This represents fixation with the actions of the more glamorous, better known, and better studied *10th SS Panzer Division*.[2] However,

---

1   Additional *Wehrkreis VI* forces were dispatched to Arnhem and fought in the defeat of the British 1st Airborne Division there but that story is outside the scope of this study.
2   On the role of the *10th SS Panzer Division* in delaying the U.S. capture of Nijmegen see: Robert Kershaw, *It Never Snows in September: The German View of Market Garden and the Battle for Arnhem, September 1944* (London: Ian Allen, 2008), pp. 162-168, 231-236; Tim Saunders, *Nijmegen: U.S. 82nd Airborne and Guards Armored Division, 1944* (Havertown: Pen and Sword, 2008.), ch. 7; David Bennett, *A Magnificent Disaster: The Failure of Market Garden. The Arnhem Operation, September 1944* (Philadelphia, PA: Casemate, 2008), pp. 92-94, 105-108; Rolf Michaelis, *10. SS Panzer Division Frundsberg* (Dörfler Verlag, 2009), pp. 79-92; Jean-Luc Leleu, *10. SS-Panzer-Division Frundsberg* (Bayeux: Heimdal, 1999); Michael Reynolds, *Sons of the Reich: The History of II SS Panzer Corps* (London: Pen and

scholars have paid less attention to the countermeasures of *Wehrkreis VI's Corps Feldt* and its subordinate *406th Division* on the eastern flank of the Allied airborne lodgment as well as the division's direct contribution to the protracted defense of Nijmegen. The division's counterthrusts out of the Reichswald forest toward the Groesbeek Heights fixed most of the 82nd Airborne into a protracted defense of the strategically vital heights as well as the village of Mook to the southeast, thereby preventing the US airborne forces from seizing Nijmegen when the opportunity existed prior to the *Waffen-SS* reinforcements arriving in strength. What follows therefore is a more detailed examination of the role that the *Ersatzheer* – and the *406th Division* in particular – played in delaying the fall of Nijmegen, thereby directly contributing to the ultimate failure of Operation Market Garden.

The Allies considered capture and retention of the Groesbeek Heights as a vital prerequisite for the capture of Nijmegen. Therefore, the counterattacks by *Wehrkreis VI*, even though it failed to regain the heights or to successfully interdict Allied supply lines, nonetheless absorbed most of the 82nd Airborne's attention and resources, leaving it insufficient strength to capture the Nijmegen bridges when they were most vulnerable to seizure – in the first 24 hours after landing. Undoubtedly the 82nd Airborne had sufficient strength to take Nijmegen, yet the *406th Division's* diversion of its attention and resources helped delay for four days the capture of the Nijmegen bridges. Since this delay prevented the successful relief of the British 1st Airborne Division at Arnhem, the *406th Division* thereby directly contributed to the failure of Market Garden.

Several reasons explain the relative lack of study of the *406th Division's* role in Market Garden. Existing scholarship has tended to focus on the ground advance of the British XXX Corps and on the beleaguered 1st British Airborne Division at Arnhem. Thus scholars have viewed the battle for the Groesbeek Heights as an uneventful side story, particularly given the German's failure to retake the heights. Additionally, none of the *406th Division's* records survived the war; nor did most of its senior leaders: its commanding officer, Lieutenant-General Scherbening and its Chief Operations Officer were both killed later in 1944.[3] Several small studies were written by German officers – including the divisional adjutant – while prisoners of the US Army after the war but these were written entirely from memory without any records and are replete with errors.[4] Moreover, the German officers involved largely glossed over a

Sword, 2009), chs. 12-19; Wilhelm Tieke, *In the Firestorm of the Last Years of the War, II. SS-Panzerkorps with the 9. and 10. SS-Divisions Hohenstaufen and Frundsberg* (Manitoba: J.J. Fedorowicz, 1999).

3   US Army Historical Division (USAHD) Foreign Military Studies (FMS) Collection C-085 Maj-Gen. Hellmuth Reinhardt, "Commitment of the *406th Division* Against the Allied Airborne Landing at Nijmegen in September 1944," (Königstein, Germany, 1950), p. 8.

4   A few, largely peripherally involved officers from these commands recorded their recollections after the war, exclusively from memory, in several reports written for the

prior partial mobilization of the *406th* in their post-war reports perhaps because they desired to emphasize their accomplishments in rapidly mobilizing and committing poor quality troops against the crack US airborne forces.[5] Only much later did fragments of the *Corps Feldt* war diary surface that shed a little more illumination.[6] Thus extant primary source material is extremely fragmentary. We must reconstruct the division's contribution from a disparate array of German and Allied sources, including memoirs and Ultra-decrypts of intercepted German messages.

Moreover, it is very clear that during the early days of Market Garden, the German high command had inadequate information regarding the strength, dispositions, and operations of the *406th Division*. This reflected several realities: the degree of strategic surprise the Allies achieved; the complete lack of combat experience of *Wehrkreis VI*; and the dislocation caused by a hasty redeployment of a rear-area administrative staff to conduct active combat operations. Thus even at the time, the German Armed Forces High Command or *Oberkommando der Wehrmacht* (OKW) – was poorly informed about what was occurring in and around Nijmegen during the first 36 hours of Operation Market Garden.

As a consequence, every published study of Market Garden has underemphasized the prior partial mobilization of *Wehrkreis VI*. In reality, the *406th Division* had already been partially mobilized and forward deployed on 12 September into the Reichswald Forest to rehabilitate the West Wall frontier defenses.[7] This saw lightly armed troops with very limited munitions move into field camps within the Reichswald where they slept rough and begun digging field fortifications and rehabilitating the West Wall. This under-acknowledged partial mobilization allowed the division to intervene more rapidly and more significantly in Market Garden than the Allies thought possible.

　　U.S. Army's History Division in its Foreign Military Studies collection. These include USAHD FMS B-044 Lt-Gen. Franz Mattenklott, "Part II: The Rhineland, 15 September 1944-31 March 1945 (Königstein, Germany, 1950); USAHD FMS B-665 Lt-Gen. Ernst Fäckenstedt, "The Activities of the Western Military Districts (*Wehrkreise VI and XII*) and their Cooperation in the Defense of the Front of O.B. West from September 1944-March 1945 (Allendorf, Germany, 1947); USAHD FMS C-085 Maj-Gen. Hellmuth Reinhardt, "Commitment of the 406th Division Against the Allied Airborne Landing at Nijmegen in September 1944," (Königstein, Germany, 1950); C-085, Kav-Gen Kurt Feldt, "Part Two: Corps Headquarters Feldt and 406th Division from 17 to 21 September 1944, (Königstein, Germany, 1950); USAHD FMS C-085a Lt-Gen Hellmuth Reinhardt, "Supplement to the Report of 1 December 1950 Concerning the Operations of the 406th Division in September 1944" (Königstein, Germany, 1951).

5　USAHD FMS C-085a, p. 9.

6　US National Archives and Records Administration (hereafter NARA), Washington, DC., Captured German Records Collection Record Group 242 series, T-314, microfilm reel 24, Kriegestagebuch Ia (Ops.) Korps Feldt, Stand: September 1944.

7　NARA T-314, 24, Kriegestagebuch (KTB) Korps Feldt Ia, Stand: 12 September 1944; USAHD FMS C-085, p. 2; Steven Zaloga, *Defense of the Rhine, 1944-45* (Oxford: Osprey Publishing, 2011), pp. 12-16.

This paper therefore examines the mobilization, commitment, and impact of *Corps Feldt's 406th Division* in the protracted defense of Nijmegen and in the Battle for the Groesbeek Heights during 17-18 September 1944, the first crucial 48 hours of the operation that denied the U.S. their immediate opportunity to seize Nijmegen and pave the way for the XXX Corps to reach the 1st Airborne at Arnhem more rapidly. It thereby sheds greater illumination on the division's important contribution to thwarting Market Garden.

Published studies of Market Garden therefore stress that *Wehrkreis VI* mobilized on 17 September in reaction to the landing of Allied airborne forces astride the Reich frontier.[8] Though Allied intelligence intercepted the German partial mobilization order for the *406th Division* into the *Reichswald* to rehabilitate the West Wall defenses insufficient time existed for this intercepted information to filter fully through to the US Airborne forces, nor was the full import of it recognized at the time.[9] Thus the *406th Division* was actually closer to the US landing zones than Allied intelligence had fully appreciated. By early September 1944, Allied intelligence had – based on Ultra intercepts of German radio messages (and Dutch Resistance information) in the weeks prior to Market Garden – come to recognize the possibility that German troops were deployed in some strength in the dense Reichswald forest.[10] Hence General Gavin, the commander of the 82nd Airborne Division – with the assent of his corps commander, General Browning – modified in his final briefings the Allied operational plan for Market Garden which gave priority to capture the Nijmegen and Grave bridges. Instead Gavin shifted emphasis to the division's second mission – that of first securing and holding the strategic high ground east and southeast of Nijmegen – the Groesbeek Heights to protect his division's landing zones.[11] Gavin therefore de-emphasized the immediate capture of the Nijmegen bridges and downgraded this mission to be accomplished only after the division had first secured the Groesbeek Heights, its defensive perimeter, and its drop zones.[12]

This erroneous shift in emphasis unfortunately played directly into the hands of the logical counter-measures launched by *Corps Feldt* which prevented the 82nd Airborne Division from capturing Nijmegen when it was weakly defended – during 17-18 September 1944. In retrospect, Gavin erred: Nijmegen should and could have been

---

8   Saunders, *U.S. 82nd Airborne*, p. 97; Kershaw, *It Never Snows*, pp. 36-37.
9   The U.K. National Archives (hereafter TNA), HW 1/3205, Ultra Decrypt, CX/MSS/T296/93, XL 9090, intercepted 1630 hrs 2 September 1944.
10 TNA, CAB 106/1056, Operation Market, Holland, 1944 "A Graphic History of the 82nd Airborne Division," p. 2; Kershaw, *It Never Snows*, pp. 36-37.
11 TNA, CAB 106/1056, p. 1; Bennett, *A Magnificent Disaster*, pp. 36-37; Charles MacDonald, *The Siegfried Line Campaign* (Washington, D.C.: OCMH, reprint ed. 1990), pp. 155-57.
12 CAB 106/1056, p. 1; James Gavin, *On To Berlin: Battles of an Airborne Commander, 1943-1945* (New York: Random House, reprint ed. 1992), pp. 162-64; Stephen Badsey, *Arnhem 1944* (Oxford: Oxford University Press, 1997), p. 29.

taken during 17-18 September before SS reinforcements arrived in sufficient numbers to delay its fall until 20 September.[13]

So what were the German forces defending Nijmegen and in the Reichswald on 17 September 1944? Unfortunately we do not have a precise picture due to the loss of most of the German war diaries. At best we can partially reconstruct the German order of battle and dispositions. What we do know is that Allied intelligence overestimated German ground troop strength and underestimated the antiaircraft defenses in the area.[14] The forces in the Reichswald belonged to *Corps Feldt* – a small, improvised headquarters formed on 4 September from the remnants of the Military Commander Southwest France, a small administrative staff that had extricated itself with some difficulty and at considerable cost from Operation ANVIL – the Allied invasion of Southern France and subsequent advance to the German frontier.[15] General Karl Feldt was an overage, 'old fashioned' cavalry officer no longer classified as fit for combat command.[16] His small headquarters had been grandiosely re-styled as *Corps Feldt* on 4 September to administer two *Wehrkreis VI* divisions that were deployed on 12 September into the Reichswald from Aachen to the Dutch frontier. The *406th* was the northernmost of these two formations. Feldt's was a miniscule staff that bore no correspondence to a frontline corps headquarters – it had no communications, transport, or administrative units save a military police troop: it thus relied entirely on *Wehrkreis VI* for supplies, communications, and transportation.[17]

The *406th Division* staff was likewise a small administrative headquarters that traditionally oversaw home defense units guarding Allied POWs in Westphalia. It had few combat experienced officers and its commanding officer, Lieutenant General Gerd Scherbening, was likewise another 'over the hill' officer relegated to home station staff duties.[18] When the division mobilized for frontier fortification duties on 12 September, the division inherited three training and replacement battalions

---

13 On the historical controversy that has raged around whether Nijmegen could have been captured on 17-18 September 1944 see Saunders, *U.S. 82nd Airborne*, pp. 28-32; MacDonald, *Siegfried Line*, pp. 163-165.

14 The Allies overestimated German strength in the vicinity of the 82nd Airborne drop zones as 8 battalions: TNA, CAB 106/1056, p. 2.

15 USAHD FMS c-085, p. 15.

16 Aged 57, Feldt was a career cavalry officer who had commanded the 1st Cavalry Division until its conversion to a panzer division in 1942. He then became the commander of an administrative occupation headquarters in southwestern France. His military career is summarized from www.wehrmachtslexicon.de/Personen-Register/F/Feldtkurt.htm.

17 NARA T-314, 24, KTB Korps Feldt, Kriegsgliederung, 12 September 1944.

18 His name was routinely misspelled Scherbenning in both Allied and German records. He was 55 years old and died in action on 12 December 1944. He served as a junior infantry officer during the Great War and then in infantry and administrative positions between the wars. He rose to command the 406th Division in October 1939 but his only active combat experience was in the Great War as a junior officer. His military service record is summarized at www.wehrmachtslexicon.de/personenregister/scherbeninggerd.htm.

comprising recruits in training and three composite battalions hastily assembled from demoralized and splintered stragglers retreating from the Western Front, whose morale were low. These poorly equipped battalions were only fit for construction tasks, not for combat deployment. The division's instructional cadre comprised experienced, if maimed, combat veterans no longer fit for frontline service.[19]

On 17 September the *406th* controlled nine battalions deployed in the Reichswald from Cleve to Kaltenkirchen. These units were the *39th Grenadier Replacement & Training Battalion*; the *1st Home Defense Training Battalion* of *Military District VI*; *Composite Battalion Klein*; the *303rd* & *304th Western Army Battalions* (newly formed from stragglers); the *Wehrkreis VI* NCO Training Course (comprising two grenadier and one heavy weapons battalions); and the *1224th Grenadier Battalion* (ear injured) – consisting of hearing impaired convalescents. The *406th* Division was small and weak – it totaled only 6,669 troops and its heavy weapons comprised: seven 120mm heavy mortars, two 150mm heavy field howitzers; three 75mm light infantry guns; one 150mm heavy infantry gun; one 37mm medium antiaircraft gun; three 50mm medium antitank guns; and one heavy 75mm antitank gun.[20] Moreover, most of the division was deployed several hundred miles away from Nijmegen in the northern Reichswald and dispersed in small company field camps across a wide geographical area.

On 17 September the 82nd Division in its first air lift alone deployed more troops and substantially greater firepower than the entire *406th Division* possessed. But the most significant dichotomy between the two formations was in manpower quality. The 82nd was an elite, cohesive, well equipped, and veteran combat experienced airborne division with marked esprit de corps. The *406th Division* was an indifferent, third rate formation thrown together six days before from a motley array of trainees, convalescents, and stragglers. It had relatively few combat experienced personnel, few heavy weapons, and minimal cohesion or esprit de corps. The *406th* was absolutely no match for the 82nd Airborne.

The stark reality was that the *406th Division* was ill-equipped, ill-prepared, ill-trained, and utterly unsuited for offensive operations against elite US airborne troops. The mobilized units had been deployed 'light' into field camps in the Reichswald with minimal equipment and provisions. They were equipped predominantly with just light arms and with minimal ammunition – just half a standard issue. Their task was construction duty not combat preparedness. Service support was nonexistent – the

19   Undoubtedly the best unit of the division was the regimental sized District VI NCO training school that included a reserve officer training course which comprised experienced enlisted personnel and new recruits undergoing training as NCOs under the auspices of crippled veteran NCOs and officers. But it was deployed on the southernmost part of the divisional sector astride Kaltenkirchen and would play no role in the Nijmegen battles during the critical first 48 hours which are the focus of this paper. Only the reserve officer training course would be committed as Battalion Göbel at Mook under *Kampfgruppe Hermann* on 18 September. USAHD FMS C-085, pp. 6-9, 15-16.

20   NARA T-314, 24, Kriegsgliederung der Division 406., Stand: 17 September 1944.

troops drew rations and supplies from adjacent *District VI* depots at Goch and Gelder. *Corps Feldt* had no armor, almost no artillery, and no signals units on September 17th and relied entirely on the local phone network for communications. Motor transport was exceedingly scarce and troop marched mainly on foot. The troops were also very tired from heavy manual labor alongside, for many, continued basic training and they typically had been laboring and training from sun up to sunset. All this reflected a partial mobilization of a rear area Replacement Army district for a tertiary task in a secondary theater. Consequently the *406th* had very minimal combat capabilities on 17 September 1944 and was incapable of defeating an elite American airborne division. That it gave the 82nd a run for its money – as the former was still consolidating and regrouping after its drops – is testimony to the skill, determination, and bravery of the *406th's* officers and men.

The partial mobilization and forward deployment of *Corps Feldt*, however, did allow the *406th* to intervene more rapidly at Nijmegen and on the Groesbeek Heights than the Allies conceived possible. Grudgingly, the 82nd Airborne conceded in its after action report the promptness of the *406th* reaction.[21] Besides the forward deployed elements of the *1st/6th* Home Defence Training Battalion which had moved into Nijmegen and onto the Groesbeek Heights just a couple of days before (of which more later), the closest unit deployed in the Reichswald – the 39th Grenadier Replacement & Training Battalion some 110 miles away from Nijmegen – began to engage US forces within six hours of their landing; testimony to the alacrity with which the *406th Division* reacted. In fact, the *406th* exceeded all doctrinal expectations with the rapidity of its response.[22]

The first warning of Allied airborne landings reached the *406th Division* Headquarters at Geldern at 1410 hours on 17 September from its forward elements stationed at Nijmegen.[23] Naturally these early reports were very fragmentary. The first warning order to the 406th Division went out at 1430 hours – it was intercepted and deciphered by Ultra the next day.[24] Within an hour the scale of the landings had become apparent to the senior German commanders and at 1530 hours Field Marshal Model's *Army Group B* headquarters ordered *Corps Feldt* and *406th Division* mobilized to attack out of the Reichswald to secure and to hold Nijmegen.[25] Later that afternoon the *406th Division's* battalions in the Reichswald frantically mobilized for combat deployment and rapidly marched westward toward the Reich frontier to engage the enemy.

21   TNA, CAB 106/1056, p. 1.
22   TNA, CAB 106/1056, p. 1.
23   NARA T-314, 24, KTB Korps Feldt, 17 September 1944; USAHD C-085, p. 15.
24   TNA, DEFE 3/901, Special Messages sent to Washington, D.C., Sunset Report 930, 12 September 1944.
25   Kershaw, *It Never Snows*, pp. 88-89.

Defense of Nijmegen 17 September 1944

The first *406th* units to join action were three understrength companies of the *1st Military District VI Home Defense Training Battalion* (hereafter the *1st/6th Battalion*). This unit has often been misidentified in secondary sources.[26] This was a home defense unit – consisting of Great War veterans and overage reservists classified as unfit for combat deployment due to age, health, or physical limitation. They had idled away the war on routine prisoner of war and internal security duties and some had never even ever fired their rifles.[27] After the partial mobilization on the 12th, elements of the *1st/6th* subsequently were further forward deployed beyond the Reich frontier to Nijmegen and onto the Groesbeek Heights where they had arrived a couple of days later. After the US landings, Parachute Colonel Henke and his headquarters of the Herman Göring Parachute Replacement and Training Regiment (which was largely deployed in the Netherlands) but whose headquarters and a single training company had been moved into Nijmegen orchestrated the defense of the town. Henke assembled every soldier he could muster to defend the town. However, the bulk of his estimated 750 troops came from the three companies of the *1st/6th Battalion*.[28]

Field Marshal Model, recognizing the strategic importance of the Nijmegen bridges, ordered that same afternoon the *10th SS Panzer Division's* Battle Group Reinhold and Battalion Euling of the *9th SS Panzer Division* to reinforce the town's garrison, but these reinforcements were badly delayed by the British blocking of the Arnhem Bridge.[29] For the vital first 24 hours, when the 82nd Airborne had its best opportunity to take the Nijmegen bridges, *406th Division* troops comprised the backbone of the German defense.

As Henke frantically improvised a defense, the first SS reinforcements arrived at 1700 hours – Captain Gräbner's *10th SS Armored Reconnaissance Battalion*. But finding everything secure and quiet, Gräbner returned to Arnhem and joined the fight for the bridge, leaving a small force, likely only in platoon strength with a few armored personnel carriers, at Nijmegen to reinforce Henke. The spirited defense of the town over the next day therefore fell overwhelmingly on the three companies – around 600 troops – of the *1st/6th Battalion's* third-rate home defense trainees who were unfit for front-line combat duty. Most were 45-55 year olds recently transferred from formerly 'essential' industrial and blue collar positions. The battalion therefore had

---

26 Kershaw identifies it as the 6th Replacement Battalion. Kershaw, *It Never Snows*, p. 112.
27 USAHD FMS C-085a, p. 7.
28 The *1st/6th Battalion* Headquarters was deployed at Groesbeek and would be quickly overrun by American paratroopers and its superior officer, Reserve Major Alemeyer, Sector Commander Cleve, killed early on in the fighting. The only other unit in Nijmegen was part of the Julich NCO Training course. NARA T-314, 24, Kriegsgliederung Korps Feldt Stand 16 September 1944; USAHD FMS C-085a, p. 2; Kershaw, *It Never Snows*, pp. 112-113.
29 Kershaw, *It Never Snows*, pp. 113-14.

very minimal combat experience – only its instructional cadre (invalided veterans) had any prior battle experience. These poor quality and partially trained reservists were utterly unprepared for combat against elite American airborne forces. These understrength companies – detachments had been dispersed in neighboring villages – had only 1-2 light machine guns per company and limited munitions for only a very short period of heavy combat. They had no offensive power whatsoever and only very limited defensive capability. It was this unremarkable rabble which held off elite US paratroopers.[30]

Forgoing an immediate push on Nijmegen as originally conceived, Gavin had committed the bulk of the 82nd Airborne to securing the strategically vital right flank along the Groesbeek Heights. Thus it was not until the evening of the 17th that A & B Companies, 508th Parachute Regiment pushed into Nijmegen aiming to seize the Waal rail and road bridges. This represented too little, too late. In the interim, Henke had vigorously organized a defense in depth with the meager assets at his disposal. By 2200 hours Henke's home defense troops had stopped the two American companies at the traffic circle short of the bridges. A vigorous counter-attack by the ill-trained and lightly armed home defense troops of the *1st/6th* then partially overran A Company and isolated its 2nd Platoon in the Post Office where it precariously held out for the next four days.[31] Indeed the 82nd Airborne Division officially character-ized the *1st/6th's* resistance as "severe" – a tribute to the *406th Division's* determined resistance and confirmation that the division was primarily responsible for thwarting the 82nd Airborne Division's attempt to take the bridges on 17 September.[32]

What about the rest of the *406th Division* on September 17th? General Feldt ordered Lieutenant General Scherbening and his *406th Division* staff to move to a forward command post at Krugers-Gut on the Kranenburg-Nijmegen road to direct countermeasures in person.[33] The closest unit capable of intervening was the *39th Grenadier Training and Replacement Battalion* in the Cleve Defense Sector, which comprised 3 weak companies totaling 6 officers and 506 enlistees. It was also very lightly equipped: only seven light machine guns, two heavy machine guns, four light, two medium, and one heavy mortar, four *Panzerfaust* antitank rocket launchers and

---

30   On 13 September the 5 company battalion reported 14 officers and 1366 enlistees on establishment. This included personnel on leave, sick and unfit with the unit, as well as detached personnel. So its effective strength was likely around 1000-1100 troops. It had 7 light German machine guns, 7 light Czech machine guns and 4 Panzerfaust antitank grenade launchers. The 3 companies in Nijmegen therefore probably had around 600 personnel. NARA T-314, p. 24, Kriegsgliederung Korps Feldt, 13 September 1944. On their poor quality see: USAHD FMS C-085, pp. 15-16, 18-19.

31   Phil Nordyke, *All American All the Way from Market Garden to Berlin: The Combat History of the 82nd Airborne Division in World War II* (Minneapolis: Zenith Press, 2010), pp. 69-74; MacDonald, *Siegfried Line*, p. 164.

32   Nordyke, *All American*, p. 74.

33   USAHD FMS C 085, p. 16.

eleven rifle grenade launchers.[34] General Scherbening appears to have been away from divisional headquarters that day – where is unclear but the evidence strongly suggests his staff covered for his absence – because he did not "reappear" to speak to his adjutant, Major Rasch, to discuss the relocation of the divisional staff until 2100 hours and only rejoined his HQ at 0200 hours on the 18th.[35] His actual whereabouts remain a mystery.

Feldt ordered the *406th* to advance and gain the line of the River Maas from Nijmegen via Zyfflich, Wyler, and the eastern edge of Groesbeek to Venlo and to prevent a US advance into the Reich using all units deployed west of Cleve.[36] Feldt further ordered the *406th* to counterattack at 0600 hours on the 18th and throw the enemy back behind the River Maas.[37] However, recognizing the impossibility of this mission for a formation as weak as the *406th*, Model promised Feldt reinforcements from the *II Parachute Corps*, but these could not arrive in time for the 18 September counterattack.[38]

The two final companies of the *1st/6th* were deployed astride the Groesbeek Heights, alongside various *Luftwaffe* light antiaircraft artillery platoons, and these *406th* elements also helped thwart the fall of Nijmegen that day. These troops endeavored to resist the numerically stronger and better equipped US Airborne troops but were largely overwhelmed by the evening of the 17th. However, their resistance did delay the 82nd Division's securing of the Groesbeek Heights well into the evening and multiple pockets of isolated resistance continued to hold out through the 18th.[39] This in turn delayed the Americans from turning to take Nijmegen and fixed in situ two entire regimental groups of the 82nd Division, elements of which that otherwise could have been redeployed to capture Nijmegen. Preoccupied with clearing the heights, Gavin did not order the withdrawal of a battalion of the 508th Parachute Regiment to take Nijmegen until 1600 hours and, as we have seen, continued resistance by the *1st/6th* ensured only two companies could initially be withdrawn.[40] This was too little, too late to secure Nijmegen in the face of Henke's resistance.

Even more important in the failure of the 82nd Division to take the Nijmegen bridges the following day on the 18th was General Feldt's recognition that the 82nd Airborne would need to be rapidly reinforced and resupplied by air drops – and therefore the American drop zones were the enemy's Achilles heel.[41] Appreciating that the American paratroopers outnumbered and outgunned his motley troops moving up,

34   NARA T-314, 24 KTB Ia Korps Feldt, Kriegsgliederung Korps Feldt, Stand 13 September 1944.
35   Kershaw, *It Never Snows*, p. 138.
36   Kershaw, *It Never Snows*, p. 138.
37   Kershaw, *It Never Snows*, p. 140.
38   Kershaw, *It Never Snows*, p. 140-41.
39   MacDonald, *Siegfried Line*, pp. 160-161.
40   Saunders, *U.S. 82nd Airborne*, p. 95; MacDonald, *Siegfried Line*, p. 162.
41   USAHD FMS C-085, p. 17.

Feldt on the evening of the 17th ordered the *406th Division* to infiltrate between the widely interspersed US airborne defensive positions during the night and encroach onto the U.S. drop zones by daylight in order to forestall, delay, or disrupt a follow up drop and exact heavy losses on the enemy.[42] It was a vital order, from an experienced field commander, that ensured Nijmegen stayed in German hands throughout September 18th.

During the evening hours of the 17th the vanguard of the *406th Division* probed the widely spread 82nd Airborne positions and having identified the main defenses infiltrated between them. The *39th Grenadier Training Battalion* absorbed the remnants of the two companies of the *1st/6th* that had been pushed off the Groesbeek Heights after the death of their commanding officer in combat, Reserve Major Alemeyer, forming the composite Battalion Stargard. It probed the 505th Parachute Regiment's positions overrunning its weak outposts southeast of Groesbeek.[43] An understrength platoon of the Regiment's 1st Battalion, was surrounded on the edge of the Reichswald and had to fight its way back to its own lines suffering heavy losses.[44]

The 39th launched its first probing counterthrust along the Gennep-Nijmegen road that same evening while a *1st/6th* machine gun team narrowly missed killing General Gavin near Groesbeek as he personally reconnoitered the defenses.[45] As early as 1800 hours the 82nd had recognized that 'much activity' was occurring in the Reichswald as *406th* vanguard reconnaissance patrols began probing outside Reithorst.[46] Having identified during the evening dusk hours through vigorous battlefield reconnaissance many of the main American defensive positions, during the night Battalion Stargard quietly infiltrated between these dispersed positions – particularly at Berg-en-Dal and Wyler – and by day break had taken up defensive positions behind the US defensive perimeter and astride probable drop zones. Here they joined isolated light antiaircraft artillery detachments and survivors of the two decimated *1st/6th* companies from the Groesbeek Heights that had continued to resist even though isolated behind enemy lines.[47]

Monday 18 September

By 0600 hours the *406th Division* had assembled three additional battalions into jump off positions for a counterattack: Battalion von Fürstenberg (the *3rd Battalion, 66th Grenadier Replacement Regiment* reinforced by an armored reconnaissance company including 3 light armored cars and 5 half-tracks); Battalion Greschick (the three companies of *17th Luftwaffe Fortress Battalion*); and Battalion Göbel, comprising 3

---

42   Nordyke, *All American*, pp. 58-59.
43   USAHD FMS C-085a, p. 2; Nordyke, *All American*, p. 58.
44   Nordyke, *All American*, p. 76.
45   Nordyke, *All American*, pp. 49-50.
46   Nordyke, *All American*, pp. 50-51.
47   Nordyke, *All American*, pp. 51-52; MacDonald, *Siegfried Line*, p. 166.

grenadier companies and a bicycle mobile company formed from the *Wehrkreis VI* Reserve Officer Training Course and totaling 350 troops. These battalions were supposed to be supported by a three battery artillery battalion that happened to be in the vicinity.[48] However, the battalion's guns were stuck at some unknown railway siding courtesy of Allied air action and so the battalion was unable to support the attacks that went in on the morning of the 18th. The attack was therefore supported only by the few mortars the units possessed and several 88mm heavy antiaircraft guns.[49]

At 0630 hours the *406th Division's* battalions counterattacked. The Germans estimated their attack force at 2,671 troops, 14 mortars, 3 light armored cars and 5 armored half-tracks. There was no armor, no artillery, no airpower, and minimal munitions. Moreover, the Germans overestimated their true strength: which was actually fewer than 2,000 troops. So hasty was the German mobilization that no accurate head count was taken: strengths were estimated based on the last "actual" strengths reported some four days earlier.[50] Feldt immediately and aggressively threw these troops into a spoiling attack to: throw the Americans off balance; deceive them as to German strength; force the enemy onto the defensive and disrupt their operations while further reserves were mobilized and rushed up.[51] Having fought American troops in Southern France, Feldt did not believe the attack could gain any ground with what he later referred to as his "motley crew" but much to his surprise the counterattack initially gained ground against the widely dispersed American parachutists, making what he later characterized was "remarkable" progress.[52] But by 1030 hours the attack had stalled, however, in the face of the superior experience, firepower, and élan of the elite US Airborne forces.

Nonetheless, the counterthrusts caused the 82nd Division considerable difficulties. A company of the 39th infiltrated to Voxhill where it isolated during the morning two platoons of D Company, 508th Parachute Regiment and threatened to overrun

---

48   USAHD FMS MS C-085, p. 17.
49   A mixed antiaircraft artillery battery of several heavy and light antiaircraft guns supported the attack. USAHD FMS MS C085a, p. 7.
50   The reported combat strength on the morning of the 18th is clearly exaggerated. Most units had not had time to take accurate headcounts. Most of the reported strengths clearly were those returned in the last official strength return of 13 September. These reported actual strengths of the units (Iststärke) not day strength (Tagesstärke). The "actual strength" figures included sick and wounded personnel, those on leave and detached for temporary duty elsewhere. Actual strength reports normally exceeded day strength by at least one quarter. Two thousand troops is therefore a more accurate approximation of actual strength that morning. NARA T-314, 24, Kriegsgliederung Korps Feldt, Stand 18 September 1944 Morgens; USAHD FMS MS C-085a, p. 7; TNA, HW 5/589, Ultra Decrypt CX/MSS/T313/55 intercepted 0122 hrs 21 September of *Wehkreis VI* Ia Message to Heeresgruppe B, 1800 hours, 18 September 1944.
51   USAHD FMS C-085, p. 17.
52   USAHD FMS C 085, p. 18.

LZ T, the main glider landing site slated for reinforcement landings that day.[53] This threat compelled Gavin to withdraw the 1st Battalion, 508th Parachute Regiment then poised to renew the assault on the Nijmegen bridges. Given that Battle Group Henke had suffered heavy losses on the 17th and only been very minimally reinforced by SS troops, the planned U.S. attack on the morning of the 18th had real prospects of seizing the two Nijmegen bridges before SS reinforcements arrived in strength. However, the *406th's* encroachment onto 'LZ T' compelled Gavin to abandon the attack and to throw immediately the battalion into clearing the drops zones ahead of the scheduled imminent glider drop.[54] Feldt's ingenious infiltration tactics therefore almost certainly saved the Nijmegen bridges from falling that day.

The *406th* attacked on a broad front from the Cleve-Kranenburg area towards Beek, Wyler, Groesbeek, while Battalion Göbel on the southern flank counterattacked toward Mook, causing significant local difficulties for the Americans. Uncommitted reserves holding the defensive line brought the *406th Division* up to a once again overstated estimated strength of 3,400 troops, 24 mortars and a few heavy AA guns.[55] The *406th Division* strongly contested the small community of Wyler which spanned the German-Dutch border. American paratroopers were perplexed by the enemy's determination to retake this seemingly strategically insignificant village. But to the Germans Wyler was the gateway to the Reich and the *406th* Division was determined to eject American forces from German territory. It seems obvious in retrospect that the Germans would do everything possible to defend the frontier of the Reich and surprising that the Americans found such a vigorous response here perplexing. The *406th* counterattacks on the 18th isolated an American paratrooper company in Wyler which had to fight it way out to safety, taking appreciable casualties in the process.[56] Indeed, on several occasions on the 18th, the 82th Airborne officially reported to higher headquarters its situation at multiple locations as "serious."[57]

Gavin therefore had to personally scrape together all possible airborne reserves and counterattack in the early afternoon in strength to overrun the now two companies of the 39th Grenadier Battalion ensconced astride Voxhill to secure LZ T ahead of the impending landing, inflicting heavy German casualties. But the German battalion's sacrifice saved the Nijmegen bridges from falling.[58] American clearing was still in

53　Nordyke, *All American*, pp. 83-84.
54　TNA, CAB 106/1056, p. 3.
55　NARA T-314, 24, KTB Korps Feldt, Tagesmeldung 17 September 1944, 2300 hours; Tagesmeldung 0700 hours, 18 September 1944; Tagesmeldung 1220 hours, 18 September 1944; During 17-18 September a total of 4927 troops were mobilized and allocated to the 406th Division. TNA HW 5/589, Ultra Decrypt, CX/MSS/T313/55, 0122 hrs 21 September of *Wehrkreis VI* message to Heeresgruppe B, 1800 hrs, 18 September 1944.
56　Kershaw, *It Never Snows*, p. 142.
57　Kershaw, *It Never Snows*, p. 142.
58　The Americans reported killing 50 German soldiers and capturing another 149 prisoners, essentially writing off the two companies. TNA CAB 106/1056, p. 3; Nordyke, *All American*, pp. 84-91.

progress as the main parachute and glider drop unfolded directly on top of the rest of the attacking *406th* battalions. The sudden appearance and dramatic landing of several thousand airborne troops in front of, astride and behind the inexperienced German troops caused panic that broke the German counterattack. Fearful of being cut off, the Germans retreated in disorder, suffering heavy casualties in the process. The counterattack dissolved into a wild flight as the inexperienced troops fled back to their start lines, where their veteran cadres finally halted them and threw them into a defensive line along their original jump off positions.[59]

The *406th Division's* minimal offensive capability was therefore completed depleted on the 18th and it was unable to continue a major attack on the 19th as it waited promised reinforcements to resume a concerted attack on the 20th. Even though the *406th Division* spoiling attack had failed at heavy loss, it did successfully distract and divert the 82nd Airborne from taking Nijmegen on the 18nd. In total, the Germans suffered 50 killed, 150 POW, and probably 400 wounded – close to 30 percent of their attack strength, heavy losses indeed.[60] But this price paled in comparison to the strategic advantage of thwarting the fall of Nijmegen.

Nijmegen on 18 September

And what of the battle for Nijmegen on the 18th? The arrival of SS Battle Group Reinhold of the *10th SS Panzer Division* to reinforce Battalion Euling of the *9th SS Panzer Division* at Nijmegen was badly delayed by British denial of the crossing of the Arnhem road bridge. Instead the SS troops had to cross the Rhine via the ferry at Pannerden. A company of the *10th SS Engineer Battalion* finally arrived at Nijmegen during the morning of the 18th but was committed to prepping both bridges for demolition.[61] *SS Battalion Euling* arrived around midday but only deployed into Nijmegen during the afternoon. Moreover, it was very weak – really only of company strength with 100 combatants.[62] Meanwhile, US paratroopers renewed their attacks on the road bridge in the morning but were once again stalled by the *1st/6th* defenders.[63] The *406th* probing attacks, deep reconnaissance, and infiltration tactics, compelled Gavin to retain the bulk of the 82nd Division deployed on its eastern flank and prevented any substantial reinforcement of the forces committed to taking Nijmegen. The pulling back of US forces before Nijmegen during the late morning to counterattack the *406th Division* shifted the initiative back to the Germans. But the Waal bridges was too threatened to be openly crossed and further SS reinforcement has to cross to the south bank via rubber dinghies, which further delayed reinforcement. Thus the defense of

---

59   USAHD FMS MS C-085, p. 18; Kershaw, *It Never Snows*, pp. 143-144.
60   Kershaw, *It Never Snows*, p. 144; MacDonald, *Siegfried Line*, p. 167.
61   Kershaw. *It Never Snows*, p. 164.
62   Ibid., p. 164.
63   Ibid., pp. 164-65.

Nijmegen remained predominantly in the hands of *406th Division* troops through nightfall.[64] Only in the late afternoon did *10th SS* troops begin to arrive in numbers and *SS Battle Group Reinhold* formally took charge of the defense of Nijmegen late on the evening of the 18th.[65] By that time, most of the troops of the *1st/6th Battalion* had become casualties and it had essentially ceased to exist as a unit.

The 406th counterattacks on the 18th thus compelled the 82nd Airborne to abandon temporarily its efforts to take Nijmegen and instead wait for the arrival in strength of the British Guards Armored Division. The spoiling attacks of the *406th* on the 18th, though unsuccessful, combined with the resolute defense of the *1st/6th* at Nijmegen – rather than the intervention of the *10th SS Panzer Division* – primarily prevented the 82nd Airborne from capturing Nijmegen during 17-18 September. Moreover, fear over the vulnerability of the eastern flank to a stronger counterthrust out of the Reichswald led General Browning to countermand General Gavin's plan to launch a concentric assault on Nijmegen to take the bridges on the 19th and instead order him to stay on the defensive until the vanguard of the XXX Corps, the Guards Armored Division, arrived in strength.[66] As a consequence of this decision, the seizure of the Nijmegen bridges had to wait until 20 September and a brave, audacious, and daring opposed river crossing by the 82nd Airborne Division. The delay imposed by the *406th* in the American seizing of Nijmegen thus contributed directly to the failure of the XXX Corps ground advance in reaching the 1st Airborne in time to relieve it and capture Arnhem.

The *406th Division* therefore played an important, and under-recognized, role in the defeat of Operation Market Garden. The *406th* imposed appreciable friction on the US Airborne forces, distracting them and siphoning off reserves that could other-wise had been committed to take the Nijmegen bridges. The 82nd Airborne Division could of, had it not been for the intervention of the *406th*, taken the Nijmegen bridges during 17-18 September. The *406th* troops formed the backbone of the spirited defense of Nijmegen town by Battle Group Henke and the divisional counterattacks on the 18th, particularly its infiltration of the American landing zones, prevented the 82nd Airborne Division from taking the Nijmegen bridges that day.

In conclusion, historians have under-examined and underemphasized the *406th* Division's contribution to the defeat of Market Garden for several reasons. They have viewed the operations on the eastern flank as a side show to the apparently more important battles for Arnhem. Moreover, scholarly attention has focused on the 'sexier' troops of the *9th* and *10th SS Panzer Divisions* in the defense of Nijmegen. Additionally, that most of the *406th's* senior officers died in the war, and few records of its actions survived either, has hampered a fuller understanding of its role. Nonetheless, mining the surviving records – the fragmentary war diaries, the post-war after-action reports,

---

64   Kershaw. *It Never Snows*, p. 165.
65   Ibid., p. 166.
66   MacDonald, *Siegfried Line*, pp. 168-69.

the records of the 82nd Airborne Division, as well as memoirs, it is possible to discern more clearly the actual role that the *406th Division* played in the defeat of Operation Market Garden. Certainly its role requires greater examination and more emphasis, for a motley crew of hastily assembled recruits and overage reservists went up against elite US paratroopers. And while they were bested, the third rate troops of the *406th* imposed sufficient friction to delay the Allied capture of the Nijmegen bridges for long enough to ensure the failure of Operation Market Garden.

Select Bibliography

PRIMARY SOURCES – UNPUBLISHED
US National Archives and Records Administration (NARA), Washington, D.C.
Captured German Records Collection, Record Group 242, Microfilm Series T-314, Roll 24, Korps Feldt, September 1944.
The National Archives (UK) (TNA), Kew, London.
Cabinet Papers (CAB).
Defense and Foreign Office Records (DEFE3).
Government Communications Headquarters records (HW).
War Office Papers (WO)

PRIMARY SOURCES – PUBLISHED
U.S. ARMY HISTORICAL DIVISION (USAHD) FOREIGN MILITARY STUDIES (FMS) COLLECTION
Manuscript B-044, Lt-Gen. Franz Mattenklott, "Part II: The Rhineland, 15 September 1944-31 March 1945" (Königstein, Germany, 1950).
Manuscript B-665, Lt-Gen. Ernst Fäckenstedt, "The Activities of the Western Military Districts (*Wehrkreise* VI and XII) and their Cooperation in the Defense of the Front of O.B. West from September 1944-March 1944" (Allendorf, Germany, 1947).
Manuscript C-085, Maj-Gen. Hellmuth Reinhardt, "Commitment of the 406th Division Against the Allied Airborne Landing at Nijmegen in September 1944," (Königstein, Germany, 1950).
Manuscript C-085, Kav-Gen Kurt Feldt, "Part Two: Corps Headquarters Feldt and 406th Division from 17 to 21 September 1944" (Königstein, Germany, 1950).
Manuscript C-085a, Lt-Gen Hellmuth Reinhardt, "Supplement to the Report of 1 December 1950 Concerning the Operations of the 406th Division in September 1944" (Königstein, Germany, 1951).

SECONDARY SOURCES
Stephen Badsey, *Arnhem 1944: Operation Market Garden*, (Westport, CT: Praeger, 2004).
David Bennett, *A Magnificent Disaster: The Failure of Market Garden, The Arnhem Operation, September 1944*, (Drexel Hill, PA: Casemate Publishing, 2008).

Donald R. Burgett, *The Road to Arnhem: A Screaming Eagle in Holland*, (Novato, CA: Presidio Press, 2001).

T. Moffatt Burriss, *Strike and Hold: a Memoir of the 82nd Airborne in World War II*, (Washington, D.C.: Potomac Books, Inc., 2001).

Lloyd Clark, *Arnhem: Operation Market Garden: September 1944*, (Stroud, U.K.: Sutton Publishing, 2002).

James Gavin, *On To Berlin: Battles of an Airborne Commander, 1943-1945*, (New York: Random House, reprint ed. 1992).

Christopher Hibbert, *Arnhem*, (London: B.T. Batsford, 1963).

Robert Jackson, *Arnhem: The Battle Remembered*, (Shrewsbury, UK: Airlife Book, 2003).

Robert Kershaw, *It Never Snows In September: The German View of MARKET-GARDEN and the Battle of Arnhem, September 1944*, (London: Ian Allan Publishing, 1994).

Jean-Luc Leleu, *10. SS-Panzer-Division Frundsberg*, (Bayeux: Heimdal, 1999).

Tim Lynch, *Operation Market Garden: The Legend of the Waal Crossing*, (Stroud, U.K.: The History Press, 2011).

Charles MacDonald, *The Siegfried Line Campaign*, (Washington, D.C.: OCMH, reprint ed. 1990).

John C. McManus, *September Hope: The American Side of a Bridge Too Far*, (London: Penguin Books, 2012).

Rolf Michaelis, *10. SS Panzer Division Frundsberg*, (Eggolsheim: Dörfler Verlag, 2009).

John Nichol and Tony Rennell, *Arnhem: The Battle For Survival*, (London: Viking, 2011).

Phil Nordyke, *All American All the Way from Market Garden to Berlin: The Combat History of the 82nd Airborne Division in World War II*, (Minneapolis, MN: Zenith Press, 2010).

R.G. Poulussen, *Lost At Nijmegen: A Rethink on Operation "Market Garden,"* (NP: R.G. Poulussen, 2011).

Michael Reynolds, *Sons of the Reich: The History of II SS Panzer Corps*, (Drexel Hill, PA: Casemate Publishing, 2002).

Cornelius Ryan, *A Bridge Too Far: The Classic History of the Greatest Battle of World War II*, (New York: Simon and Schuster Inc., 1974).

Tim Saunders, *U.S. 82nd Airborne and Guards Armored Division*, (Barnsley: Pen and Sword Books Ltd., 2001).

Wilhelm Tieke, *In the Firestorm of the Last Years of the War, II. SS-Panzerkorps with the 9. and 10. SS-Divisions Hohenstaufen and Frundsberg*, (Manitoba: J.J. Fedorowizz, 1999).

Frank Van Lunteren, *The Battle of the Bridges: The 504th Parachute Infantry Regiment in Operation Market Garden*, (Havertown, PA: Casemate, 2014).

Frederick D. Worthen, *Monty's Folly: Operation Market Garden: 2nd Air Division*, edited by Carroll A. Berner, (Carlsbad, CA: California Aero Press, 1999).

Steven Zaloga, *Defense of the Rhine, 1944-45*, (Oxford: Osprey Publishing, 2011).

7

"Dangerously Overexposed?" – Divisional Operations on the flanks of MARKET GARDEN, September to December 1944[1,2]

Philip McCarty

A perennial problem for the historian is the selective adoption of partial narratives and selective truths for the purposes of drama in popular entertainment. Although the use of dramatic licence and time compression are understandable to fit the needs of a script or screenplay, there is always a risk that in the public imagination this can become the abiding popular perception. Due in no small part to William Goldman's screenplay for Richard Attenborough's film *A Bridge Too Far* in 1977 (based on the Cornelius Ryan book of the same name from 1974)[3] – the viewing public could be excused for believing that the September 1944 battles in the Low Countries were a matter solely for the 1st Allied Airborne Army from the air and British XXX Corps on the ground, the latter reduced yet further to the Guards Armoured Division and to the 3rd Battalion Irish Guards in particular. Notwithstanding scenes where the chain of command melts away and the Corps commander (Lieutenant General Brian Horrocks, played by Edward Fox) briefs the commanding officer of 3rd Battalion Irish Guards (Lt. Col. J.O.E. Vandeleur, played by Michael Caine) directly,[4] this story

---

1   The author wishes to record his acknowledgments and thanks to Jonathan Ware, whose advice and assistance in the preparation of the original lecture from which this chapter is derived, was of great help. Jonathan is in the process of completing a new history of 53rd Welsh Division in World War 2.

2   The title is derived from Montgomery's view that Eisenhower's broad front policy in Tunisia had dangerously exposed his flanks to attack, a concern which would recur in North West Europe. See for example Crosswell, *The Chief of Staff: The Military Career of General Walter Bedell Smith*, p.160.

3   Ryan, *A Bridge Too Far*.

4   Although Horrocks refers to Vandeleur directly (and his brother and fellow commanding officer of 2nd Battalion Irish Guards, Giles – who features briefly in the film, portrayed by Michael Byrne) and in a complementary fashion in both his autobiographical works, *A Full Life* and *Corps Commander* he does not suggest such direct circumvention of the chain of command took place.

arc overlooks the actions on the flanks by British VIII Corps, under Sir Richard O'Connor, XII Corps under Sir Neil Ritchie and the "follow up" divisions of XXX Corps itself. The part these cinematically overlooked formations would play in the long hard slog to the borders of Germany after the failure to 'bounce the Rhine' in September was critical.

The intention here is not to dwell in great detail on the Corps level operations, but instead to focus on the actions of two specific British divisions in the autumn of 1944 in order to compare and contrast how they performed, how they were commanded and their long-term fate. The divisions are the 50th (Northumbrian) Division, commanded by Major General Douglas Graham and the 53rd (Welsh) Division led by Major General 'Bobby' Ross.

These were two divisions which had had rather different experiences of the war prior to the landings in Normandy in June 1944. Both were divisions originally drawn from the Territorial Army (TA) and still had (at least nominally) TA battalions within them in 1944. 50th Division had had four solid years of operational experience in France, the Western Desert and the Mediterranean. It had landed on GOLD Beach on D-Day – Operation NEPTUNE was the third amphibious assault landing of the war for the Division's 231st Brigade. 53rd Division was brand new to combat having spent the war thus far training in the UK. It would not land in France until nearly three weeks after D-Day on 23-24 June, but its introduction to action would be quick, shocking and typical of the high attrition of the battles through July and August.

Additionally, 50th Division carried with it the stigma of having been involved in the so-called "Salerno Mutiny" of September 1943, where some 1500 soldiers and Non-Commissioned Officers of both it and the 51st Highland Division in X Corps initially refused to fight after learning that they had not been shipped to Sicily to rejoin their units, but instead to the Salerno beachhead to reinforce 46th Division. This gave rise to a grievance that they had been deliberately misled. New recruits were quickly dispatched to units, but a core of some 500 veterans remained, of whom 300 were isolated. The intervention of the Corps commander, Lt. Gen. Richard McCreery, who told the remainder that an error had been made and that they would be returned to their units, left a core of 192 who were charged with mutiny and removed to face court martial and imprisonment.[5] Although there was an element of injustice in the treatment of the mutineers, the largest single number of charges of mutiny ever levied on members of the British Army reflected badly on their divisions. Although by the time of the Normandy landings there had been considerable change in both divisions' command staff and in their manpower and the mutineers charged had been isolated, the stigma had not completely vanished from these veteran formations Montgomery had specifically picked to "stiffen" the inexperienced formations coming from the United Kingdom.

---

5   David, *Mutiny at Salerno: An Injustice Exposed* and Hansard "Salerno Mutineers" (Commons Debates, 22 March 2000, Columns 242-249WH).

Divisional Organisation

The infantry organisation of each division in early September 1944 was as follows:

50th Division
Divisional Commander: Maj Gen DAH Graham (Wounded in November)
69th Brigade – Brigadier FYC Knox (wounded 29 October); Brigadier JMK Spurling:
5th Battalion East Yorkshire Regiment
6th Battalion The Green Howards
7th Battalion The Green Howards

151st Brigade – Brigadier DS Gordon:
6th, 8th and 9th Battalions Durham Light Infantry

231st Brigade – Brigadier Sir Alexander Stanier Bt:
2nd Battalion The Devonshire Regiment,
1st Battalion The Dorset Regiment,
1st Battalion The Hampshire Regiment,

53rd Division
Divisional Commander Maj Gen RK Ross
71st Brigade – Brigadier V Blomfield (wd. 21 Sep) then Brigadier M Elrington (k.
    Apr 45):
1st Battalion Oxfordshire & Buckinghamshire Light Infantry
1st Battalion Highland Light Infantry
4th Battalion Royal Welch Fusiliers

158th Brigade – Brigadier GB Sugden (From August 1944; k. Jan 45):[6]
7th Battalion Royal Welch Fusiliers
1/5th Battalion The Welch Regt
1st Battalion East Lancashire Regiment

160th Brigade – Brigadier CFC Coleman:
2nd Battalion The Monmouthshire Regiment
6th Battalion Royal Welch Fusiliers
4th Battalion The Welch Regiment

Both Divisions, originally regionally based TA Divisions, were made up of sub units which reflected their respective recruiting areas, the north east of England and Wales. By the late summer of 1944, however, casualty rates had made sustaining such arguably

---

6   The National Archives (TNA) WO171/689, 158 Brigade HQ, January – December 1944.

artificial distinctions impossible to sustain and units plugged manpower gaps with reinforcement drafts as they became available. (This did not stop the waggish description of 71st Brigade as being "the International Brigade" for having and English, Scottish and Welsh battalions in it). The divisional commanders themselves were very of differing personalities but with one unifying factor: they owed their appointments to Montgomery's support.

The Commanders

Douglas Graham had had a fighting war already; 51 on D-Day, he had commanded a Brigade in 9th (Scottish) Division in Home Forces in 1940 and later had a "good war" in the desert. Brigade command in the Middle East brought a trio of decorations; a Distinguished Service Order for the Second Battle of El Alamein, to which a Bar was added six months later for the Battle of the Mareth Line in Tunisia. He would also receive the award of Commander of the Order of the British Empire (CBE) for his work in the desert, all these adding to his Western Front Military Cross awarded in 1918. Passing Staff College at Camberley in 1925, by the outbreak of war in 1939 he was Commanding Officer of 2nd Battalion The Cameronians (The Scottish Rifles), serving with them in Palestine during the Arab Uprising there in 1936-39. In April 1940, he was appointed to command 27th Brigade of the 9th (Scottish) Division, the Second Line duplicate of 51st Highland Division. When the former division was used in the summer of 1940 as a cadre to re-establish the latter after its loss in the Battle of France, 27th Brigade was redesignated 153rd Brigade and Graham went with it in command. Despite being a Lowlander Scot with impeccable Clan credentials, he performed sufficiently well in 51st Highland Division to retain a post under the eyes of Maj. Gen. Douglas "Tam" Wimberley, whose determination to have only Highlanders in his Division was well known throughout 8th Army. Described as tough, blunt-spoken and a "fighting soldier", it was also perceived when Graham arrived from 51st Highland Division that he was a favourite of Montgomery's – yet he quickly gained the trust and loyalty of his divisional staff. When the opportunity arose in Tunisia, Montgomery personally recommended Graham for the command of the 56th (London) Division. He remained in post as the Division entered Tunis, and again at Salerno where he was wounded, and the capture of Naples. Graham's service in Italy added a Companion of the Order of the Bath (CB) to his tally of British decorations. For his service alongside the Americans on the Volturno Line he was appointed to the US Legion of Merit and the French would also appoint him Knight of the Legion of Honour. Graham's wounds in Italy were insufficiently serious to prevent him succeeding Maj. Gen. Sidney Kirkman in taking command of 50th Division in the UK on 19 January 1944, when the latter went to Italy to command XIII Corps on promotion to Lieutenant General.[7]

7   Smart, *Biographical Dictionary of British Generals of the Second World War*, entries for GRAHAM and KIRKMAN.

Graham therefore had extensive battle experience, and had impressed his superiors both in control of a Brigade and a Division; the awards from allies also suggested an ability to function well in coalition and some political skill.

RHK "Bobby" Ross had also had a "good" 1914-18 war, arguably an even better one than Graham, as he ended it with both a DSO and an MC at the age of 25. Originally commissioned into The Queen's (Royal West Surrey) Regiment in 1913, he served first on the Western Front and then with the Egyptian Expeditionary Force. From 1923-32 he was attached for service with the Egyptian Army and the Sudan Defence Force, returning to command his regimental depot. He commanded the 2nd Battalion of his regiment in Palestine, – where he was mentioned in dispatches – from 1937-1940.[8] In August 1940, he was appointed to command 160th Infantry Brigade in 53rd (Welsh) Division, rising to command the Division in September 1942 in succession to Maj Gen Gerry Bucknall. In 1944, he too was 51 years old but with the exception of Palestine had not seen any active service since the First World War.

Subordinates

The Brigadiers subordinate to both Graham and Ross had, as may be expected at this stage of the war, a broad mixture of postings and active service experience, or rather lack of it. In 50th Division, Fergus Knox, originally from the Royal Ulster Rifles, had been awarded a DSO for command of his battalion at Dunkirk but had had no combat experience since, commanding 130 Brigade in 43rd (Wessex) Division in the UK from 1941-43. Wounded in October 1944, he would be replaced by John Spurling, a 1939 Staff College graduate and former Leicestershire Regiment officer. Spurling had served mostly as a Staff Officer at Divisional level in the United Kingdom before spending time as a liaison officer in the Middle and Far East. Held as a reserve battalion commander for casualty replacement, he went to Normandy to command a Territorial battalion in 59th Division, remaining there until that Division was broken up to provide in-theatre reinforcements in August. He was subsequently appointed to command 69th Brigade and remained there until December when posted to 7th Armoured Division[9] on the breakup of 50th Division. Brigadier Desmond Gordon of 151st Brigade, formerly an officer of the Green Howards, had had combat experience commanding a Territorial battalion of The Queen's Regiment in the later stages of the Tunisian Campaign for which he received the DSO. Sir Alexander Stanier, originally from the Welsh Guards, had also, like Knox, been awarded the DSO for Dunkirk. He commanded two Home Defence Brigades from 1940-43, unfortunately losing an eye

8   Information derived from The Queen's Regiment Museum website: http://www. queensroyalsurreys.org.uk/colonels_and_co/commanding_officers/queens_west_ surrey/023.shtml (Accessed 15 August 2014 and 1 February 2015).

9   Biography from the Royal Leicestershire Regiment website: http://www. royalleicestershireregiment.org.uk/have-you-a-tiger/record/55350/ He retired from the Army in 1958 as a Major General, in the post of Chief of Staff, Northern Command.

in a grenade training accident when in command of 183rd Brigade of 61st Division; however, this injury was not an obstacle to his taking over the experienced 231st Brigade in February 1944.[10]

The commander of Ross' senior Brigade, Valentine Blomfield, although a veteran of the North West Frontier between the wars, had had no active service since Dunkirk, spending 1940-43 in staff postings. This included a spell as the Deputy Director of Staff Duties at the War Office. He took over 71st Brigade on Christmas Eve 1943. His eventual replacement, Brigadier Maxwell 'Goldfish' Elrington was another officer relocated from the disbanded 59th Division, where he had commanded 177th Brigade; he was originally commissioned into the Border Regiment and had commanded a battalion of the Queen's Regiment in Italy.[11] He had been awarded a DSO for Palestine pre-war. Stanley Jones, the original commander of 158th Brigade from August 1941, spent a year and a half as Commandant of the Senior Officers' School in Sheerness from May 1942 to September 1943 simultaneously with his Brigade command; he received an OBE for services in the so-called "Phoney War" in France, in 1939-40. He had taken charge of 6th Brigade in the UK in the immediate aftermath of Dunkirk. Wounded in August 1944, he would be replaced by Gwynne Sugden who had been appointed CBE for command of his battalion of the South Wales Borderers in Sicily but was recalled from the post of Deputy Director of Military Training at the War Office to fill the gap. Charles Coleman had, until early 1944, spent most of the war as Commanding Officer of 4th Battalion, The Welch Regiment in the United Kingdom. He was a youngish Brigade commander, holding temporary command of 160th Brigade in 1943 at the age of 39 before being appointed its full time commander in early 1944. Although a pre-war regular officer (he had been Adjutant of his Battalion, 2nd Welch Regiment from 1932-35) he had no combat experience prior to landing in Normandy.[12]

Although it has not been possible to trace any documentary evidence to either confirm or deny this assertion, it appears that the county and Territorial identity of 50th Division had little influence on the appointment of its Brigade commanders or any of their replacements; the constant rotation of combat operations and a Scot as its commander may have been an indirect factor. In 53rd Division, however, despite its "International" brigade, there appears to have been some effort to sustain a sufficiently Welsh identity in its replacement Brigade commanders. Except for Max Elrington, most were from Welsh regiments. Although Ross himself was not Welsh or from a Welsh regiment, his long service in the Division could have rubbed off on him.

---

10   Sir John Stanier Bart. Obituary, *The Times* (London) 25 January 1995 p.17.
11   Biography derived from The Queen's Regiment Museum website: http://www.
      queensroyalsurreys.org.uk/colonels_and_co/commanding_officers/queens_west_
      surrey/038.html (Accessed 16 August 2014).
12   Lieutenant General Sir Charles Coleman; Obituary, The Times (London) 24 June 1974
      p.12

However, neither Graham nor Ross owed their advancement directly to patronage, despite Montgomery's support or advocacy for their appointments. Graham was certainly at the Staff College when Alanbrooke was an instructor there in 1923-26, but he is not listed in the group of General officers cited by David French who may have been talent spotted by him.[13] Ross did not attend Staff College, either at Camberley or Quetta. By 1944, however, in the face of demand outstripping supply, the proportion of Staff College graduates commanding at Divisional level was dwindling, and fell below 75% as active service experience was taken more into account.[14] As noted, Montgomery had recommended Graham personally on the basis of his performance in 51st Highland Division. Some accounts suggest,[15] but at second-hand, that Ross knew Monty well; there are no immediately apparent connections but they could have met in Palestine when Montgomery commanded 8th Division there in 1938-39. (This could equally apply to Graham, but neither of their Battalions was under Montgomery's direct command).

The Campaign in Europe So Far

50th Division had landed on D-Day and was in action from the very outset. The reticence of veterans of the desert and Mediterranean towards being chosen to fight in France is well known and often recorded, "Many felt we had already done our share... Why does it have to be us? Some have never struck a bat... We didn't like that".[16] But a Company Sergeant Major of 7th Green Howards noted, "We didn't take to it kindly... we'd done our fair whack... but Monty's way was to keep you going and going."[17] The division as a whole fought hard in the ultimately successful attempts to capture Tilly sur Seules and again in Operation BLUECOAT. 69th Brigade was particularly badly affected in the July battles in the bocage and on 5th August the Division as a whole was pulled out of the line to rest, re-equip and embody reinforcement drafts. Brigadier Knox had expressed concerns to Graham in July and August that his Brigade "was not fit for further offensive action" and seemed to have lost faith in his men. Conversely, some of Knox's battalion commanders were concerned that he was out of touch with them and their troops. In particular Robin Hastings, formerly on Montgomery's HQ staff, who had been sent in to take over 6th Battalion Green

13   David French, "Colonel Blimp and the British Army: British Divisional Commanders in the War Against Germany, 1939-45." *English Historical Review.* 111 (1996), p.1193.
14   French, Colonel Blimp, p.1185.
15   For example in Delaforce, *Red Crown and Dragon: 53rd Welsh Division in NW Europe 1944-45.*
16   Private of the 5th Battalion East Yorkshire Regiment, quoted in Barnes, *The Sign of the Double T*, p.62.
17   Ibid, p.62.

Howards prior to D-Day, felt this.[18] Desmond Gordon of 151st Brigade would also ask for "battle weary" troops to be replaced around the same time.[19] The Division had fought well in the Battle of Normandy, but with high attrition from battle casualties and battle exhaustion. In June, July and August the Division had lost (excluding exhaustion cases) 848 killed and 4058 wounded all ranks (85/763 killed; 257/3801 wounded).[20] Stephen Hart notes that the Division's battle exhaustion casualties in that period were so notably high that concerns were raised that they were being feigned, causing the Division's chief medical officer to launch an investigation. The number of convictions for desertion or being absent without leave within 50th Division in the period June – September 1944 exceeded those of the whole of 2nd British Army combined.[21]

53rd Division had also taken high casualties in the battle for the bridgehead in late June and July, despite its later entry into theatre after D-Day. The Division suffered particularly in the operations on the Odon and Guighe rivers and the hard fighting during the two attempts to take Evrecy during Operation GREENLINE, the feint operation designed to distract from GOODWOOD. Hastily planned, GREENLINE achieved little and was described as "a pointless muddle."[22] However, a detailed history of the Division's support arms written after the war shows that 53rd Division by this point had specifically allocated two of its Field Dressing Stations as Divisional Exhaustion Centres which remained in operation until the war's end.[23] The rest of July was described by one divisional historian as being raids and patrols after a series of complicated moves, counter-moves and brigade reliefs within the Division.[24] Ross decided also to realign his Royal Welch Fusiliers battalions around the brigades at the beginning of August, a move which caused some resentment and had an impact on morale, but which was driven by necessity due to the dual causes of heavy casualties in 158th Brigade and the arrival of new COs and reinforcement drafts who needed to settle in.

Into mid-August the division played a key role in putting pressure on the roads to Falaise from the south and south west – where casualty rates again started to climb, although there was an increase in "Normandy stomach" alongside battlefield causes.[25]

---

18   Knox and Hastings' concerns are cited in Converse, *Armies of Empire: The 9th Australian and 50th British Divisions in Battle 1939-1945*, p.203.
19   Converse, *Armies of Empire*, p.203.
20   Figures primarily from Barnes, *The Sign*, p.227.
21   Hart, *Montgomery and 'Colossal Cracks'*, p.29.
22   Col. JW Tweedie, quoted in Buckley, *Monty's Men*, p.98.
23   Anon, *Team Spirit: The Administration of 53rd (Welsh) Division during Operation OVERLORD, June 1944-May 1945*. The Field Dressing Stations were Numbers 13 and 26.
24   Delaforce, *Red Crown*, pp.58-60.
25   Contrary to popular belief this was not predominantly caused by drinking immature Calvados, or apple brandy; rather it was a particularly aggressive form of diarrhoea caused by ingesting food infected by the ubiquitous and unavoidable flies which fed on the carcasses of dead animals.

In 6th Battalion Royal Welch Fusiliers a whole company had to be disbanded due to lack of reinforcements; divisional reserves had been depleted and drafts from regiments outside the division were appearing. In the Battle of Normandy and up to the end of August 53rd Division lost 585 killed, 2856 wounded and 378 missing.[26]

In early September, up to the beginning of MARKET GARDEN on the 17th, both 50th and 53rd Divisions were involved in bridgehead operations on the flanks. 50th Division crossed the Albert Canal towards Gheel on 7-8 September. 151st Brigade took the town, but was quickly repulsed by a German counter-attack taking advantage of the Division's wide dispersal. The town was retaken on 12 September as the Germans – true to Normandy form – over extended their counterattack. Although 151st Brigade prevailed, the German response had badly affected some sub-units and 6th Battalion Durham Light Infantry partly broke. Allan Converse states that although the Brigade had recently absorbed experienced reinforcements from disbanded formations, they were still not fully organised; veteran accounts cite anger from the supporting armour (the Sherwood Rangers Yeomanry) towards the infantry, but the Durham war diary gives little hint of such trouble.[27] 50th Division was relieved by 15th (Scottish) Division, and the idea of using a bridgehead across the Meuse-Escaut Canal at Aart to develop the operation was abandoned. The belief that German resistance across the canal line was a 'thin crust' which could quickly be overwhelmed was soon disabused – and the hope that an easy advance from the canals to guard XXX Corps' flanks on 17 September was dashed.

After a period of comparative quiet in the first half of September – with occasional bouts of street fighting, wood clearances and aggressive patrolling, (a visit to Ross by Monty on 13 September led one officer to remark "the real war starts again"), 53rd Division had a major part in the main XII Corps task to develop and protect the left base and left flank of Operation MARKET GARDEN and to force the Canal de Jonction north of Lommel. For many of the battalions in the Division this would be their first assault crossing, and a costly one. Brigadier Blomfield of 71st Brigade and a number of his brigade staff were wounded on the enemy bank on 21 September. The Brigade would be under temporary command for eleven days, a period described by a divisional historian as comprising "half a dozen nasty unit battles." Blomfield's replacement, Maxwell Elrington had been serving in 21st Army Group Headquarters following the disbandment of 177th Brigade on the break-up of 59th Division in August; he would temporarily command the Division in early 1945 but was killed in a mine explosion before the war's end.

By D-Day for MARKET GARDEN on 17 September, neither XII nor VIII Corps had been able to deploy sufficiently to protect the flanks of the main advance up the XXX Corps corridor. 50th Division was transferred to XXX Corps command

---

26   Derived from Delaforce, *Red Crown*, p.85; Barclay, *The History of 53rd (Welsh) Division in the Second World War*, and Anon, *Team Spirit*, Chapter 1, pp.5-6.

27   Converse, *Armies of Empire*, p.185.

for D-Day to assist in the breakthrough, with 231st Brigade attached to the Guards Armoured Division to penetrate the initial defences, but the division would rapidly revert to VIII Corps after D+1. VIII Corps was still trailing back from the start line and guarding XII Corps' flank. Thus, Dempsey's strategic vision of a general Second Army advance in a broad front would be untenable. Additional tasks levied on the two flank Corps would detract even more from simply protecting XXX Corps' flank. XII Corps' broadened mission was to advance to Turnhout and on to the Maas; VIII Corps was to diverge yet further, to extend 2nd Army's base of operations in Holland and then to cover the Maas. Under such conditions it is perhaps unfeasible that either Corps could have assumed the role of immediate flank protection of XXX Corps' advance as it drove up the corridor to Valkenswaard, Eindhoven, Nijmegen and Arnhem. David Bennett contends that there never was a plan to converge with XXX Corps flanks, given the diversity of the Corps objectives.[28]

50th Division ground slowly north; with 69th Brigade being cut in two by a German counter-attack in the area of Uden, five miles south of Grave, on 22 September. 69th Brigade then moved twice; to the Guards Armoured Division in the midst of the counter-attack at Uden, and thence to 43rd (Wessex) Division on 29 September. There was a considerable struggle to hold Halderen from 26 September-4 October; factory chimneys there were being used for artillery spotting and needed neutralisation. German forces released from the Arnhem area after 1st Airborne Division's failure to hold on there would constantly attack, driving the British back towards Nijmegen; a further counter-attack by 50th Division on 4 October led to Halderen's eventual capture on 6 October. From now until the end of November, 50th Division would be contained in "The Island", the rough triangle of land between the Rhine and the Waal containing the final stretch of road between Nijmegen and Arnhem. The onset of autumn and the ensuing tactical conditions of heavy rain and mud would drain divisional morale, with a brief fillip during the battles of Aam-Bemmel between 25 September and 4 October. It was to be the Division's last battle; its brigades were rotated back through Nijmegen throughout October and November for rest and refit – but this would be the end for the Division as a contained formation. It was announced in early December that 50th Division was to be broken up and returned to the UK as a holding and training formation. On hearing of this decision from Sir Alan Brooke, the Chief of the Imperial General Staff, an infuriated Churchill ordered Montgomery to reverse the decision; he only withdrew his order when Montgomery responded that the disbandment had already begun; he added, and Brooke and the Chiefs of Staff agreed, that any reversal of the order would have detrimental consequences for 2nd Army fighting power in Europe.[29]

---

28   Bennett, *A Magnificent Disaster: The Failure of Market Garden, September 1944*, p.75.
29   Hart, *Montgomery*, p.57. Also referred to in Baker and Rust, *A Short History of the 50th (Northumbrian) Division*, p.56.

53rd Division, after expanding out of the Lommel Bridgehead, would also face stiff resistance in the area of The Island; 1st Battalion Oxfordshire and Buckinghamshire Light Infantry had ten miserable days in the area of Ressum and 4th Battalion Royal Welch Fusiliers was shelled during pay parade on 28 September. On 19 October, 158th and 161st Brigades were pulled out to prepare for the planned attack on s'Hertogenbosch. In order to exploit Antwerp, the road from there to Nijmegen had to be opened, and s'Hertogenbosch (or Den Bosch) would need to be taken due to its strategic position sitting across road, rail and canal communications. A rapid seizure of the town would also prevent German 15th Army from retreating across the Meuse. The attack on the city was known as Operation ALAN; it took place under the general umbrella of Operation PHEASANT, the overall liberation of southern Holland. After a preparatory bombardment by all of XII Corps' artillery, 53rd Division advanced from a start line seven and a half miles to the east of the city at 0630 on Sunday 22 October. Ross' operational scheme was conventional; 71st and 160th Brigades forward, with 158th Brigade following on behind ready to exploit crossings across the canals. 160th Brigade, facing more open ground and with tank support, made reasonable progress. 71st Brigade fared less well. Ross ordered 158th Brigade to pass through 160th Brigade to seize and cross the canals. The advance was short-lived as the lead units ran into minefields. Progress slowed, and did not increase much on 23rd; Ross ordered a night attack to ease the path of 71st Brigade. The assault by 1st Battalion East Lancashire Regiment on 23/24 October – assisted by "artificial moonlight" – managed to infiltrate around the German defensive line into the city, but it would take another four days to suppress German opposition due to determined resistance, intense house-to-house fighting and the fact that all the bridges across the city centre had been destroyed. The eventual pacification of the city required close co-operation by British ground units as bad weather precluded close air support. Infantry-armour work was especially close, in particular the use of Crocodile flame thrower tanks to clear multi-storey buildings. The city fell to 53rd Division on 28th October. In October alone 53rd Division had suffered nearly 1,000 casualties.[30]

For the next two months, the weather became even worse with heavy rain rendering already poor ground conditions appalling going. 53rd Division would spend its time attempting to reduce pockets of resistance west of the Maas and, with 51st Highland Division on its right (to the south) to seek to force the Wessem Canal. On 23rd November, the Maas broke its banks, and for the next month the Division guarded an extended front of over 20 miles along the river. Although the concurrent set-piece operations in this period, MALLARD and NUTCRACKER, intended to pinch out the German salient west of the Maas around Venlo, were facing increasingly less resolute German opposition, the poor conditions prevented full exploitation by the infantry. This was so even though by now use of rudimentary armoured personnel carriers (de-turreted Canadian Ram tanks known as Kangaroos) was commonplace.

30   Delaforce, *Red Dragon*, p.123.

Thus, as the end of 1944 approached, both Divisions were now "veteran"; the "Tynesiders" of 50th Division with five years' combat experience and the arriviste "Welshmen" of 53rd Division now blooded after six months' spent in battle. Both had seen their pre-war regional identities eroded as the North West Europe campaign progressed, due to heavy, but not particularly atypical, casualty rates. On 29th November, 50th Division was withdrawn to Belgium – and it would not fight as a formation again. So why was 50th Division broken up and 53rd Division left to press on to the war's end?

Prevailing conventional wisdom has stated that the three "desert" divisions were burnt out by 1944, tactically hidebound and poorly led. But more recent writing[31] suggests that such criticism only emerged post-war and was not voiced at the time. For example, Maj. Gen. 'Pip' Roberts was critical of Monty's leavening out of the assault force with formations from the desert and Mediterranean, thinking it "unsound" as they "lacked dash".[32] Yet this was not a fair charge against 50th Division in the immediate aftermath of the D-Day landings – one of their historians has asserted that the infantry brigades showed too much readiness to engage the enemy before full support – particularly armour – was ready to act in a co-ordinated manner. It is undeniable that in the later stages of the battle of Normandy 50th Division was suffering from considerable morale and discipline problems, and battle exhaustion; but it was not the worst, either of the Divisions on the continent or of the "desert divisions" of which it was part. Graham was perhaps less sympathetic to "battle exhaustion" in comparison with other divisional commanders, having a robust attitude towards such casualties, although he cannot be accused of ignoring the issue as his senior medical officer's investigation demonstrates. Whilst analysis of 50th Division's performance varies in the literature, Graham himself is almost universally praised. He was popular with his officers and men, and visited his Brigades more frequently than any of his predecessors, on some occasions while they were heavily engaged. Horrocks labelled him "an old war horse never far from battle".[33] Ethan Williams, in his study for the US Army War College, asserts that 50th Division believed that following its experiences in Sicily "…it did not require any specialist training for fighting in the close countryside of Normandy", perhaps with undue hubris.[34] By the autumn it had shown tactical adaptability and had been praised for overcoming its earlier problems in this area. When Graham was wounded in October, he was temporarily replaced by Maj. Gen. Lewis Lyne, Montgomery's "trouble-shooter" who would later take command of another supposedly 'problematic' veteran division, 7th Armoured. Two of his Brigades mainly retained the same commanders during the period June-December 1944 thus

---

31   Buckley, *Monty's Men* pp. 142-143.
32   Ibid., p.143.
33   Horrocks, *A Full Life*, p.182.
34   Lt. Cdr. E.R.Williams, "50 Div in Normandy: A Critical Analysis of the British 50th (Northumbrian) Division on D-Day and in the Battle of Normandy" Master's Degree Thesis, (Fort Leavenworth US Army Command and General Staff College, Kansas 2007).

ensuring continuity; when Knox of 69th Brigade was wounded in late October, he was replaced by Spurling, whom Converse labels "mediocre" without further amplification (even though he would retire as a Major General thirteen years later as Chief of Staff, Northern Command).[35] Stanier of 231st Brigade was arguably one of the better Brigadiers on the Continent and adept at infantry-armour co-operation; even critics of the Division concede that it was approaching a "tactical peak" by October 1944.[36]

Ross was mostly popular with his officers; as noted, he was comfortable with Montgomery, reportedly a frequent visitor to his headquarters. Ross was an adherent of the old military adage that "any fool can be uncomfortable", ensuring that his headquarters mess sought out good food and drink in the field via a specific ADC; he also ensured that the Division as a whole was well entertained out of the line, indicating awareness of morale maintenance. Yet although he was described as gregarious, having a good sense of humour and not being over-bearing, his Orders Groups were often merely business-like and he was reserved and introspective. His ADC noted that Ross and Horrocks did not have a cordial relationship and that he got along better with Neil Ritchie at XII Corps. There was occasional criticism of Ross' handling of the Division; then-Brigadier Michael Carver of 4th Armoured Brigade described his Orders Groups as tending to be "more like a council of war than the issuing of clear, succinct orders."[37] It is, however, possible that this remark was driven by personal animus as Ross had declined Carver's advice on the use of his Brigade in Normandy. There was also some criticism from within. Major Nick Cutliffe of 4th Battalion Royal Welch Fusiliers complained about "penny packet" tactics and inadequate preparation during the August battles. He also claimed that his superior officers showed indifference to battle exhaustion. Ross' juggling of the RWF battalions was also unpopular, but arguably necessary. Delaforce criticises the "musical chairs" of Brigade reliefs in late September and early October especially citing 69th Brigade for this. It could be argued that Ross should have paid closer attention to a Brigade under temporary command, but he already had a reputation for leaving his Brigadiers to their work. 53rd Division's use of co-ordinated artillery and armour attacks improved throughout the summer and culminated in the successful attack on s'Hertogenbosch, where the Division performed "perhaps the best example in modern times of a successful assault on a large town held by a resolute and skilful enemy. Larger and more important towns were captured during the campaign, but they either capitulated at an early stage or were comparatively easily reduced."[38]

Graham would contribute a narrative to the 1947 Staff College Course notes on the Normandy Campaign[39] which does not assign criticism to Montgomery. He did not,

35   Converse, *Armies of Empire*, p.225.
36   Ibid., p.226.
37   Field Marshal Lord Carver, *Out of Step*, p.193.
38   Barclay, The History of 53rd Division, pp.85-87.
39   TNA, WO 233/7, 50th Div – Notes by Maj Gen Graham, 1943-44.

however, write any personal memoir after the war where he could to express his views of the treatment of him, or of his Division. Ross died relatively young at the age of 58 in 1951, and did not leave any assessments or memoirs at all, let alone of his time in Divisional command.

So why was the 50th Division selected for disbandment? That it was "burnt out" is the usual verdict, but this is not a completely adequate answer. 51st Highland Division had suffered markedly in Normandy with high casualties and marked disciplinary problems; Sir John Crocker of I Corps thought the Division was not up to standard through the Normandy battles and was in need of a considerable shake-up. Brooke and Montgomery clearly agreed, the latter sacking its commander, Maj. Gen. Bullen-Smith, in July and replacing him with Tom Rennie from 3rd Division when he had recovered from wounds received early in the Normandy campaign. Both 50th and 53rd were held to be "among the eight most effective divisions" in 21st Army Group, although they were admittedly fourth and fifth in that list.[40] Both had dealt with disciplinary and psychological issues with some success and overcame difficulties not of their making – such as erratic reinforcement and the unpredictable nature of these drafts in time and quality. Finally, both retained their commanders until the end, save for a brief period when Graham was wounded and Ross was away from the Division from March-May 1945. Converse notes that although discipline improved in 50th Division through August and September, court-martial rates started to climb again through October and November and supporting formations remarked that the Division's troops appeared demoralised.[41]

Could it be that Monty's decision was a snap one? He was not universally popular among the 'old hands' in 50th Division due to its being withdrawn not to rest, but to fight again; the shadow of the Salerno Mutiny still hung over the Division, despite a new commander with no connection to it. The Field Marshal could turn quickly on those he previously supported and then criticise them accordingly; Graham seems to have fallen out of favour with Montgomery post-war, but it is not readily apparent why this may have been so and as has been noted Graham was in good favour with Montgomery before and during the Normandy campaign. 51st Highland Division had also started to overcome its operational and discipline problems and operated effectively alongside 53rd Division in Operation ALAN. 50th Division was not alone in suffering a resurgence of discipline and morale problems with the onset of winter and markedly poor campaigning conditions. The fluctuating morale state – a problem which had trailed behind the Division since the Mediterranean – must have contributed to the decision to disband it. An officer of the Division, Major Peter Martin, offered his own view, whilst highlighting the piecemeal manner in which the decision was passed down to the troops:

---

40   Hart, *Montgomery*, p.45.
41   Converse, *Armies of Empire*, p.225.

People began to wonder if we were going home – there were rumours emanating from the HQ clerks. I told that this was going to happen: we would be reduced to twelve officers and one hundred and nine other ranks and sent home to train surplus RAF and naval recruits as infantry for the Rhine Crossing. The reason? Not only had 50 Div done its stuff, but its standard of training was getting shaky and it was time for someone else... This was a betrayal... We pleaded with the CO to launch an objection.[42]

51st Highland Division, despite its own difficulties in this regard, did have the presentational advantage of its being resurrected from the ashes of defeat to now being part of the road to victory. In the public imagination perhaps the image of its pipers at El Alamein in the film *Desert Victory* and the division's propensity to put its distinctive formation sign everywhere – leading to its being dubbed "the Highway Decorators" by the rest of the Army – gave it what would now be called "brand recognition" and its disbandment might have resulted in public uproar. This may be rather an exaggeration (the "Double T" for Tyne-Tees badge of 50th Division was also well-known) of an intangible factor; the decision to break up Graham's division may not have been entirely "fair" but operational decisions in wartime rarely are.

Bibliography

Anon, *53rd (Welsh) Division: Team Spirit: The Administration of 53rd (Welsh) Division during Operation Overlord June 1944-May 1945*, Germany, Privately published, 1946.

Army Staff College, *50th (Northumbrian) Division Battlefield Tour: Normandy Assault*, Camberley, Privately published, 1947.

Barclay, C.N., *A History of the 53rd (Welsh) Division in the Second World War*, London, William Clowes, 1956.

Barker, A.H.R. and Rust, B., *A Short History of the 50th Northumbrian Division*, Berwick upon Tweed, The Tweeddale Press, 1966.

Barnes, B.S., *The Sign of the Double T: The 50th Northumbrian Division, July 1943-December 1944*, York, Sentinel Press, 1999.

Bennett, D., *A Magnificent Disaster: The Failure of Market-Garden, the Arnhem Operation September 1944*, Oxford, Casemate, 2011.

Buckley, J., *Monty's Men*, London, Yale, 2012.

Carver, M., *Out of Step: A Memoir*, London, Hutchison, 1989.

Clay, Ewart W., *The path of the 50th: the story of the 50th – Northumbrian – Division in the Second World War, 1939-1945*, Aldershot, Gale & Polden, 1950.

Converse, A., *Armies of Empire: The 9th Australian and 50th British Divisions in Battle 1939-1945* (Australian Army History Series), Cambridge, Cambridge UP, 2011.

42   Barnes, *The Sign*, p.159.

Crosswell, D.K.R., *The Chief of Staff: The Military Career of General Walter Bedell Smith*, New York, Greenwood, 1991.

David, S., *Mutiny At Salerno: An Injustice Exposed*, London, Conway, 2005.

Delaforce, P., *Red Crown and Dragon: 53rd Welsh Division in NW Europe 1944-45*, London, Tom Donovan, 1996.

French, D., "Colonel Blimp and the British Army: British Divisional Commanders in the War Against Germany, 1939-45", *English Historical Review*. 111 (444), 1996.

French, D., *Raising Churchill's Army*, Oxford, Oxford UP, 2000.

Hart, S., *Montgomery and Colossal Cracks*, London, Greenwood, 2000.

Horrocks, B., *A Full Life*, London, Collins, 1960.

Horrocks, B., *Corps Commander*, London, Sidgwick and Jackson, 1980.

Ryan, C., *A Bridge Too Far*, New York, Simon and Schuster, 1974.

Smart, N., *A Biographical Dictionary of British Generals of the Second World War*, Bradford, Pen and Sword, 2004.

Williams, Lt. Cdr. E.R., *50th Div in Normandy: A Critical Analysis of the British 50th (Northumbrian) Division on D-Day and in the Battle of Normandy*, Master's Thesis, United States Army Command and Staff College, Fort Leavenworth, Kansas, 2007.

The National Archives (TNA) London

WO 233/7: 50th Div – Notes by Maj Gen Graham, 1943-44.

WO 171/689: 158 Brigade HQ 1944: January to December.

Electronic Sources

Website of the Museum of The Queen's Royal Surrey Regiment http://www.queensroyalsurreys.org.uk

Website of the Museum of the Royal Leicestershire Regiment http://www.royal-leicestershireregiment.org.uk/

8

The Viktor Graebner Assault, 0900 hrs Monday 18th September 1944

Peter Preston-Hough

The majority of the papers given in the two days of the 'Highway to the Reich' conference concentrated on grand strategy, doctrine and policy. This paper will reassess one controversial attack during Operation MARKET GARDEN which has been misinterpreted for many years, namely *SS Hauptsturmfuhrer* Viktor Graebner's assault on Arnhem Bridge during the morning of Monday 18th September 1944. This paper will examine the historiography, the background reasons why the attack was carried out and then reassess the eventual outcome of the assault. Firstly it is necessary to provide some background to the attack.

Viktor Graebner joined the German army in 1937 and served as a soldier with the rank of Leutnant during Operation BARBAROSSA in 1941 as a front line soldier. In October 1941 Graebner was appointed as commander of the 2nd Company of the *256th Reconnaissance Battalion* and subsequently served with distinction on the Eastern Front gaining military honours. In January 1943 he transferred to the *9th SS Panzer Division (Hohenstaufen)* and during June 1944 participated in repelling the Allied advance firstly on Caen and later in France itself. For his bravery and leadership during the Normandy battles he was awarded the Knights Cross on 23rd August but did not receive the award until 17th September, the day before his death in Arnhem. His final transfer was to the *9th Hohenstaufen's Reconnaissance Battalion* in August 1944 a month before the commencement of MARKET GARDEN.

When the British 1st Airborne Division landed close to the Dutch village of Wolfheze on Sunday 17th September, Graebner, following the award of his Knights Cross, was sent South to Nijmegen at 1800hrs to reconnoitre the area. Following some light fighting with American paratroopers in Nijmegen he decided to travel back North towards Arnhem, but before withdrawing he left two armoured half-tracks with German troops at Nijmegen Bridge to reinforce their resistance against the expected American assault. Stopping in Elst overnight, which is roughly half-way between Arnhem and Nijmegen, Graebner was in an ideal position to travel to either city if the situation demanded.

The original plan for the 1st British Airborne Division after landing on 17th September was to move off from their landing grounds at great speed towards Arnhem Bridge, being preceded by heavily armed jeeps of the Reconnaissance Squadron who would initially seize the Bridge. The remaining troops would capture three bridges (rail, pontoon and road) and then form a perimeter around the river, North and South, whilst waiting for XXX Corps arriving from the South. However, owing to a series of delays and initial enemy action a reduced force reached Arnhem town with no airborne troops on the Southern bank. During Sunday evening, the Northern area around Arnhem Bridge had been taken by elements of 1st Airborne Division: 2nd Battalion of the Parachute Regiment minus one company; C Company of 3rd Battalion Parachute Regiment; five six pounder anti-tank guns of the Airlanding Anti-Tank Battery Royal Artillery; and soldiers from the Royal Army Service Corps (RASC), the Royal Army Medical Corps (RAMC), the Royal Engineers (RE), the Royal Army Ordnance Corps (RAOC), some of the Reconnaissance Squadron, the Glider Pilot Regiment, and the Royal Military Police (RMP). According to available sources the British force at the bridge numbered about 740 soldiers. 2nd Battalion paratroopers were engaged during Sunday evening in an attempt to take the Southern end of the bridge, and during early Monday morning, 18th September, German counter-attacks by troops carried in lorries and later by tanks were successfully beaten off. At 0900 hours that morning a column of German armoured cars and half-tracks followed by a number of lorries carrying soldiers attempted to cross Arnhem Bridge from the South. Although the first five armoured cars were successful in crossing the bridge, the remaining half-tracks, lorries and soldiers following were cut down by a hail of airborne small arms fire, anti-tank guns and grenades. Viktor Graebner was the leader of this doomed column.

Over the years since the attack the event's historiography has not been kind to Graebner, the assault being usually classed as the work of an enthusiastic young man who was a 'typical' SS reconnaissance officer who took the situation into his own hands. Cornelius Ryan wrote:

> Against paratroopers armed with only rifles or machine guns, Graebner expected little difficulty. His powerful armoured units would simply smash through the lightly-held British defences and knock them over.[1]

Robert Kershaw wrote in 1990:

> Only conjecture and a piecing together of fragmentary reports can ever recreate these last few hours during which he condemned himself and much of his unit to death.[2]

1   Ryan, Cornelius, *A Bridge Too Far*, 1974, p.248.
2   Kershaw, Robert, *It Never Snows in September*, p.128.

A.D. Harvey was much more critical:

> Other units were of much higher quality, though even these sometimes bungled things badly; for example SS-Hauptsturmfuhrer Graebner, an experienced officer who had just been decorated with the Knight's Cross, showed a completely amateurish crassness in his attempt to drive his column of reconnaissance vehicles across the Arnhem bridge in the face of a newly established defence line.[3]

Similar views exist in other works and has been a long held view, but did Graebner actually act on his own initiative without orders?

An alternative view to Graebner's alleged incompetence appeared in a book written by a Dutchman, Peter Berends. The book, *Een Andere Kijk op de Slag bij Arnhem* [*Another look at the Battle of Arnhem*], may not be widely known in Britain as it has sadly not been translated into English.[4]

Peter Berends' book was published in 2002 and during its preparation the author had been in correspondence with Wilfried Schwarz, former Chief of Staff of the 9th *SS Hohenstaufen Division*. Schwarz informed Berends that Graebner had received verbal orders from Schwarz's staff following detailed instructions that had been received from SS General William Bittrich's headquarters of the *II SS Panzer Corps*. Graebner was to cross Arnhem Bridge, break British resistance and then form a defence line to the West.[5] Berends also wrote that Schwarz emphatically denied the notion that Graebner had acted on his own initiative, acting instead on the orders of superior officers.[6]

This account raises various questions and possible explanations. Firstly why had it taken Schwarz nearly sixty years to come forward with this revelation? Possible answers are that he had decided to put the record straight as increased interest in Operation MARKET GARDEN since 1974 and the publication of Ryan's *A Bridge too Far* had persistently portrayed Graebner, a recognised German war hero, and Schwarz's own colleague, in a very bad light. Another possibility was he had decided to re-write history to give the action, and particularly Graebner's memory, an honourable conclusion. Schwarz's decision to tell what may, or may not be, the truth in 2002 is even more interesting as he was interviewed by Robert Kershaw for his 1990 book, *It Never Snows in September*, where Kershaw wrote:

---

3   Harvey, A D, *Arnhem*, p.189.
4   Berends, Peter, *Een Andere Kijk op de Slag bij Arnhem* [*Another look at the Battle of Arnhem*].
5   Berends, Peter, *Een Andere Kijk op de Slag bij Arnhem*, p.111.
6   Ibid.

Schwarz, whilst not understanding his [Graebner's] decision to attack the Arnhem bridge, admitted nevertheless 'that this was typical of Graebner – always the first to get stuck in!' This remark provides the key to his subsequent actions.[7]

Schwarz did not and was not pressed by Berends to explain his change of heart so it may therefore be a matter of some conjecture as to why he changed his mind and story in that intervening ten or so years.[8]

The second factor lies with the alleged order from Graebner's superiors to attack. The difficulty with verbal orders, as all historians know, is proving their existence and what they actually said, especially after such a long passage of time. Furthermore, to continue Schwarz's involvement, it is entirely possible that he misheard or misremembered the orders. However, is it also feasible that even if the orders had been written down, they were conveniently lost once the disaster had overcome Graebner's force, so therefore does the evidence represent a cover-up?

The Germans clearly did not fully appreciate 1st Airborne's strength at the bridge, both in terms of soldiers and anti-tank artillery. According to Ryan:

However, from radio messages, he [Graebner] had learned that some British troops were on one side of the bridge. Harzer's headquarters had merely called them 'advance units'.[9]

Given the uncertainty it would have been natural to send a reconnaissance unit over the bridge in force to gain intelligence and possibly obtain an advantage if British strength was weak and could be easily overcome. However, when the venture ended in disaster German commanders may have wished to distance themselves from the debacle, by placing the blame on someone who could not speak for himself, e.g. the dead Graebner. Verbal orders could be denied, written ones lost and witnesses sworn to secrecy.

What evidence did Peter Berends' have to support this theory? There was no mention of the attack in the German magazine publication, *Signal*, which trumpeted the German success at Arnhem even as Nazi spin on Graebner's heroism.[10] More substantial evidence is that neither Bittrich, SS Lieutenant-Colonel Walther Harzer (Commander 10th SS) nor SS Colonel Heinz Harmel (Divisional Commander 10th SS) mentioned Graebner's attack in their post-war reports, which is a suspicious

---

7   Kershaw, Robert, *It Never Snows in September*, p.128.
8   Unfortunately Peter Berends passed away a few years ago.
9   Ryan, Cornelius, *A Bridge Too Far*, p.246.
10   Berends, Peter, *Een Andere Kijk op de Slag bij Arnhem*, p.113.

omission. Similarly the Dutch historian, Lieutenant Colonel Theodoor Boeree, interviewed Bittrich after the war and, again, there is no mention of Graebner.[11]

Whether there is substance to the theory that Graebner's orders to assault the bridge was covered up or not, there is some veracity in the belief that Graebner received some definite orders from his superiors. The column of vehicles accompanying him consisted of about 10 to 12 lorries, which were equipped with oil drums or sand bags to absorb enemy fire. The numbers of these suitably equipped vehicles combined with their troops suggest that this was a planned assault that required the right man to lead it. However, the sandbag-equipped lorries would also add weight to the theory that the Germans had no idea of the 1st Airborne's strength at Arnhem Bridge as they were quite inadequate to deal with anything but very small arms fire.

The second part of this paper will examine the outcome of Graebner's attack. The traditional view is that the Germans came out of it badly; Graebner was killed as were about 70 of the assault troops; eight armoured half-tracks were lost, which the Germans could ill-afford to lose; and no ground was taken. At the very most the Germans had discovered that British strength on the bridge was much stronger than previously thought and would take a greater effort to displace, but this would not be from the South whilst the fighting continued in Nijmegen. The British Airborne soldiers on the Northern bridge ramps are generally considered to have emerged victorious; few casualties had been sustained and the first major German counter-attack had been successfully repelled. 1st Airborne's morale was thus left very high as Private James Sims later recalled:

This was now a very hazardous place and we felt more than pleased with ourselves. Despite Jerry's local superiority in tanks and manpower, we had been giving him a good hiding.[12]

However, in closer analysis of the attack it is clear it had a significant effect in shortening the Airborne soldiers' hold on the bridge in terms of their ammunition reserves.

To explore this theory it was necessary to compare the amount of ammunition taken onto the bridge against the amount fired during Graebner's assault. It was soon apparent that this task was very difficult. Each airborne soldier was issued with a minimum of 100 rounds of .303 ammunition, a Sten gunner with eight magazines, each containing 32 rounds, and a Bren gunner with 24 magazines, each containing 30 rounds.[13] This included the soldiers from the RE, RASC, RAOC party, reconnaissance unit and all committed units. However, as soldiers the world over know, men will always put an additional few rounds or grenades into their pockets, just in case. Furthermore, it is difficult to quantify how much reserve ammunition was taken to

11   Airborne Assault Museum, papers not referenced.
12   Sims, James, *Arnhem Spearhead*, p.85.
13   Airborne Archive, Duxford, Box 4, F1 2.10.1.

the bridge by the RASC party. Initial accounts of four jeep/trailer combinations and their loads vary from man to man in the 250th Light Composite Company, and a story of a commandeered lorry filled with ammunition has been disproved.[14] In operational orders for MARKET GARDEN (left over from Exercise TRANSFIGUATION and Operations LINNET and COMET) each unit, for example, should have had four containers each with a load of 16,000 rounds of .303 ammunition, a total of 64,000 rounds.[15] It is unclear from all the available evidence whether all this reserve amount made its way through to the bridge.

Just as it is difficult to quantify how much ammunition was taken to the bridge, it is impossible to gauge how much was expended during Graebner's attack. In the feature film, *A Bridge Too Far*, the attack lasts four and a half minutes, whereas in reality it lasted between nearly two and two and a half hours and soldiers were too busy to note down how many rounds they were using. It is clear from some of the accounts that the airborne soldiers expended lots of ammunition rounds. The HQ Brigade diarist wrote in the unit's diary, "Most of these vehicles were fairly full of Germans who provided very good target practice for the Brigade HQ who were in the attic."[16] Corporal Geoff Cockayne, was in the Brigade HQ building and later said:

> I had a German Schmeisser and had a lot of fun with that. I shot at any Gerry that moved… We didn't stay in the room we were in but came out to fire, keeping moving, taking cover and firing from different positions. The Germans had got out of their troop carriers – what was left of them – and it became a proper infantry action. I shot off nearly all my ammunition.[17]

The commanding officer of the 2nd Battalion, Lieutenant Colonel John Frost, wrote:

> All round the battle raged… There were no exceptions from the fighting line, all ranks and trades were in it. Staff officers, signallers, batmen, drivers and clerks lent a hand. For a while I couldn't understand how what sounded like German machine-guns were firing from immediately below our windows. By craning out, one could just see Freddie Gough in action behind the twin K-guns on his jeep, grinning like a wicked uncle.[18]

Signalman Bill Jukes' later recollection gives a good impression of the weight of fire and the Airborne's eagerness to get into action:

14   Middlebrook, Martin, *Arnhem 1944*, p.160.
15   The National Archive (TNA), WO 171/592, War Diary 1st Parachute Brigade, July, August and September 1944.
16   TNA, WO 171/592, War Diary 1st Parachute Brigade, September 1944.
17   Quoted in Middlebrook, Martin, *Arnhem 1944*, p.294.
18   Frost, John, *A Drop too Many*, p.220.

The first vehicle which drew level with the house was hit, and the second rammed into it, blocking the roadway. The rest didn't stand a chance. The crews and passengers, those still able to, began to pile out, and those of us armed with Stens joined in the general fusillade. One of the radio operators grabbed my Sten gun which was leaning against the wall, but I snatched it away from him, telling him to go and get his own. I hadn't waited five years to get a shot at the enemy like this only to be denied by some Johnny-come-lately to the section. It was impossible to say what effect my shooting had. There was such a volley coming from the windows along the street that nobody could have said who shot who.[19]

There are many more similar accounts to these usually using various combinations of the three words: hail, murderous and fire.

The accounts of the action suggest a number of factors. Firstly, they reinforce what is now known that early communications between the bridge and to the rest of the Airborne Division in the West around Oosterbeek were poor as the bridge defenders were expecting to be reinforced and, more importantly, resupplied during Monday 18th September. They did not know MARKET GARDEN had started to deteriorate between Oosterbeek and Arnhem from Sunday night as the remainder of 1st Airborne were trying to push through to the bridge but had been held up in various German ambushes and blocking lines. Secondly, there may have been a lack of control exerted over the use of ammunition during the attack. In the available accounts none states senior NCOs or officers advising against profligate use of small-arms ammunition. To fire for over two hours would require some remarkable self-discipline as munitions were expended. Returning to Corporal Cockayne:

I shot off nearly all my ammunition. To start with, I had been letting rip, but then I became more careful; I knew there would be no more. I wasn't firing at any German in particular, just firing at where I knew they were.[20]

The high rate of ammunition usage probably should come as little surprise as it is symbolic of the British Airborne's policy of aggressively engaging the enemy whenever possible. Faced with the targets on Arnhem Bridge it is clear that the soldiers acted in the way they had been trained and upheld their regiment's tradition. William Buckingham suggests that the 1st Airborne Division had suffered from a lack of training in the months prior to MARKET GARDEN which may have affected its performance during the operation.[21] However, there is nothing to suggest that the 2nd Battalion's actions on the bridge were as a result of inadequate training or discipline problems. Furthermore, fighting in a built-up area uses larger amounts of ammunition

---

19   Quoted in Middlebrook, Martin, *Arnhem 1944*, p.294.
20   Quoted in Middlebrook, Martin, *Arnhem 1944*, p.294.
21   Buckingham, William, *Arnhem 1944*, pp.50-51.

owing to the enemy's proximity and nature of the surroundings.[22] Taking these factors together the high use of ammunition was expected, if not problematical.

After Graebner's demise and the end of his assault, there was a short sharp German attack which was repelled, followed by another short fierce action by German tanks which was mainly beaten off by 6 pounder anti-tank guns and PIATs.[23] Finally there were a few minor attacks by German troops during the same afternoon which were successfully dealt with. The shortage of ammunition now became a problem; during Monday evening whatever reserve ammunition brought in by the RASC had been issued; there was to be no more. Major Digby Tatham Warter, commanding A Company 2nd Battalion, wrote in a 1944 report whilst in a Prisoner of War camp, "The small Bn reserve of ammunition was distributed mostly to troops East of the bridge."[24] The following morning, John Frost ordered that all sniping had to cease, and ammunition had to be conserved for beating off assaults at close quarters. This decision, as John Frost wrote, would have serious consequences:

> This was an advantage to the enemy, in that he could risk a certain amount of movement, and it enabled him to improve his positions in some respects.[25]

One result was that the Germans were able to secure better firing positions which eventually removed British anti-tank guns from the defence and although anti-tank ammunition was available until the end, their crews could not approach the guns in the face of German small arms sniping fire.

It is accepted that this theory may be tenuous based on this fragmentary and unsubstantiated evidence, although it is also suggested the firmer evidence is compelling. Graebner's Monday morning assault was the single most sustained attack that 1st Airborne had faced since arriving at Arnhem Bridge and had clearly expended more small arms ammunition than any other encounters. It was the German troops' devotion to duty and the attack which saw them press on even when their vehicles had been shot from underneath them and forced the British into firing for over two hours.

Viktor Graebner's attack poses various questions. Does it actually matter whether Graebner was given the order to attack or not? The answer is probably not, but an explanation for that aspect of the attack should be established to, possibly, clear a brave man's reputation. Wilfried Schwarz holds the key to whether Graebner was given specific orders to rush the bridge or whether he decided to take a gamble on crossing the bridge on his own initiative as his character may suggest. However, it should be recognized that whatever the reasons behind the assault there is one irrefutable

22   I am grateful to Robert Kershaw for pointing this factor out to me during our conversations.
23   PIAT: Projectile Infantry Anti-Tank.
24   Quoted in Peatling, Robert, *Without Tradition, 2 Para 1941 – 1945*, p.146.
25   Frost, John, *A Drop too Many*, p.222.

fact and that is it certainly occurred. The varying Battalions and units of the British 1st Airborne Division did not reach Arnhem Bridge in the strength it intended in their operational plan, but it would appear that a significant problem was the lack of ammunition brought with the troops. Despite the difficulties quantifying the amount brought to the bridge, even if the barest minimum as specified in the operational orders is considered as arriving, and there is no way of verifying that, Graebner and his troops' sustained action resulted in the entire ammunition reserve being issued after approximately 24 hours with all its attendant consequences. Although the British Sten Gun could use German 9mm ammunition, limited amounts of .303 rounds, required for Lee Enfield rifles and Bren guns, eventually presented profound difficulties. The attrition of 1st Airborne's ammunition was not a goal for the attack, but it clearly had a profound subsidiary effect.

Viktor Graebner's attack was obviously not the sole reason for the British 1st Airborne's eventual failure to hold the bridge, but was a much more significant event in the operation to capture Arnhem Bridge that should be regarded as such.

Bibliography

Primary Sources

The Airborne Archive, Duxford Box 4 F1 2.10.1, Operation MARKET GARDEN.
The National Archive, Kew
WO 171/393 War Diary, 1st Airborne Division, 1st September 1944 to 31st December 1944.
WO 171/592 War Diary, 1st Parachute Brigade, 1944.
WO 171/1511 War Diary, 4th Parachute Squadron, Royal Engineers, 1st March 1944 to 30th September 1944.
WO 219/5137, Report on Operation MARKET GARDEN, 1st Airborne Division, September 1944.

Secondary Sources

Berends, Peter, Een Andere Kijk op de Slag bij Arnhem [Another look at the Battle of Arnhem], Soesterberg, Uitgeverij Aspeky, 2002.
Buckingham, William, Arnhem 1944, Stroud, Tempus, 2004.
Clark, Lloyd, Arnhem, Grangemouth, Headline Review, 2009.
Frost, John, A Drop Too Many, London, Sceptre, 1983.
Harclerode, Peter, Wings of War, London, Cassell, 2006.
Harvey, A.D., Arnhem, London, Cassell, 2001.
Jackson, Robert, Arnhem: The Battle Remembered, Shrewsbury, Airlife, 1994.
Kershaw, Robert, It Never Snows in September, Hersham, Ian Allan, 2004.
—— A Street in Arnhem, Hersham, Ian Allan, 2014.
Middlebrook, Martin, Arnhem 1944, London, Viking, 1994.
Peatling, Robert, Without Tradition 2 Para 1941 – 1945, Barnsley, Pen and Sword, 2004.

Ritchie, Sebastian, *Arnhem: Myth and Reality*, London, Hale, 2011.
Ryan, Cornelius, *A Bridge Too Far*, London, Hamish Hamilton, 1974.

Articles
Zwarts, Marcel, 'SS-Panzer-Aufklärungs-Abteilung 9 and the Arnhem Road Bridge', *Newsletter of the Friends of the Airborne Museum*, June 2003, Newsletter Number 90, Mini-story Number 78, pp.1-12.

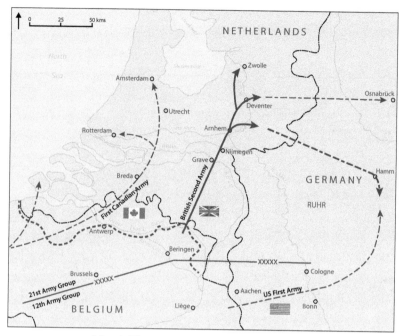

Map 1 The strategic situation, autumn 1944.
(Map drawn by George Anderson © Helion & Company Ltd)

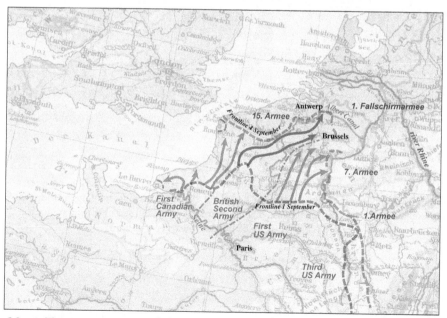

Map 2 The situation in the West on 4 September 1944. (Map © Didden/Swarts collection)

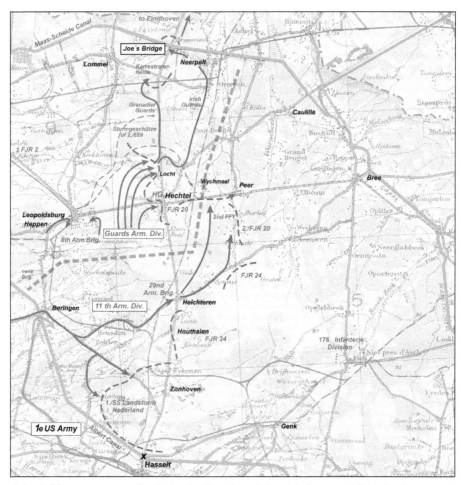

Map 3 The engagements fought by the Guards and the 11th Armoured Division between 6
September (establishing the bridgehead at Beringen, left) and the capture of 'Joe's Bridge' on
11 September (top centre). Chill was responsible for the left-hand sector, Erdmann for the
right-hand one. (Map © Didden/Swarts collection)

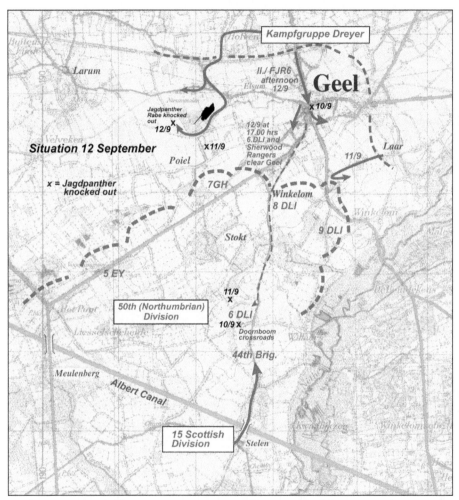

Map 4 The British bridgehead at Geel. Amazingly Kampfgruppe Chill managed to retake the town on 11 September. (Map © Didden/Swarts collection)

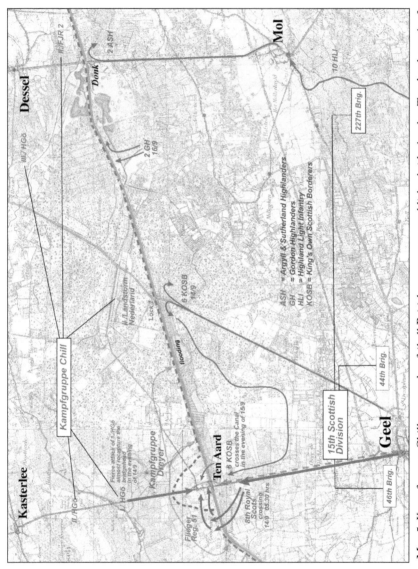

Map 5 Kampfgruppe Chill managed to foil all British attempts to establish a bridgehead at Ten Aard, north of Geel. This seriously frustrated the British plan to protect the left flank of Operation Market Garden effectively.

(Map © Didden/Swarts collection)

D

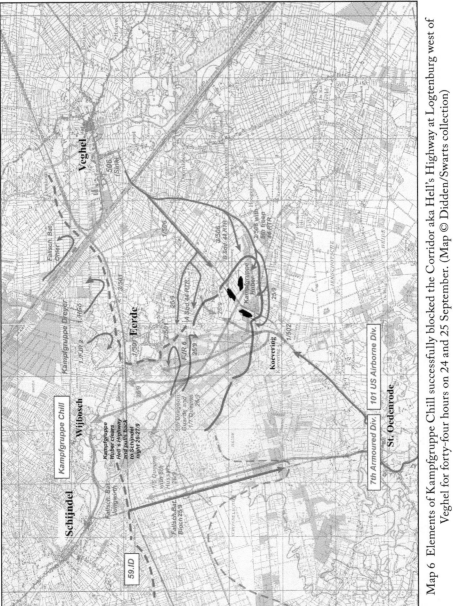

Map 6 Elements of Kampfgruppe Chill successfully blocked the Corridor aka Hell's Highway at Logtenburg west of
Veghel for forty-four hours on 24 and 25 September. (Map © Didden/Swarts collection)

E

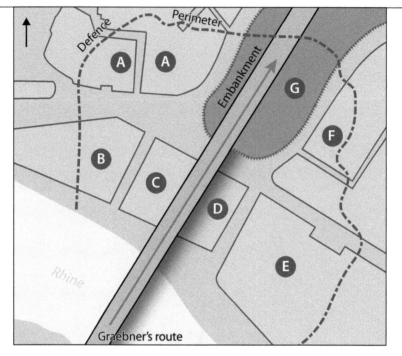

Map Key

Approximate British positions during Graebner's attack during the morning of 18th September 1944. (All 2nd Battalion Parachute Regiment unless stated.)

A
Part of Brigade HQ Defence Platoon
Brigade HQ
2nd Battalion (Batt.) HQ
Part of Mortar Platoon
3rd Platoon RASC
HQ Support Companies
Glider Pilots
2nd Platoon 9th Field Company (Coy) RE
1st Airlanding Anti-Tank Battery HQ

B
Field Security Section and Military Police
Part of 4th Platoon B Coy
B Coy HQ
5th and 6th Platoon B Coy

C
1st Platoon A Coy
Machine Gun Platoon
Anti-Tank HQ

1st Para Squadron RE
A Coy HQ
2nd Platoon A Coy

D
3rd Platoon A Coy

E
8th Platoon C Coy 3rd Batt.
Part of Brigade Defence Platoon

F
Part of Brigade HQ Defence Platoon
RAOC
Part of Brigade Signals Section
1st Para Squadron RE

G
1st Para Squadron RE
C Coy HQ
9th Platoon 3rd Battalion

Map 7 Graebner's assault. (Map drawn by George Anderson © Helion & Company Ltd)

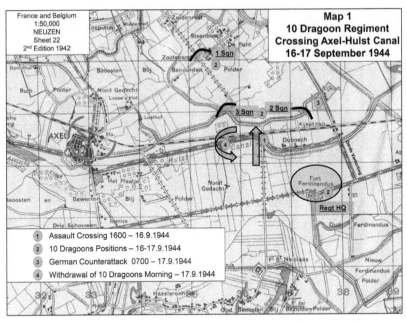

Map 8 10 Dragoon Regiment's crossing of the Axel-Hulst Canal,
16-17 September 1944. (Map © Paul Latawski)

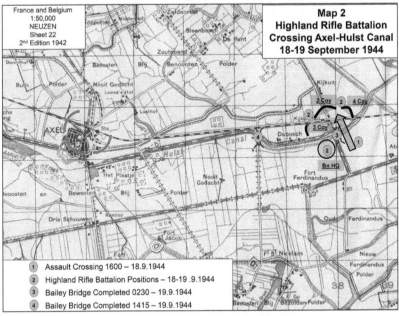

Map 9 Highland Rifle Battalion's crossing of the Axel-Hulst Canal,
18-19 September 1944. (Map © Paul Latawski)

G

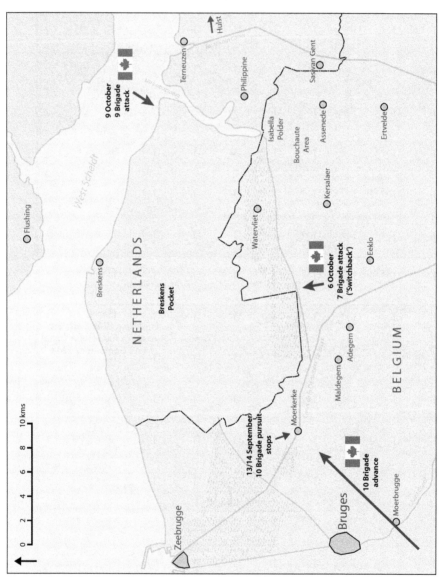

Map 10 Breskens Pocket and 10 Canadian Infantry Brigade Area. (Map drawn by George Anderson © Helion & Company Ltd)

9

Taking the Nijmegen Bridges:
Personal Stories from the Cornelius Ryan Collection

Doug McCabe

I have never seen a more gallant action.
> Lieutenant General Frederick 'Boy' Browning, commander of the
> 1st Airborne Corps, reacting to the crossing by the 504 PIR[1]

The crossing of the Waal River and the taking of the Nijmegen bridge on the part of the 3rd Battalion, 504th Parachute Infantry Regiment have taken their rightful place in all military archives. This action is ranked as one of the great military operations of all time. Corps and Army Commanders galore have congratulated our Regimental commander who has in turn been personally thanked by the King and Marshal Montgomery as the man whose Regiment crossed the Waal.
> Captain Henry Keep, 82nd Airborne Division[2]

There are two main reasons for the huge success of Cornelius Ryan's three battle books – *The Longest Day, The Last Battle* and *A Bridge Too Far*. First, he was a hell of a good writer. Second, he collected personal accounts from hundreds of the people who participated in the events. For *A Bridge Too Far* alone he was in contact with 452 Americans, 426 British, one Canadian, 271 Dutch civilians, 14 Dutch military personnel, 66 Germans and 12 Poles for a total of 1,242 people. Personal files directly or indirectly related to the taking of the Nijmegen bridges total 24 from the 82nd Airborne Division Headquarters, 50 from the 504th Parachute Infantry Regiment, 18 from the 508th Parachute Infantry Regiment, 103 from the 505th Parachute Infantry

---

1   Cornelius Ryan Collection, Mahn Center, Alden Library, Ohio University (hereafter (CRC), Box 108, Folder 1.
2   CRC, Box 103, Folder 2.

Regiment, 67 from the Guards Armoured Division, 33 from Nijmegen civilians and 6 from the 10th SS Panzer Division. These numbers do not include materials from American, British, Dutch and German sources containing such items as after action reports, planning reports, photographs and maps.

The original plan for capturing the highway bridge and possibly the railroad bridge was for the 508th PIR to enter the city along the Waal River, specifically avoiding the built up area of Nijmegen. This was not done and the fight with the Germans through the streets resulted in the repulse of the Americans. The next attempt had to wait for the arrival of British forces. This second attempt would be a coordinated effort using the 508th PIR and British tanks pushing through the city to the southern approaches of the highway bridge while elements of the 504th PIR paddled across the Waal in assault boats while supported by British tanks on the south bank of the river and with aid from British artillery and tactical air forces. This was General Gavin's idea – take the bridges from both ends simultaneously.

General James Gavin, commander of the 82nd Airborne Division, explained to Ryan his planning regarding the Nijmegen Bridges. "General Browning directed that nothing be done to jeopardize the seizure and retention of the high ground around Groesbeek. As I continued to evaluate the situation, I finally decided, about 24 hours before going in, that Lindquist could spare one battalion. I stood with him over a map and pointed out that the way to get the bridge was to go down into the flatland to the east of the city and approach it over the farms without going through the built-up area. We had had considerable fighting in towns in Sicily and Italy, and some in Normandy, and I cautioned him about the dangers of getting caught in streets. One Kraut with a machine gun can hold up a battalion under such circumstances, as we had learned earlier."[3]

Agardus 'Gas' Marinus, 20 year old unemployed resident of Nijmegen, was recruited by Lieutenant Wilde of the 508th PIR. "'They asked us the strength of the Germans around the bridge and if they had any fortifications there. I knew the Germans had pillboxes and when Wilde asked if we would guide them toward the bridge, we agreed to do it.' Leegsma went with one of the three columns in to the bridge. He went with Lieutenant Wilde to a large apartment building on Barbarossastraat. They climbed to the fourth floor and from there could see the bridge. From there the patrol worked its way up closer to the bridge and were only a few hundred yards away from it when the Germans opened up on them with 88 fire and mortars. 'Suddenly I heard the Americans shouting among themselves. They were shouting, 'We're surrounded! They've got us surrounded!' Wilde was on his radio and he suddenly said, 'We've got to fall back.' I did not know what he meant at first. Fall back? We had just got there. I could not understand why. The artillery was certainly a nuisance, but not that much of a threat.' Leegsma says of course he has 23 years behind him 'to make me look wise' but he was certain even then that they could have overpowered the gun crews

3   CRC, Box 100, Folder 3.

and taken the bridge. He learned later they pulled back on orders from Lieutenant Colonel Lindquist."[4]

Colonel Ruben Tucker, commander of the 504th PIR noted, "On the night of 19 September, I was informed by Division Headquarters that the 504th was to make an assault crossing of the Nedu Rhine (should be the Waal) and to establish a bridgehead on the North end of the road and railroad bridges. I was directed to contact British XXX Corps at General Horrocks headquarters where I would meet a British armored commander who would support the 504th crossing with tank fire. The Division directive to me said to make the crossing 20 September, establish the bridgehead and to contact the British armored. This was not a written order but was given to me by Jack Norton, Division G-3."[5]

Tucker told Major Julian Cook, commander of the 3rd battalion to move his unit up closer to Nijmegen and report to Division headquarters. It was there that Cook found Gavin, who told him of the planned assault crossing. "I was dumbfounded. I had to say I didn't have any boats and he said well, you should have been looking around. Then in the process I was told that the bank on the north side of the river where I was going to make the crossing was over 20 feet above the water level. Straight up, like a wall or something. I was wondering what kind of mountain climbing instrument I would be able to get ahold of. It was very disturbing." Once he got to the power station he was able to get a look. "I remember we went half-way up an peeked out of the window and were readily relieved to finally see that the other bank wasn't a sheer cliff or wall 20 feet high above the water and the water looked pretty swift and it looked pretty damn far but the relief, and by that time we also knew that we were going to get the boats from the British."[6]

Lieutenant Colonel Giles Vandeleur, commander of the 2nd Armoured Battalion of the Irish Guards was assigned to cover the 504th PIR. "I did not object to a plan being laid on quickly. Speed is usually of the essence in warfare. What worried me were such things as communication. Colonel Tucker asked me to remain in the command post, which I did. There were two main problems in this. Communications between his troops and the command post, where they sent their demands for targets, and my problem of passing on the targets to my two squadrons of tanks. Being a tank battalion, we had no telephones, only wireless, and all of our wireless sets were jeep-mounted and not portable. I therefore had the problem of being in the command post, receiving target orders and having to relay them to my tanks. The only possible way to do this was to put one of my scout cars with a wireless downstairs and relay the messages to my tanks that way. I asked Tucker to have his people run a cable upstairs from the scout car to me and put us on a telephone link-up so I could talk to Captain Fitzgerald directly and he could relay my orders. This was done eventually, but I seem

---

4   CRC, Box 123, Folder 6.
5   CRC, Box 103, Folder 23.
6   CRC, Box 102, Folder 17.

to recall that the telephone wasn't fully operational for 15 or 20 minutes after the assault was launched. I therefore had to resort to sending messages up and down stairs via a runner, which cost us valuable minutes."[7]

Cousin Lieutenant Colonel J.O.E. Vandeleur, commander of the 3rd Battalion of the Irish Guards, whose tanks were assigned to dash across the highway bridge from the south remembered a conference discussing the two-pronged attack but he felt so rotten due to too many apples and champagne he paid little attention. Shortly afterward he turned command over to the Group and stretched out on the floor in a kitchen. He slept through the entire battle.[8]

Sam Appleby, a Staff Sergeant with 2nd Battalion, 505th PIR reported, "At 1300 hours the company C.O. joined the Battalion Commander and received the attack order on Nijmegen. We were with the British armor and mechanized infantry to attack and cross the Nijmegen Bridge and set up a bridgehead on the North side of the Waal River. The Battalion C.O. had ordered that Company E would lead the assault supported by eight Sherman tanks and six Bren carriers from the Coldstream Guards. Company F would follow with Company D having the mission of attacking the railroad bridge also supported by British armor. Dutch underground assistance was invaluable at this time as they had intimate knowledge of the German dispositions and their latest movements. A hand to hand battle followed in which the 2nd platoon had to literally drive the Germans from their positions with cold steel and grenades. This final assault along with the Company F moving up on our left flank enabled British armor to cross the bridge..."[9]

Private Michael Brilla of 505th PIR noted, "I lost my right eye in the park in Nijmegen right at the bridge and stayed in an old barn for about 10 days before they got me out."[10]

James Megallas, a 1st Lieutenant with H Company of the 3rd Battalion in the 504th, said, "At 3:00 pm in the afternoon our Battalion Commander, Lieutenant Colonel Julian A. Cook, blew a whistle and we charged over the dike towards the river carrying the boats with us. The Germans were well ensconced on the bridge well within the range of small arms fire and from Fort Lent on the other side of the river. This was no doubt the most hectic time I experienced during the war. The strong current played havoc with the course of our very light boats. There were not enough paddles in the boat to maintain a straight course [so] we used the butts of our rifles to gain additional momentum. Halfway across a mortar or artillery shell hit the boat carrying one half of my platoon and the boat sank at that point with no survivals. Several other in my boat were hit by small arms fire. Those of us who were lucky to make it across the river ran into a barrage of automatic and small arms fire from

7   CRC, Box 115, Folder 36.
8   CRC, Box 115, Folder 37.
9   CRC, Box 104, Folder 3.
10   CRC, Box 104, Folder 10.

German-entrenched forces from behind a protective dike. I believe the 3rd Battalion sustained perhaps the largest number of casualties experienced during the war in such a brief engagement."[11]

Jacobus Brouwer, member of the resistance and a worker at the PGEM power plant, said, "I do remember the arrival of great numbers of small boats, which meant that a crossing would take place. Our request to go along was rejected of course. Of the crossing of the big river Waal with its strong current I remember the gruesome picture of many men who got hit and often had to drop the paddles and how the others tried to keep the boats in the right direction. It seemed to go on forever. Those who reached the other side had no shelter to speak of and fired while they ran straight for the rifle and gun positions of the enemy. After the run across the outer marches they rushed up the dike. The gunfire and explosions of shells did not abate when they had disappeared behind the dike. A small number of boats returned with wounded and dead. Again paratroopers crossed the river. Though the enemy shots directly opposite to us had been silenced, the eastern and western gun positions had not and they once more took their toll of the crossing troops who were taken under fire already when they walked in the outer marches on our side. From their firing we gathered that the paratroopers made their way to the northern part of the bridge while firing and that they had to fight for every single metre. The only thing we could do after the first troops had crossed was lending assistance in carrying the returned wounded soldiers to safe places."[12]

Private Jack Bommer, Headquarters Company of the 504th stated "Not proudly, I tell you, I killed boys not over 15 and men over 65 in their foxholes in the crossing of the Maas Waal. It was such an operation, everything went so fast and so hectic, it's hard to explain. Surrender – I saw few of, there wasn't time. I did see old German men grab our M1's and beg for mercy. They were shot point blank.

Such is war."[13]

1st Lieutenant Virgil Carmichael of the 504th recorded, "There was one area near the end of the railroad bridge which contained many, many dead Germans. One of the men is supposed to have counted the bodies and counted over 260. You must remember that we were on an airborne mission... the Germans were concentrating heavily... Lieutenant Wisniewski's death incensed and angered and frustrated us all... the small number of men we were able to transport across the river... the amount of ammunition which we could carry across the river with us could be expended within about three or four minutes so that we were highly vulnerable on the north shore of the river. In these circumstances, our men, who were exceedingly brave, felt that they had been placed in very desperate circumstances and they responded by very aggressively attacking every position from which enemy fire came. The task of taking a large

---

11   CRC, Box 103, Folder 10.
12   CRC, Box 123, Folder 15.
13   CRC, Box 102, Folder 12.

number of prisoners would have imposed a burden on us and would have impeded our actions. Under those circumstances the men in H Company, who largely accumulated around the north end of the railroad bridge refused to take any prisoners, and even though a good many Germans attempted to surrender as they retreated across the bridge, our men shot them down."[14]

In an interview with Lieutenant Richard La Riviere of the 504th he noted that on the way to the railroad bridge they ran right into a bunch of German soldiers who wanted to surrender. He estimated there were 30 to 40 of them, ordinary run of the mill soldiers, but there were only 15 to 20 Airborne – what was left of La Riveiere's platoon and part of I Company – so they shot the Germans. It took about two hours to make their way from the railroad bridge to the traffic bridge. They got to the traffic bridge at about 1700 hours and spent the rest of the night clearing out the Germans. The first British tank came along just as they were getting to the bridge. Two tanks came across and stayed at the north end of the bridge all night.[15]

Professor Frits Van Der Meer of Lent reported, "From time to time the professor and Dr. Huygen would climb a staircase [in the Convent] the Germans did not know about and go into the building upstairs. One evening they saw that a gap suddenly seemed to open up in the barrier which had been thrown up on the Lent side. Small figures were jumping backward and forward. All of a sudden vehicles from the Nijmegen side started to cross the bridge. The bridge had been captured by the Allies! In the background was the dreadful sight of burning Nijmegen. And everywhere there was shooting and projectiles were exploding. 'It was,' the professor said, 'Dante's inferno' all over again."[16]

T. Moffat Burriss, Captain in the 504th, claimed that when the British armor came through their [504's] bridgehead there were two lead tanks which were destroyed by the Germans and the column came to a halt. When they came across the bridge, "it was the most beautiful sight I had ever seen," he said. He concluded, "any time you're on foot and you just have a rifle and armor comes up, you feel like you can lick the world when you see them coming to support you."[17]

"Somewhere around 6 o'clock, I would say, I received orders to go up and see Major Trotter, who was by the bridge," related Sergeant Peter Robinson of the Grenadier Guards. "The Major didn't waste any time. He just said we had to take that bridge and that he wanted me to do it. 'You've got to get across at all costs,' he said. 'Don't stop for anything.' I remember he shook hands with me as I left and said not to worry, that he knew where I lived and would let my wife know if anything happened to me. 'Well, I said,' 'you're bloody cheerful, aren't you sir?'" Once across the bridge, Robinson indicates he did not see any Americans until after driving under the railroad bridge. "We

14   CRC, Box 102, Folder 16.
15   CRC, Box 103, Folder 7.
16   CRC, Box 123, Folder 8.
17   CRC, Box 102, Folder 14.

just got around when I saw some figures duck into the ditches and run. They fired at us and I figured they were Jerries. Just then there were two explosions in front of us. As the dust cleared I caught sight of a couple of the figures in the ditch. From the shape of their helmets I could see they were Yanks. I shouted to stop the firing and stop the tank. I think I said they were our 'feathered friends' the name we used to call the airborne. One of them said to me, 'You're the sweetest guys we've seen in years.'"[18]

Lieutenant A.G.C. 'Tony' Jones, 14th Field Squadron engineer, followed the fourth tank across the highway bridge. "The first thing I saw were six or eight wires coming up over the railings and laying on the footpath. I used a pair of wire cutters to cut them." He walked to a point just north of the second pier from the north bank of the river. There he discovered a set of charges laying alongside the footpath on each side of the road. Obviously, they had been placed there specifically to cut the concrete roadway. "Tony Vivian and I pried a manhole cover up and got down onto the pier and had a look around. I got halfway down when a voice said, 'Do not shoot.' Christ! It was another Kraut! The German spoke excellent English and offered to show me the charges. We went back up on the bridge and into the next pier, which was the second one from the northern end. There were windows in the sides of the compartments and through them you could see the girders. In the girders we found the charges. They were directly under the place where I had found them on the road, just to the north of the pier. When I arrived, there was no evidence of any sort to convince me that anyone had removed any of the charges. Everything was perfectly in order and I couldn't tell you to this day why that bridge wasn't blown."[19]

Major General Heinz Harmel, commander of the 10th SS Panzer Division, was on the north side of the Waal. "I realized that the bridge could not be held when the pressure from the advancing Americans became too strong and they finally took this traffic circle where Euling had formed his defense line. When I gave the order, finally, to blow the Nijmegen bridge I did not contact Bittrich beforehand. There was no time and besides the bridge was prepared for demolition. It was on the 20th, about 18:30 when I first received a report that the British tanks had reached the southern bank of the Waal and that they were starting over the bridge. Almost simultaneously the message reporting this heavy smoke screen arrived. Nothing could be seen but it was obvious that the Americans were making an attempt to cross the river. I was near Lent and I had my driver drive me to the edge of Lent. I crossed the town on foot till I reached the eastern edge. The detonator box was hidden in a garden, well camouflaged. I was waiting for them to reach the middle of the bridge before giving the order. Then I gave it, 'OK let it blow.' It took me a couple of seconds to realize that the charge had not gone off. It was quite a shock I can tell you to expect to see one thing and then to see another. I expected to see the bridge collapse and the tanks to be plunged into the river. But instead I could see the tanks moving forward relentlessly.

18   CRC, Box 115, Folder 22.
19   CRC, Box 115, Folder 12.

They got bigger and bigger, came closer and closer. Then we dove for cover behind a bush."[20]

Corporal Fred Baldino, A Company of the 1st Battalion in the 504th, gets the last words. "We were withdrawn across the Nijmegen bridge and still remember a German soldier on the Nijmegen side of the bridge who was dead and his arm was up in the air and seemed to be pointing across the bridge." Twenty years ago a photograph turned up in a section of the Ryan Collection of that very German soldier.[21]

Perhaps the most controversial result of the taking of the Waal highway bridge was (and is) just who – the Americans or the British – were the first to reach the northern side and disable the explosives. Additional personal stories in the Ryan Collection show rather decisively that the members of the 504th Parachute Infantry Regiment, 82nd Airborne Division were already at the north side of the bridge before British Armour crossed the structure. Besides the interviews in the Ryan Collection, elaboration on the American presence at the bridge comes from the books of T. Moffett Burris (*Strike and Hold*) and James Megellas (*All the Way to Berlin*). Both men and Private James Musa (quoted in Magellas's book) reveal they had their men on and below the north end of the bridge and had killed or captured German defenders before the British tanks attempted their crossing from the south.[22] Additionally, Burris noted the Americans were unsure whether the approaching tanks were German or British and allowed the first two tanks to clear the bridge by several hundred yards. Only when they were sure the vehicles were British did the Americans reveal themselves to the third tank. This is when Burris said, "You guys are the most beautiful sight I've seen in years."[23]

For his part, tanker Peter Robinson of the Grenadier Guards did not know the Americans were on the north side of either bridge until he approached the railroad span having passed the hidden paratroopers at the highway bridge. It is also likely that A.G.C. 'Tony' Jones, the 14th Field Squadron engineer, who followed the fourth tank over the bridge and began cutting wires near where the charges were hidden, did not see any Americans in the fading light. Neither the Americans nor the British could have known that Major General Heinz Harmel, commander of the 10th SS Panzer Division, had ordered the bridge blown when the tanks were at the middle of the span, some minutes before Jones came close to any wires. Finally, as General Gavin pointed out, it was standard operating procedure for paratroopers to immediately sever any communication and demolition wires they encountered. Thus the British and the Germans could not have known the Americans had already cut all wires leading onto the bridge.

20   CRC, Box 130, Folder 11.
21   CRC, Box 102, Folder 11.
22   Burris, T. Moffett, *Strike and Hold: A Memoir of the 82nd Airborne in World War II* (Washington, DC: Brassey's, 2000) p. 122 and Magellas, James, *All the Way to Berlin: A Paratrooper at War in Europe* (New York: Ballantine Books, 2003) pp. 128 and 134.
23   CRC, Box 104, Folder 14.

10

The Defence of the Most High:
The Role of Chaplains in the Battle of Arnhem

Linda Parker

On the 22nd February 1919 the Army Chaplain's department received the accolade of becoming the Royal Army Chaplain's Department in recognition of what the king described as "the splendid work which has been performed by the department."[1] The Great War had been a steep learning curve for the chaplains (3,475 by the end of the war)[2] and despite some criticism in the anti-war reaction in the late twenties and early thirties, it is generally accepted that chaplains had found a role that went beyond both the purely material and purely spiritual and which involved them in a variety of roles, from base camps to field dressing units.

At the beginning of the Second World War, therefore the department was assured of a role which would be regarded as helpful and in many minds, essential. 3,629 chaplains served in the Second World War and their role as in the previous conflict revolved around ministry at base camps and hospitals, in combat and, in far greater numbers than in the first war, they experienced the opportunity to minister in prisoner of war camps. A major difference, was that in the Great War although many chaplains showed great acts of bravery in the front line, they were as a rule discouraged from 'going over the top' with their men (there were of course exceptions to this), in the Second World War they were expected and encouraged to be with their men at every stage of their combat experience. The Revd Paul Abram, an airborne chaplain who began writing a history about airborne chaplains in the 1970s summed up his opinion their role:

> The man who felt out of depth or needed reassurance, especially when they were in action, could not help being inspired by the unarmed chaplain appearing with

---

1   Army Order no. 92, 22nd February 1919, cited by Smythe, *In This Sign Conquer*, p.203.
2   Snape, *God and the British Soldier: Religion in the British Army*, p. 90.

a cheery smile. War is a vile business and the chaplain is a key man in ensuring that soldiers retain their humanity, but to do this he must be with them.[3]

During the war airborne chaplains fulfilled this requirement to be with their men serving with airborne forces in North Africa, Sicily, Italy, Greece, D-Day, Arnhem, the crossing of the Rhine and in Palestine

The Revd Freddie Hughes, chaplain to the 8th Army had managed to achieve a high profile for army chaplaincy in General Montgomery's opinion, hence his famous words: "I would soon think of going into action without my artillery as without my chaplains."[4] Historians of military chaplaincy have debated the use of chaplains as promoters of military morale,[5] but there is no doubt that by 1944 army chaplains had a very real function and regard in the eyes of military commanders

In September 1941 the idea of an airborne division, which had the enthusiastic support of Churchill, started to become a reality with the formation of the First Parachute Brigade, followed by the First Airborne Division. The first two chaplains to be posted to airborne units were a Roman Catholic chaplain, Father Bernard Egan and a Methodist chaplain, R.T. Watkins. They did not initially volunteer to be parachutists. Watkins commented wryly that they were posted as "Penguins" or non-flying birds and their arrival at Hardwick Hall came as a surprise to them. They soon realised that they would do no useful work among the men and officers if they did not participate fully and undergo jump training. Paul Abram commented: "As long as the chaplains did not parachute, Egan and Watkins realised that they did not and could not belong. However freely they might meet and talk to those men."[6] The chaplains had the support of General Browning, commander of the 1st Airborne Division who also realised the importance of chaplains jumping.[7] Egan and Watkins realised that if chaplains waited too long they would be left out of aspects of operational planning. Abram commented: "They felt that they had to know something of a soldier's job so that they would not be out of place in the confusion of an airborne operation... It made the men realise that the chaplains cared for them to the extent that he was prepared to stand in their shoes."[8] They completed their parachute course at Ringway airfield, Manchester on 3rd January 1942.

---

3   Museum of Army Chaplaincy Archives, Airborne Chaplains papers deposited by Rev P R C Abram CVO, 'Lower than Angels', p.ii.
4   Hamilton, *Monty the Field Marshal, 1944-1976*, p. 44.
5   For example Louden, *Chaplains in Conflict: The Role of Army Chaplains since 1914*; Wilkinson, "The Paradox of the Military Chaplain", *Theology*, 1984, p.249; Snape, "Church of England Army Chaplains in the First World War: 'Goodbye to All That'", *Journal of Ecclesiastical History*, Vol. 62, No. 2, April 2011.
6   Abram, 'Lower than Angels', p. 3.
7   Robinson, *Chaplains at War: The Role of Clergymen During World War II*, p. 111.
8   Abram, 'Lower than Angels', pp.3-4.

An example of the role enhancement of chaplains who were able and willing to of being able to jump came when four men died in an accident jumping at Ringway and Watkins, the Lt Colonel and the medical officer were able to each lead a stick on that afternoons exercise to improve morale. Egan and Watkins were breaking new ground and in a way creating the role of an airborne chaplain. In very short time they created the pattern that was to be expected of airborne chaplains subsequently.

Just before the 1st Parachute Brigade left for North Africa to take part in Operation TORCH in November 1942, the senior airborne chaplain, the Revd John Hodgins managed to persuade the Chaplains' Department to allow airborne chaplains to adopt the red beret and also organised the first version of the airborne chaplains' field communion set, a small paten and chalice and two cruets designed to fit in to the web belt. At about this time he also wrote the airborne force's collect based on the book of Malachi, chapter 4, verse 2:

> May the defence of the most high be above and beneath, around and us and within us in our going out and our coming in, in our rising up and in our going down, through all our days and nights, until the dawn when the sun of righteousness shall arise with healing in his wings for the peoples of the world. Through Jesus Christ our lord. Amen.

The parachute padres subsequently saw action in North Africa and Sicily and were parachuted in behind enemy lines with 9 Para on D-Day. Several padres who subsequently served in Arnhem took part in these operations, the Revd G. Pare in Normandy, the Revd R. Watkins in Sicily and Fr B. Egan in North Africa,

Fifteen British chaplains landed at Arnhem. Nine became prisoners of war, one was sheltered by the Dutch until liberation, two died of wounds, and three escaped during Operation BERLIN, the retreat over the River Rhine. Three Polish chaplains landed at Driel and took part in the evacuation over the Rhine. One of these was killed. The situation of the British chaplains was in some ways unique, even for airborne chaplains, as there was no possibility of retreat. They were performing their spiritual and practical duties under constant fire and all showed physical and moral courage, mostly on the front line of battle. Any concerns about role conflict did not appear to have prevented the variety of tasks carried out, taking services, bringing in wounded, tending wounded under horrendous conditions, keeping up morale by material and spiritual comfort, and in some cases directing the course of military action. Denominational issues and rivalries were few. The Revd Maclusky had commented in training, "While one denomination or another might be held most efficacious for man's upward ascent, Church and Chapel, Protestant and Roman Catholic, bow alike all to gravity and fall with equal force."[9] Fr Danny MacGowan was censured by the church on his return for giving Holy Communion to non-Catholics at St Elizabeth's

9   McLuskey, *Parachute Padre*, p. 25.

Hospital, but was unrepentant, considering that he had acted wisely in the circumstances of war.[10]

The plans for the operation did not proceed as expected and the chaplains found themselves in the thick of the battle, often ministering to the wounded and dying in aid posts which formed the frontline of battle, as at Oosterbeek, and becoming prisoners of war. Very few were able to keep to their planned tasks with their units. In the fog of war, some were active in helping in organising action although not bearing arms.

The Revd G.A. Pare wrote an account of his experiences in 'Arnhem Aftermath'.[11] After celebrating Holy Communion on the 17th September, he set out as chaplain to the 1st wing of the Glider Pilot Regiment and travelled in the glider of the commanding officer, Lt. Col. Ian Murray. Also in the same glider was General Urquhart. Pare commented on the way out on the "great fleet of accompanying gliders." After a good safe landing Pare set out to see if any of the gliders who had overshot needed help. He buried a young sapper who had been killed in the landing and eventually found the divisional HQ. He spent the evening visiting the field ambulance. He waited at the drop zone for the second lift due to drop on the 18th at Wolfheze.

At 3 o'clock the second lift landed into heavy opposition and flak. Pare attached himself to a regimental aid post and joined a party with the regimental doctor in two ambulance jeeps sent to find wounded. Having found a group of wounded men and arranged for them to be escorted back to the aid post Pare decided to try and get near the dead and wounded men lying in the open around the crashed gliders. Pare described the action:

> I grasped a Red Cross flag, beckoned to two of the stretcher bearers to follow me with a stretcher and the others to await my signal, and then with a palpitating heart and waving my flag, set out across the open, the two bearers following me. Five of the Gliders were just heaps of ashes, and bodies could be seen at different points stretched out on the grass. I was still wearing my dog collar, and I mentally committed myself.[12]

Finding some alive, Pare signalled to the ambulance jeeps to join him and the wounded were evacuated. However, as soon as the first aid party made it back to the trees a "fusillade of shots rang out." He realised that they had been in the enemy's sights all the time, but fire had been deliberately withheld. Later, Pare realised that the German troops "respected the Red Cross scrupulously."[13] After what he described

---

10   A letter to Paul Abram from Sir John Hackett, 1st December 1971. Museum of Army Chaplaincy Archives, Airborne Chaplains papers deposited by Rev P R C Abram CV.
11   11 Pare, *Arnhem Aftermath*, p.2c.
12   Ibid., pp.11-12.
13   Ibid., p.13.

as a "nightmarish" journey back to the first aid post, Pare spent the night there before moving on to Divisional HQ at the Hartenstein Hotel, Oosterbeek, where he was reunited with many men of his regiment who were dug in around the grounds, beginning to establish a defensive position, and where he was able to consult the Senior Chaplain, the Revd Harlow. That morning he was given the task of burying Major-General Kussin, the Arnhem garrison commander, who had been killed in his car at Wolfheze crossroads. Pare was given two young SS troopers to help him and they buried Kussin, his driver and interpreter, and also managed to bury some British troops, a German soldier and a Dutch civilian. He was able to share out some chocolate and cigarettes with the SS troopers, who were young, hungry and scared.

That afternoon (Tuesday) Pare was witness to the disastrous glider landing and supply drop, "prayers must have come to all our heads as we watched this terrible drama which resulted in many casualties."[14] For the first time he realised that the operation was facing considerable opposition but still placed faith in the eventual appearance of the Second Army. He decided to stay at the field hospital set up at Schoonoord Hotel at the Oosterbeek crossroads. Together with the Vreewijk Hotel and the Tafelberg Hotel, this became the main hospital area and the place where the chaplains felt they could best meet the wounded and minister to them spiritually and practically. Here he met Padre Irwin and had a conversation with him about the merits of wearing a dog collar. Pare advised him to wear one so that the men could identify him as a padre without effort. This Irwin did, but was killed by an exploding mortar shell at the door to a first aid post the following day, Wednesday 20th September.

The hospitals at the crossroads were of course on the front line at this point. The Schoonoord took a direct hit and a R.C Chaplain, Father B.J. Benson, lost his arm. Fr Benson seemed to lose the will to live, as he felt he would not be able to perform the mass without his arm. He died on the 27th September and was buried by Fr Danny MacGowan at St Elizabeth's Hospital. In the course of the next few hours the Germans took control of the crossroads and started evacuating walking wounded, both British and German. However, the hospitals were once again in British hands after few hours and Pare started visiting all the wounded and on Wednesday 20th was able to hold a service on each floor of the hospital. He remembered, "in the evening when the men had been bedded down I went around the wards holding short services. It was helpful to these helpless men and our prayer for relief was heart felt." The situation at the crossroad hospitals was deteriorating as more and more wounded came in and Pare found himself increasingly ministering to dying men, "I remember one unfortunate Scots boy telling me that he was dying and dictating a message to his mother... somehow I was given the power to settle and comfort."[15] On the 23rd the water and food situation was desperate and Pare devised a system of draining off water from the guttering to provide more water.

---

14 Ibid., p.25.
15 Ibid., p. 25.

During Saturday the Schoonoord was now back in German hands, but Pare's routine of visiting and practical help continued as the Germans evacuated the walking wounded and the lines of battle moved across the hospital/hotel area. Pare was invited to go with a German jeep under a white flag and Red Cross flag, to visit St Michael's Hospital near Arnhem where he was able to catch up with Revd Harlow who was awaiting interrogation, before returning to the Schoonoord. Pare was prevented from having a large Sunday service by renewed fighting and shelling in the area but recounts the poignant singing of "Abide with me." The text for his sermon that day was from the Gospel of St Matthew, Chapter 6, "Therefore, take no thought for your life, what you shall eat, or what ye shall drink, nor for your body what you shall put on, Is not the life more than meat and the body more than raiment?" He recalled, "at this particular service, with men stretched out on the floor and a couple of lamps flickering, I really felt the presence of the almighty with his sheltering wings over this place."[16]

Pare fell asleep exhausted on the evening of Monday 25th, still hoping that the sounds of battle outside heralded the eventual arrival of the Second Army. When he awoke it was to the news that the British forces had retreated across the Rhine, leaving the badly wounded in the care of the medics and chaplains. Later in the afternoon he was taken to Apeldoorn, but before he went around the piles of dead British at the back of the Schoonoord, noting down the names of the soldiers in his notebook. On Friday 6th of October he was sent on a hospital train, accompanied by Padre Thorne, which was heading back to Germany. Pare, who had assembled a great deal information that he thought would be useful to the army authorities at home, decided to take the opportunity to escape. After being helped by some Dutch resisters, he ended up being passed from family to family in the guise of Piet Baas, a deaf mute evacuee. He had to wait for liberation by the Canadians in April 1945 before returning home.

The Revd R. Watkins, as we have seen, was a pioneer of airborne chaplaincy. He had been attached to the 16th Parachute Field Ambulance at Sicily, but by 1944 was chaplain to the 1st Parachute Battalion his activities after landing at Drop Zone X show how a chaplain had sometimes to compromise on a strictly pastoral role. The 1st Parachute Battalion took the northern route towards the bridge. In the heavy fighting in the woods between Wolfheze and Oosterbeek he tended the wounded, but in the confusion of the fighting became separated from the main medical unit and gave first aid wherever possible, helped by Dutch civilians. On Tuesday 19th the men of the 1st Battalion were scattered. While the transport officer Lt J. L. Williams coordinated the rearming force, Watkins went on reconnaissance. They seemed to be the only ones trying to restore order and re-group the men. It was at this point that Watkins realised that he was acting as a soldier rather than a chaplain, but continued to play a dual role, taking control and giving orders in the confusion that existed as the British forces retreated to the perimeter. He took a jeep out from St Elizabeth's Hospital to pick up wounded in the gardens and houses in the vicinity and later took some wounded to the

16   Ibid., p. 36.

Schoonoord and visited the HQ at the Hartenstein Hotel where he had a conversation with General Urquhart and caught up with the situation, also briefing the general on the situation at St Elizabeth's Hospital.

Lt Williams' exhausted men and Watkins were assigned to a position on the south eastern part of the perimeter. On Thursday afternoon they were withdrawn from the polder where they had been coming under heavy fire and rendezvoused in the church, where Watkins heard a part of Major R.T.H Lonsdale's address. On Friday and Saturday Watkins used his red cross flag to move freely around the units in his part of the perimeter, and as well as moving wounded into the vicarage, praying and helping raise morale. His freedom of movement allowed him to keep some of the pinned down units in touch with each other. For example, he was able to pass on information that the Guards Armoured Division would probably reach the southern Rhine on the Friday night. Sunday saw fierce fighting and many more casualties arriving at the vicarage aid post. Watkins was with young major when he died and his body was swiftly removed to the garden to make way for another wounded man. This upset him and Abram recalled, "He was filled with hopeless fury that such a man should be reduced to the status of disposable flesh." However, he did not feel he could share this with others, and Abram commented, "Battle is something that a chaplain can share with others, but there are certain aspects which he cannot share, which he must carry alone and which have no place in the military histories."[17]

In preparation for the evacuation on Monday Watkins was given the task of ensuring that every unit and group received their written orders. He arranged that even though wounded were to be left behind, the vicarage was so near the river he could take a group of less wounded men to the boats, and he escorted them across the river. He then returned to collect more wounded, but dawn was breaking and he was not able to. Now stuck on the wrong side of the river and separated from the troops remaining on the north side of the river, he decided to swim across to the south side and joined the men who had been evacuated. Watkins was awarded the Military Cross. His citation read:

> During the entire operation at Arnhem 17th-25th September 1944 Padre Watkins conducted himself with considerable fortitude and dash. Operating within the divisional perimeter he made himself responsible for carrying information from commander to commander invariably through intense shell and mortar and always when the need was greatest. His endless tending of the wounded under fire, and his continued organising of their evacuation to dressing stations, often made possible by his untiring personal effort and example, afforded an unparalleled example to all ranks. His demeanour throughout, his unfailing courage and

---

17   Abram, 'Lower than Angels', p. 98.

his complete disregard for his own safety guaranteed the morale of the whole force which never wavered in the least.[18]

The activities of the Revd Selwyn Thorne form a different but complementary picture of the chaplain's role at Arnhem. He landed by glider, attached to the Light Regiment Royal Artillery and on landing joined the advance on Arnhem reaching the area of the Concert Hall in Oosterbeek-Lang on Monday. Here the regimental aid post was set up in the old vicarage, the house of Kate ter Horst. At first they only dealt with minor casualties, as the badly wounded could still be evacuated to the hospitals set up at the Oosterbeek cross roads. But as the perimeter formed and then shrunk, the post was overcrowded with serious casualties and from the Wednesday onward was under fire. It became so full that it was only possible to reach the wounded by walking on the handles of the stretchers.[19] The dead were piled up outside and Thorne managed to bury 14 men despite gunfire on Saturday 23rd. Thorne gave Kate ter Horst, who was helping in any way she could, his bible in English and asked her to read the 91st psalm to the groups of the wounded, beginning with the words, "He that dwelleth in the secret place of the Most High /shall abide under the shadow of the Almighty" and ending with the verse 7, "A thousand shall fall at thy side/ and ten thousand at thy right hand/ but it shall not come by thee."

Thorne was described as being "Small, neat and quiet"[20] and "a model of calm and meticulous neatness."[21] He simply got on with his job of assisting the doctor, acting as an orderly and fulfilling his priestly functions to the wounded and dying showing God's love at all times He was willing to any job that came along, including cleaning the lavatory. Another side to his character was shown when a Tiger tank approached the vicarage and prepared to shell. Bombardier Bolden and Thorne rushed out, flourishing a Red Cross flag and yelling to the commander to cease fire as it was an aid post. The tank commander agreed as long as the machine gun on the roof was removed. Although Kate ter Horst and Watkins remembered that there was not a machine gun. Thorne distinctly remembered giving the order for it to be brought down, as he reckoned that was the only military order he had ever given. On an occasion when Watkins returned to the hospital rendered unrecognizable with mud and blood, Thorne quietly set him down, calmed him, and cleaned him up. When the evacuation commenced, Thorne stayed with the wounded and became a prisoner of war.

Other chaplains had varied experiences. The senior chaplain Bill Harlow was at the Oosterbeek crossroads when the cease fire to evacuate the wounded was arranged and despite already having been a prisoner of war in the western desert, agreed to accompany the 150 walking wounded into captivity. Fr B Egan had been chaplain to the

---

18   van Roekel, *The Torn Horizon, The Airborne Chaplains at Arnhem, p.*65.
19   Abram, 'Lower than Angels', p. 100.
20   Ibid., p. 101.
21   van Roekel, *The Torn Horizon, p. 55.*

2nd Parachute Battalion since 1942, and had been through the North African, and Italian campaigns with them, being awarded the Military Cross in March 1944. Egan got through with the 2nd Battalion to the bridge and helped the two doctors in the aid station set up in a cellar at the northern end of the bridge. As the battle raged on Tuesday and Wednesday the cellar became crowded with injured British and German troops. Egan left the relative safety of the cellar to visit soldiers in other hideouts around the north end of the bridge and was hit while returning to the aid post. He was wounded in the back and legs and on surrender of the bridge was captured and taken to Municipal Hospital and then became a POW at Mühlhausen until its liberation in 1945.

Fr Danny MacGowan parachuted in with the 4th Parachute Brigade and was responsible for members of the Royal Army Medical Corps. After a disastrous jump in which he had become entangled with his kit bag, he went with his unit to search for any injured members of their brigade. After spending the night at Wolfheze, he went the next day to the Schoonoord crossroads. On Thursday morning he was taken prisoner at Oosterbeek and then ministered to German and British Patients at the Municipal Hospital and at St Elizabeth's Hospital. While there on the 24th September he received reports that there were still wounded British soldiers hiding in the woods and set out, hitching a lift with a German jeep to Oosterbeek, where, right under the noses of the Germans, he proceed to roam the battlefield for 14 days. His impeccable appearance, red beret and Red Cross arm band apparently gave him free passage and he was able to make contact with hiding airborne troops, giving them rations and passing on the details of where they were hiding to the resistance. At the hospital he took part in a mock funereal which succeeded in smuggling spare small arms to the resistance, "The two blanketed corpses were three Bren guns, a German light machine gun, some grenades, and several magazines of ammunition."[22] On 16th October, he escaped with Lt Col Harford, only be to recaptured few days later, within a few yards of the Rhine. He was awarded a Military Cross and the last paragraph of his citation reads:

> [He] even contrived to make contact with unwounded members of the division who were lying up and leave food and other necessities. He was frequently under fire from our own guns and aircraft whilst doing so. The material services provided by this priest to the wounded were great. But far more important was the example he gave of cool, calculated courage and devotion to what he saw his duty.[23]

Daniel MacGowan was unable to settle to parish life in the post war Catholic Church and left Holy Orders, becoming a probation officer and marrying and having a family.

---

22   Abram, 'Lower than Angels', p. 113.
23   Quoted by van Roekel, *The Torn Horizon*, p. 114.

The Revd W.R. Chignell, after arriving by glider with the 2nd Glider Pilot Regiment, was mentioned in despatches for his time in the defence of the perimeter, and also found himself being taken up with the militaristic aspects of his situation, "It is awful how bloodthirsty one gets and how soon one loses all sense of the peace and Christian charity when one is in the thick of battle."[24] With Watkins and Padre Rowell, Chignell was one of three chaplains who made it back over the Rhine. When they returned it was to empty camps, where the survivors were gathered. They took memorial services on the first Sunday they were back which was two weeks from when the first lift had taken off.

The Revd E.L.Phillips landed with the 3rd Battalion who ran into fierce opposition. Taking cover in a three storey house on the Utrechtseweg, he found himself on a floor below the room where Brigadier Urquhart had taken cover. Managing to get to St Elizabeth's Hospital, he was captured and became a prisoner of war. The Revd A.C.V. Menzies headed towards Arnhem with the 156th Parachute Battalion after landing but was taken prisoner on Tuesday 19th. The Revd R.F. Bowers landed badly, breaking his ankle, but carried on helping at the dressing station and taking some burial services, but the next day was captured taking some wounded troops to the Wolfheze dressing station. Another padre who was captured quite early on in the battle was The Revd A.A. Buchanan, but not before he had played his part in the care of the wounded in the grounds of the municipal museum and taken part in the military action by giving an order for 7th platoon to occupy a house opposite the museum. The Revd G.J. Morrison landed at Reijerskamp farm on 17th September and found himself with the troops defending the perimeter at Krugerstraat. When the order came for evacuation over the Rhine he stayed with the wounded and was taken prisoner of war.

The Polish Independent Parachute Brigade parachuted into the Driel area, south of the Rhine on 21st September, and had three padres on their strength. Father Mientki was attached to Brigade Headquarters dealing with the many wounded, Father Bendorz found the local Roman Catholic parish priest, who gave him a crucifix in thankfulness for their liberation. Father Misiuda crossed the Rhine with the 3rd Battalion to support the British troops, despite the efforts of his commanding officer to prevent him. After digging in to support of the Border Regiment, they received orders on the 25th September and Misiuda was killed while escorting a groups of walking wounded towards the river.

Abram, in his introduction to his draft history of airborne chaplains, said that the main jobs of a chaplain were to pray and to care, "Soldiers expect their chaplain to pray, they know instinctively that he is an intermediary between themselves and God... Sometimes the prayer through the liturgy, at other times informally with a small group. Most often the prayer is offered in the quiet of the chaplain's heart." The

---

24   Chignell, 'Diary of the Battle of Arnhem', quotation from diary excerpts reproduced in van Roekel, *The Torn Horizon*, pp. 73-75.

second is to care, "This is most obvious in times of tragedy. At such time men look to him for hope and encouragement... it is Christ who can speak through him." In Abram's opinion, "The only way he can do this is by giving himself without reserve."[25] The history of the chaplains at Arnhem demonstrates the extent to which they lived up to the ideals of the military chaplaincy.

Select Bibliography

Archival Sources

Museum of Army Chaplaincy Archives, Airborne Chaplains papers deposited by Rev P R C Abram CVO. Typescript, 'Lower than Angels', 1971.
Ohio University, the Cornelius Ryan Collection of World War II Papers, G.F. Pare, 'Arnhem Aftermath'.

Books

Hamilton, Nigel, *Monty the Field Marshal, 1944-1976*, London: Sceptre, 1987.
Louden, Stephen, *Chaplains in Conflict: The Role of Army Chaplains since 1914*, London: Avon Books, 1996.
McLuskey, J.F., *Parachute Padre*, London: SCM Press, 1951.
Robinson, A, *Chaplains at War: The Role of clergymen During World War II*, London: Tauris, 2012.
Smythe, John, *In This Sign Conquer*, London: Mowbray, 1968.
Snape, M.F., *God and the British Soldier: Religion in the British Army*, Woodbridge: The Boydell Press, 2008.
van Roekel, Chris, *The Torn Horizon, The Airborne Chaplains at Arnhem*, Oosterbeek: t'Horst and Van Roekel, 1998.

Journals

M.F.Snape, "Church of England Army Chaplains in the First World War: Goodbye to'Goodbye to All That'", *Journal of Ecclesiastical History*, Vol. 62, No. 2, April 2011.
Alan Wilkinson 'The Paradox of the Military Chaplain', *Theology*, 1984.

---

25   Abram, 'Lower than Angels', p. iii.

11

A Medical Bridge Too Far:
Medical Support to Operation *Market-Garden*, September 17-26, 1944

Stephen C. Craig, DO, MTM&H FRCP (Ed.)
Colonel, Medical Corps, US Army (retired)

Operation Market-Garden was the failed attempt of Allied airborne and armored forces to secure a crossing of the Lower Rhine River at Arnhem from 17-26 September 1944.[1] At the end of those nine days the American 82nd and 101st Airborne, British 1st Airborne Divisions, and 1st Polish Parachute Brigade had sustained tremendous casualties [See Table].[2] These figures reflect hard fighting, but could also suggest an

---

1   References to military operations in this paper were taken from the following sources: Charles B. McDonald, *The Siegfried Line Campaign* (Washington, D. C.: Center for Military History, 1990); Cornelius Ryan, *A Bridge Too Far* (Norwalk, CT: Easton Press, 1974), Geoffrey Powell, *The Devil's Birthday: the Bridges to Arnhem 1944*, (New York: Franklin Watts, 1984), Phil Nordyke, *All American, All the Way: The Combat History of the 82nd Airborne Division in World War II* (St. Paul, MN: Zenith Press, 2005), and Leonard Rapport and Arthur Norwood, *Rendezvous with Destiny: History of the 101st Airborne Division* (Old Saybrook, CT: Konecky & Konecky, 1948); Robert Kershaw, *It Never Snows in September* (Surrey: Ian Allen, 2008); John Frost, *A Drop Too Many: A Paratrooper at Arnhem* (Mechanicsburg, Pennsylvania: Stackpole Books, 2008); and Roy E. Urquhart, *Arnhem* (Barnsley, South Yorkshire: Pen And Sword Books, Ltd., 2008).
2   Casualty figure estimates and total troop strengths derived from National Archives and Records Administration, College Park, Maryland, File 319.1-2, Box 385, *Annual Report of Medical Department Activities*, ETO 1944, 82d Airborne Division and *Annual Report of Medical Department Activities*, ETO 1944, 101st Airborne Division, [Hereafter cited as *Ann. Rpt. Medical 82nd* and *Ann. Rpt. Medical 101st*, respectively] and RG 331, E65, Box 2, *Operation 'Market' Report on Airborne Medical Services*, Deputy Director of Medical Services, First British Airborne Corps, [Hereafter cited as *Rpt Abn Med Services, DDMS*]; Public Record Office, Kew, AIR 37/1214, *Airborne Operations in Holland, September-November 1944*, First Allied Airborne Army; McDonald, *The Siegfried Line Campaign*, pp. 145, 159, 198n, 206; Ryan, *A Bridge Too Far*, p. 599; Powell, *The Devil's Birthday*, p. 10; Nordyke, *All American, All the Way*, p. 420; Rapport and Norwood, *Rendezvous with Destiny*, pp. 269, 313, 271; and Urquhart, *Arnhem*, 181.

Allied medical planning and execution failure. A review of pertinent documents at the National Archives in Washington and London, medical histories, and personal memoirs of the participants indicate that such a suggestion is more apparent than real. Successful airborne assaults – and their medical support – are dependent upon adequate planning, efficient execution resulting in a secure and consolidated tactical perimeter, and rapid reinforcement by robust conventional forces. This paper will review British and American medical operations in this battle in light of medical capabilities, planning, execution, and the German battlefield response.

The Plan

At the time newly promoted Field Marshal Sir Bernard L. Montgomery conceived *Market-Garden* German forces had been in full retreat from the Normandy hedgerows since late July 1944. The Allies were quite optimistic that this state of affairs would continue. Montgomery had taken Antwerp on 4 September. General Eisenhower was eager to clear German defensive positions along the Scheldt Estuary so port facilities at Antwerp could be secured, thereby shortening the Allied logistical chain in preparation for a broad front drive into Germany's industrial Ruhr and Saar Valleys. Field Marshal Montgomery contended that his 21st Army Group could not seize Antwerp unless his northern flank, the Lower Rhine River, was secure. To achieve this, he advocated a rather daring combined airborne and ground attack. Three simultaneous airborne assaults – code named *Market* –just north of Eindhoven and at Nijmegen by the US 101st Division commanded by Major General Maxwell D. Taylor and the 82nd Brigadier General James M. Gavin, and at Arnhem by British Major General Roy Urquhart's 1st Division and Major General Stanilaw Sosabowski's Polish Parachute Brigade were to seize bridges along the 64 miles of road from the Belgian border to Arnhem. As these landings took place the British XXX Armored Corps, commanded by Lieutenant General Brian Horrocks, with the VIII and XII Corps protecting its flanks, would initiate the ground attack – code named *Garden* – rolling up the road, across the bridges, and into Arnhem in 48 hours to secure and consolidate this northern thrust. General Eisenhower agreed the Lower Rhine had to be secured and approved the plan on 10 September.[3]

Montgomery believed if the northern thrust was successful he would also be in a position to completely flank the Siegfried Line, dash east across the northern German plain to Berlin, and, hopefully, end the war. For logistical reasons Eisenhower disagreed, but this strategy was not lost on the Germans. With the fall of Antwerp Hitler ordered Field Marshal Walther Model, Army Group B commander, to stop retreating and begin to consolidate his remaining forces in the s'Hertogenbosch-Arnhem-Wesel

---

3   Montgomery was promoted on 1 September 1944. Bernard Montgomery, *Memoirs of Field Marshal Montgomery* (New York: World Pub., 1958), p. 242. Dwight D. Eisenhower, *Crusade in Europe* (New York: Doubleday, 1948), p. 307.

area and building fortified positions along the Albert Canal in preparation for an Allied thrust.

The State of Military Medicine, 1944

By the time of Operation *Market-Garden*, British and American military medicine had achieved a level of efficiency and efficacy that was second to none. The injured soldier entered a medical treatment and evacuation system that provided state-of-the-art medical, surgical, psychiatric, and rehabilitative care from point of injury to general hospitals in the rear.

Progress in resuscitation and shock therapy – such as volume expanders and whole blood transfusion – general, orthopedic, neurologic, and maxilla-facial surgical specialties, and psychiatry that came out of World War I developed and matured largely in the civilian medical community during the interwar years. These years also saw the development of synthetic sulfa-based anti-microbials, synthetic anti-malarials, and a host of vaccines, such as those against tetanus, chlolera, plague, yellow fever, and louse-borne typhus. However, when Hitler's armies marched through Europe in 1939–40 these pharmaceuticals were just being tested in, and adapted to, the military field medical environment.

The military medical establishments of Britain in 1940 and America in early 1942 were not prepared to support a highly mobile army in the field. Both scrambled to fill the medical ranks with qualified physicians and surgeons and create more efficient field medical assets. Britain's field ambulances (FA) were made lighter and more ambulance cars added, the field dressing station (FDS) and forward surgical unit were established,[4] and her well organized and functional Army Transfusion Service – the only one in any army at the time – established mobile field units.[5] The American field medical establishment, much of which existed only on paper due to interwar budgetary constraints, was organized for a small army and mobilized using First World War experience. Through trial and error the Auxiliary Surgical Group, a US Corps level asset, came to work in conjunction with a field hospital platoon, rather than with the division clearing station, creating a mobile priority surgical hospital.[6]

Sadly, from the disaster at Dunkirk through the North Africa and Sicily campaigns, both armies also had to relearn medical lessons from the First World War. New drug and vaccine prophylaxis modalities did not replace well organized and disciplined

---

4   F. A. E. Crew, *The Army Medical Services, Administration*, vol. 1 (London: Her Majesty's Stationery Office, 1953), pp. 466–7.

5   F. A. E. Crew, *The Army Medical Services, Administration*, vol. 2 (London: Her Majesty's Stationery Office, 1955), pp. 372–421.

6   John Boyd Coates, ed., Activities of the Surgical Consultants, vol. 1, *Surgery in World War II* (Washington, D. C.: Office of the Surgeon General, 1962), pp. 304–6, 308–10; Clifford L. Graves, *Front Line Surgeons: A History of the Third Auxiliary Surgical Group* (privately published, 1950), pp. 70–1.

field sanitation and hygiene. Treating psychiatric casualties at the front immediately after injury with the expectation of a return to full duty significantly reduced manpower loss. Sulfonamides, plasma, and new methods of anesthesia could not replace adequate debridement, whole blood, and ether anesthesia in the treatment of the severely wounded soldier.

By spring 1944 British and American airborne forces had been tested and proven in North Africa, Sicily, and Italy. Providing medical support to these forces required creativity and innovation in organization, mission requirements, and equipment.[7] Regimental medical detachments, field ambulances, and medical companies had to be personnel heavy and equipment light, yet have a self–sustaining capability for 72 hours. While many of the nuances of airborne medical support had been worked out prior to the Normandy invasion, the scattered night landings of American paratroopers on the Cotentin Peninsula highlighted the requirement for putting adequate numbers of personnel and transportation on the drop zone simultaneously to collect casualties and retrieve equipment and supplies. The campaign also demonstrated the unreliability of air resupply to airborne medical assets.[8]

By summer 1944 allied airborne medical care at the division level included the routine use of whole blood and oxygen for resuscitation, triage, and surgical exploration of the abdomen and chest supported by state-of-the-art anesthesia techniques, positive-pressure breathing apparatus, and anti-microbials [sulfas and penicillin]. Psychiatric injuries were well understood and treated at the division level by psychiatrists according to the proximity, immediacy, and expectancy protocol.

Medical Planning

American medical planning for *Market* benefitted from airborne operational experience in the Sicily and Normandy campaigns. Planners addressed the medical challenges – personnel, equipment and supplies, and transportation – inherent to airborne operations that had to be self-sustaining for 48–72 hours. Too few personnel in, and dispersion of, these detachments, exhaustion of supplies, and lack of transportation for casualty collection or retrieval of supplies, were major flaws during the Normandy drop. Immediate casualty collection and treatment on Dutch drop zones would be performed by larger regimental medical detachments accompanied by lightly equipped medical company elements.[9] These regimental medical detachments jumped heavily loaded with a variety of rigger manufactured kit bags which carried everything from

7   Allied parachute operations were concerned with physical training and wastage, optimum conditions for troops during air transit, development of a system for collection and treatment of battle casualties on the drop zone, equipment preparation and delivery. Crew, *Army Medical Services, Administration*, pp. 506–7.

8   *Ann. Rpt. Medical 82nd*, Annex I, "Medical Service in Operation Neptune, p. 8; *Ann. Rpt. Medical 101st*, pp. 3–4.

9   *Ann. Rpt. Medical 82nd*, pp. 3–4; *Ann. Rpt. Medical 101st*, pp. 1–3.

bandages and tape to plasma.[10] Additional equipment and supplies were pushed out the doors or released from under the aircraft during the drop. These assets would be reinforced by more medical company elements in glider landings which immediately followed the parachute insertion. American planners decided that for *Market* the glider lift accompanying the paratroops would be allocated enough gliders to carry collecting detachments from the medical company, and two jeeps with trailers loaded with equipment and supplies for each regimental detachment. The initial glider lift would also carry surgical assets. Two teams from the Third Auxiliary Surgical Group accompanied by two field hospital platoons from the 50th Field Hospital per division would establish an initial forward surgical element near the drop zone then as soon as practical move into civilian facilities in their area of operations.[11] Planners took no chances ensuring the adequacy of the follow on package to arrive on D+1. This second echelon package would not only would deliver the remainder of the medical companies and field hospital platoons to support the surgeons, but enough equipment and supplies that 121 gliders were required to transport it all.[12]

The British were confident that three field ambulances transported in 24 gliders on D-Day and D+1 with daily air re-supply would be adequate to support the Arnhem force until a medical supply depot could be established at Deelen Airfield north of Arnhem. British surgical support resided in the Parachute and Air-landing Field Ambulances organic to their airborne divisions. Surgical and nursing personnel were increased in these. Once Arnhem was liberated the 16FA would be established at St Elizabeth's Hospital, the 133FA at Municipal Hospital, and the 181FA would maintain a hospital in the brigade area. An exhaustion center under the direction of the corps psychiatrist was to be established as soon as possible.[13]

The Polish Parachute Brigade would be supported by three medical detachments and one field ambulance. Once initial casualties had been collected and treated, Polish medical assets were to move into the Catholic boy's school in Driel.[14]

---

10 Michael De Tretz, *The Way We Were: Doc McIlvoy and his Parachuting Medics* (Wezembeek–Oppem, Belgium: D-Day Publishing, 2004). This is a well-illustrated and well-composed dedication to one 82nd Airborne physician and his medics. Their exploits during Normandy and Holland are undoubtedly representative of many of their colleagues in the 1st British, and 82nd and 101st American Airborne Divisions.

11 *Ann. Rpt. Medical 82nd*, Annex III, "Medical Service in Operation Market," p. 1; *Ann. Rpt. Medical 101st*, p. 5; National Archives and Records Administration, College Park, Maryland, File 319.1–2, 50th Field Hospital, ETO 1944-1945, "Report of the 50th Field Hospital," p. 1.

12 Six CG-4A gliders carried two trucks, two trailers, and fifty-two men. *Ann. Rpt. Medical 101st*, p 5.

13 *Rpt Abn Med Services, DDMS*, pp. 838–40; Niall Cherry, *Red Berets and Red Crosses: The Story of the Medical Services in the 1st Airborne Division in World War II* (Renkum, Netherlands: R. N. Sigmond, 2000), pp. 14–17, 84–5.

14 *Rpt Abn Med Services, DDMS*, pp. 885-87.

The equipment and supplies for all airborne medical assets included tables, lamps, instruments, and packing materials all designed for airborne insertion. They included sulfonamide and penicillin antimicrobials, ether anesthesia, oxygen and intermittent positive pressure breathing equipment, portable radiographic apparatus, as well as whole blood and blood plasma. All of these critical elements would be resupplied to *Market* forces by air for the first five days.[15] This was robust, state-of-the-art health care adapted to modern combat operations which allowed surgeons – for the first time in history – to deal successfully with severe chest and abdominal wounds directly on the battlefield.

Medical planning for *Garden* was composed of four parts. First, the 14 Field Dressing Station and 24th Evacuation Hospital, positioned at Bourg Leopold and Hechtel, Belgium respectively, were to receive the early casualties.[16] Evacuation would be by ground until airheads were established at Nijmegen and north of Arnhem. Second, ambulances would move with the van of the column, make initial contact with the 101st at Zon, and evacuate casualties south as required. These ambulances would then move on to Nijmegen, establish contact with the 82nd and set up casualty clearing station (CCS) and field dressing station capability there in conjunction with civilian assets. Third, 163 FA and 3CCS were to move with high priority up the road to reinforce and resupply field ambulances with the 1st Division and Polish Brigade in Arnhem and assist with collecting and evacuating patients to the rear. And fourth, the ground operation was also to resupply US medical assets at Eindhoven and Nijmegen.[17]

However, by the time the first C-47 aircraft took off on Sunday 17 September, Lieutenant General Sir Frederick Browning's demand for thirty-six gliders to fly his staff to Nijmegen and Lieutenant General Louis H. Brereton's lack of transport aircraft and adamant support for crew rest set the stage for mission failure. Rather than risk tired air crews making a second flight the same day, Brereton let the US 82d and British 1st Divisions shoulder the risk of not having sufficient fire power and

---

15   National Archives and Records Administration, College Park, Maryland, File 319.1.2 (82nd ABN Div), 382–Med-03, 307th A/B Medical Company, "Report of Unit Operations, HOLLAND," p. 4. [Hereafter cited as "Report of Operations," 307th Med. Co.]; *Rpt Abn Services, DDMS*, p. 840. Blood may have been supplied by ground to 82nd and 101st medical units by Detachment B, 152nd Station Hospital, Tréviérs, France. For the operational history of the 152nd Station Hospital see Douglas B. Kendrick, *Blood Program in World War II*, Medical Department, United States Army (Washington, D. C.: Office of the Surgeon General, 1964), pp. 498–513, 515–22. Soldiers with matching blood types and 'universal' donors, those soldiers with blood type O, could also be a source of blood if supplies ran short.

16   Crew, *Army Medical Services, Campaigns*, v4, pp. 293-294; National Archives and Records Administration, College Park, Maryland, File 319.1–2, 24th Evacuation Hospital, ETO, "Annual Report 1944," p. 2.

17   Crew, *Army Medical Services, Campaigns*, v4, pp. 294–5; *Ann. Rpt. Medical 101st*, p. 6; "Report of Operations," 307th Med. Co., p. 2.

medical support for the first 24 hours of battle. Furthermore, anti-aircraft positions around Arnhem cowed planners into putting the 1st Division eight miles northwest of their objective at Renkum Heath.[18]

Medical Execution in the Face of German Response

In the clear sunny afternoon British and American paratroopers floated down onto broad Dutch heaths relatively well consolidated, with the majority of personnel and equipment undamaged, and virtually unopposed, and Horrocks' XXX Corps rolled across the Belgian-Dutch border headed for Eindhoven.[19]

Immediate casualty clearing and treatment was accomplished on all drop zones, albeit slower and with more difficulty in the 82nd area for lack of personnel, surgical support, and transportation.[20] Surgical assets from the 101st began set up tents and two operating tables near the drop zone by late afternoon. Early in the evening they established themselves in the civilian hospital at Zon.[21] From Renkum Heath the 1 British Parachute Brigade raced down three converging avenues of approach to the Arnhem bridge: Lieutenant Colonel D. Dobie's First Battalion down Amsterdamseweg [Leopard], Lieutenant Colonel J. A. C. Fitch's Third Battalion down Utrechtseweg [Tiger], and Lieutenant Colonel John Frost's Second Battalion along the Lower Rhine river [Lion]. The 181FA, tasked to establish a Brigade area hospital, set up a Dressing Station near the railway station in Wolfheze by 1630 hours. The 16FA, which accompanied Second Battalion down Lion route, set up two operating teams assisted by Dutch medical staff at St Elizabeth's Hospital by 2200 hours. Battalion Regimental Aid Posts set up in houses along each route evacuated wounded to St Elizabeth's.[22]

Late in the evening of 17 September, all 1st Division units had been ordered to move closer to Arnhem. Division headquarters was established in the Hartenstein Hotel on the Utrechtseweg in Oosterbeek. Assistant Director of Medical Services, Colonel Graeme M. Warrack, directed the 181FA, commanded by Lieutenant Colonel Alfred Marrable, to move into the Schoonoord Hotel, 150 yards east of Division headquarters. However, the Schoonoord did not provide sufficient space to treat and hold an increasing number of patients, and Warrack had 181FA surgical teams set up in the Tafelberg Hotel, 200 yards south on Pietersbergweg.[23]

Over the next 48 hours the timidity of *Market-Garden* planners would be compounded by a competent and violent, if not wholly rapid German response. The

18 Ryan, *A Bridge Too Far*, pp. 129, 190; Powell, *Devil's Birthday*, pp. 235–6; *Ann. Rpt. Medical 82nd*, p. 1.
19 *Ann. Rpt. Medical 101st*, pp. 5-6; "Report of Operations," 307th Med. Co., p. 1; Kershaw, *It Never Snows*, pp. 74–5, 78, 137.
20 *Ann. Rpt. Medical 82nd*, p. 1-2; "Report of Operations," 307th Med. Co., p. 1.
21 *Ann. Rpt. Medical 101st*, p. 6.
22 Cherry, *Red Berets and Red Crosses*, pp. 87–91.
23 Graeme Warrack, *Travel By Dark After Arnhem* (London: Harvell Press, 1963), p. 23.

German forces collected under Field Marshal Walther Model's Army Group B were a hodge-podge of *Kriegsmarine* and *Luftwaffe* personnel, Paratroops, Infantry, Training Battalions, Engineers, and Armor. However, the officer and senior non-commissioned officer leadership was competent and experienced, and they improvised battle groups quickly. Initially, the Germans fought a rearguard action, striking XXX Corps at Valkenswaard and destroying bridges at Zon, which required the construction of a Bailey Bridge for the Allies to cross, and later at Best. These actions delayed XXX Corps by 12 hours at Valkenswaard and by 24 hours at Zon. Lieutenant General Wilhelm Bittrich, commander of the *SS II Panzer Corps*, directed the *9th Panzer* to Arnhem to crush the British assault and the *10th Panzer Division* to Nijmegen to check the ground force advance.[24]

In Arnhem on D+1, 1st Division began to feel resistance from this capable and determined enemy. St Elizabeth's hospital was captured temporarily by the Germans early that morning, however mounting casualties at all fourteen regimental aid posts continued to be evacuated downtown due to a lack of radio communications. The Germans allowed surgical teams to continue operating, but a large number of other Royal Army Medical Corps (RAMC) personnel went into captivity before British control was regained.[25]

Heavy fog over airfields in England delayed second echelon paratroopers and gliders until mid-afternoon. American personnel and equipment in the 54 gliders carrying the remainder of the 326th Medical Company arrived at Zon without loss.[26] The entire 307th Medical Company of the 82nd Division landed in good condition in sixty-seven gliders near Groesbeek, but two trailers and equipment were never recovered. A clearing station, composed of a clearing element, a platoon of the 50th Field Hospital, and the two auxiliary surgical teams, was set up two miles west of Groesbeek and casualties from the day before were moved to this location. Before the day was out 82nd casualties were in surgical hands just four to six hours after wounding, an injury-to-treatment time that was considered very good under existing conditions. A relatively successful air re-supply of both US divisions followed the gliders, however, these drops were never adequate to the needs of the medical units. "Many items requested," wrote 82nd Division Surgeon, Lieutenant Colonel William C. Lindquist, "were either not dropped or not recovered ... though in practice adequate care of the casualties was not seriously affected. Once evacuation began all supplies were available and British sources insured adequate supplies for the remainder of the

24 Kershaw, *It Never Snows*, pp. 80, 83, 95.
25 Kershaw, *It Never Snows*, pp. 147–8; Powell, *Devil's Birthday*, pp. 104–5; Cherry, *Red Berets and Red Crosses*, pp. 92–3; Warrack, *Travel by Dark*, p. 24.
26 National Archives and Records Administration, College Park, Maryland, 3101-MED-03, 326th Airborne Medical Company, "After Action Report," p. 1. [Hereafter cited as "After Action Report, 326th Med Co."].

Campaign. The generosity and whole hearted cooperation of all the British agencies left nothing to be desired."[27]

The 1 Air Landing Brigade, 4 Parachute Brigade, reserve section of 181FA, and the entire 133FA – dropped 8 miles from drop zones on Ginkel Heath – followed in support of 1st Division, but the Germans hotly contested these landings, shooting paratroopers as they descended, and large numbers of casualties were sustained.[28]

Early on Tuesday, September 19, XXX Corps crossed the river at Son. Sixteen ambulances were sent forward and evacuated 450 casualties to the 24th Evacuation Hospital at Hechtel.[29] Traffic moving north precluded further evacuation until the following day when elements of the 326th Medical Company made contact with 101st units at Veghel.[30] At this point in the battle plasma, whole blood, oxygen, tetanus toxoid, sulfonamides, and penicillin were available in sufficient quantity to both the British and Americans. Standard surgical procedures were employed in the treatment of all cases. By noon British armor had linked up with Gavin's paratroops. Two to three hundred 82nd casualties were evacuated south, but German counterattacks on the road between Veghel and Nijmegen soon precluded further evacuation.[31] Fierce fighting for the control of this road would earn it the epithet, Hell's Highway.

At the same time in the Wolfheze–Oosterbeek–Arnhem area, the 181FA Reserve and 133FA joined their colleagues in Oosterbeek to consolidate medical care against strengthening German resistance. Regimental aid posts were set up in any available building, such as the home of the ter Horst family next to the Oosterbeek Old Church, and with continually increasing casualties medical care expanded into the Vreewijk Hotel, Paasberg School, and other surrounding buildings in Oosterbeek.[32]

A determined British attack on Tuesday forced the Germans to fall back. British control of St Elizabeth's was regained for a time allowing a number of wounded and some medical officers to get in. However, by mid-afternoon the British, without air, artillery, or armor support, had been fought to a standstill by Model's well-equipped soldiers without linking up with Frost's battalion at Arnhem Bridge. At 1600 hours, the heavy equipment for the Polish Brigade landed by glider. Resupply flights dropped containers, but regrettably most fell into German lines. By evening German forces are once again in control of the area around St Elizabeth's. Once stabilized British

27   "Report of Operations," 307th Med. Co., pp. 1, 4; *Ann. Rpt. Medical 82nd*, Annex III, "Medical Service in Operation Market," quote p. 1.
28   Cherry, *Red Berets and Red Crosses*, pp. 96-97; Ryan, *A Bridge Too Far*, pp. 369–70; Powell, *Devil's Birthday*, pp. 108–9.
29   Crew, *Army Medical Services, Campaigns*, v4, p. 295.
30   "After Action Report, 326th Med Co.," p.1.
31   Crew wrote that 300 82nd casualties were evacuated, but the 82nd Division surgeon reported 200. Crew, *Army Medical Services, Campaigns*, v4, p. 295; *Ann. Rpt. Medical 82nd*, Annex III, "Medical Service in Operation Market," p. 1.
32   Cherry, *Red Berets and Red Crosses*, pp. 100-101, 116; Urquhart, *Arnhem*, pp. 125–6, 151; Powell, *Devil's Birthday*, p. 188.

wounded were evacuated to William III Barracks in Apeldoorn and then interned in Germany.[33]

On Wednesday, 20 September, while fog and rain kept the Polish Brigade in England, Field Marshal Model was well on his way to gathering a total of 82,000 fighting men from *Fifteenth Army* still holding positions in western Holland and units arriving from Germany.[34] He began a counteroffensive with the goal of controlling the highway to Arnhem, thereby isolating each airborne element so they could be destroyed piecemeal. This counteroffensive marked the turning point in the battle, both from a combat action and a medical care delivery perspective, as Allied forces contended with a strengthening enemy reaction. In Oosterbeek–Arnhem the Germans overwhelmed Frost's force at the bridge and begin to squeeze what was left of 1st Division from east, north, and west. They captured the Schoonoord and Tafelberg Hotels, and the Paasberg School. Here the confusion of battle was so great that lightly wounded British soldiers were able to receive treatment guarded by the enemy and then surreptitiously slip away to their line to fight again.[35] This came to an end later in the day, and although the Germans allowed the field ambulances to continue caring for the nearly 1,000 British, German, and Dutch casualties in Oosterbeek, the majority of RAMC personnel became prisoners-of-war.[36] The Pietersburg Hotel was taken over to relieve crowding and St Elizabeth's continued to receive and treat casualties. In all of these hospitals British surgeons, assisted by Dutch physicians and nurses, used Dutch equipment, supplies, and whole blood.[37]

At Nijmegen, the Germans hammered at the 82nd Division perimeter, and continually jabbed at the 101st along Hell's Highway from Zon to Uden. Remarkably however, with the Germans attempting to cut that road at various points between Zon and Nijmegen from 20–24 September, Allied medical support in this area was actually strengthened and consolidated. In the rear, just south of Eindhoven, the 48 FDS, 49 Forward Surgical Unit, and 7th Field Transfusion Unit opened another surgical hospital. One auxiliary surgical team was sent from the 326th Medical Company to the 50th Field Hospital platoon at Veghel, dividing 101st surgical assets to handle casualties more efficiently.[38] The 82nd clearing station were settled in relative comfort

33 Powell, *Devil's Birthday*, pp. 122–4; Cherry, *Red Berets and Red Crosses*, p. 103.

34 Ryan, *A Bridge Too Far*, p. 452.

35 Powell, *Devil's Birthday*, pp. 187–8; Stuart Mawson, *Arnhem Doctor* (Stapleton, United Kingdom: Spellmount, 1981), pp. 89-91; Urquhart, *Arnhem*, p. 113. Mawson's personal account of the conditions and events at the Schoonoord Hotel and its environs is a moving story and one that ties together many other medical accounts.

36 Cherry, *Red Berets and Red Crosses*, pp. 112–13.

37 Daniel Paul, *Surgeon at Arms* (New York: W. W. Norton, 1958), pp. 4–5. Alexander Lippman-Kessel, RAMC was a surgeon with the 16FA at St. Elizabeth's hospital and wrote under a pseudonym.

38 "After Action Report, 326th Med Co.," p. 2. Surgical assets with the 82nd could have been split as well, but the tactical situation did not require it. *Rpt Abn Med Services, DDMS*, p. 875.

in a Jesuit school, re-modeled by the Germans into a 'Hitler Mother' obstetrical hospital, in the south end of Nijmegen, and 3CCS and 35 FDS opened in the Jonker Bosch Hospital also in Nijmegen.[39] Dutch physicians and nurses assisted in all of these hospitals throughout the campaign knowing very well that should the Allies be defeated, German retribution would be severe.

German attacks along the Hell's Highway, especially between St. Oedenrode and Veghel and just north of Veghel, intensified interrupting 101st and 82nd casualty evacuation from 25–26 September and 18 September until the end of the battle, respectively.[40] British medical elements, especially the critical 163FA and 3 and 10CCS, continued to move with difficulty toward Nijmegen. These assets included psychiatrist and venereologist to deal with the minor sick, exhaustion, and venereal disease cases. The British seaborne medical element arrived at Valberg, just northeast of Nijmegen, and joined 163FA.[41]

By Thursday, 21 September, Lieutenant General Browning was aware the 1st Division was in extremis north of the Lower Rhine. He determined to send the British 43rd (Wessex) Division in a rescue attempt. The 163FA and 3 and 10CCS were positioned at Driel to support the assault on the evening of Friday, 22 September.[42] Also on Thursday the weather finally allowed a portion of the 1 Polish Parachute Brigade to make an afternoon drop near Driel and lend support to the British 43rd Division. Early on the 22nd the Polish field ambulance established a dressing station in Driel as planned.[43] That evening British and Polish forces made a vain attempt to relieve Urquhart leaving the 43rd Division severely pummeled and the Polish command nearly destroyed for no gain whatsoever.

By this time in Oosterbeek, Urquhart, unable to reach the bridge, had drawn his remaining forces into a tight perimeter. Frost and 2nd battalion were captured. Over the next four days the Germans squeezed them from west, north, and east. The Medical Dressing Station (MDS) crossroads as it was known soon became part of the eastern perimeter where the battle ebbed and flowed. Remnants of 133 and 181FAs cared for nearly 1,500 casualties in the MDS crossroads area as the Germans continued to press against the perimeter. Medical care went on, whether controlled by the British or Germans, hindered by a lack of supplies and equipment, and in the end personnel.[44] These buildings were repeatedly hit by tank and mortar fire, which

39   *Ann. Rpt. Medical 82nd*, Annex III, "Medical Service in Operation Market," p. 1; Crew, *Army Medical Services, Campaigns*, v4, p. 295.
40   *Ann. Rpt. Medical-101st*, p. 6; *Ann. Rpt. Medical 82nd*, Annex III, "Medical Service in Operation Market," p. 1.
41   Crew, *Army Medical Services, Campaigns*, v4, pp. 295, 297.
42   Ibid., 297.
43   "Report of Senior Polish Medical Officer," *Rpt Abn Med Services, DDMS*, pp. 888–9.
44   Mawson commented that as early as 21 September everything was "running short: rations, ammunition, morphia, blood for transfusion, penicillin, and other drugs and medicaments, bandages and dressings." Mawson, *Arnhem Doctor*, p. 77.

wounded medical personnel and re-wounded patients, made evacuation to this area was hazardous and surgical care difficult.[45]

Late on the evening of Saturday, 23 September elements of the Polish Brigade attempted a crossing of the Lower Rhine to take in medical supplies and join the Oosterbeek battle. Intense German resistance halted the attempt and increased the workload of the Polish medical company.[46]

Short of supplies, space, food, and water, regimental aid posts were directed to hold on to their patients as better care was no longer possible at the dressing stations. Of the original fourteen aid posts only five were still functioning, including the home of the family ter Horst which contained 300 British wounded.[47] Lieutenant Colonel Arthur T. Marrable, commander 181FA and medical officer in charge at Schoonoord, also persistently resisted German efforts to fortify the Schoonoord and demanded Geneva Conventions be observed. The Germans noted that their wounded were being properly cared for as well and agreed to remove their soldiers, provide food and medical supplies, and remove the seriously wounded.[48] However, even if well intentioned, the Germans in Holland did not have sufficient quantities, or quality, of supplies to provide much assistance. Moreover, it appeared that many of the British wounded would not survive until relief forces broke through.

On Sunday morning, 24 September, Colonel Warrack explained to Major General Urquhart in the Hartenstein Hotel that the facilities had become completely inadequate, supplies of morphia, penicillin, and bandages were nearly gone, and performing surgery had become impossible; only minimal medical care was now possible. Although he had some "qualms of conscience," Warrack was convinced that captivity in German hospitals would be more humane for these casualties and proposed a temporary ceasefire to accomplish the task.[49] Urquhart agreed so long as the Germans understood that Warrack was a "doctor representing [his] patients and not an official emissary from the division."[50] Warrack was taken to General Bittrich's headquarters by Captain Egon Skalka, the Divisional physician and Commanding Officer of the *SS–Sanitäts Abteilung* [Medical Detachment] in the German area, where he gained the German commander's agreement to the temporary cease fire. Later that afternoon nearly 500 wounded were evacuated through the German lines.[51]

45   Mawson, *Arnhem Doctor*, pp. 80-81, 101; Warrack, *Travel By Dark*, p. 30; Urquhart, *Arnhem*, p. 112.
46   "Report of Senior Polish Medical Officer," *Rpt Abn Med Services, DDMS*, p. 888.
47   Cherry, *Red Berets and Red Crosses*, pp. 114–15.
48   Mawson, *Arnhem Doctor*, pp. 135–36.
49   Warrack's description of the truce and evacuation of wounded to German care is quite low key and modest in the extreme. Warrack, *Travel By Dark*, pp. 40–5, quote p. 46.
50   Urquhart, *Arnhem*, quote p. 154.
51   Warrack noted that "at least 300 casualties had been evacuated." Warrack, *Travel By Dark*, quote p. 46; Urquhart, *Arnhem*, pp. 156–8 ; Cherry, *Red Berets and Red Crosses*, pp. 117–19.

That same evening Urquhart informed his staff, including Warrack, that Horrocks' XXX Corps was not able to relieve them. A decision had been made for their withdrawl south of the river the following night.[52] The seriously wounded, medical staff, and chaplains would have be left behind.[53] A number of lightly wounded would also remain to provide an appearance of battle strength until the withdrawal was complete. At 2100 hours on Monday evening an echeloned, ferry-borne evacuation began with assistance from British guns around Nijmegen. The 163FA examined all returning troops and the 130FA from XXX Corps collected, treated and evacuated casualties during the operation. Nearly 2,300 soldiers managed to get across; 244 medical personnel and chaplains remained behind with 1,600–2,000 wounded.[54]

On Tuesday, 26 September, Warrack met with the Germans, conducted rounds on all aid posts and dressing stations, and assisted in removing all casualties into hospital at William III Barracks in Apeldoorn. Operation "Market" was over and Oosterbeek had fallen silent.[55]

Conclusion

Urquhart remembered Browning commenting to Montgomery as they planned Market-Garden that they "may be going a bridge too far."[56] The operation and that expression have come to represent overconfidence in one's own resources and abilities, with too little consideration of one's adversary.

Allied planners largely ignored the offensive and defensive capabilities of the Germans in Holland. From a medical planning and execution perspective it was also a bridge too far. Decisions above division level, which failed to take an enemy response into account, set the stage for medical failure: 1) British 1st Division landed too far from objectives, 2) second lift on D+1 to all 3 divisions would be in time, 3) British 1st and US 82nd did not have full medical capability, that is casualty collection and surgery, for the first 24 hours, and 4) adequate resupply and ground and air evacuation depended on securing assigned objectives rapidly and British XXX Corps arriving in Arnhem in 48–72 hours.[57]

Although the German response was considered slow and not well organised it was enough to significantly impact all of these Allied decisions. The delaying actions south of Arnhem put the British XXX Corps permanently off schedule, delayed dependable resupply and ground evacuation, and put all US 82nd surgical assets at risk during the second glider lift. However, those less than optimal reactions also allowed both

---

52   Urquhart, *Arnhem*, pp. 160,163, 165–7; Warrack, *Travel By Dark*, p. 47.
53   Urquhart, *Arnhem*, p. 168.
54   Cherry, *Red Berets and Red Crosses*, p. 122; Urquhart, *Arnhem*, p. 181; Warrack, *Travel By Dark*, p. 50.
55   Warrack, *Travel By Dark*, p. 52–7.
56   Urquhart, *Arnhem*, p. 4.
57   Ryan, *A Bridge Too Far*, pp. 131–3, 159–60.

American divisions to secure immediate objectives and establish a perimeter within which medical assets could function in relative security.

In Wolfheze–Oosterbeek–Arnhem, essentially the area where German forces had marshaled to make a stand, larger numbers of enemy troops and armor made an immediate impact on British attempts to seize objectives and provide medical care. The 16FA achieved its objective, but was almost immediately captured. The 133 and 181FAs did not achieve their objectives, the Municipal Hospital and the Deelen Airfield, respectively. Germans controlled Deelen Airfield and soon all the drop zones thereby rendering resupply depot or air-evacuation impossible.

A relatively secure perimeter which allowed treatment and holding of wounded, the fact that US medical planners initially brought large amounts of supplies and equipment with them, and a re-supply and evacuation route, fragile as it was, allowed American medical support to be successful in spite of the German counterattack.

Not so north of the Lower Rhine. The German response precluded evacuation and dependable resupply either by air or ground. It had captured the majority of British medical facilities halfway through the battle, putting large numbers of medical personnel in captivity and established a conduit to prison for all British wounded. Moreover, the main British medical facilities extending south from the MDS cross-roads became the leading edge of the battlefield by 20 September. Fighting armor in an urban environment, the British took greater casualties and were less able to care for them than their US colleagues. From the standpoint of a medical operations planner it was a military medical failure of the first order.

Yet when one reads any of the accounts which discuss British medical care failure is not a word that comes to mind. The leadership and technical skills – both tactical and clinical – the devotion to duty, unflagging courage, and loyalty to patients and colleagues displayed by Colonel Graeme Warrack, Lieutenant Colonels Arthur Marrable and E. Townsend, commander of the 16FA, surgeons such as Alexander Lippman-Kessel and Clifford, all the regimental medical officers, RAMC enlisted personnel, and dozens of nurses and orderlies, as their world literally collapsed upon them, were decisive in saving the lives of hundreds of British, German, and Dutch casualties. A medical bridge too far perhaps, but a medical battle far from lost.

Table 1 Operation *Market* Casualty (Killed/Wounded/Missing) Rate Estimates, 17-15 September 1944

Unit	Strength	Casualties	Casualty Rate/1000/Day	Casualty Average/Day
US 82nd	9,856	1,430	16	159
US 101st	9,348	2,140	25	235
British 1st	10,005	6,977	77	775
Polish 1st	750	383	128	96

12

Exploiting "Market-Garden"?
Operation "Gatwick" – The Offensive That Never Was[1]

Stephen Ashley Hart

Given the extensive historiography on the September 1944 Allied "Market-Garden" offensive and its immediate aftermath, one would expect that historians have extensively analysed every aspect of this subject. There is, however, one exception to this. Operation "Gatwick", the planned follow-up offensive to "Market-Garden", has been virtually forgotten in the historiography of the 1944–45 North–west Europe campaign.[2] There is a simple explanation for this; "Gatwick" was never implemented, as subsequent events overwhelmed the intent to initiate it. But the failure to launch "Gatwick" conceals the underlying reality that the 21st Army Group devoted extensive planning and preparatory activity for the offensive over a protracted five-month period.[3] Indeed, it could be argued that "Gatwick" was indeed eventually implemented in that the 8 February 1945 "Veritable" offensive represented the eventual realisation of the "Gatwick" operational concept, albeit with key modifications. Thus, from its first public announcement of the "Gatwick" concept on 27 September 1944,

---

1   The chapter's title is a play on words related to Evan Montagu, *The Man Who Never Was*, (London, Evans Brothers, 1953), an account of Operation "Mincemeat", the famous 1943 Allied deception scheme related to the planned invasion of Sicily.

2   The planned offensive toward Krefeld (otherwise known as "Gatwick") is mentioned but twice in the British Official History of the campaign, and even then without mentioning its operational code-name; Major L.F. Ellis, *Victory in the West* II (History of the Second World War, U.K. Military Series), (London, HMSO, 1968), pp.80, 98. It was then ignored until this author's *Montgomery and "Colossal Cracks": The 21st Army Group in North-west Europe, 1944–45*, (Westport, CT., Praeger, 2000), pp.87, 122, 145-47, 167, 175. Even renowned scholars of "Market-Garden" attending the conference where these ideas had their first public articulation – the University of Wolverhampton's September 2014 "Highway to the Reich" Conference – confessed to not even having heard of "Gatwick".

3   Peculiarly, the planned operation was designated Operation "Gatwick" by the Second British Army but termed "the Krefeld operation" or the offensive "toward Krefeld and the Ruhr" by Montgomery; why this was so remains unclear.

after the stalling of "Market-Garden", the 21st Army Group took 155 days to initiate the realisation of the "Gatwick" intent. This chapter aims to put right the unjustified dearth of discussion of Operation "Gatwick". It will do this by examining the origins of the operation and its underlying intent. The chapter will then examine the extensive efforts undertaken by the 21st Army Group to plan, prepare for and execute the offensive. These examinations will be delivered within an analysis of the unfolding wider operational, strategic and political contexts in which these activities occurred.

The "Gatwick" concept revolved around the notion of mounting an assault from the south-eastern flank of the 21st Army Group front during autumn 1944. The assault was to be launched from the bridgeheads recently established east of the Rivers Waal and Maas (Meuse) in the Groesbeek–Boxmeer region of the south-eastern fringes of The Netherlands. This assault aimed to strike south-eastward toward the Wesel–Krefeld area in the north-western fringes of the Rhineland. The main objective of the operation was to secure one or more bridges over the River Rhine in the Emmerich–Wesel region. The planned operation thus constituted the principal element in any 21st Army Group advance toward the north-western fringes of the Ruhr. This thrust toward the northern Ruhr should be seen in the context of Montgomery's ideas on a possible double envelopment of the northern and southern fringes of the Ruhr, Germany's principal industrial region, to be mounted by the 21st Army Group and elements of the 12th United States Army Group.

In turn, Montgomery's s concept of securing the Ruhr, whether by encirclement or not, formed a key part of his so-called concentrated narrow-thrust strategy – a concentrated offensive eastward into Germany from the entire sector north of the Ardennes, to be spearheaded by the 21st Army Group.[4] The debate over whether to follow Supreme Allied Commander Eisenhower's preferred broad-front approach rather than Montgomery's so-called narrow-thrust strategy raged across the Allied higher commanders during autumn 1944. This complex disagreement about theatre strategy, which fused associated divisions over command, operational art, inter-Allied politics, and logistical priorities, formed the wider context within which 21st Army Group operations developed.[5] Any activity concerning Operation "Gatwick" unfolded within these wider operational and theatre-level strategic considerations.

---

4   Bernard Montgomery, *The Memoirs of Field Marshal Montgomery*, (London, Collins, 1958), pp.265-87.
5   This issue has been exhaustively examined in (all *passim.*): Nigel Hamilton, *Monty* III, (London, Hamish Hamilton, 1986); David Irving, *The War Between the Generals*, (London, Allen Lane, 1981); Russell Weigley, *Eisenhower's Lieutenants*, (London, Sidgewick & Jackson, 1981); see also Ellis, *Victory* II, pp.3-4, 9-10, 16-20, 77-80, 84-94, 165-69, 199-203. For key archival sources, see Liddell Hart Centre for Military Archives, King's College, London, [LHCMA], Field Marshal Alanbrooke Papers 14/26-33, and Imperial War Museum [IWM], Montgomery-Simpson Correspondence, both *passim*. For the historiography of this debate, see: G. E. Patrick Murray, *Eisenhower versus Montgomery: The Continuing Debate*, (Westport, CT., Praeger, 1996).

Another facet in these inextricably intertwined issues was that, as Montgomery later admitted, "ever since the Battle of Normandy had been won, my eyes had been fixed on the Rhine and the Ruhr."[6] Montgomery fully recognised that once the key industrial region of the Ruhr had been captured, Germany could only continue the war for another 4–8 months. Indeed, one could argue that this aspiration – even fixation – formed the heart of the "Gatwick" concept.

The Context Within Which the "Gatwick" Concept Emerged

The "Gatwick" concept crystallised during September 1944 within a particular and peculiar wider operational and strategic context. After the stunning defeat of the German Army in Normandy secured during August 1944, the higher command echelons of the 21st Army Group were pervaded with an atmosphere of optimism, or more accurately over-optimism. The common perception was that the German Army was all but defeated and that "the end of the war in Europe was most certainly 'within reach'."[7] Even the Supreme Allied Headquarters (SHAEF) was infected to some degree with this sentiment. The army group's senior commanders believed that if their forces could resume the offensive, the fragile enemy front could be decisively broken. In the wake of this, rapid exploitation to the north, north-east or east would allow Anglo-Canadian forces to secure an intact bridge over the Rhine. These commanders hoped that if this was achieved, Eisenhower – having recognised the operational implications of this triumph – would bestow logistical priority to the 21st Army Group.

This bestowal of logistical priority would allow Montgomery's forces to mount their concentrated "narrow thrust" offensive into the North German Plain to deliver the final strategic defeat of Germany, with the American forces largely relegated to secondary efforts. Operation "Market-Garden" was the first attempt to realise this operational scheme to secure an intact Rhine bridge. The existence of this over-optimistic, eastward-looking, Ruhr-fixated atmosphere provided the wider context in which the 21st Army Group made its decisions concerning "Gatwick". It is hard to pin down precisely the impact of this atmosphere but it is nonetheless clear that 21st Army Group planning and decision-making unfolded differently than that during the earlier Normandy battles. Particularly, the caution and tight control so evident in earlier planning seemed more muted during September–October 1944.[8] Perhaps most significantly, this optimistic atmosphere seemed to endure throughout the autumn, despite an unfolding battlefield situation that gave plenty of evidence to suggest that this paradigm no longer, if indeed it ever, reflected the realities on the ground. The

6   Montgomery, *Memoirs*, pp.274, 297.
7   Montgomery, *Memoirs*, p.266.
8   Hart, *Colossal*, pp.79-127.

German forces had to some extent already recovered the cohesion lost in the wake of the debacle in Normandy.

The existence of this optimistic atmosphere during autumn 1944 was crucial because it connected with the British politico-strategic aspirations that underpinned the campaign.[9] Senior British commanders recognised that if their forces suffered devastating losses defeating the Germans in North-west Europe, British influence on post-war Europe would be diminished: Britain had not just to win the war but also the ensuing peace as well.[10] Montgomery's dispute with Eisenhower over theatre strategy and command reflected his determination "to maintain" the campaign on "lines most suitable to Britain,"[11] because "it was of no avail to win the war strategically if we lost it politically."[12] The maintenance of Britain's international influence necessitated that British forces played a prominent role in the prosecution of the vital North-west Europe campaign; Britain's post-war political prestige rested in part on the glory that her soldiers won on the battlefields of Europe.[13] The 21st Army Group, however, scarcely possessed sufficient forces to achieve such prominence. However, if Britain maintained such a high profile, with the 21st Army Group spearheading the Allied onslaught against the German Army in the West (*Westheer*), its forces would incur severe casualties. These partly irreplaceable losses would compel the army group to disband formations, thus reducing its already meagre peak strength of 16 divisions.[14] The fewer the divisions with which the British army emerged at the war's end, the weaker its influence on Europe would be in the face of the growing might of two nascent superpowers. Indeed, by 1945, the American forces deployed in the theatre outnumbered the British Commonwealth's forces by three to one. Montgomery's generalship sought to achieve a high British military profile while paradoxically avoiding the casualties that went with such a profile.[15]

The longer the war lasted, moreover, the smaller would be the British effort in North-west Europe comparison with that of the ever increasing American forces. Thus the British remained more interested in achieving victory quickly than the Americans, since "the British economy and man-power situation demanded victory

---

9   Hart, *Colossal*, pp.62-67.
10   Dominick Graham and Shelford Bidwell, *Coalitions, Politicians and Generals: Some Aspects of Command in Two World Wars*, (London, Brassey's, 1993), p.209.
11   R. W. Thompson, *Montgomery the Field Marshal: A Critical Study*, (London, Allen and Unwin, 1969), p.20.
12   Montgomery, *Memoirs*, p.332.
13   Hamilton, *Monty* III, p.158.
14   For a discussion of the dimension of losses, replacements and casualty conservation within 21st Army Group operations, see Hart, *Colossal*, pp49-77.
15   Churchill, for example, "greatly" feared "the dwindling of the British Army" in France "as it will affect our rights to express our opinion upon strategic ... matters", The UK National Archives [TNA] WO216/101, folio 21, Message, Churchill to Montgomery, 12 December 1944. see also Hart, *Colossal*, pp.62-67.

in 1944: no later."[16] The 21st Army Group, however, possessed insufficient resources to achieve early victory by itself, unless the Germans collapsed unexpectedly. Equally, Montgomery could not afford to sustain the heavy casualties that would be incurred in a British-dominated attempt to secure swift strategic victory over the *Westheer*. Should such a full-blown British offensive effort fail, Montgomery's emasculated army group might be reduced to a secondary role in the theatre, left merely to observe America's defeat of the *Wehrmacht*.

The launching of Montgomery's atypically bold "Market-Garden" offensive is more intelligible in this context. The operation reflected his attempt to exploit an apparently unique fleeting battlefield opportunity. With the *Westheer* seemingly all but defeated, now was the time for the 21st Army Group to gamble that its forces might secure for Britain a prominent profile in an Allied victory over the Germans achieved during 1944.[17] Despite the failure of the "Market-Garden" gamble, the "Gatwick" concept represented an attempted continuation of this risk-embracing mentality. If the Germans remained uncohesive to a degree, and if the "Gatwick" offensive could swiftly secure a bridgehead over the Rhine, Montgomery might secure logistical priority for his proposed "narrow-thrust" offensive astride the Ruhr into the north German plain. If the enemy could not rapidly recover, this gamble might just deliver the crucial knock-blow to end the war, without the army group's forces being devastated in the process. The 21st Army Group's implementation of the "Gatwick" concept was, therefore, inextricable interlinked with the connected issues of theatre strategy, operational art, command, inter-Allied politics, and logistical priorities.[18]

The Genesis of the "Gatwick" Concept

The first obvious articulation of the ideas that formed the basis of the "Gatwick" concept emerged during early September 1944. The concept revolved around the intent to secure an intact crossing of the Rhine in the area of the north-western fringes of the Ruhr. At this time plans were mooted suggesting the employment of airborne forces to capture by surprise coup-de-main an intact Rhine bridge. These were but a small part of many hastily thrown-together plans for airborne drops to support the rapid ground advance developed during this period. One such plan was Operation "Comet" outlined on 3 September 1944, which proposed the seizure by air assault of the Rhine Bridge at Arnhem.[19] This formed a possible element in Second British Army's ground advance on the Rhine between Arnhem and Wesel, ordered in Directive M523 and

---

16 Montgomery, *Memoirs*, pp.270-71; Arthur Bryant, *Triumph in the West*, (London: Collins, 1959), p.366

17 Such an opportunity presented "the moment for boldness" that required the senior commander "to throw [his] bonnet over the mill and soar from the known to seize the unknown": Montgomery, *Memoirs*, p.353.

18 Hart, *Colossal*, pp.62-67.

19 Ellis, *Victory* II, p.7.

initiated on 6 September. At some point in these discussions the idea of mounting an air assault at Wesel was suggested. However, this idea was rejected by the air force planners involved. As part of the wider flak defence system that protected the German Reich's key industrial region, the Ruhr, the town of Wesel had deployed around it a very heavy concentration of flak. Any airborne insertion into this area would suffer, the air forces planners argued, intolerably high casualties as the transport aircraft fell prey to the German anti-aircraft assets.[20]

With events on the ground unfolding at break-neck pace, "Comet" was abandoned and replaced by Operation "Market-Garden". In the latter plan, three airborne divisions from First Allied Airborne Army would be dropped to secure various bridges running from south-to-north from Eindhoven up to the Rhine crossings at Arnhem. These seizures would facilitate a rapid ground advance by British XXX Corps, part of Second British Army, northward through Arnhem and on toward the Zuider Zee. Securing a sizable bridgehead north of the Lower Rhine at Arnhem might allow 21st Army Group forces subsequently to strike east toward Osnabrück and Hamm, enveloping the northern approaches to the Ruhr.[21]

During 9–10 September, as "Market-Garden" planning unfolded apace, the Commander of Second British Army, Lt-Gen Miles Dempsey, expressed reservations about the concept. Since the axis of advance of "Market-Garden" was northward, it created a lengthening exposed east-facing flank for Second British Army's meagre forces to defend. Moreover, a northward advance also created an increasing gap between Dempsey's forces and their right (southern) flank formation, the First United States Army. With the latter advancing on a broadly eastward axis toward Cologne, this meant that the two armies were advancing at right angles to one another, in other words, on divergent lines. Dempsey apparently preferred the north-eastward axis of ground advance associated with airborne forces seizing the Rhine Bridge at Wesel rather than that at Arnhem. So Dempsey's thinking prior to "Market-Garden" being launched suggests that he favoured a north-easterly advance toward Wesel.[22]

Despite these reservations raised by his senior subordinate, Montgomery nevertheless decided to proceed with "Market-Garden" as planned. The Field Marshal explained that the new enemy V-2 rocket threat to the United Kingdom had swayed his decision. A successful "Market-Garden" that secured a significant advance north beyond Arnhem to close on the Zuider Zee would threaten the lines of communication of the V-2 rocket launcher units deployed in the Rotterdam–Amsterdam region of The Netherlands. The other advantage of "Market-Garden" was that if a bridgehead north of the Lower Rhine was successfully established, this could be exploited with advances to the west, north, or east.[23]

20   TNA, WO229/27/10, M523, 21 Army Group Directive, dated 3 September 1944.
21   TNA, WO229/27/10, M525, 21 Army Group Directive, dated 14 September 1944.
22   Montgomery, *Memoirs*, pp.274-75. Hamilton, *Montgomery* III, pp.50-56.
23   Montgomery, *Memoirs*, pp.274-75.

Operation "Market-Garden" commenced on 17 September and the 9th Parachute Battalion secured the Arnhem Bridge as planned, even though it unfortunately remained isolated from the bulk of 1st British Airborne Division. But by the morning of 21 September, however, with XXX Corps' spearheads still just north of Nijmegen, ferocious German counter-attacks overwhelmed 9 Para's heroic resistance at Arnhem bridge. However, "Market-Garden" continued to limp on until the morning of 26 September, when the withdrawal of 1st Airborne Division from the Oosterbeek perimeter back south across the Lower Rhine was completed. Crucially, at 1445 hours on 21 September, just a short time after the loss of the Arnhem bridge, Montgomery sent Message M221 to Eisenhower that proposed that "if we are to take quick advantage of the favourable situation in the Nijmegen area [sic] it is essential that the right corps of Second Army should develop at once a strong thrust on the axis Gennep–Cleve–Emmerich", presumably with the intent to seize a bridge over the Rhine at this latter location. In his accompanying notes to Freddie de Guingand, his Chief of Staff, Montgomery explained that the corps would advance south-east between "the Rhine and Meuse directed on the N.W. corner of the Ruhr." The map accompanying M221 depicted a simultaneous advance by other forces from Second Army northward from Nijmegen through Arnhem that then swung right through 90 degrees to advance eastward toward Hamm. The proposal to advance toward Emmerich and Wesel and seize Rhine bridges in this area would seem to be the first public discussion of the intent to initiate the "Gatwick" concept.[24]

The first formal articulation of Montgomery's intent to initiate the "Gatwick" concept, however, did not occur until 27 September when he issued Directive M527. This announced the Field Marshal's vision of how the 21st Army Group should exploit the by-now irrevocably stalled "Market-Garden" offensive. M527 noted the two key features of the current situation. First, it observed that the previous day's withdrawal from the bridgehead across the Lower Rhine at Oosterbeek implied that any further advance north in the near future would be problematical. Second, it noted that that Second British Army's possession of crossings of the Rivers Maas (Meuse) and Waal in the Eindhoven–Grave–Nijmegen area meant that Allied forces could thrust south-east between these two rivers toward the Ruhr.[25]

In Directive M527's "intent" paragraph Montgomery gave each of his armies a task. First Canadian Army was to continue its ongoing offensive to open the vital port of Antwerp by clearing the enemy-held Scheldt Estuary. He also ordered Second

---

24   TNA, M221, Message Montgomery to Eisenhower, 1445 21 September 1944 and accompanying map. Montgomery also gave written guidance to his Chief of Staff, Freddie de Guingand, who was to discuss this message with Eisenhower: TNA, WO205/247, folio 23a, Notes for Chief of Staff, 21 September 1944. For "Freddie's" relationship with Montgomery, see Stephen A. Hart, "Francis de Guingand" in David Zabecki (ed)., *Chiefs of Staff* II, (Annapolis, Md., Naval Institute Press, 2008), pp.89-102.

25   TNA, WO205/5G, M527, 21st Army Group Directive, 27 September 1944; Montgomery, *Memoirs*, p.294.

British Army, in conjunction with First United States Army, to "destroy all enemy forces that were preventing the Allies from capturing the Ruhr." To deliver this intent, Second British Army would "operate strongly from [the] area Nijmegen–Gennep" with a south-easterly advance toward the north-western corner of the Ruhr in the Wesel–Duisburg–Krefeld region.[26] Although not specifically articulated here, the phrase "strongly" would suggest that Second British Army would mount a powerful two-corps offensive backed by heavy supporting artillery firepower.

M527 also allocated to Second Army's other forces the task of "maintaining a firm bridgehead" north of the Waal at Nijmegen to create a "constant threat of advance" north over the Lower Rhine. M527's Task paragraph outlining the new Second British Army offensive directed that its right (southern) flank should mount an advance aimed on Krefeld. Simultaneously, the Army's left (northern) flank was to advance ESE toward the Rhine, which was to be "crossed as and where opportunity offers and in particular every endeavour will be made to get a bridgehead at Wesel." The offensive was "to begin" as soon as the "maintenance situation will allow." Indeed, showing some recognition of how far the enemy had recovered since the start of "Market-Garden", Montgomery warned that the proposed offensive might be "a hard dog-fight battle, or killing match."[27]

M527 also directed that the First United States Army meanwhile mount a "strong offensive movement toward the Rhine" at "Cologne and Düsseldorf". While these two operations unfolded, the American 7th Armoured Division was to clear the enemy-held salient located west of the Maas in the Deurne–Venlo–Roermond area; this was to link-up Second British Army's front with that of the American forces to the south. Once these initial operations had been successfully completed, the Second British and First United States Armies were to secure "bridgeheads over the Rhine" to the "north and south of the western face of the Ruhr". Both armies would subsequently "isolate [the] Ruhr" through a double envelopment.[28]

The Preparations Undertaken to Implement "Gatwick"

The issuing of Directive M527 ushered in extensive planning efforts by the Second British Army to implement this new offensive, which by the end of September was being referred to as Operation "Gatwick". Lt-Gen Dempsey held a conference with his corps commanders on 1 October and the next day Second British Army held a major planning conference on the intended operation.[29] These meetings articulated that the offensive's main objectives were "Krefeld, Venlo, Wesel [and the] Rhine

---

26   TNA, WO205/5G, M527, 21st Army Group Directive, 27 September 1944.
27   TNA, WO205/5G, M527, 21st Army Group Directive, 27 September 1944.

28   TNA, WO205/5G, M527, 21st Army Group Directive, 27 September 1944.
29   TNA, WO285/16, Dempsey's 'Notes on Conference with Commanders VIII and XXX Corps', 1 October 1944; WO171/120, War Diary, 21st Army Group, October 1944,

crossing south of Emmerich." Interestingly the articulation of which Rhine bridge to secure was at variance with M527, which emphasised the Wesel crossing; the map accompanying M527, meanwhile, implied that bridges would be secured at both locations. This modest inconsistency in stated objectives perhaps suggests that both the planning for "Gatwick" and the wider operational situation were still fluid, and that the former was being delivered at considerable pace.[30]

These conferences also confirmed that the offensive would be mounted by two corps. Three divisions from the British VIII Corps would operate on the offensive's right (south) flank, striking south-east toward Krefeld. Critically, this thrust would have its southern flank anchored secure along River Maas (Meuse). Meanwhile, three divisions from the British XXX Corps would mount the left (northern) thrust that would establish bridgeheads over (that is, north of) the Rhine in the Emmerich–Wesel area. This flank would be largely unprotected and thus potentially susceptible to powerful enemy counter-attacks. These conferences also stated that the offensive would begin on 8 October, but added the caveat that if the administrative preparations were not ready, particularly the dumping of artillery rounds, the offensive would be postponed until the 10th.[31] This again suggests that "Gatwick" was conceived as a powerful firepower-reliant set-piece offensive that was being rushed to initiation. This haste aimed to exploit extant enemy weakness, since every day that passed gave the *Westheer* time to reorganise, reconstitute and bring up reinforcements, thus incrementally regaining the cohesion lost during the debacle in Normandy.

The chief problem with this plan to launch "Gatwick" during 8–10 October 1944 was that this intent sat increasingly uncomfortably with the unfolding battlefield situation within the 21st Army Group sector. A sense of unease about this had been growing in Montgomery's mind for several days, and he made these concerns public in his 7 October appreciation of the situation. This document began with the frank admission that the Field Marshal was "not happy about [the] overall battle situation". It observed that the enemy had "reacted very violently" to the "Market-Garden" offensive and had "concentrated strong forces against Second [British] Army". The statement went on to observe that the hard-pressed 21st Army Group now faced three onerous immediate commitments, together with a fourth envisaged commitment – the launching of "Gatwick". When the demands of accomplishing these four missions

Appendix L, folio 18, 'Minutes of Chief of Staff's Conference Held at HQ XXX Corps on 2 October', dated 3 October 1944.

30   TNA, WO205/5G, M527, 21st Army Group Directive, 27 September 1944; WO285/16, Dempsey's 'Notes on Conference with Commanders VIII and XXX Corps', 1 October 1944.

31   TNA, WO285/16, Dempsey's 'Notes on Conference with Commanders VIII and XXX Corps', 1 October 1944; WO171/120, War Diary, 21st Army Group, October 1944, Appendix L, folio 18, 'Minutes of Chief of Staff's Conference Held at HQ XXX Corps on 2 October', dated 3 October 1944.

were combined, the document stated, these requirements outstripped the army group's overall combat and logistical capabilities. The possible consequences of this reality, Montgomery suggested, was that the situation could get "very awkward" and "unbalance the whole business in the north."[32]

The army group's first mission was to open the vital port of Antwerp to Allied shipping, which required First Canadian Army to continue clearing the surrounding territory astride the Scheldt Estuary. This involved the capture of the South Beveland peninsula, Walcheren island, and the Breskens area located on the south-western shoulder of the estuary. Montgomery recognised that he had to reinforce these operations if Antwerp was to be opened in a timely fashion. The second task required Second British Army to defend the "none too strong" but strategically significant bridgehead that jutted north of the River Waal around Nijmegen toward the Lower Rhine at Arnhem. This was "daily being threatened by the enemy" and therefore needed to be reinforced by two infantry divisions. The third task required the right flank of Second British Army to clear the enemy from the potentially threatening salient that jutted west across the River Maas (Meuse) in the region Boxmeer–Deurne–Roermond–Venlo. This enemy-held enclave threatened the southern flank of the envisaged "Gatwick" offensive, which remained exposed unless it could be anchored on the Maas after the clearance of this salient.[33]

After considering the combined burden imposed by these three missions, Montgomery concluded that his forces "definitely cannot carry all three [tasks], and also launch Second [British] Army toward Krefeld" in Operation "Gatwick".[34] If Second British Army's XXX and VIII Corps were launched eastward toward Krefeld on 10 October 1944 as now planned, then they would "have two hostile [exposed] flanks" and would also face "strong frontal opposition". This reality constrained the prospects of significant success. Moreover, Montgomery feared that a successful German counter-attack against the thinly-held Nijmegen bridgehead would threaten the lines of communications of the two corps involved in "Gatwick". This would "unbalance completely" Montgomery's forces, cause the premature termination of "Gatwick", and ultimately might cause these forces to be "possibly unable to hold [their] gains." Finally, the appreciation concluded that Montgomery could not "launch Second [British] Army toward the Ruhr" in "Gatwick" until after the operations to open Antwerp had been "finished" and the enemy had been pushed "back over the Meuse" around Deurne–Venlo. The appreciation finished with the direction that "the attack of Second [British] Army toward Krefeld and the Ruhr be postponed" until these conditions had been met.[35]

---

32   TNA, WO205/5G, Montgomery's Statement "7 October", dated 7 October 1944.
33   TNA, WO205/5G, Montgomery's Statement "7 October", dated 7 October 1944.
34   TNA, WO205/5G, Montgomery's Statement "7 October", dated 7 October 1944.
35   TNA, WO205/5G, Montgomery's Statement "7 October", dated 7 October 1944. See also CAB44/255, "Liberation Campaign North-west Europe", Chapter VI, Section D,

In the ensuing days, the situation continued to develop in ways that decreased the likelihood that Operation "Gatwick" would be launched in the immediate future. First, Supreme Allied Commander Eisenhower became increasingly concerned about the time First Canadian Army was taking to dislodge the dogged German defence of the Scheldt Estuary and thus open up the key port of Antwerp to Allied shipping. The latter's significant capability to receive supply shipments would prove of immense value in supporting any future Allied advance eastward into Germany.[36] This was particularly relevant because the Allies were still landing a proportion of their supplies on the Normandy beaches, and because the Germans were still tenaciously defending five isolated port-enclaves along the French Atlantic Coast, as well as the Channel Islands, thus denying vital port facilities to the Allies.[37] The swift opening of Antwerp was therefore crucial.

On 9 October, meanwhile, Eisenhower messaged Montgomery that "of all our operations on our entire front from Switzerland to the Channel, I consider Antwerp of first importance."[38] Yet despite this statement by his superior, the lure of the offensive eastward to the Ruhr continued to loom large in Montgomery's thinking, possibly beyond that which was logical given the circumstances. The new 21st Army Group Directive M530 issued on 9 October, therefore, still stated that its forces would soon initiate the Krefeld operation, but only after they had also "securely held" the Nijmegen bridgehead and "cleaned up" the enemy salient west of the Maas (Meuse) around Venlo. When these two tasks had been completed, M530 directed that Second

Phase 6, Book I, WO Telegram 83859, Vice-Chief of the Imperial General Staff to Chief of the Imperial General Staff, relaying Montgomery's views, 11 October 1944.

36   On the extremely significant contribution Antwerp made to Allied resupply of the European Theatre of Operations, see CAB106/992, Anon., *The Administrative History of the Operations of 21 Army Group on the Continent of Europe, 6 June 1994 – 8 May 1945*, (Germany, 1945), pp.74-77, 100, 106-08, Appendix H.

37   As late as 1 May 1945 some 120,000 German military personnel continued to hold five enclaves along the French Atlantic Coast and the Channel Islands, namely Dunkirk, Lorient (and the adjacent islands), St. Nazaire, La Rochelle, and the Île d'Oléron off the Gironde Estuary. Bundesarchiv-Militärarchiv [BAMA], Freiburg-im-Breisgau, Germany, RW44-I/33, folio 132, Message, Jodl am Festungs-Kommandanten Dünkirchen, St.Nazaire u. La Rochelle, dated 28 April 1945. TNA, WO106/2996, folio 397a, dated 13 May 1945; WO219/1962, SHAEF Scavenger Intelligence Report, No.3, dated 15 May 1945. For the defence of Dunkirk, see TNA, WO205/1223, Appendix H, German Army Strength Return, dated 8 May 1945. For Lorient and St-Nazaire, see ETOUSA, *66th: The Story of the 66th Infantry Division*, (Paris, Desfosses-Neogravure, 1945), p.12. For the defence of La Rochelle and the Gironde estuary, see TNA, WO219/1890, SHAEF G-2 Division, Operational Intelligence Sub-Division, file GBI/01-C/371-1-32, Estimate of German Forces in Specific Areas, August 1944-April 1945, Message, M.R. Watkin to Assistant Chief of Staff, 12th United States Army Group, "Enemy ORBAT in Western France", dated 20 March 1945; Charles de Gaulle, *War Memoirs: Salvation 1944–1946*, (London, Weidenfeld & Nicolson, 1960), pp.157-59.

38   Montgomery, *Memoirs*, p.283.

British Army would "at once regroup" to launch the Krefeld operation. However, the Directive did add the significant caveat that the final decision to launch this offensive "toward the Ruhr" was still dependant on "the Antwerp situation".[39] Montgomery's intent seems still to have been to strike east toward the Ruhr while simultaneously striving to clear the Scheldt Estuary and open Antwerp to Allied shipping.

On 16 October, however, Montgomery's Directive M532 postponed the initiation of "Gatwick", at least for the medium term. The Field Marshal had finally recognised his folly in attempting to continue operations eastward toward the Ruhr before the key logistical node of Antwerp's harbour had been opened for traffic. Because of this split intent neither mission could be the army group's main effort. Consequently, Montgomery had given First Canadian Army the tough mission of clearing the Scheldt Estuary with forces insufficient for the task; this had led to delay in exploiting the immense resupply potential of Antwerp's docks. Belatedly, Directive M532 gave the task of opening Antwerp to shipping "absolute priority" within 21st Army Group. Montgomery later admitted that he had made "a bad mistake" in attempting both to advance toward the Rhine while simultaneously clearing the Scheldt Estuary.[40]

To support this now obvious main effort in the Scheldt Estuary, M532 directed that Second British Army forces be redeployed to the Canadian eastern flank. From here they were to launch an offensive north-westward toward Breda, an assault designed to assist First Canadian Army's attacks to open up the Scheldt Estuary to the west. All other Second British Army offensive operations were to be closed down while this offensive was mounted. Thus Dempsey's forces could not undertake offensive operations to clear the enemy from the potentially dangerous salient west of the Maas in the Deurne–Venlo–Roermond area, which was now viewed as a pre-requisite for mounting Operation "Gatwick".[41] With the enemy still reconstituting every day, the prospects that "Gatwick" would be launched in the immediate future seemed slim.

By 3 November 1944, however, Montgomery and Dempsey's continuing desire to mount Operation "Gatwick" had received a boost. By then First Canadian Army, finally given forces sufficient for the task, had come close to completing the operations required to open the vital port of Antwerp.[42] Between 27 October and 10 November, therefore, significant elements of First Canadian Army redeployed eastward, thus taking over the western sector of Second British Army's front. This enabled the latter to redeploy forces over to its eastern flank in prelude to initiating Operation "Gatwick". As early as 27 October, for example, Second British Army Movements staff were wrestling with the logistical complications of moving 400 tracked and 9,500 wheeled

39   TNA, W205/5G, M530, 21 Army Group Directive, 9 October 1944.
40   Montgomery, *Memoirs*, p.297.
41   TNA, WO205/5G, M532, 21st Army Group Directive, 16 October 1944.
42   TNA, CAB44/255, "Liberation Campaign North-west Europe", Chapter VI, Section D, Phase 6, Book I; CAB101/319, Colonel Joslen, "Unpublished Narrative: The Opening of the Schelde Estuary"; WO179/2599, War Diary, First Canadian Army HQ, October 1944; WO205/758, Report on the Opening of the Scheldt.

vehicles from I British Corps sector to the Second British Army area. These vehicles came from the British 49th Infantry Division, various artillery units, and the specialised armour of 79th Armoured Division.[43]

But even as the forces that would be required to mount "Gatwick" began to move to the south-eastern flank of the 21st Army Group sector during late October and early November, the concerns expressed in Montgomery's 7 October Statement remained extant. For the Germans still held the potentially threatening salient that jutted west across the River Maas in the Deurne–Roermond–Venlo region.[44] The existence of this enemy-held enclave threatened the exposed southern flank of the envisaged "Gatwick" offensive. This threat violated one of Montgomery's basic operational tenets; that an offensive should wherever possible have at least one non-vulnerable flank, protected either by the shape of the Allied front or by a physical geographical barrier such as a river.[45] As the geostrategic realities of "Gatwick" meant that its northern flank was bound to be exposed, having secured several bridgeheads north of the Rhine, the fact that the offensive's other flank might be exposed represented a significant detriment to its perceived chances of success. The perceived threat posed by this salient was reinforced during 27 October–4 November, moreover, when the enemy mounted a surprise local counter-attack from the Meijel area within the enclave.[46]

As a result of these concerns on 2 November Montgomery's Directive M534 ordered that the dangerous enemy-held salient west across the Maas had to be eliminated before "Gatwick" could be launched.[47] Montgomery's cautious operational planning, seen so clearly in Normandy, had fully re-asserted itself after the over-optimism of early autumn, and rightly so as the enemy by now had significantly recovered their cohesion. As the completion of the clearance of this salient subsequently took much longer than imagined, this effectively delayed the initiation of "Gatwick" for a significant period. During 4–13 November Second British Army redeployed its forces and undertook the necessary administrative preparations required to launch offensive operations to clear the Roermond–Venlo salient.

Finally, on 14 November 1944 Dempsey's forces commenced two offensives designed to clear this enclave (now known officially as the Venlo salient), codenamed Operations "Mallard" and "Nutcracker". In the former the British XII Corps attacked the south-western face of the salient along the Wessem Canal. During the

---

43   TNA, WO205/318, "Operation "Gatwick" Regrouping of Formations", 'Preliminaries for Gatwick', 27 October; 'Regrouping of Armies', 29 October 1944; 'Minutes of Meeting Held at 21st Army Group on 2 November 1944 to Discuss the Re-grouping of 21 Army Group', dated 2 November.

44   TNA, WO205/5G, Montgomery's Statement "7 October", dated 7 October 1944.

45   For a discussion of the principle of flank protection within 21st Army Group operations, see Hart, *Colossal*, pp.122-123.

46   TNA, WO205/757, Immediate Report IN-116, Action at Asten 28-30 October 1944; Ellis, *Victory* II, pp.159-60; Hart, *Colossal*, p.115.

47   TNA, WO229/72, folio 32, M534, 21st Army Group Directive, 2 November 1944.

next four days XII Corps fought itself east over the Zig Canal and captured Beringe. Meanwhile, in "Nutcracker" the British VIII Corps had attacked the central face of the German salient centred on the town of Meijel and hinged along the Deurne Canal. Both corps continued their attacks eastward until by 25 November the whole salient had been cleared up to the Maas bar for a small enclave centred on Blerick and Venlo. By 3 December Second British Army's forces had cleared the remaining small salient at Venlo, thus removing the threat to the southern flank of the proposed "Gatwick" offensive.[48] The fact that it had taken four weeks to clear the Venlo salient meant that the initiation of "Gatwick" had been pushed back to mid-December.

After the completion of Operations "Nutcracker" and "Mallard" all the preconditions required for the launch of Operation "Gatwick" as articulated on 7 October had been fulfilled. However, Montgomery nevertheless still perceived the operational situation as not conducive to the initiation of the offensive toward the Ruhr. For to the south of the now-cleared Venlo salient the Allied front still remained rather "untidy", in that the German XII-SS Corps held a salient that jutted west beyond the River Roer, subsequently termed the Heinsberg (or Roermond) Triangle.[49] The north-western face of this triangular enclave ran south-west down the River Maas from Roermond to Maeseyck, where it turned to run south-east back to the Roer near Linnich.

Back on 2 November Montgomery's Directive M534 had decided that the Second British Army front south of the proposed "Gatwick" axis of advance could be held more economically if this was anchored entirely on the more easily-defended line of the Rivers Maas and Roer; if this was done, it would thus free up more forces to undertake "Gatwick".[50] With a total Second British Army strength at this juncture of just 10 divisions and four independent brigades, freeing-up the maximum number of these formations for "Gatwick" by securing an easily-defendable front anchored on the Maas and Roer made tactical sense. Moreover, at this time Montgomery had realised that the intended Ninth United States Army assault toward Cologne was not strong in allocated forces. So he ordered Second British Army's southernmost corps to conduct a limited operation in the Heinsberg area that would provide flank-protection assistance to this American attack. But the consequence of these decisions concerning the Heinsberg Triangle was that the initiation of Operation "Gatwick" was again delayed.

On 18 November 1944 Second British Army's XXX Corps initiated Operation "Clipper". This was an eastward thrust through Geilenkirchen toward Linnich on

---

48 TNA, WO171/311, War Diary XII Corps; TNA, WO171/289, War Diary VIII Corps; LHCMA, Papers of Lt-Gen H.E. Pyman, Account of Operations of Second British Army in Europe 1944-5, Vol. 1, August 1945, p.269; Ellis, *Victory* II, pp.160-161.

49 For a discussion of "tidiness" as part of the principle of "balance" within 21st Army Group operations, see Hart, *Colossal*, pp.116-117.

50 TNA, WO229/72, folio 32, M534, 21st Army Group Directive, 2 November 1944; see p1, paragraph 8 in particular.

the River Roer, designed to protect the northern flank of the Ninth United States Army in its drive on Cologne. The assault was timed to exploit any redeployment of German reserves to deal with the "Nutcracker" and "Mallard" offensives against the Venlo salient to the north. "Clipper" cleared a small part of the southern fringes of the Heinsberg salient but did not significantly reduce the size of the enemy-held enclave. Therefore, for Second British Army to hold the front economically along the Maas and Roer Rivers, so as to free-up the maximum forces for "Gatwick", the remainder of the Heinsberg Triangle still needed to be cleared.[51]

The Eventual Realisation of the "Gatwick" Concept

During the ensuing weeks the combination of prolonged bad weather, the ensuing bogged terrain, as well as the need to reorganise and replenish, prevented the Allies from making much progress in initiating any operation to complete the clearance of the Heinsberg Triangle. Despite this planning continued for such an operation. In the meantime, however, Montgomery's resolve to implement the "Gatwick" concept remained strong. Indeed, at the major planning conference held on 7 December 1944 at the Supreme Allied Headquarters (SHAEF), the initiation of a 21st Army Group offensive, code-named Operation "Valediction", and slated to commence on 1 January 1945, was publically announced.[52]

The "Valediction" offensive, subsequently renamed "Veritable", in many ways represented the final realisation of the "Gatwick" concept, even though there were some significant differences. Whereas the map sketch of "Gatwick" accompanying Directive M527 depicted the northern corps crossing the Rhine downstream (that is, west and north) of both Emmerich and Wesel, "Veritable" operated with the Rhine forming a protecting boundary to the otherwise exposed northern flank of the offensive. The operation aimed to clear the entire Rhineland between the Rhine and Maas (Meuse) up to the line Wesel–Xanten–Geldern. The Rhine, therefore, would be crossed after "Veritable" had been completed, rather than during the offensive as in the original "Gatwick" concept. Given that by the time that "Veritable" was being planned, the enemy was far stronger than when "Gatwick" was first contemplated in late September 1944, this modification of the plan to exploit flank protection based along a major water obstacle made much tactical sense.

Another key difference was that "Veritable" was ultimately mounted by First Canadian Army (albeit spearheaded by British XXX Corps) rather than by Second

---

51   TNA, WO171/481, War Diary 43rd Division, November 1944; WO171/838, War Diary, 4th/7th Royal Dragoon Guards, November 1944; Charles MacDonald, *The Siegfried Line Campaign*, (Washington D.C., OCMH, 1963), pp.545-57.

52   Library and Archives of Canada [LAC], RG24, Vol. 13608, War Diary, First Canadian Army G(Plans), December Diary, Pangman's Note "Valediction", 7 December 1944; WO229/72/10, 'Montgomery's Note on Grouping for Operation Valediction', dated 9 December 1944.

British Army as intended by "Gatwick". This change was due to some complex inter-related issues within the 21st Army Group concerning lines of supply, geographical space, axes of advance, and the balance between concentration of force and economy of effort.[53] A final key difference was that the vague notions of an American southern assault north-eastward to link up with "Gatwick" had become a formal part of Montgomery's scheme for "Veritable". Operation "Grenade" was to be simultaneously launched by the Ninth United States Army, striking north-east from the River Roer toward Wesel, where it would link-up with the Anglo-Canadian advance. In fact "Veritable" in its final form bore considerable similarity with the right corps' axis of advance depicted on the map of an intended offensive that accompanied Montgomery's message M221 to Eisenhower of 21 September 1944.

During the first half of December 1944, First Canadian and Second British Armies undertook the preliminary preparations and initial redeployments required to mount Operation "Veritable". On 16 December, moreover, Montgomery's Directive M536 confirmed that the next operation to be mounted would be "directed south-east from the Nijmegen area, between the Rhine and Meuse", as originally ordered in M534 of 2 November. These preparations, however, were rudely disturbed that very same day, when the Germans initiated their surprise counter-offensive in the Ardennes. During the rest of December, elements of the 21st Army Group – particularly XXX Corps – were redeployed to assist the American defence against this surprise enemy riposte. As a result of the major impact the German counter-offensive exerted on the Allies, the ongoing preparations for "Veritable" all but ceased.[54]

By early January 1945, however, the Allied forces had first contained the German counter-offensive and then driven it back to its start lines. This success subsequently enabled the 21st Army Group to complete the final tidying-up of its front prior to the initiation of "Veritable". For the enemy still held the Heinsberg salient – the triangular enclave that jutted west of the River Roer. Second British Army still had to clear this salient if was to hold an economic front along the Rivers Maas (Meuse) and Roer, so as to free-up the maximum possible forces for "Veritable". On 14 January 1945, there-fore, the three divisions of the British XII Corps initiated Operation "Blackcock" to clear the Heinsberg Triangle. Amid poor weather conditions, the offensive against

53   LAC, RG24, Vol. 13608, War Diary, First Canadian Army G(Plans), December Diary; LAC, Crerar Papers, CP/2, File 1-0-7/11. See also Hart, *Colossal*, pp.176-78.

54   For the best of the extensive literature on the Battle of the Ardennes, see: Michael Reynolds, *Men of Steel: 1SS Panzer Corps – The Ardennes and Eastern Front 1944–45*, (Staplehurst, Spellmount, 1999); Danny S., Parker, *Battle of the Bulge: Hitler's Ardennes Offensive*, (London, Greenhill, 1991); Roger Cirillo, *Ardennes-Alsace*, (The Campaigns of World War II, CMH-72-26), (Washington, DC., OCMH, 1992); Gerald Astor, *A Blood-Dimmed Tide: The Battle of the Bulge by the Men Who Fought It*, (NY., Dell, 1992); Jean Paul Pallud, *Battle of the Bulge: Then and Now*, (London, Battle of Britain, 1984); Charles B. MacDonald, *The Battle of the Bulge*, (London, Weidenfeld & Nicholson, 1984); Cole, Hugh M., *The Ardennes: Battle of the Bulge*, (US Army in WW2: ETO), (Washington, DC., OCMH, 1965).

well-prepared defences proved a difficult slog and it took until the 26th to complete the clearance of the salient.[55] With the completion of "Blackcock" the final preliminary deemed necessary for "Veritable" to be launched had been completed.

Consequently, back on 21 January 1945 – as soon as it looked likely that "Blackcock" would clear the Heinsberg Triangle, Montgomery's issued a new Directive, M548. This ordered First Canadian Army to complete the preparations required to mount "Veritable", which was slated to commence on 8 February 1945. The "Veritable" offensive was indeed a bitter slugging-march, as Montgomery back on 27 September 1944 had feared the assault toward the Ruhr might be.[56] Indeed, it took a protracted series of bloody engagements that lasted until 10 March for the British XXX Corps and the II Canadian Corps to complete the capture of the Rhineland up to the area Xanten–Geldern–Wesel; in the process the Allies inflicted grievous losses on the powerfully-reinforced German First Parachute Army.[57] Operation "Gatwick" had been finally accomplished – some 165 days after it was first publically announced in Directive M527 of 27 September 1944. The analysis delivered in this chapter on the intent, origins, preparations for, and final execution of the "Gatwick" concept have, it is hoped, finally filled the unjustified silence about this operation in the historiography of the 1944–45 North-west Europe campaign.

55   Imperial War Museum, Bernard Montgomery Papers, BLM/152, 21st Army Group Report "Blackcock".
56   TNA, WO205/5G, M527, 21st Army Group Directive, 27 September 1944.
57   BAMA, ZA1/954, B-601 von Bernstoff Report on XLVII Panzer Korps; ZA1/1191-92, B-843 Fiebig Report on 84th Infantry Division; LAC, CMHQ Reports 185–86, "Veritable"; Crerar Papers, CP2, File 1-0-7/11; TNA, CAB106/1020, MORU Report "Veritable"; WO106/5846, Battlefield Study "Veritable"; WO205/953, 21st Army Group Final Report "Veritable"; WO205/1020, folios 49-72, Special Interrogation Reports on Generals Schlemm and Straube; WO205/1022, folios 19-35, 61-67, Special Interrogation Reports on Generals Plocher, Meindl, and Fiebig.

13

Starvation and Sacrifice: The Reality of MARKET GARDEN

Tim Jenkins

Introduction

The obvious and continuing admiration of the Dutch civil population of those who participated in the allied attempt to liberate the country in September 1944 remains one of the most incredible legacies of MARKET GARDEN. Buckingham comments that:

> There can be no place in Europe more fervent and diligent in its thanksgiving for its liberation than where the airborne battle was fought in 1944, particularly at Oosterbeek.[1]

However, the immediate consequences of the operation for those that remained under German occupation was intense suffering and fleetingly, in the eyes of the Dutch Government in exile, betrayal. Prince Bernhard of the Netherlands is reputed to have commented in the aftermath of the battle that 'my Country can never again afford the luxury of another Montgomery success.'[2]

The above is a particularly succinct and poignant appraisal of the operation from the perspective of a sovereign of an occupied nation. The military experience of Operation MARKET GARDEN and the courage of the allied forces involved have been consistently well documented. However, the effect of the operation upon the civilian populace of northern Holland has remained rather neglected in comparison and will form the basis of discussion in this paper.

---

1   Middlebrook, *Arnhem 1944: The Airborne Battle*, p.451.
2   Ryan, *A Bridge Too Far*, p.267.

Civilian Sacrifice

In early September 1944 celebrations broke out throughout the country when it appeared that liberation was only a matter of days away. However, those festivities, in which precious stocks of food were consumed in merriment and presented in gratitude to allied troops proved nearly eight months premature, months in which many of the revellers died of starvation. Approximately 18,000 deaths occurred during the winter months alone.[3] The following extract from an article in *The New York Times* published on 8 April 1945 indicated the despair and disillusionment of the Dutch civil population:

> They are past caring what happens. News of the great Allied offensive across the Rhine will stir painful memories more than hope. They can never forget "Mad Tuesday," Sept. 5th 1944, when victorious Allied armies sweeping through Belgium into the Netherlands came to an abrupt halt. They had spent their stocks of food and drink in joyous anticipation and now in the ensuing months they have spent their last reserves of hope.[4]

The Rhine offensive to which the article alluded was Operation VARSITY which took place on 24 March 1945. Unlike its Dutch predecessor, Operation VARSITY became the most successful divisional strength airborne operation of the war in Europe.

However, following the evacuation of the remnants of the 1st Airborne Division across the Rhine on the night of 24 and 25 September the Germans ordered 100,000 civilians out of an area to the north of the lower Rhine. The region was then systematically plundered for materials with which the remaining German forces in northwest Holland bolstered their defences against any future allied offensives. Furniture and other household items were actually removed and sent to bombed-out civilians in Germany.[5]

The consequences for the Dutch civil population were disastrous. H. Terwindt, an Arnhem citizen, managed to stay in the vicinity until early November 1944 before being forced to leave along with his sisters and girlfriend:

> On the 4th of November we pulled out and walked all the way to The Hague where we arrived on the 11th.[6] Here the food situation was bad, but got worse and as we had no supplies whatsoever, starvation was facing us. I lost 20 pounds the first month, as I was getting underfed, we started buying on the black market. It cost us a small fortune but we got through. 50,000 people died of starvation

---

3   Buckingham, *Arnhem 1944*, p.227.
4   'Starving Holland Soon To Get Help', *The New York Times*, 8 April 1945, p.56.
5   Buckingham, *Arnhem 1944*, p.227.
6   A distance of approximately 120 kms.

in Holland, all in the west part of the country. If the Germans could they would have starved us all, as they have stolen everything and looted the country, they wanted to destroy what was left out of spite because they were losing the war and because they could not make us take their side.[7]

Arnhem was not liberated until 15 April 1945 and regions further north were not cleared of German occupying forces until Admiral Friedeburg, appointed as head of the German Navy, surrendered all forces in north-west Germany, Holland and Denmark to Field Marshal Montgomery on 4 May 1945.

Much of the hardship suffered by the Dutch population in areas that the Allies failed to liberate in September 1944 was a direct result of SHAEF (Supreme Headquarters Allied Expeditionary Force) appeals for civilian strike action in support of Operation MARKET GARDEN. On the day the airborne operation was launched both Eisenhower, and more reassuringly for citizens, the Dutch Government in exile, promised the populace that liberation was imminent and ordered railway workers to strike in order to disrupt German transport capabilities:

> Prime Minister Pieter S. Gerbrandy said there was every reason to believe that the blow struck today by the people of the Netherlands and their allies, who included American, British and Polish troops, would lead to the liberation of Holland. He added "The great thing is that the people living in Holland will now get a chance to show their worth."[8]

The loyalty of the Dutch people was proved as they answered their country's call but unfortunately the operational aspect of the liberation strategy failed to deliver what had been previously promised. However, it is also worth briefly exploring the relationship between Montgomery, the Dutch resistance and Dutch military in order to begin to understand why the opinion of the British held by Dutch civilians was so different from that of their government and monarchy.

Essentially, intelligence received by the Dutch resistance was consistently ignored by the British who believed it had been compromised by the Germans. Prince Bernhard conceded in his biography that he did not blame Montgomery for not acting upon information which he did not fully rely upon,[9] yet he could not forgive the British Field-Marshal for his dismissal of intelligence received from senior members of the Dutch military, particularly during the planning of MARKET GARDEN:

> For three days before the battle my Chief of Staff, Major-General P. Doorman, an experienced General Staff officer, and I were with him – and we knew a little

---

7   L.H.A., 9/28/84, Misc. 51, Letter from H. Terwindt to Mrs Y. Lugg, November 1944.
8   'Appeal to Dutch Timed to Landing', *The New York Times*, 18 September 1944, p.4.
9   Hatch, *H.R.H. Prince Bernhard of the Netherlands*, pp.112-113.

more than he about conditions in Holland. We told him about the lie of the land, the state of the soil, and the roads; what the tanks could do and what they could not do, and where the infantry should be and where they should not be.[10]

Bernhard believed that if Montgomery had accepted such advice Arnhem may have been a victory, or at least mitigated the consequences of defeat for both the British airborne and Dutch civilian population.

Following the failure of Arnhem, and despite warnings made by SHAEF to the Germans that reprisals against Dutch civilians would be punished, the show of defiance by the population only antagonised Dutch-German relations further when it became obvious that the operation, and corresponding liberation attempt, had failed. The Royal Institute of International Affairs concluded that the general strike, initiated at the request of SHAEF and the Dutch government in exile, was not broken until long after the allied advance was thwarted at Arnhem. However, once it gradually started to subside the German response was ruthless:

> The Germans tightened their grip on those parts of the country which were still held, and the strike began to recoil, not only on the strikers, but on the whole population. The Germans, considering the Dutch to have now forfeited all right to consideration, began a systematic and ruthless destruction and pillage of the country's assets.[11]

Allied warnings were blatantly ignored by the occupiers and the consequences for the Dutch civilians were devastating.

Starvation – The Hunger Winter

Secretary of State for War, Sir P.J. Grigg, delivered a report to the War Office on 4 November 1944 which detailed the direct consequences of the failure of MARKET GARDEN upon the civilian population. Grigg admitted that Holland presented the most serious problem in northern-Europe with regard to food shortages but also drew attention to the fact that it was incredibly difficult to give any accurate appreciation of the situation. This was largely because only a small percentage of the country had actually been liberated. Grigg continued to report that Dutch civilians were undernourished to a worse extent than their Belgian and French counterparts and referred

---

10   Ibid, p.114.
11   Viscount Chilston, 'The Occupied Countries in Western Europe,' in Royal Institute of International Affairs, *Survey of Internal Affairs 1939 – 1946: Hitler's Europe*, (London, 1954), p.505.

to disturbing reports of malnourishment amongst citizens in the towns of Eindhoven and Nijmegen.[12]

It was certainly true that the nutritional situation in Holland was far more severe than that which existed in liberated France and Belgium. This was partly due to the fact that Holland was still a battle zone and military supplies took precedence over civilian aid, but Grigg argued that it was also due to the attitude of the occupying forces:

> For some time past the German attitude towards Holland has been increasingly severe, and with the recent calling by the Allies of a railway strike in Holland the Germans have practically cut off supplies from the deficiency areas. Some damage has already been done in these areas by flooding and it is estimated that 500,000 acres are out of production from this cause, though the flooding is fresh water flooding and the land can be brought into production again within a comparatively short period after it has been pumped dry. It is clear, therefore, that at best we shall have to meet a serious situation in Western Holland, where liberation will find the population not only without any stocks of food, but probably in a state of semi-starvation.[13]

The destruction of dykes and the flooding of large areas of Holland by the Germans to disrupt allied military operations severely impeded the Dutch capability for food production which resulted in acute shortages. Hatch succinctly stated that:

> If ever the night was darkest before dawn it was in the Netherlands during the terrible winter of 1944-45. Nature seemed to have joined the Nazis in brutal indifference to the sufferings of the Dutch people.[14]

Consequently, Grigg estimated that once the country had been liberated 2,000 tons of foodstuff and 1,000 tons of other necessities would be required daily to sustain life for '3½ million destitute and largely homeless people.'[15]

However, the question as to whether the Allies would be capable of feeding Europe after the liberation of each country in turn had actually been raised in the media as early as July 1944. In an article in *Picture Post*, Dr F. Le Gros Clarke, a prominent British nutritionist who founded the 'Committee against Malnutrition,' wrote the following:

12 TNA, CAB 66/57/7: The Position with regard to Food, Agriculture and Nutrition in France, Belgium and Holland, by P.J. Grigg, 4 November 1944.
13 Ibid.
14 Hatch, *H.R.H. Prince Bernhard of the Netherlands*, p.126.
15 TNA, CAB 66/57/7.

Europe will present a strangely diverse pattern of misery, destitution and hunger. The precise nature of that pattern we cannot predict; it will depend on the course taken by the invasion, both from the west and east. A German in retreat seems usually to be a systematic incendiary; and he will do what he can to damage bridges, flourmills, rolling stock and mines.[16]

In Holland this was certainly the case as demonstrated in the German systematic destruction of windmills, which were not only crucial to the production of flour, but had a military purpose as observation posts.

By October 1944 the situation regarding food supplies was also being raised in the House of Commons as evidenced in the following exchanges between various MPs and government officials. On 24 October the following exchange took place between Mr Harvey and the Parliamentary Secretary to the Ministry of Economic Warfare:

Mr. Harvey (M.P. Combined English Universities)
Asked the Parliamentary Secretary to the Ministry of Economic Warfare whether he will give the latest available information as to the shortage of food in Holland; and what measures are being taken for the relief of the civilian population.

Mr. Foot
I have received information from the Dutch authorities that the shortage of food in Holland is acute. His Majesty's Government and the United States Government, in consultation with the Netherlands Government, are endeavouring to make arrangements for bringing relief to the civilian population.[17]

Despite initial discussions between the parties referenced above a satisfactory plan was not developed and agreed upon until early 1945, and even then took far longer than anticipated to instigate and start to achieve results.

By January 1945 the food situation for the Dutch populace remained critical in both liberated and occupied regions. In the case of the liberated areas the fact that they were still effectively a battle ground and that no Dutch port was in operation severely curtailed the ability of the military authorities to supply and distribute aid. The lack of an allied secured sea port is particularly important here as MARKET GARDEN was launched in preference of an operation to open up shipping and alleviate subsequent materiel supply.

The relationship between the Dutch and the German occupiers continued to deteriorate to such an extent that at one point the nutritional value of daily rations available to civilians only constituted between 800 and 1,000 calories. In the occupied areas

16 F. Le Gros Clarke, 'Can the Allies Feed Europe', *Picture Post*, 17 June 1944, pp.7-9, p.9.
17 Hansard Parliamentary Debates: HC Deb 24 October 1944, Vol. 404, c48w.

food shortages were far more acute and the Germans continued to restrict the import of supplies. An unfortunate indicator of the level of animosity experienced can be found in the German refusal to allow two neutral Swedish ships loaded with supplies to pass the blockade and dock at Rotterdam.[18]

It is true to suggest that the situation in Holland had not been anticipated by either allied civil or military authorities, possibly due to over confidence following the successful advance since D-day. However, it soon became apparent that they were not prepared for the humanitarian crisis that ensued post-September 1944. The destruction of supplies and equipment as part of the scorched earth policy of the Germans and the diversion of labour to Germany had damaged both agricultural and industrial production. This, coupled with the cessation of internal transportation systems, meant that the distribution of supplies was impossible.

In a report investigating the logistics of supplies for liberated Europe written on 25 January 1945, Clement Attlee, the author of the paper, listed the following major causes of the supply difficulties:

> The planning of the allies before D-day was based on the assumption that the campaign would be one of attrition and slow retirement, and that arrangements would be worked out gradually in the light of experience gained, or that it would proceed so swiftly that the military period and the interval before the normal civil government was restored and material could be diverted from military production and requirements would be a short one. In fact, neither of those expectations has been realised. The war is lasting much longer than anticipated six months ago, and the problems of demand, supply, transportation, &c., which confront us in respect of liberated areas, are only one aspect of the consequence of this.[19]

The above statement is evidence that the situation in Europe had caught the Allies entirely unprepared with consequent serious implications for the Netherlands. Holland remained a battle ground with much of the country still under German occupation in January 1945, a situation that the allied planners had not predicted. Clement Attlee wrote the following with specific reference to the plight of Dutch civilians:

> In particular, it had, we understand, been anticipated that the bulk of the fighting would be in France and that Holland and Belgium would escape very lightly. In fact France and Belgium have escaped relatively lightly but a burden far greater than anticipated has fallen on Holland.[20]

18   TNA, CAB 66/61/13: Supplies for Liberated Areas in Europe, by C.A. Attlee, 25 January 1945.
19   Ibid.
20   Ibid.

In early 1945 there was strong evidence that the critical situation in Holland risked an irreparable fracture in relations between the Netherlands Government in exile and its British and American allies. Political tension between the Netherlands government and their British hosts had in fact been gradually building ever since the first day that exiled Dutch statesmen arrived in Britain, particularly concerning the future of the Dutch overseas territories.[21]

The Dutch Government in Exile

The British relationship with the Dutch government did not quite start on the best possible terms during the *Blitzkrieg* of 1940. On 10 May the British government casually informed the members of the Netherlands administration that they had decided to send British troops to the Dutch colonies of Curacao and Aruba in order to protect the Royal Dutch Shell oil refineries against the eventuality of German attack. Although the official communiqué declared that the arrangements had been made by means of mutual consent the decision had been an entirely British one. Far from a display of benevolence the action was undoubtedly taken to protect British interests, the simple fact of the matter being that the Dutch refineries supplied over 80% of the aviation fuel consumed by the Royal Air Force. Consequently, the Anglo-Dutch relations remained predominantly influenced by British foreign policy for the remainder of the war, a situation that the exiled Netherlands government grudgingly accepted.[22] In fact Churchill alluded to the situation during an address on the war and international situation to the House of Commons during the aftermath of MARKET GARDEN on 28 September 1944:

> I trust that the day is not far distant when our forces will also have completed their task of liberating the territory of our staunch and sorely tried friends and allies in Holland—allies in the war of the Spanish succession and in all the struggles for the establishment of freedom in Europe. They are also very near to us in thought and sympathy and their interests at home, and also abroad, command British support and are largely interwoven with our own fortunes.[23]

Nevertheless, although the exiled Dutch government realised it was dependent upon Great Britain, it was certainly not prepared to watch in silence whilst its people suffered the consequences of the failed liberation attempt.

---

21   H.W. von der Dunk, 'Holland: The Shock of 1940', *Journal of Contemporary History*, Vol. 2, No.1, 1967, pp.169-182, p.179.
22   A. Kirsten & M. van Faassen, 'Goodbye Mr Churchill: Anglo-Dutch Relations during the Second World War,' in N.J. Ashton & D. Hellema (ed.) *Unspoken Allies: Anglo-Dutch Relations Since 1780* (Amsterdam, 2001), p.155.
23   Hansard Parliamentary Debates: HC Deb 28 September 1944, Vol. 403, cc.421-604.

On 7 March 1945 Churchill received an emotional letter in which the Dutch Premier, Dr Gerbrandy, outlined the disillusionment of his Government at the apparent allied reluctance towards relieving the plight of his nation. He requested that the allied forces mounted a special operation aimed specifically at securing the liberation of northern Holland. Gerbrandy had previously approached General Bedell-Smith with a similar appeal but had been told that the Allies did not possess the necessary divisions or war materiel to achieve a decisive outcome.

Bedell-Smith predicted that the earliest date any such operation could be attempted was late May 1945 and upon hearing this news Gerbrandy decided he had little choice but appeal directly to Churchill:

> The situation in north-west Holland is desperate. In Rotterdam, according to the report of a trustworthy official who escaped through the lines, it may happen that when you ring the doorbell of a house you get no answer. On enquiry you may find that every single member of the family is dead. Cases of deaths by the roadside or in the rest shelters provided in schools, and other places, are common. Even in the most favourable circumstances there are people who try to still the pangs of hunger with flower bulbs.[24]

The desperation experienced by the population of northern Holland was further increased by hugely inflated food prices for any items outside the usual meagre rations. Gerbrandy continued:

> The prices offered for one single potato, one piece of bread, and so on, off the ration, are fantastic. According to one partly confirmed report from occupied Holland, already in January there was difficulty in burying the bodies in one town owing to the inordinate demand for coffins. When this happened bodies were buried in mass graves.[25]

The Dutch premier placed the responsibility for ensuring that the provision of aid was plentiful once the remaining occupied territories had been liberated firmly with the Supreme Command of SHAEF.

During negotiations in January 1945 between Eisenhower, Gerbrandy and the Dutch Merchant Marine Minister, J.M. De Booy, the Supreme Commander promised to sanction a series of measures by which relief could be carried out immediately after the liberation. In further discussions with General Bedell-Smith the method(s) by which aid would be delivered were summarised into the following three points:

---

24   TNA, CAB 66/63/9: Relief for North-West Holland, by W.S. Churchill, 9 March 1945.
25   Ibid.

i)   21st Army Group were given responsibility for instigating the relief plan under the sole leadership of General Galloway.

ii)   Relief was to be brought to the Dutch people by three routes:
  • Road transport from Oss (where 30,000 tons of food had been assembled)
  • Sea transport from West Brabant
  • Transport by sea of supplies from England

iii)   Aircraft were to be utilised as far as was possible although it was made clear to the Dutch authorities that this may well be more of a token gesture than substantial assistance.[26]

The assurances given to the Dutch Government in January by SHAEF undoubtedly gave them initial satisfaction and reassurance. However, this quickly turned to despair when it was realised that the plan was not achieving the desired result, or worse, not being carried out at all.

Betrayal?

By March 1945 the situation had changed considerably for the worse, a fact that Gerbrandy was determined to bring to the attention of the British Prime Minister:

> Since these proposals had to a certain extent set the minds of the Netherland Government at rest, it was all the more disappointing to learn that General Galloway had been appointed commander of a division instead of being placed at the head of the relief operations, and that the supplies already available to OSS (in Brabant) for relief of Western Holland after liberation had been so reduced that, out of 30,000 tons only about 5,000 remained, while there was no question of collecting supplies anywhere else. Nothing further had been done about the transport problem.[27]

Gerbrandy conceded to Churchill that, despite an excellent liaison in General Clark, head of the SHAEF mission to the Netherlands government, faith in Montgomery and his forces had been severely tested:

> I cannot conceal the fact, however, that the trust of the Netherlands government has been shaken by the course events have taken. The fact that, in spite of the promise given to us, there has been neglect on the part of the 21st Army Group,

26   Ibid.
27   Ibid

and that an intervention by General Bedell-Smith has been necessary, is most disquieting.[28]

The letter closed with a reminder to Churchill that the Dutch government had placed all the resources they possessed, including ships, men and supplies, at the disposal of the allied war effort. When one considers the situation alongside Montgomery's attitude toward intelligence and advice during the planning for MARKET GARDEN, it is easy to empathise with the Dutch situation and their feeling of betrayal.

Consequently, the Dutch had become entirely dependent upon SHAEF, not only for the liberation of their country, but also the provision of supplies once freedom had been secured. Gerbrandy reminded Churchill that should the Dutch people suspect that the Allies had not done everything in their power to relieve their sufferings at the earliest possible opportunity the result would be disillusionment and outrage with the blame being firmly placed not only with the Dutch Government, but also at the door of the British administration. Interestingly, the continued admiration of the Dutch people, particularly the residents of Arnhem, would suggest that the attempted liberation was worth the consequent suffering. However, one must concede that such a retrospective observation is much easier to make some seventy years after the event.

The frustration of the exiled government at the apparent nonchalance of SHAEF, and in particular 21st Army Group, is entirely understandable but there was a genuine concern amongst senior military planners that any attempt to liberate northern Holland by force would ultimately prolong the suffering of its residents. Eisenhower made the following justification for the decision:

> We knew that conditions in Holland had been steadily deteriorating and, after advance of our armies had isolated the area from Germany, the Dutch situation became almost intolerable. Judging from the information available to me I feared that wholesale starvation would take place and decided to take positive steps to prevent it. I still refused to consider a major offensive into the country. Not only would great additional destruction and suffering have resulted but the enemy's opening of dykes would further have flooded the country and destroyed much of its fertility for years to come.[29]

Eisenhower's concerns regarding the flooding of Holland were in fact justified but large scale damage had already been done. The Germans had utilised the tactical application of flooding throughout the length of the MARKET GARDEN route to devastating effect as an alternative to organising local counter attacks.

28 Ibid.
29 Eisenhower, *Crusade in Europe*, p.454.

One of the most successful examples of this defensive method occurred in December 1944 and was reported in the minutes of a Meeting of the American General Council on 11 December 1944:

> On the night of 4-5 December, the Germans succeeded in breaking a dike on the south bank of the lower Rhine, south west of Arnhem. Waters from the swollen river immediately commenced inundating the lowlands between Arnhem and Nijmegen. By the end of the week, flood waters had spread over two-thirds of the country between the lower Rhine and the Waal and had forced a general Allied retirement in this area.[30]

In January 1945 a report by Sir Jack Drummond, the scientific advisor to the Ministry of Food, was presented to the Cabinet by the Minister for Food concerning the food situation in both Holland and Belgium. Drummond submitted his report on 24 January and concluded that:

> If the position of these people is not alleviated materially and soon, many thousands will die, directly or indirectly, of starvation. People cannot survive at calorie levels such as those that are believed to be current in these towns for more than two or three months.[31]

However, it is worth highlighting that Drummond also identified economic disruption as a factor in the malnutrition in the civilian population due to lack of funds for the purchase of additional food on the black market.

Conclusion

The desperate situation in northern Holland was not relieved until April 1945 when allied bombers began a large scale aid operation. From 29 April to 8 May 1945 almost the entire Lancaster and Mosquito strength of Bomber Command, over 1,000 aircraft, was employed on Operation MANNA.

During the operation over 7000 tons of food supplies were dropped to the starving population of Rotterdam and The Hague. Despite the determination of the bomber crews the suffering endured by the Dutch was a direct result of the failure of Operation MARKET GARDEN.[32] The extent of the airpower displayed during the relief operation does raise one potentially interesting question. Had such air power been available

---

30   A.H.C.O., Minutes, Meeting of the General Council, 11 December 1944.
31   TNA, CAB 66/61/28: The Food Situation in Belgium and the Netherlands, by J.J. Llewellin, 30 January 1945.
32   Longmate, *The Bombers*, p.347.

in September 1944 to deploy the airborne forces in divisional strength on the first day of the operation could such suffering have been avoided?

Montgomery certainly believed that the additional airpower would have made a significant difference:

> If the operation had been properly backed from its inception, and given the aircraft, ground forces, and administrative resources necessary for the job it would have succeeded.[33]

He concluded the episode in his memoirs by conceding that he remained 'MARKET GARDEN's unrepentant advocate.'[34] However, even with such an extensive additional airpower resource there were still not enough aircraft available to deliver the First Allied Airborne Army in one-lift and it is doubtful that the outcome would have been significantly altered.[35]

With regard to the phenomenon of continuing Dutch civilian admiration for the British 1st Airborne Division, the following contemporary account by Commander Prior in the House of Commons on the 18 January 1945 following a visit to northern Holland may well form part of the explanation:

> So much do the Dutch prize liberty that we were met everywhere by smiling welcoming people and there was no complaint that we were the means of their undoing. The industry, cheerfulness, and friendliness of the Dutch were a great inspiration and example to us all. Food unfortunately is very scarce. Milk is practically non-existent, the people are on the verge of starvation, the cattle are dying, there is no pasture. It might be possible for the Allied Governments to use part of the great liberated ports to land more sustenance for the civilian people.

Churchill further acknowledged the courage of the Dutch people in a speech to the Commons on 14 March 1945:

> I am sure that the House would wish me to take this opportunity of expressing the deep concern and sympathy which we all feel for the Dutch people in their present ordeal and our admiration of the magnificent spirit shown by those in the still occupied areas in resisting the repeated efforts of the enemy to exploit their distress.[36]

33   Montgomery, *The Memoirs of Field-Marshal Montgomery*, p.308.
34   Ibid.
35   Hansard Parliamentary Debates: HC Deb 18 January 1945, Vol. 407, cc376-493.
36   Hansard Parliamentary Debates: HC Deb 14 March 1945, Vol. 409, cc223-4223.

Despite the devastation caused it is testament to the Dutch people that they recognised, and continue to acknowledge, that the consequent suffering was born of allied sacrifice and endeavour rather than the malice of an occupying force. This factor remains the true, and eternal legacy of MARKET GARDEN.

Bibliography

Primary Sources
The National Archives (TNA)
CAB 66/57/7: The Position with regard to Food, Agriculture and Nutrition in France, Belgium and Holland, by P.J. Grigg, 4 November 1944
CAB 66/61/13: Supplies for Liberated Areas in Europe, by C.A. Attlee, 25 January 1945
CAB 66/61/28: The Food Situation in Belgium and the Netherlands, by J.J. Llewellin, 30 January 1945
CAB 66/63/9: Relief for North-West Holland, by W.S. Churchill, 9 March 1945

Hansard Parliamentary Debates:
HC Deb 28 September 1944, Vol. 403, cc421-604
HC Deb 24 October 1944, Vol. 404, c48w
HC Deb 18 January 1945, Vol. 407, cc376-493
HC Deb 14 March 1945, Vol. 409, cc223-4223

Liddell Hart Archive:
L.H.A., 9/28/84, Misc. 51, Letter from H. Terwindt to Mrs Y. Lugg, November 1944

Journals and Newspapers
F. Le Gros Clarke, 'Can the Allies Feed Europe', *Picture Post*, 17 June 1944, pp.7-9
'Appeal to Dutch Timed to Landing', *The New York Times*, 18 September 1944, p.4
'Starving Holland Soon To Get Help', *The New York Times*, 8 April 1945

Published Diaries and Memoirs
Hatch, Alden, *H.R.H. Prince Bernhard of the Netherlands*, London, Harrap, 1962.
Eisenhower, Dwight, *Crusade in Europe*, London, Heinemann, 1949.
Montgomery, Bernard, *The Memoirs of Field-Marshal Montgomery*, London, Collins, 1960.

Secondary Sources
Buckingham, William, *Arnhem 1944*, Stroud, Tempus, 2004.
H.W. von der Dunk, 'Holland: The Shock of 1940', *Journal of Contemporary History*, Vol. 2, No.1, 1967

A. Kirsten & M. van Faassen, 'Goodbye Mr Churchill: Anglo-Dutch Relations during the Second World War,' in N.J. Ashton & D. Hellema (ed.) *Unspoken Allies: Anglo-Dutch Relations Since 1780,* Amsterdam, Amsterdam University Press, 2001.

Longmate, Norman, *The Bombers,* London, Hutchinson, 1988.

Middlebrook, Martin, *Arnhem 1944: The Airborne Battle,* London, Viking, 1995.

Ryan, Cornelius, *A Bridge Too Far,* London, Coronet, 1977.

Viscount Chilston, 'The Occupied Countries in Western Europe,' in Royal Institute of International Affairs, *Survey of Internal Affairs 1939–1946: Hitler's Europe,* (London, 1954)

14

Crossing Water Obstacles in the Low Countries:
The First Polish Armoured Division's Forcing of the Axel-Hulst Canal
16-19 September 1944

Dr Paul Latawski

For the formations of 21st Army Group, the advance into the Low Countries introduced new terrain features in the form of numerous rivers, canals and other water courses. Surmounting water obstacles became one of the major tactical problems during operations in the Low Countries. The pursuit northwards from Normandy had provided a glimmer of the scale of the problem to be later encountered. In a Royal United Services Institute (RUSI) lecture published in 1946, Major General Sir J D Inglis, a senior Royal Engineer officer, noted that the advance from the Seine and the Albert canal had necessitated the construction of 127 bridges.[1] Crossing these water obstacles in the pursuit northwards had been relatively easy. A disorganised German enemy had conducted incomplete demolitions of bridges. Moreover, the German inability to mount a coherent defence of these water obstacles ameliorated the problem of getting across the rivers and canals found between Normandy and Belgium. This, however, was all to change as 21st Army Group formations reached the Low Countries. Between the Seine and the line running between Antwerp and Brussels, 21st Army Group engineers constructed 8,000 feet of bridging. Moving northwards into northern Belgium and southern Holland to the Meuse River absorbed 41,000 feet of bridging in crossing water obstacles.[2] The terrain of the Low Countries undoubtedly presented enhanced difficulties in surmounting obstacles criss-crossed as they were with a denser network of water courses and canals. Adding to the challenges was a coalescing of the German defence. The disarray experienced in the Allied pursuit gave way to more complete German demolitions of bridges linked to coherent and effective defence of water obstacles.

---

1   Major General Sir J.D. Inglis, 'The Work of the Royal Engineers in North-West Europe, 1944-45', *Royal United Services Institution, Journal*, 91:591 (1946), p. 184.
2   'Holdfast', 'Bridging in North-West Europe', *The Army Quarterly*, 51:2 (January 1946), pp. 211-212.

The 1st Polish Armoured Division, like other formations in 21st Army Group, was confronted in its operations in the Low Countries with the tactical problem of crossing water obstacles. Although this was something that was anticipated in doctrine and training, inevitably it meant that forcing a crossing of a defended water obstacle led to the assimilation of operational lessons. This chapter will look at the experience of 1st Polish Armoured Division by examining as a case study its forcing of the Axel-Hulst Canal 16-19 September 1944. It will first examine the then current doctrine employed by the 1944 British pattern armoured division for crossing water obstacles, the bridging and engineer capabilities organic to the division and the division's experience in crossing water obstacles in the operations preceding entry into the Low Countries.

Doctrine and Bridging Capabilities

The 1st Polish Armoured Division was organized and equipped in the pattern of the 1944 British armoured division. The integration of Polish land forces in the West extended to the translation and utilization of British Army doctrine. In terms of coalition operations, this level of practical interoperability makes the Polish armoured division an interesting non-British prism to view the employment of British doctrine. Inevitably, Polish doctrine and operational experience would shape the utilization of British doctrine by officers of the Division. Given the technical and enabling nature of the engineering branch of any army, the military roles of engineers in the British and Polish Armies were in broad terms identical. Polish interwar engineering doctrine for crossing water obstacles was necessarily well developed for a country replete with water obstacles and a relatively underdeveloped transportation infrastructure as compared to Western Europe in the period. Use of local materials such as wood was evident in Polish engineering doctrine pointing to a culture of adaptation when circumstances required.[3] In this regard, Polish military engineering resembled the experience of the Royal Engineers in less developed corners of Empire. The war, as was the case for the British Army, introduced technical modernization to Polish military engineering driven by the widespread use of tracked and wheeled motor vehicles.

The crossing of water obstacles is scarcely a new military problem. During the Second World War, the widespread emergence of mechanization in armies gave a new flavour to an old problem. Writing in the RUSI Journal in 1923 on 'The Crossing of Rivers in Warfare', Col D. J. C. K. Bernard presciently predicated the difficulties water obstacles would present to armoured fighting vehicles:

---

3   See: *Instrukcja saperska do użytku wszystkich rodzajów broni*, (Warszawa: Ministerstwo Spraw Wojskowych, 1929) and *Instrukcja saperska kładki bojowe*, (Warszawa: Ministerstwo Spraw Wojskowych, 1931).

Whatever the value of small streams may have been during previous warfare, there is no doubt that they will be increasingly used in future wars. The reason for this statement is to be found in the advent of the Tank. Tanks can cross wire and most other obstacles, but at present quite an insignificant stream can hold them up. A stream is just as formidable an obstacle to the Tank as wire is to Infantry and Cavalry.[4]

Twenty years later the significance of water obstacles raised in the pre-war article was not lost on wartime planners. A 1943 study of the Directorate of Tactical Investigation assessing the forces required for the forthcoming campaign in North West Europe highlighted the challenges posed by water if defended by a resolute enemy:

The Germans will probably base many of their main and rearguard positions on river obstacles. The opposed river crossing, one of the most difficult operations of war, is therefore likely to be one of the most frequent.[5]

Prior to operations on the continent in1944, the British Army produced two doctrine pamphlets designed to give guidance on river crossing operations. The first of these documents *Operations Military Training Pamphlet No. 23 Part VIII River Crossings* appeared in December 1940. Work on MTP 23 1940 undoubtedly preceded the disastrous campaign in France in the summer of 1940, but it is clear that those events shaped the content of this doctrine for crossing rivers. The opening paragraph of MTP 23 1940 made clear why rivers and canals in the current war enjoyed greater significance as obstacles in a defence:

The development of armoured fighting vehicles has considerably enhanced the importance of rivers and canals as defensive obstacles, while the increased weight of vehicles has added to the technical difficulties of passing a force over a water obstacle.[6]

Defensive positions organised along water obstacles, however, did not offer enemy forces a defenders' panacea. Establishing positions along a river or canal often saw the defending force overlooked from high ground on the opposite bank. Flood plains adjacent to rivers were often featureless, 'low-lying and waterlogged'.[7] High banks or

4   Colonel D. J. C. K. Bernard, 'The Crossing of Rivers in Warfare', *Royal United Services Institution, Journal*, 70:479 (August 1925), p. 426.
5   The National archives (TNA) WO 231/18, 'The Balance of Arms', Paper prepared by the Directorate of Tactical Investigation, 1943, p. 4.
6   *Operations Military Training Pamphlet No. 23 Part VIII River Crossings*, The War Office, 21 December 1940, p. 1. Hereafter referred to as MTP 23 1940.
7   MTP 23 1940, p. 1.

levees created dead ground close to the water's edge. Whether straight or meandering, a river could present a defender with wide frontages to cover.

Having set out an analysis of the terrain's benefits and liabilities to the defender, MTP 23 1940 turned to the problem of crossing a water obstacle. The doctrine postulated two types of offensive action: an 'encounter crossing' and a 'deliberate crossing'.[8] This methodology clearly reflected something of the full gamut of the German experience in June 1940 of crossing river lines in Belgium and France. These German operations embraced both the rapid and opportunistic crossings of river lines in the Ardennes in Belgium and the 'set-piece' crossing of the Meuse at Sedan.

The 'encounter crossing' took advantage of a weak, disorganised or ill-formed enemy defence of a water obstacle. In an encounter crossing, offensive action was anticipated as taking three forms. The first was by a *coup de main* attack seeking to surprise an enemy force and pre-empt demolition of a bridge. Speed and surprise were key ingredients to a successful *coup de main* attack of a crossing point. The second was 'attack by infiltration'. In this scenario it was envisaged that gaps in the enemy defences along a river line could be exploited to establish bridgeheads and take from the rear defended crossing points. The third was 'quick attacks' where risk would be accepted in the interest of keeping initiative and maintaining momentum in operations. Follow-up of reserves was seen as vital to a successful crossing to consolidate and hold a bridgehead with the Royal Engineers providing rafting or building bridges to pass forces across the water obstacle.[9]

In contrast, the 'deliberate crossing' required a more carefully planned approach to crossing a water obstacle in the face of a coherent enemy defence. As MTP 23 1940 stated: 'Unlike the encounter crossing, the operation must be planned as a whole from the outset, consideration being given when the plan is made to the sites of the road bridges.'[10] The latter point underscored implicitly the fact that most crossings needed to be conducted in proximity to roads and where bridges had been placed. Not doing so created the complication of more engineering work to build connecting roads and additional work at the river bank to support the construction of a bridge. Creating necessary infrastructure meant significant resource and time penalties. MTP 23 1940 devoted over a dozen pages to conducting a deliberate crossing taking into account, preparation, surprise, location of crossing, timing, fire support, phases of a crossing operation and engineering capabilities to support the assault and afterwards.[11] Despite the set-piece operation in a 'deliberate crossing' taking place against a prepared enemy, the importance of supporting fire was not emphasized. Indeed MTP 23 1940

8   MTP 23 1940, p. 2.
9   MTP 23 1940, pp. 2-4.
10   MTP 23 1940, p. 5.
11   MTP 23 1940, pp. 5-19.

maintained that 'the greatest measure of success is likely when the crossing can be carried out silently without the employment of covering fire'.[12]

Doctrine in wartime is seldom static and by 1942 MTP 23 was reissued in a much revised form entitled *Operations Military Training Pamphlet No. 23, Part VIII Infantry and Armoured Divisions in the Opposed Crossing of a Water Obstacle 1942*. Despite the extensive revisions, the changes were more in emphasis and in the greater elaboration of technique. MTP 23 1942, as its title indicated placed considerably more importance on overcoming enemy opposition in crossing a water obstacle. It dropped the concept of 'encounter crossing' but still stressed that 'no opportunity of capturing bridges intact or incompletely demolished must be missed'.[13] The other categories of types of attack remained unchanged in the doctrine and included: coup de main, infiltration, quick assaults and deliberate assaults. What did change was the elaboration of the planning requirements and sequencing of the crossing operation that recognised whether a bridgehead had been established by a rapid *coup de main* or of grinding deliberate assault, for a division to establish, consolidate and exploit a bridgehead was a complicated business requiring substantial effort of planning in a compressed timeframe.[14] The complexities were reflected in the eight sections making up MTP 23 1942 that covered 'general considerations', 'reconnaissance', 'planning', 'assembly and preparation', 'the assault', 'the establishment of bridgeheads', 'construction of bridges and crossing of main body' and 'methods of crossing'.[15]

MTP 23 1942 in comparison with the 1940 version of river crossing doctrine indicated that 'difficulties have grown' in conducting such operations thus requiring a 'new technique' and the 'closest cooperation between all arms'.[16] The emphasis on a river crossing operation being an 'all arms' battle pointed to the fact that orchestration of the various arms involved was crucial to success. The role of 'supporting and covering fire' in mounting an assault received more elaboration than in the previous version of the river crossing doctrine. The 'silent crossing' conducted without fire support was something only to be attempted at night. The daylight crossing, however, was to be conducted with the 'maximum amount of supporting fire'. Achieving obscuration of movements, weather conditions permitting, was to be achieved by employing 'a liberal amount of smoke'.[17] Forward Observation Officers (FOO) were to cross early with the leading echelons of the assault to provide necessary support to assault troops encountering centres of enemy resistance.[18]

---

12   MTP 23 1940, p. 7.
13   *Operations Military Training Pamphlet No. 23, Part VIII Infantry and Armoured Divisions in the Opposed Crossing of a Water Obstacle*, The War Office, August 1942, p. 24. Hereafter referred to as MTP 23 1942.
14   MTP 23 1942, pp. 8-18.
15   MTP 23 1942, pp. 1-44.
16   MTP 23 1942, p. 1.
17   MTP 23 1942, pp. 29-30.
18   MTP 23 1942, p. 30.

The other supporting arm that had a crucial role was the engineers. Their role was to get the force across the water obstacle by boat, raft, footbridge and vehicle bridge. The degree to which the engineers could succeed was conditioned by the capacity of the enemy to interfere with the engineer's work especially the construction of a bridge capable of taking vehicles. The erection of a bridge was critical to the passing of the main force across the obstacle into the bridgehead and to further exploitation. From a technical point of view, erecting a new bridge on the site of a demolished one or repairing a bridge presented a more 'straightforward engineer task' and utilized the existing road network to the bridge. On this latter point, having to construct approaches and exits capable of carrying vehicles was seen as a 'more difficult task' than erecting a bridge.[19] Hence securing the area of an established bridge crossing, however damaged, was desirable for a variety of practical reasons. Nevertheless, these were the points most likely to be well defended.

MTP 23 1942 gave more attention to the problem of establishing and consolidating a bridgehead after crossing a water obstacle. In many respects the bridgehead in its early stages was the most exposed aspect of an operation to cross a water obstacle. The 1942 doctrine noted that 'the bridgehead force will be vulnerable to counterattack, especially by A.F.V.s, until some of the heavier supporting weapons and transport are across'.[20] As a consequence, MTP 23 1942 stressed that 'the commander's aim is to get his main striking force as a whole across the obstacle as rapidly as possible'.[21] Underscoring this point, *Army Training Memorandum* No. 45, published in May 1943 indicated the priorities in passing a force across a water obstacle:

> In normal circumstances there will be no necessity to get tanks across in the initial stage of a bridge crossing, the essential weapons at that stage being those required to establish a bridgehead, *e.g.*, infantry, anti-tank guns, and mortars. Every effort will be devoted to getting these weapons over quickly.[22]

Key variables in establishing a bridgehead included levels of enemy resistance, 'extent and timing' of enemy counterattacks and the technical issues related to the engineering tasks associated with the construction of rafts and bridges.[23]

The Bailey Bridge

The doctrine for crossing water obstacles ultimately relied on the engineer's bridging capability. The bridging to support armoured division operations required a number

19   MTP 23 1942, p. 34.
20   MTP 23 1942, p. 31.
21   MTP 23 1942, p. 31.
22   *Army Training Memorandum* (ATM) No. 45, The War Office, 29 May 1943, p. 49.
23   ATM No. 45, p. 32.

of critical features. In battlefield conditions it had to be designed to be quickly erected and yet have the capacity to take the weight of the heaviest armoured fighting vehicles. The use of a simple design with standard components that could be easily assembled with a minimum of amount of specialist equipment was desirable in meeting military requirements for simplicity and standardization.[24] What is remarkable is that at the outbreak of war, the British Army lacked such a modern bridging capability suitable for the operational conditions to be encountered in the new war. This capability gap, however, would be rectified by a remarkable piece of British engineering – the Bailey bridge.

In December 1940, the British Army's 'Experimental Bridging Establishment' (EBE) began the task of designing a new bridge. Largely the result of the ideas of Donald Bailey, the EBE's Chief Designer, the 'Bailey' bridge was designed, tested and put into production in an extraordinarily short period of time. Work began on the project in December 1940 and one year later the first production examples reached the field Army. By the end of the war, British industry manufactured 400,000 tons of components for Bailey bridges which were enough to assemble 200 miles of Bailey bridge.[25] Manufacture of the Bailey bridge utilized non-critical medals and its design meant that a wide range of firms could be employed in its production. Most importantly, its 'Meccano' set of standard components conferred flexibility and adaptability in the range of bridge types that could be constructed including a pontoon variant.[26] The post war British Army study of wartime field engineering described the principal features of the Bailey bridge:

> The basic idea of the bridge is the bolting together in a variety of combinations, depending on the job required, of a number of flat panels or frames. The main girders are built up of these panels, which can be arranged either in one, two, or three trusses side by side, and in one, two, or three stories high, with almost any combination between. Panels are attached to each other by the insertion of steel pins through holes in overlapping jaws. The roadway is carried on steel transoms resting on the bottom chord of the girders to form a "through" bridge. For the heaviest loads the number of these transoms is increased. The panels, which can be carried by six men, and each of the other parts can be packed into a 3-ton G.S. lorry and so no special transport is required.[27]

24   Donald Coleman Bailey, Robert Arthur Foulkes and Rodman Digby-Smith, 'The Bailey Bridge and Its Developments', in *The Civil Engineer in War: A Symposium of Papers on War-time Engineering Problems Vol. I Airfields, Roads, Railways, and Bridges*, London: The Institution of Civil Engineers1948, p. 374.

25   Major General Pakenham-Walsh, *Military Engineering (Field)*, (London: The War Office, 1952), pp. 259-260.

26   See: *Military Engineering Volume III – Part III, Bailey Bridge – Normal Uses 1944*, The War Office, 18 March 1944.

27   Pakenham-Walsh, *Military Engineering (Field)*, pp. 259-260.

Wartime engineers possessed a range of capabilities to support the crossing of water obstacles that included assault boats, kapok foot bridges and pontoon rafts that could carry light vehicles.[28] Although these other capabilities were important when mounting an operation to cross a water obstacle, they were only a prelude to the erection of a Bailey bridge.

Engineering Capability in the 1st Polish Armoured Division

As the 1943 British doctrine for the armoured division stressed, 'the primary role of the engineers is to assist the armoured division in maintaining its mobility'.[29] Toward this end, 519 officers and other ranks served in the engineering component of the 1944 British pattern armoured division. The chief engineering officer in divisional headquarters (Commander Royal Engineers – CRE) controlled the engineering resources centrally and allocated units and sub-units to particular tasks or assigned them to combined arms groups. In the 1st Polish Armoured Division, the CRE role was filled by the forty-five year old Lieutenant Colonel Jan Dorantt, an experienced professional soldier whose career included a three year posting to the Military Engineering School (*Wojskowej Szkoły Inżynierii*) as a lecturer and command of a motorised sapper battalion in 1939. The engineers of the division were distributed in four units: a Field Park Squadron, two Field Squadrons and a Bridging Platoon.[30] The Field Park Squadron provided workshops, engineering stores and operated heavy plant such as bulldozers. The two Field Squadrons, one for each brigade, did the full range of engineering tasks from clearing mines to building bridges. The bridging platoon provided the organic bridging capability and possessed enough Bailey bridge material to build 130 feet of Class 40 bridge capable of carrying the heaviest armoured vehicles in the division.[31] The engineering element in the 1st Polish Armoured Division followed this organizational template with unit titles reflecting Polish practice. The Field Park Squadron was called the Sapper Park Company (*kompanii parkowej saperów*), the two Field Squadrons were the 10 and 11 Sapper Company respectively (*kompanii saperów*) and divisional Bridging Platoon was the *dywizyjnego plutonu mostowego*.

28   MTP 23 1942, pp. 37-39.
29   *Military Training Pamphlet No. 41, The Tactical Handling of the Armoured Division and its Components Part 1 The Tactical Handling of Armoured Divisions*, The War Office, July 1943, p. 18.
30   George Forty, *Companion to the British Army 1939-1945*, (Stroud, Gloucester: The History Press, 2009), p. 161.
31   John Church, *Military Vehicles of World War 2*, (Poole, Dorset: Blandford Press, 1982), p. 107.

Pursuit: Normandy to the Low Countries

On 29 August 1944, the 1st Polish Armoured Division left its rest area in Normandy with orders to move north as part the allied pursuit. Two days later it crossed the Seine and moved to within fifteen km (nine miles) east of Rouen. On 1 September, five years after the outbreak of war in Poland, the 1st Polish Armoured Division joined the pursuit northwards of the German forces defeated in the battle for Normandy.[32] Its route to the France-Belgium border took it through Elbboeuf, Buchy, Neufchatel, Blancy, Abbeville and St Omer. Between 30 August and 9 September the division's march covered a distance of 470 km (292 miles) averaging forty-two km (twenty-six miles) per day. The armoured reconnaissance regiment, 10 Mounted Rifles (*10 Pułk Strzelców Konnych*), in the van of the divisional line of march, covered about 900 km (559 miles) probing for enemy forces, clearing pockets of resistance and looking for suitable crossing points of water obstacles.[33] The speed of the advance and distance covered was greatly facilitated by the weak resistance of a disorganized and retreating enemy force. As the Polish Armoured Division's after-action report for the period of the pursuit noted, opposing enemy forces consisted mostly of ad hoc *Kampfgruppen* made up of soldiers from a mishmash of units.[34] This incoherent and weak enemy resistance precluded in the pursuit northwards the utilization of the major river and canal lines encountered for effective defence.

The first opposed crossing of a water obstacle by the 1st Polish Armoured Division occurred in Normandy in mid-August in the context of Operation Tractable. Against crumbling German resistance the 1st Polish Armoured seized two crossing points over the river Dives. This operation led to the construction by divisional engineers of an improvised bridge and two Bailey bridges at Jort and Vendeuvre.[35] It was, however, a prelude to the problem of crossing water obstacles encountered in later operations after Normandy. In the path of the advance of the allied forces northwards were a series major water obstacles including the rivers Seine, the Somme and the Lys Canal. Although these and other lesser water obstacles were surmounted against light or no enemy resistance, a major engineering effort was necessary to keep the lead divisions of 21st Army Group moving.

The first major undertaking of the engineers of the 1st Polish Armoured Division was the construction of a large pontoon Bailey bridge across the Seine. On 28 August, the two Sapper Companies of the Division, as the result of a Corps directive, were

32   Stanisław Maczek, *Od podwody do czołga Wspomnienia wojenne 1918-1945*, (Edinburgh: Tomar Publishers, 1961), p. 188.

33   Instytut Polski i Muzeum im. Gen. Sikorskiego, Londyn, [Polish Institute and General Sikorski Museum, London], (IPMS), AV 1/1, 'Raport Nr 3 Raport bojowy Dowodcy 1 Dywizja Pancernej, walki za okres 23.8 – 9.9.44 r,' 10 September 1944, p. 2.

34   IPMS: 'Raport Nr 3 Raport bojowy Dowodcy 1 Dywizja Pancernej, walki za okres 23.8 – 9.9.44 r,' 10 September 1944, p. 1.

35   IPMS: C-191-A War Diary, 10 Sapper Company, August 1944.

given the task of constructing a pontoon Bailey bridge at Crique sur Seine. Major Władysław Podgorzelski, the Commander of 11 Sapper Company was placed in command of the bridge building operation with both of the Division's sapper companies committed to the effort. Following a reconnaissance the site and the acquisition of bridging materials, construction of the pontoon Bailey bridge began with the two Polish engineer companies completing the 518 foot (157 m) Warszawa (Warsaw) bridge across the Seine on 29 August after 13 hours of effort.[36] With the drive northwards by the 1st Polish Armoured Division beginning in earnest on 1 September, the two sapper companies were kept busy building, repairing or adapting bridges to convey the division's vehicles. During the pursuit, Polish sappers constructed two Bailey bridges across the Somme River and the Neuf Fosse canal. In addition, three existing bridges were repaired or adapted, fords strengthened and a makeshift bridge improvised that could take vehicles, all in a period of nine days. This intense work helped to maintain the rapid tempo of the advance of the Polish armoured division but stretched the division's engineering resources.[37]

By 5 September the 1st Polish Armoured Division, advancing on two axes, approached the France-Belgium border. Against stiffening if still disorganized enemy resistance, the Division cleared St Omer and after a night assault crossing by the Highland Rifle Battalion (*Batalion Strzelców Podlański*) seized a bridgehead on the northern side of the Neuf Fosse canal near Blaringhem. By the morning of 6 September the Polish sappers completed a bridge over the waterway. On 7 September the 1st Polish Armoured Division crossed into Belgium and liberated Ypres. The 9th Rifle Battalion (*9 Batalion Strzelców*) cleared the town encountering significant enemy resistance. The Division's operations on 7 September captured the towns of Roulers, Hooglede and Gits in west Flanders. Clearing these towns was in the face of increasing and better organized German resistance. For example, it took heavy fighting until dawn of 8 September to clear Roulers by 9 Rifle Battalion supported by elements of the Highland Rifle Battalion. Operations on 8 September saw a similar pattern of heavy fighting to clear the towns of Thielt (Tielt) and Ruysselede (Ruiselede). As the 1st Polish Armoured Division moved closer to the border with Holland, the disorganized and ad hoc German resistance encountered during the pursuit was giving way to a coherent German defence.

It was not only levels of German resistance that were changing. The terrain of the Belgian-Dutch borderlands heralded the beginning of a landscape typical of Holland. Flat, low lying and prone to flooding, roads and built-up areas resided on natural or man-made elevated ground with the country criss-crossed by canals and watercourses. Although the quality of roads was generally good, movement nevertheless

36 IPMS: C-192-I 'Budowa mostu na rz. Sekwanie w Criquebeuf, Most Nr 2 "Warsaw Bridge"', enclosure in War Diary, 11 Sapper Company, July-August 1944.
37 IPMS: C-191-B, War Diary, 10 Sapper Company, September 1944 and IPMS: C-192-II-A, War Diary, 11 Sapper Company, September 1944.

was restricted. Roads had to be constructed on built-up earth embankments that had the effect of limiting and channelling movement. These features did not make for ideal tank country. The landscape also had an urban dimension as it was dotted with towns and villages. Fields of view were often restricted. The after action report of the 1st Polish Armoured Division covering operations in this area noted that the landscape resembled the Pripet marshes (*Polesie*) of eastern Poland. For an army fighting a defensive battle, this landscape possessed abundant features to be exploited by the defender. The arrival of the 1st Polish Armoured Division in the Belgian-Dutch borderlands coincided with the recovery of the German Army's capacity to mount a coherent and effective defence.

These changed circumstances were made amply clear to the 1st Polish Armoured Division on 9 and 10 September in its attempt to cross the next major water obstacle – the Ghent canal. The Division's line of advance north toward the Scheldt estuary required it to cross the Ghent canal. Major General Stanisław Maczek, GOC 1st Polish Armoured Division gave this task to a battlegroup consisting of 2 Armoured Regiment (*2 Pułk Pancerny*), 10 Dragoon Regiment (*10 Pułk Dragonów*), a squadron of self-propelled anti-tank guns and supporting engineers. The attempted night crossing of the Ghent canal on 9-10 September failed with the commander of the 10th Dragoon Regiment, Lieutenant Colonel Władysław Zgorzelski being seriously wounded.[38] The assault of the 10th Dragoons was unsuccessful due to a combination of factors: the steep five metre banks of the canal, inadequate numbers of assault boats, poor fields of observation and strong and well masked enemy positions.[39]

The repulse of 10 Dragoons after repeated attempts to cross the canal was an indication that the German Army was no longer in disarray. The 1st Polish Armoured Division now faced the more formidable opponents of the *712th German Infantry Division* under the command of Lieutenant General Friedrich-Wilhelm Neumann. Its main elements consisted of the *732nd* and *745th Infantry Regiments* supported by the *652nd Artillery Battalion*. This German Division occupied a sector of the Belgium-Netherlands coast near Bruges and was a fresh and reasonably up-to-strength formation that knew the ground well over which it would fight as it had been assigned to the area in 1942.[40]

The failure of the Dragoon's to cross the Ghent canal led Maczek to order his 3 Rifle Brigade (*3 Brygada Strzelców*) to plan a deliberate attack to force a crossing of the

38 IPMS: AV 1/1, 'Raport Nr 3 Raport bojowy Dowodcy 1 Dywizja Pancernej, walki za okres 23.8 – 9.9.44 r,' p. 8 and Eugeniusz Piotr Nowak, *10 Pułk Dragonów Tom II*, (Kraków: Barbara, 2006), 115.

39 IPMS: B1817, 'Dworak Relacje', p. 58. [Post-war report by the deputy division commander on the division's wartime operations].

40 *German Order of Battle: The Directory of Allied Intelligence, of Regiments, Formations and Units of the German Armoured Forces*, (London: Greenhill Books, 1994), p. D 111 and Samuel W. Mitcham, *Hitler's Legions: The German Army Order of Battle World War II*, (London: Leo Cooper, 1985), p. 312.

canal with the intention of mounting the attack on 11 September. Preparations for a second assault crossing, however, were overtaken by events and the assault cancelled. The 2nd Canadian Corps directed the 1st Polish Armoured Division instead to relieve the British 2nd Armoured Division in the region of Ghent.[41] Up until 14 September the Division's 3 Rifle Brigade had the job of clearing Ghent and adjacent areas and 10 Armoured Cavalry Brigade (*10 Brygada Kawalerii Pancernej)* took control of Stekene, St Gill and the area around La Tromphe.[42]

Crossing the Axel-Hulst Canal 16-19 September 1944

On 15 September, Maczek issued a fresh directive in line with 2nd Canadian Corps objectives to launch an attack to clear German forces from a sector running north from the Axel-Hulst canal to the Scheldt. This was to lead to the 1st Polish Armoured Division's first deliberate assault crossing of a water obstacle in the Low Countries. The western flank of the 1st Polish Armoured Division was anchored in Ghent. Maczek assigned this defensive role to a battlegroup consisting of 8 Rifle Battalion (*8 Batalion Strzelców*), 24 Lancer Regiment [Armoured] (*24 Pułk Ułanów*), an artillery battery, an anti-tank battery and sapper platoon. This battlegroup was under the command of Lieutenant Colonel Władysław Dec, the deputy commander of 3 Rifle Brigade. The 10th Armoured Cavalry Brigade screened the eastern flank of the Division with two of its three armoured regiments and a self-propelled anti-tank battery. The main effort of the 1st Polish Armoured Division was to be undertaken by 3 Rifle Brigade in the central sector of the Division's area of operations. The Brigade had the task of crossing the Axel-Hulst canal at a point somewhere along a five kilometre stretch of the canal to the east of Axel. After crossing, 3 Rifle Brigade was to move northwest to Terneuzen and clear enemy forces from an area running from a north-south line marked by the Ghent-Terneuzen canal in the west and to the north and east by the Scheldt.[43] Colonel Franciszek Skibiński, Commander of 3 Rifle Brigade, described the area his brigade was to clear as the 'Axel island', a natural fortress with water obstacles forming the boundary on every side. Elements of the *712th* and *59th Infantry Divisions* defended 'Axel Island'. The German forces had the combined strength of six infantry battalions, an anti-tank battalion, two batteries of light artillery, an armoured car company and a composite company of tanks and self-propelled guns.[44]

For the task of crossing the Axel-Hulst canal and clearing the area to the Scheldt, Skibiński had 3 Rifle Brigade's own Highland Rifle Battalion and 9 Rifle Battalion.

---

41   Franciszek Skibiński, *Axel*, (Warszawa: Książka i Wiedza, 1979), pp. 20-21 and Franciszek Skibiński, *Pierwsza Pancerna*, (Warszawa: Czytelnik, 1966), pp. 314-315.

42   Skibiński, *Axel*, p. 21 and IPMS: C 97, '1 Dywizja Pancerna Kalendarzyk Działan Dywizja', p. 6.

43   IPMS: C 96/II, 'Rozkaz Szczegolny do Działania w dniu 16 I 16 IX 1944 r.', War Diary, 1st Polish Armoured Division, 15-16 September 1944.

44   Skibiński, *Pierwsza Pancerna*, p. 320.

In addition, attached to the Brigade for the operation was the motor infantry battalion from 10 Armoured Cavalry Brigade, 10 Dragoon Regiment. The 10th Mounted Rifles, less one squadron (kept as a divisional reserve) provided armour support. Other supporting assets included two anti-tank batteries, one towed and one self-propelled. The 3rd Brigade was allotted full support of divisional artillery less the one battery in Ghent. The 10th Sapper Company less one platoon was to support the Brigade attack.[45]

On 15 September, Skibiński finalized his Brigade plan. At an orders group at 1900 in the Brigade headquarters held in a secondary school in St Paul, Skibiński briefed his senior officers on their role in the attack. The 3rd Rifle Brigade would advance on two axes. On the left, 9 Rifle Battalion with an anti-tank gun battery, a heavy machine gun company and with a platoon of engineers attached moved north through Kemseke and Koewacht. The 9th Rifle Battalion had responsibility for conducting a reconnaissance of the stretch of the Axel-Hulst canal running east from Axel to Nooit Gedacht looking for suitable crossing points. On the right, 10 Dragoon Regiment with an attached anti-tank gun battery and platoon of engineers moved north from La Tromphe to Drie Hofijers. Upon reaching the Axel-Hulst canal, the Dragoons had responsibility for conducting a reconnaissance for crossing points running east from Nooit Gedacht to Hulst. For supporting fires, all of the division's artillery regiments were allocated to the attack under the direction of the commander divisional artillery. In the second echelon of the attack was the brigade reserve that included the Highland Infantry Battalion, the armoured 10 Mounted Rifles and the remaining engineers of 10 Sapper Company following mainly on the left. The Brigade plan established three reporting lines: 'Roman One' following the line of the Dutch frontier forts, 'Roman Two' further to the north following the highway running from Sas van Gent to Hulst and 'Roman Three' on the northern bank of the Axel-Hulst canal. The operation was set to begin the morning of 16 September.[46]

Before 3 Rifle Brigade could traverse the Axel-Hulst canal and clear to the Scheldt, the Brigade had to cross over the Belgium-Netherlands border and control the southern approaches to the canal. The Brigade attack in this initial stage was an advance to contact. The area it moved through contained difficult terrain with enemy demolitions and destruction potentially slowing the attack. After crossing the border into the Netherlands, the Brigade would encounter in the border area a line of fortified towns and forts running east-west that formed part of a seventeenth century defensive system. These features still had defensive potential. Skibiński's plan, however, had built in flexibility contingent on what his Brigade ran into south of the Axel-Hulst canal. Depending on enemy resistance and what his two columns

45   IPMS: C 96/II, 'Rozkaz Szczegolny do Działania w dniu 16 IX 1944 r.'.
46   IPMS: C 106/I-B, 'Rozkaz Bojowy na dzień 16 IX 1944', War Diary, 3 Rifle Brigade,15 September 1944 and Skibiński, *Axel*, pp. 65-67.

found, his dispositions allowed a crossing attempt on each axis of advance or just one. Skibiński saw his two groups reaching Koewacht and Drie Hofijers as 'the basis for further operations'.[47]

At 0700 on 16 September, 3 Rifle Brigade launched its attack. The 9th Rifle Battalion group on the right captured its initial objective of Koewacht at 0900 without a fight. The town had been the headquarters of the German *712th Infantry Division* and in its hasty withdrawal 9 Rifle Battalion captured papers left behind by the divisional staff. The 10th Dragoon group on the right enjoyed similar progress reaching and clearing its objective of Drie Hofijers against very light resistance. By mid-morning, the reports of 9 Rifle Battalion and 10 Dragoons indicated that the advance faced only light resistance south of the Axel-Hulst canal. Skibiński now faced the decision how to further develop his Brigade's operations.

The western (left) group of 9 Rifle Battalion he directed on a line of march through Het Zand and Halt that would take it to the canal line south of Axel. When Skibiński issued his revised orders in late-morning he believed that his western (left) group was likely to be his main effort.[48] Proof of this can be seen in his written confirmatory order issued at 1300 for verbal orders issued at 1115. In it Skibiński warned his engineers to be ready to build a bridge on the area of operations of 9 Rifle Battalion.[49] However, the increasing German resistance encountered by the 9 Rifle Battalion group made a crossing in their sector more problematic. Reflecting the increased levels of German resistance, Skibiński ordered one squadron of armour of the 10 Mounted Rifles to support the attack. When 3 Company of 9 Rifle Battalion with the armour support of 1 Squadron, 10 Mounted Rifles advanced toward Axel from Drie Schouwen in the late afternoon, the combined arms group ran into heavy fire suffering four dead and twenty wounded in a matter of minutes. This setback halted the advance before Axel. The 9th Rifle Battalion group found the enemy defence on the northern bank of the canal robust and built around what proved to be two German battalions in Axel.[50] Lieutenant Colonel Władysław Szydłowski, the commander of 9 Rifle Battalion convinced Skibiński that a crossing attempt was impossible. He argued that 9 Rifle Battalion Group lacked the necessary strength and needed to consolidate for the night. Skibiński in his published account of the operations stressed his implicit trust in Szydłowski's judgement of the situation and abandoned the idea of a crossing attempt at Axel.[51] This left Skibiński with the eastern (right) 10 Dragoon group to attempt a canal crossing. Moving north from Koewacht, the 10th Dragoons moved through difficult terrain and brushed aside weak German patrols to reach the canal

---

47   IPMS: C 106/I-B, 'Rozkaz Bojowy na dzień 16 IX 1944'.
48   Skibiński, *Axel*, p. 71.
49   IPMS, C 106/I-B, 'Rozkaz Potwierdzajacy rozkazy ustne wydane o godz. 11.15', War Diary, 3 Rifle Brigade, 16 September 1944.
50   Zdzisław Szydłowski, 'Bój o Axel', in: *1 Dywizja Pancerna w Walce, Praca Zbiorowa*, (Brussels: 1947), pp. 192-193.
51   Skibiński, *Axel*, p. 73.

by noon. The biggest challenge as the Dragoons advanced to the canal was the slow-going movement in the terrain caused by destruction and obstacles. On reaching the canal, the squadrons of 10 Dragoons covered a two kilometre frontage running from Fort St Nicolaas in the west to Absdale in the east. In his revised orders Skibiński also directed 10 Dragoons to mount a crossing of the Axel-Hulst canal in their sector.[52]

Black Day for the Dragoons

The 10th Dragoon Regiment was led by Captain Wacław Kownas. As noted earlier, the Dragoons' well-respected commander since 1943 had been Lieutenant Colonel Władysław Zgorzelski, who was wounded a week earlier on 9 September in the attempt to cross the Ghent canal. That Kownas was placed in command was an indication of the heavy losses already incurred among the senior officers of the Regiment. The second in Command, Major Andrzej Szajowski, had been seriously wounded in Normandy. The most senior company commander of 2 Squadron, Captain Tadeusz Dudziński died on operations at Falaise. With Kownas the next most senior officer, command of the Dragoons' fell on his shoulders. Kownas now faced a difficult operation very soon after taking command of the Regiment. Although Kownas was well liked by the soldiers of his squadron, the same could not be said of the other officers in the Regiment.[53] Kownas was an infantry officer posted to a cavalry Regiment where he was treated by his fellow officers as the 'outsider'. To make matters worse he was seen as being both inexperienced and ambitious by 3 Rifle Brigade Commander, Skibiński.[54] These command tensions set the stage for what was to be the worst day of the war for 10 Dragoon Regiment.

The Dragoons began their assault crossing of the Axel-Hulst canal in the area near Dubosch around 1600 on 16 September (see Map 1). The axis of the attack across the canal followed the line of the road running north from Fort St Nicolaas. The 3rd Squadron under the command of Lieutenant Jacek Bielawski rapidly crossed the twenty-five metre canal in the engineer's assault boats. After taking fire from German troops in houses on the opposite bank and a machinegun from a nearby dyke, Bielawski's 3 Squadron cleared opposition in the area of the canal bank. Bielawski's squadron then moved to establish its position one and a half kilometres to the North West of Dubosch. The 1st Squadron led by Captain Zbigniew Giera crossed next and moved quickly in a north westerly direction toward the crossroads at Steenbosc two kilometres distant from the canal. The 2nd Squadron under the command of Lieutenant Zbigniew Bojanowski was last to cross the canal around 1900 and

52 Skibiński, *Axel*, p. 74.
53 Memoir of Karol Wierzgoń, 10 Pułk Dragonów in Jacek Kutzner and Aleksander Rutkiewicz (compilers), *Polacy z Wehrmachtu w polskiej 1. Dywizji Pancernej gen. Maczka*, (Warszawa: Oficyna Wydawnicza RYTM, 2011), pp. 216-217.
54 Skibiński, *Axel*, p. 79 and Skibiński, *Pierwsza Pancerna*, p. 324.

established its positions on an embankment in an area half a kilometre to the west of Kijkuit.[55] Although the Dragoons had gained a bridgehead on the northern bank of the canal against light opposition, the seeds of disaster were already being sown in their dispositions. Giera's 1 Squadron had moved too far from the canal and was out of contact with the other squadrons. It is unclear whether Kownas directed 1 Squadron to the crossroads at Steenbosc or Giera, the squadron commander, took this action on his own initiative.[56] Given the personalities involved and the difficult command relationships, either possibility offers a credible explanation for 1 Squadron's move to Steenbosc. Instead of meeting Skibiński's intent in the 3 Rifle Brigade plan of forming a tight bridgehead consisting of a hard half circle near the crossing point where the Dragoons could protect the engineers as they built a bridge, 1 Squadron overextended the bridgehead and risked being cut off and the other squadrons subsequently being rolled up.[57]

Apart from ferrying the Dragoons to the north bank of the Axel-Hulst canal, 1 Platoon of 10 Sapper Company set about building a kapok footbridge at 1800 to insure ammunition resupply and communications with squadrons in the bridgehead. The footbridge was completed about 2000.[58] Next in the sequence of engineer tasks was to build a pontoon ferry that was big enough to convey light vehicles and heavy weapons such as the anti-tank guns. While work was going on at the canal, elements of 10 Sapper Company also began surveying the location to begin preparations to build a Bailey bridge so that follow-on Polish armour and infantry could be moved into the bridgehead. The sappers had the task of building the bridge near or over the remains of the destroyed bridge on the road running north from Fort St Nicolaas that crossed the canal a few hundred metres west of Dubosch.[59] With the surrounding fields waterlogged, the use of a road raised on an embankment was necessary for the Division's vehicles.

As 10 Sapper Company completed the kapok footbridge, a liaison officer from 3 Brigade arrived with fresh orders for Kownas. The brigade commander, Skibiński, ordered that the three Dragoon squadrons be withdrawn to positions close to the canal and form a tight half circle on the northern bank to protect the engineers building the bridge. For Kownas, the fresh orders marked the beginning of the crisis for the Dragoons. The first problem Kownas faced in carrying out his orders was that his 1 Squadron was not only physically separated from the rest of the regiment but was out of radio contact making it difficult for him to pull back his overextended 1 Squadron. Kownas also understood that he needed the engineers to complete the pontoon ferry as quickly as possible. The pontoon ferry was critical as the Dragoon squadrons lacked

---

55   Nowak, *10 Pułk Dragonów*, p. 131 and Szydłowski, 'Bój o Axel', p. 194.
56   Skibiński, *Pierwsza Pancerna*, p. 325.
57   Skibiński, *Pierwsza Pancerna*, p. 325.
58   Nowak, *10 Pułk Dragonów*, p. 132 and Szydłowski, 'Bój o Axel', p. 194.
59   IPMS: C-191-B, War Diary, 10 Sapper Company, 16 September 1944.

any anti-armour capability beyond hand-held PIATs. Until the Dragoons' heavy weapons could be brought across the canal, they were vulnerable in the event of a German counterattack. The engineers only began to assemble the pontoon raft at 2300 and made a lot of noise in its construction.[60]

At 0100 on 17 September, just as the first Bren carrier was being ferried across the canal on the completed pontoon, intense German artillery and mortar fire began to rain down on the crossing point. The raft with its carrier sank and as the shelling intensified, engineering work became impossible. Kownas now could neither communicate with the 1st Squadron nor reinforce his vulnerable squadrons across the canal. The situation, however, only worsened for Kownas. His command and control problems continued to mount as he lost in succession all three of his Regimental command post radios and his vital supporting artillery fire was interrupted when the assigned FOO was wounded and his equipment smashed. In desperation, Kownas at 0200 put together a scratch patrol made up of Dragoons in his headquarters area at Fort Ferdinandus and set out to try personally to reach Giera's 1 Squadron taking advantage of a lull in German artillery fire. Kownas, however, never made contact with 1 Squadron as his patrol was pinned down after it encountered a German unit moving across its front. Although not discovered by the larger German force, Kownas was forced back and had to re-cross the canal and return to his headquarters. Skibiński would later question Kownas' decision to go forward indicating that 'this was not the work of a regimental commander'.[61] By moving forward, Kownas made worse his already tenuous command and control of his regiment.

At 0300 Kownas had his first direct contact with 1 Squadron. Giera had sent back a four man patrol with a Dutch guide to report on his situation and to convey the news that his radio was damaged and not working. Kownas sent the patrol back with orders for 1 Squadron to withdraw to the crossing point.[62] Believing that 1 Squadron was vulnerable and the bridgehead in need of reinforcement, Kownas at 0330 sent his adjutant to 3 Rifle Brigade headquarters to ask for reinforcements to take over the defence of the canal so that he could use his other two squadrons to break through to the overextended 1 Squadron. Skibiński, who had been sending liaison officers forward trying to get information on the Dragoon's situation, now received the request from Kownas for additional resources. This confirmed for Skibiński the extent of the crisis that the Dragoons' now faced. Skibiński did not agree with Kownas' plan to reinforce the bridgehead and to attempt to link up with Giera's isolated 1 Squadron. Skibiński instead decided to send forward two companies of his reserve Highland Rifle Battalion to occupy positions on the southern bank of the canal. In addition he allocated 1 Squadron of 10 Mounted Rifles to provide tank support to give covering

---

60   Nowak, *10 Pułk Dragonów Tom II*, pp. 133-134.
61   K. Jamar, *With the Tanks of the 1st Polish Armoured Division*, (Holland: 1946), p. 215-216, Szydłowski, 'Bój o Axel', p. 194 and Skibiński, *Axel*, p. 79.
62   Jamar, *With the Tanks*, p. 218.

fire. Skibiński's decision was something of a compromise.[63] Deploying the armour and infantry in this manner gave him the option of supporting a withdrawal if necessary or to reinforce quickly the Dragoon bridgehead if the engineers were able to complete a Bailey bridge. It would be daybreak before all the reinforcements would be in position.

When Kownas requested additional support from 3 Rifle Brigade headquarters, it is clear that the effort to cross the Axel-Hulst canal at Dubosch was beginning to unravel. He did not really have effective control of his squadrons with communications across the canal tenuous and the crossing point under heavy indirect fire. At 0600 Kownas received news that Giera, the commander of 1 Squadron, was moving his unit back to the crossing point. The 1st Squadron, however, after finding its route back blocked by strong enemy forces made its way to another section of the canal and eventually succeeded in crossing further west in the area of 9 Rifle Battalion. The mist that descended over the area of the canal masked Giera's withdrawal.[64] This positive development, however, was overshadowed by the final act of the black day for 10 Dragoon Regiment.

At 0700 fire erupted on the right flank of the bridgehead directed against 2 Squadron commanded by Lieutenant Bojanowski. The German counterattack consisted of a battalion plus of infantry supported by armoured cars and was launched from Kijkuit.[65] The mist that had covered Giera's withdrawal of 1 Squadron allowed the German infantry to move close to Polish positions before launching their counterattack. Taking heavy casualties and with some of its positions overrun, 2 Squadron was pushed back into 3 Squadron's location nearer to the canal. At the crossing point the two squadron commanders Lieutenant Bielawski and Lieutenant Bojanowski found no engineers or boats waiting to ferry them back across the canal. With the two squadrons facing destruction, 2 and 3 Squadron commanders in the chaotic conditions agreed to search for a way back across the canal by moving west using the cover of a railway embankment. The squadrons then moved one and a half to two kilometres to the west where they found a damaged and submerged footbridge that they utilized to cross back over the canal. The cool leadership of Bielawski and Bojanowski had saved the two squadrons from complete destruction. Kownas from his command post at Fort Ferdinandus could only helplessly watch the disaster unfold. His effort to mount a rescue with a scratch force of anti-tank gun crews, drivers and signallers was overtaken by news that the squadrons had succeeded in crossing back.[66] In any case, he had no means of crossing the canal.

The Axel-Hulst canal crossing operation on 16-17 September was the most costly action of the war for 10 Dragoon Regiment. The history of the regiment put casualty figures at seventy-five including twenty-eight dead, nineteen wounded, eleven missing

63   Skibiński, *Axel*, p. 82.
64   Nowak, *10 Pułk Dragonów Tom II*, p. 134.
65   Skibiński, *Axel*, p. 83.
66   Jamar, *With the Tanks*, p. 219 and Nowak, *10 Pułk Dragonów Tom II*, pp. 138-139.

and seventeen taken prisoner.[67] The 10th Dragoons moved to Koewacht for recovery and reorganization.[68] Kownas' first major action in command of the Dragoons' had ended in failure and with heavy losses. It was to cost him his command. Maj Bohdan Mincer, deputy commander of 2 Armoured Regiment was given command of 10 Dragoons on 17 September. Maczek, the divisional commander decided to move Kownas to 2 Armoured Regiment and had him placed in command of 3 Squadron pending investigation of the events surrounding the failed attempt to cross the Axel-Hulst canal at Dubosch. Less than a fortnight later on 1 October 1944, Kownas died in action *na polu chwały* (on the field of glory). His gallant death closed further scrutiny of his actions.[69]

The Second Crossing Attempt

The disaster that had befallen 10 Dragoons forced Skibiński to reset the priorities for 3 Rifle Brigade. His immediate concern was to organize a rescue operation for 10 Dragoons offering support and assistance to the trickle of Dragoons who were separated from their squadrons and trying to get across the canal. Skibiński also shifted the Highland Rifle Battalion and 1 Squadron of 10 Mounted Rifles into a defensive posture along the stretch of the canal running west from Drie Schouwen to Fort Ferdinandus.[70] Throughout 17 September, the shift to a defensive posture by the Highland Rifle Battalion battlegroup did not herald inactivity. Aggressive patrolling including on the north bank of the canal and a thorough reconnaissance of the stretch of the waterway accompanied 3 Rifle Brigade's pause in offensive operations. Skibiński also made a personal report on the situation to the divisional commander, Maczek, and requested additional resources from him to mount another crossing attempt. In the early hours of 18 September Maczek ordered that 8 Rifle Battalion be taken from the battlegroup in Ghent and the artillery battery assigned to the battlegroup be returned to its regiment to strengthen supporting fire. The 10th Dragoons returned to the command of its parent 10 Armoured Cavalry Brigade but 1 Armoured Regiment (*1 Pułk Pancerny*) was placed under Skibiński's command to provide additional armour support.[71] In the course of 17 September the weather improved with cloud, mist and rain giving way to clear and sunny conditions.

The reconnaissance of the Axel-Hulst canal continued through 17 September and half the following day. On 18 September, 1 Squadron of 10 Mounted Rifles, discovered that the stretch of the canal between Dubosch and a north-south road on an embankment called the Derde Verkorting was lightly defended by the German forces.

---

67   Nowak, *10 Pułk Dragonów Tom II*, p. 142.
68   Szydłowski, 'Bój o Axel', p. 195.
69   Nowak, *10 Pułk Dragonów Tom II*, p. 143 and Skibiński, *Pierwsza Pancerna*, p. 327.
70   Szydłowski, 'Bój o Axel', p. 196.
71   IPMS: C-96-II, War Diary, 1st Polish Armoured Division, 18 September 1944 and Skibiński, *Axel*, pp. 86-87.

The Derde Verkorting road ran north toward Kijkuit with the road bridge over the canal destroyed. The terrain in the vicinity of the Derde Verkorting road provided better conditions to mount an assault crossing. The infantry both during the crossing and when established in a bridgehead could be covered by supporting fire from tanks as the southern side of the canal had higher ground that provided good observation and fields of fire. The 10th Mounted Rifles regimental commander, Major Jerzy Wasilewski, did his own reconnaissance of the ground before taking the news of potential crossing site to Skibiński around mid-day.[72]

After receiving Wasilewski's report on the potential crossing site near the Derde Verkorting road, Skibiński did not deliberate long before deciding to mount another crossing of the Axel-Hulst canal. From a number of standpoints, the new location offered a number of features to recommend going ahead. The infantry would enjoy protective fire from Polish armour once established in a bridgehead. As the assault area included a road, this aided the engineering effort to build a Bailey bridge and once the bridge was complete, the means of echeloning through forces into the bridgehead for exploitation. Although the likelihood of a German counterattack and indirect fire to inhibit the construction of the bridge remained significant challenges, Skibiński assessed the risk as acceptable. Around 1300 on 18 September, Skibiński ordered the assault crossing to proceed.[73] His plan directed the Highland Rifle Battalion under the command of Lieutenant Colonel Karol Complak, to cross the canal and form a tight half-circle defensive position on the north side. Covering fire would be supplied by 1 and 3 Squadrons of 10 Mounted Rifles. With a bridgehead established 10 Sapper Company were to set about the task of constructing a Bailey bridge.[74]

The Highland Rifle Battalion began the assault at 1600 with one of the 1st Polish Armoured Division's artillery regiments in support as well as the firepower of two squadrons of Cromwell tanks of 10 Mounted Rifles (see Map 2). In complete contrast to the earlier Dragoon experience the crossing assault met little opposition. The Highland Rifle Battalion took two officers and fifty-two other ranks prisoner and established a bridgehead at the cost of one wounded soldier. The 2nd Company was first to cross establishing positions at the centre of the axis of advance. The 3rd Company followed and covered the left flank of the bridgehead facing Dubosch. The 4th Company was last to cross and took up positions on the left flank facing east. The Battalion's 1 Company, Support Company and headquarters were located to the north and east of Fort Ferdinandus. The 10th Mounted Rifle Squadrons provided over-watch of the bridgehead as the companies in the bridgehead dug in to face the inevitable German counterattack.[75]

---

72   Skibiński, *Axel*, pp. 89-90.
73   Skibiński, *Axel*, p. 91.
74   Szydłowski, 'Bój o Axel', p. 198.
75   Szydłowski, 'Bój o Axel', p. 199.

The success or failure of the second crossing attempt now hinged on whether or not the engineers of 10 Sapper Company, reinforced by additional platoons from 11 Sapper Company, could complete a Bailey bridge by the next morning. The orders given on 18 September to 10 Sapper Company under the command of Major Wiktor Neklaws were in fact to complete two bridges. The first priority was to erect a Bailey bridge quickly near where the Derde Verkorting road crossed the Axel-Hulst canal so as to allow reinforcement of the bridgehead held by the Highland Rifle Battalion. As the bridgehead expanded westwards, a second Bailey bridge was to be constructed where the road running north from Fort St Nicolaas met the canal. This location was where the Bailey bridge would have been completed to establish a link to the Dragoons' bridgehead.[76]

The construction of the Bailey bridge near the Derde Verkorting road faced enormous difficulties throughout the evening and night of 18-19 September. Not helping matters was the fact that Lieutenant Wacław Kohut-Koszut of 10 Sapper who was one of two officers directing the erection of the bridge left the area and was nowhere to be found a few hours after construction started leaving his 11 Sapper Company counterpart in sole command. The reasons for the disappearance of Kohut-Koszut have not been satisfactorily explained. The commander of 11 Sapper Company Major Wacław Pogorzelski, in his after action report on the operation, raised questions as to why Kohut-Koszut disappeared tacitly suggesting that it might be a case of dereliction of duty.[77] Thus the 'bridge' officer in charge of construction was Lieutenant Tadeusz Andrzejewski from 11 Sapper Company. Apart from access roads being in poor condition and slowing the assembly of materials, German indirect fire proved the most serious problem in completing the bridge. Intense artillery and mortar fire interrupted work on four occasions.[78] Andrzejewski described the intensity of German mortar fire around midnight of 19 September as being murderous; every two to five minutes a shell arrived between fifty and 300 metres from where the bridge was under construction.[79] Keeping the sappers at work under such conditions proved a difficult leadership challenge. Nevertheless, this young officer carrying enormous responsibility for the success 3 Rifle Brigade operations proved to be up to the task. Work began on the Bailey bridge at 1430 on 18 September with construction completed at 0230 on 19 September. The first tanks of 10 Mounted Rifles drove across the bridge at 0630.[80]

76   IPSM: C-191-B, 'Rozkaz Szczegolny', War Diary, 10 Sapper Company, 18 September 1944 and IPMS: C-192-II-A, War Diary, 11 Sapper Company, 18 September 1944.
77   IPMS: C-192-II-A, Enclosure report by Major W, Pogorzelski, War Diary, 11 Sapper Company, 26 September 1944.
78   Władysław Dec, *Narwik and Falaise*, (Warszawa: MON, 1972), p. 324 and IPMS: C-192-II-A, Enclosure report by Major W, Pogorzelski.
79   IPMS: C-192-II-A, 'Sprawozdanie z budowy mostu Bailey'a 80'DS w pkcie 380035', War Diary 11 Sapper Company, 20 September 1944.
80   IPMS: C-192-II-A, Enclosure report by Major W, Pogorzelski, Skibiński, *Axel*, p. 94. and Szydłowski, 'Bój o Axel', p. 199.

While the engineers were busy constructing the Bailey bridge, Skibiński finalized his plan for 3 Rifle Brigade's operations on 19 September to consolidate and exploit the bridgehead. At 2030 he issued a fresh directive that organized the brigade's assets into three battlegroups. Each battle group was built around one of the brigade's three infantry battalions with attachments of armour or anti-tank guns. The sequence of movement across the Bailey bridge into the bridgehead was to be first, the remaining elements of the Highland Rifle Battalion along with the tanks of the 1 and 3 Squadrons of 10 Mounted Rifles at 0600, second, 8 Rifle Battalion at 0700 and third, 9 Rifle Battalion at 0730.[81] In practice this timetable proved optimistic. Congestion on the Derde Verkorting approach road slowed units moving into the bridgehead. All of 3 Rifle Brigade was being funnelled through one crossing point. The second bridge, meant to ease movement by creating multiple crossing points, was incomplete on the morning of 19 September as German forces still controlled the north bank of the canal in the sector where the bridge was to be built. After 8 Rifle Battalion secured the area around Dubosch the same morning, the expansion westward of the bridgehead created the conditions necessary for the construction of a second bridge.[82] The second bridge was complete at 1415 that day.[83]

Despite the frictions and delays, Skibiński succeeded early on the morning of 19 September in strengthening the bridgehead over the Axel-Hulst canal and creating conditions for further exploitation of the bridgehead. As the Polish battlegroups echeloned into the bridgehead, they quickly broke out driving northwest to envelope Axel and toward the port of Terneuzen. The exploitation phase of the crossing operation maintained momentum despite the often waterlogged terrain that meant armoured movements were channelled and limited to roads built on embankments. The breaching of the Axel-Hulst canal line precipitated the collapse of the German defence and the hasty withdrawal of the German 712th Infantry Division across the Scheldt. By the end of 20 September Skibiński's 3 Rifle Brigade cleared German forces up to the Scheldt estuary from the port of Terneuzen in the east to Walsoorden Haven in the west. With the successful second crossing attempt of the Axel-Hulst canal, 'Axel Island' was secured.

Conclusion: Crossing Water Obstacles in 1944

The challenges faced by the 1st Polish Armoured Division in crossing the Axel-Hulst canal highlighted the difficulties that water obstacles presented to a formation predicated on mobility. In assessing the Polish operational experience two areas proved

---

81   IPMS, C 106/I-B, 'Rozkaz Potwierdzajacy rozkazy ustne wydane na odprawie o godz. 20.30', War Diary, 3 Rifle Brigade, 18 September 1944.
82   Skibiński, *Axel*, p. 98.
83   IPMS: C-192-II-A, War Diary 11 Sapper Company, 19 September 1944.

critical in operations to cross the Axel-Hulst canal: the application of doctrine and the exercise of command and leadership.

If doctrine is meant to be a guide rather than a template for action on the battlefield, it is clear that the then current British doctrine for crossing water obstacles, MTP 23 1942, had its concepts and principles effectively applied by the Polish armoured division. Two examples suffice to illustrate the utilization of the doctrine in the Polish crossing operation. MTP 1942 stressed the vulnerability of a bridgehead until heavy weapons and armour could be brought over. In both of the attempted crossings of the canal this was well-understood by Polish commanders as a critical priority to success even if conditions and events precluded this happening in the first attempt but were wholly successful in the second attempt. MTP 23 1942 also highlighted the importance of careful reconnaissance. The opportunity for a methodical reconnaissance of the canal was not possible in the first attempt to cross the canal as it formed part of an advance to contact. Following the failed first attempt at crossing, however, the temporary shift to a defensive posture was utilized to make a careful reconnaissance of the canal that underpinned the successful second crossing attempt. While not every Polish action might have been consistent with everything to be found in MTP 23 1942, it is worth noting that the Polish armoured division did not mount a deliberate set-piece assault crossing nor did it mount an opportunistic rapid *coup de main* assault crossing. The 3rd Rifle Brigade faced a defended water obstacle that fell between these two extremes and applied existing doctrine in a flexible manner tailoring it to the circumstances that confronted its commanders.

The senior command and leadership cadre of the 1st Polish Armoured Division by and large consisted of seasoned professional soldiers who had considerable wartime operational experience. This did not mean that those holding command appointments were immune from the frictions of war or personal conflict in the exercise of leadership. Command and leadership problems undoubtedly contributed to the failed first attempt by 10 Dragoons to cross the Axel-Hulst canal. Captain Wacław Kownas' first exercise of regimental command in a major operation ended in disaster for which it cost him his appointment. He owed his command of 10 Dragoons to a string of casualties among the senior officers of the Dragoons that led to Kownas assuming command of the regiment (motor battalion) on the basis of seniority. Among his superior officers, there is a remarkable consensus of opinion that believed Kownas was both 'ambitious' and 'inexperienced'.[84] As noted earlier, he was perceived as the infantry outsider in a cavalry regiment. The fatal tactical mistake that occurred in the first crossing attempt was the separation of 1 Squadron from the bridgehead due to overexploitation. Whether 1 Squadron's movement to Steenbosc was on the order of Kownas or due the independent action of Giera, the squadron commander, is not important as

---

84   Dec, *Narwik and Falaise*, p. 322, IPMS: B-1817, Dworak relacje, no date [1946?], Maczek, *Od podwody do czołga*, p. 195, Skibiński, *Axel*, p. 79 and Skibiński, *Pierwsza Pancerna*, p. 324.

the ultimate responsibility rested with Kownas for either a tactical misjudgement or failing to grip a subordinate. Most of Kownas' battle was spent trying to reverse the consequences of the overexploitation by 1 Squadron. In fairness to Kownas, the frictions of war also played a role in his command failure. The lack of ability to exercise command and control due to his radio net collapsing and enemy action that destroyed the engineer's pontoon raft, critical to ferry vehicles and antitank guns, also contributed to the failed first attempt to cross the canal.

The 10th Dragoon's 'black day' also led to recriminations directed against Colonel Franciszek Skibiński, Commander of 3 Rifle Brigade. Colonel Tadeusz Majewski, commander of 10 Armoured Cavalry Brigade which was the Dragoon's parent formation, was angry about what happened to the Dragoons while under Skibiński's command and insisted that a commission be set up to investigate the causes of the disaster. Colonel Kazimierz Dworak, the deputy commander of the division headed the commission. As Skibiński wrote in his memoir: 'Dworak, found that engineers were not able to complete the bridge for objective reasons and the commander of the brigade [Skibiński] undertook all the necessary remedial measures' [to assist the Dragoons].[85] There was a legacy of animosity between Majewski and Skibiński that dated from Normandy when Skibiński had been the deputy brigade commander of 10 Armoured Cavalry Brigade. Within 10 Dragoons Skibiński was also seen as bearing responsibility for the disaster. Allegedly, the well-respected Lieutenant Colonel Zgorzelski who had command of 10 Dragoons before being wounded at Ghent refused to shake hands with Skibiński when they later met.[86] In the wake of such a trauma in a regiment's history it is understandable that there would be some bitterness and a desire to apportion blame.

Did Skibiński carry some measure of blame for the disaster that befell 10 Dragoons? There can be little doubt that Skibiński did not think much of the command ability of Kownas and regarded him as inexperienced. If this was the case, then why did Skibiński not provide more command support for his inexperienced subordinate? One factor that made this difficult was that Skibiński located his brigade headquarters on the axis of his eastern column in the brigade advance to the Axel-Hulst canal. The lack of proximity meant that Skibiński's situational awareness suffered from distance that was not helped by the failure of radio equipment in the Dragoons' headquarters. As Kownas did not survive the war to provide his account of events, Skibiński's provides the dominant but still largely credible narrative of command failure on 10 Dragoon's 'black day'. Given the fundamental mistakes made in the deployment of 1 Squadron and the intensity of the German reaction to the bridgehead, it is difficult to see how Skibiński could have done more to retrieve the situation. Skibiński trusted his

---

85 Skibiński, *Pierwsza Pancerna*, pp. 326-327.
86 Franciszek Idkowiak, *Franciszek Skibiński: żołnierz, teoretyk i historyk wojskowy*, (Poznań: Wydawnictwo Wyższej Szkoły Oficerskiej im. Stefana Czarnickiego, 2002), pp. 77 and 83.

subordinate to carry out his task but Kownas was found wanting under the pressures of command.

If the first crossing attempt highlighted the consequences of command failure, then the second attempt showcased professional, adaptable and agile leadership. In the wake of disaster, Skibiński made good use of the pause in offensive operations to gather intelligence by a thorough reconnaissance of the stretch of canal in his area of operations. When 10 Mounted Rifles provided him with a location where an assault crossing could be attempted with strong fire support of armour, Skibiński swiftly moved to seize the opportunity. Within thirty-six hours after the failed first attempt, Skibiński had reorganized his forces and mounted a second assault crossing that succeeded with negligible cost. His utilization of task organised combined arms battlegroups was adroit and his subordinates understood the practice of the 'closest cooperation between all arms'. The Highland Rifle Battalion and 10 Mounted Rifles both had experienced commanders whose judgement Skibiński trusted. Indeed, Skibiński had a high regard for the 10th Mounted Rifles' commander, Wasilewski, who he described as a 'talented tactician'.[87] The ability to consolidate and exploit a bridgehead, however, was very much down to the efforts and capabilities of the sappers of the armoured division. The leadership shown by Lieutenant Andrzejewski from 11 Sapper Company insured that a Bailey bridge, critical to the success of the brigade plan, was completed in a timely fashion under highly difficult conditions. Once across, Skibiński adeptly maintained the momentum of his attack echeloning combined arms battlegroups across the canal that rapidly broke out of the bridgehead to clear 'Axel island'.

87   Skibiński, *Axel*, p. 90.

15

Command, Control, Co-Ordination and Communication at Westkapelle in November 1944 – Operation Infatuate II

Nigel de Lee

In the first week of November 1944 the 4th Special Service Brigade Group made an opposed assault landing at Westkapelle on the Island of Walcheren, then exploited along the narrow coastal strips to the south-east and north-east, taking batteries and beach defences. The operation was described as; '…one of the neatest and most complete triphibious operations of the war.'[1] But in fact the operation was hardly neat, and was less triphibious than had been intended, leaving the troops ashore to rely on their own basic skills and first principles to improvise solutions to complex problems rather than on the diverse and massive support they had been led to expect by the plans for the operation.

Opposed amphibious assault operations and subsequent exploitations are highly complex, even more so when multi-national. The preparation and performance of INFATUATE II involved elements of Air, Naval and ground forces from Belgium, Britain, Canada, The Netherlands, and Norway. In such an enterprise co-ordinated action is vital to survival and success; only close and effective co-operation can lead to the necessary synergistic action. This in turn depends on command, control and communication. The means to generate these functions consist of:

1. Command structure;
2. Formal planning, at all levels, from the grand strategic to the basic platoon 'O' Group;
3. Liaison, formal and informal, in which personalities and personal negotiation are significant;
4. Experience shared of previous operations, training, and education, leading to the use of standard operational procedures;

1   TNA ADM 202/407, Major W.R. Sendall, The Royal Marine Landing at Westkapelle.

5.   Communications; technical means such as wireless, line, and despatch riders, and personal.

All the above, but particularly experience can diminish the malignant effects of cultural dissonance-the inability of members of different services to understand each other due to distinct histories, traditions, training and working milieus, and also of corporate autism, more prevalent at senior levels, where ambition and egotism drive behaviour which is indifferent to the collective interest.

In contrast to the arrangements for NEPTUNE-OVERLORD, there was no special command structure or staff for INFATUATE II, so no basis for unified planning. This ran contrary to the lessons of the operations in Normandy, analysed in a study by the RAF which stated the need for unity of command and planning that was fully integrated and co-ordinated to maximise efficiency, especially where heavy bombers were to support ground forces.[2] The work was done within the existing allied commands most of which stemmed down from SHAEF, but some of which were beyond the authority of the Supreme Commander. The operation was carried out within the geographical sector of 21st Army Group, but that HQ and its commander showed little interest in the operation, and the responsibility for planning and command was devolved to 1st Canadian Army, whose commander did take an active interest, but handed most of the work on to the 2nd Canadian Corps. Firm decisions about the chain of command were not made until about five weeks before the actual operation. On 24th August SHAEF sent a directive to HQ 21st Army Group which mentioned as an objective that it should 'get a secure base at Antwerp...', but did not give this aim the highest priority, nor did it refer to the need to clear the estuary of the Scheldt in order to free the approaches to the port.[3] One month later decisions were made on the chain of command and on the division of command authority. The HQ of 1st Canadian Army was in charge of all military operations, and was jointly, with HQ 84 Group, RAF, to be responsible for co-ordination of air operations. Heavy bomber operations were under the aegis of Bomber Command, while the HQ of Allied Expeditionary Air Force via 2nd Allied Tactical Air Force was in command of tactical air support. Overall command of the Naval operations was in the hands of the Allied Naval Expeditionary Command, led by Admiral Ramsay.[4] The geographical dispersal of the relevant HQs was disruptive to the exercise of their functions; the 1st Canadian Army rested at St. Omer, 2nd Canadian Corps at Ghent, then Bruges, 4th Special Service Brigade was near Dunkirk, then moved to Ostend, Force 'T', the Naval component was in England until shortly before the operation. Ramsay moved

2   TNA AIR/1595, Report on OP.OVERLORD, paras 531, 532, 342-344.
3   F.H. Hinsley, *British Intelligence in the Second World War, Vol. III, Pt 2*, (London: HMSO, 1988), p.309.
4   RiksArkiv, Oslo KA 2856 COHQ, Bulletin Y/47.

himself and his Staff Officer, Plans in their Mobile HQ caravans to join the Canadian 2nd Corps, initially at Alost, then at Breskens to secure a better connection.[5]

The plans for INFATUATE were produced by a series of conferences and meetings held ad hoc. The first was a conference convened at Ghent by the commander of 2nd Canadian Corps on 22nd September to consider preliminary action. The Chief of Staff of 1st Canadian Army, and senior representatives of the Navy, Bomber Command and 84 Group RAF were in attendance. The main issue discussed was whether or not Bomber Command could and should breach the sea-dykes around Walcheren.[6] Next day General Crerar, commander of 1st Canadian Army, held a conference at St Omer, which was attended by the commander and CofS of his 2nd Corps, senior officers of Force 'T', the Air Forces, 21st Army Group, and the Allied Airborne Army, but no representative from Combined Operations. Crerar gave an outline of the general strategic position of the Canadian Army and discussed the possible courses of action to secure Walcheren. Simonds, commanding the 2nd Corps, remarked that he had not been able to study the operation in detail, but went on to give an outline plan which in general was followed in the actual operations. He also said that 4th Special Service Brigade had been warned, was planning and training, and should be ready to act in 21 days. The role of the Air Forces was also discussed, but many issues were left unresolved. In contrast, the tasks of the Naval forces were clear.[7] Simonds, now Acting GOC of the 1st Canadian Army held another conference on 29th September at which he stated that the best method of attacking Walcheren would be by a seaborne assault near Westkapelle, and endeavoured to settle questions about the operational responsibilities of Bomber Command and 84 Group, and of the means to co-ordinate their operations.[8] The last conference held by the Canadian Army was on 26th October, with the intention: 'To finalise arrangements for support of the assault on Walcheren'. The conference was attended by the senior members of the Army staff, Foulkes, the Acting Commander of 2nd Corps, with his CofS and CCRA, senior officers of 2nd TAF and 84 Group, the Commander of 155th Brigade, due to assault Vlissingen across the Scheldt, Captain Pugsley, commander of Force 'T', and Brigadier Leicester, commander of 4th Special Service Brigade. Simonds stated that air action, especially the attacks on the dykes which had flooded most of the island, had greatly weakened the defences and that the assaults on both Vlissingen and Westkapelle would be

5   Miss E. Schuter, 'A Wren's Eye View', IWM Documents, 05/62/1, p.127; A.F. Pugsley and D. MacIntyre, *Destroyer Man*, (London: Weidenfeld, 1957), p.188; R.W. E Love and J.Major, (Eds), *The Year of D-Day: The 1944 Diary of Admiral Sir A. B. Ramsay*, (University of Hull, 1994), p.157.
6   TNA DEFE 2/311, 4th Special Service Brigade, Report, INFATUATE; AIR14/1472, Group Captain Lucas, OP INFATUATE, Notes on a Conference at Ghent.
7   TNA AIR 14/1427, Main HQ, 1st Canadian Army, St. Omer, OP. INFATUATE, Conference 23rd September 1944.
8   TNA AIR 14/911, Brigadier Mann, 30th September 1944, Minutes of a conference at Main HQ, 1st Canadian Army, 29th September 1944, Ghent.

launched on 1st November, if the weather permitted, whether or not air support was available. A commando would lead the attack on Vlissingen, and if this went well, the 155th Brigade would follow up, but if not the 155th would reinforce the commandos via Westkapelle. The Canadian army on South Beveland would continue pushing towards Walcheren across the isthmus. He hoped that Bomber Command would be able to deliver the planned intense attacks in the last four days before the assaults, and that 84 Group could give close support afterwards. Arrangements for massive support by British and Canadian artillery on the south bank were in place. The Royal Navy was to provide bombardment from heavy ships, lift and delivery to the enemy shore, and close support from a Support Squadron for the operation at Westkapelle.[9]

The planning process was affected by cultural dissonance manifested particularly in two aspects; the Army and RN did not appreciate the limitations on the effectiveness of heavy bombers; and the Army did not understand the need for urgency of the RAF and RN due to the crucial effects of weather on their operations. Corporate autism was also evident in the primary concerns of the senior officers with their own services' interests, and their personal ambitions. Montgomery and 21st Army Group were most interested in invading Germany as soon as possible; Ramsay was most anxious to secure the sea lines of communications, and Bomber Command seemed intent on bombing Germany and asserting their independence above all else. The relations between the higher commanders resembled those of potentates in the court politics of the renaissance. There is not sufficient space to consider more than a modest selection of the issues that arose in the planning process which reveal the factors mentioned above in action.

At the highest level the question of most importance was whether it was necessary for the allied forces to have the use of Antwerp. As late as 5th October Montgomery expressed the opinion that there was no need to have use of the ports of Antwerp or Rotterdam.[10] In this he was opposed by senior figures; virtually all others from Churchill and the Combined Chiefs of Staff downwards, in accord with the views of Hitler, Keitel and Jodl.[11] On 5th October Montgomery's strategy was strongly criticised by the other CinCs at a conference he did not attend, and on 8th October he altered his plan for 21st Army Group to move the British 1st Corps to the west in order to allow the Canadian Army to concentrate stronger forces on the fighting to clear the approaches to Antwerp. The opposition to Montgomery was led by Ramsay, but others agreed with him, including Alan Brooke who remarked: '...he ought to have made sure of Antwerp in the first place'.[12]

9   TNA AIR 14/911, Main HQ, 1st Canadian Army, Conference, 26th October 1944, OP. INFATUATE.

10   Hinsley, op.cit. p.395; Love, op.cit. p.151.

11   Hinsley, op.cit, pp.369, 380-1.

12   Love, op.cit. pp.151, 153; Danchev and Todman, (eds.), *Alanbrooke: War Diaries 1939-1945*, (London: Phoenix, 2001), p.600.

Montgomery disagreed with his senior colleagues about the best way to defeat the enemy on Walcheren and so open Antwerp. In September he recommended that it would best be done by an airborne operation, and this idea was under consideration until Eisenhower informed him on the 21st it had been ruled out after consultation with Brereton because the terrain, being polder, was unsuitable.[13] Even so, on 23rd September, at Crerar's conference, Brigadier-General Cutler was told that the possibility of an airborne operation should be discussed again; Cutler stood firm.[14]

Montgomery's other proposed form of action was to use Bomber Command to destroy the German coastal defence batteries on Walcheren, and so make the Scheldt safe for the passage of allied shipping, or, at least minimise the need for substantial ground forces to be used to clear the island. This idea ran contrary to a RAF study of the lessons of Normandy which concluded that 'other services expect too much of the air forces from the point of view of the destruction of prepared gun emplacements, especially when completely concreted.'[15]

A number of issues disturbed relations between Bomber Command and the Canadian Army. The first to arise, and probably that of the greatest operational importance, was whether heavy bombers could and should be used to breach the sea dykes around Walcheren and flood the Island. On the 22nd September Simonds advocated breaching the dykes on the grounds that the consequent floods would isolate the narrow strips of high ground along the west coasts, 'where most of his coast defence batteries are located' which would present more concentrated targets, and that '… seaward defences on the dunes could be attacked by amphibians from the rear.' In addition, the German movement of reserves and supplies would be hindered, and many of the batteries inland drowned.[16] He repeated his views at Crerar's conference on the 23rd. But Air Vice-Marshal Oxland from Bomber Command doubted if bombing could break the dykes, and whether the flooding would be advantageous. Crerar said that such an operation would depend upon whether it was feasible and authorised by the Supreme Allied Commander.[17] Simonds repeated his arguments on 29th September, and the RAF officers at his conference again said that they could not guarantee to breach the dykes, and that attempts to do so would require long and difficult operations. A decision was made that Bomber Command would attack the dykes provided that Eisenhower gave authority and both weather and technical

13   TNA AIR 14/1427, OPERATION INFATUATE; AIR 37/531, Message, 13th September 1944, Advanced HQ AEAF to Main HQ 2nd TAF.
14   TNA AIR 14/1427, Conference, 23rd September 1944.
15   TNA AIR 20/1595, Reports on OPERATION OVERLORD, para. 497.
16   TNA DEFE 2/311, 4th Special Service Brigade, Report.
17   TNA AIR 14/1427, Conference, St.Omer, 23rd September 1944; Oxland, Notes on the conference of 23rd September 1944, Main points for Bomber Command, 26th September 1944.

conditions allowed.[18] However, once Eisenhower had given his authority, on 1st October, Bomber Command flew to attack and break open the dyke at Westkapelle, and afterwards made repeated attacks on request, until by 22nd October the flooding was assessed as successful enough to permit the amphibious assault.[19] The attacks on the dykes were extremely effective in degrading the German defence of Walcheren; the floods wiped out half of the coastal defence batteries covering Westkapelle.[20]

There was much more difficulty in relations between the Army and the RAF over what sort of attacks the air forces should make on the defences of Walcheren, and the mechanism by which they should be organised. These questions became entwined with matters connected to the relative status of the HQs involved, in which the RAF was most strongly concerned to maintain independence and resist any sign of subordination to the Army. On 21st September Eisenhower informed the Air Ministry that, '... the whole strength of all available air forces will be required to soften the defences and support the attack on Walcheren' and that Leigh-Mallory would co-ordinate the necessary air action.[21] The Air Ministry, in response, sent a message to the HQ of Allied Expeditionary Air Force specifying that 'The resources of Bomber Command should be made available for these operations. The new Directive for control of the Strategic Bomber Forces in Europe requires you to meet this commitment,' and co-ordinate action according to the requirements of the ground forces.[22] But a similar message to Bomber Command used less imperative language, and stated, '...you are requested to meet this commitment.'[23] At the Canadian Army conferences on 23rd and 29th September Crerar and Simonds demanded a campaign of sustained heavy bombing, to start at once, to degrade the defences of Walcheren, and the target list issued by the Army called upon Bomber Command to attack batteries on the Island.[24] A revised list of targets drawn up by 22nd October consisted largely of coastal batteries and other concrete works.[25] The staff of 4th Special Service Brigade believed that ' ... the heaviest possible air bombing effort would be necessary to reduce the Coastal Defence Batteries sufficiently to allow seaborne assault to succeed...', and that there

18   TNA AIR 14/1427, Air Commodore Dickens, Note on Conference, 29th September 1944.
19   TNA AIR 14/911, Message, 1st October 1944, HQ Bomber Command to Main HQ, 84 Group; Message, 05:00, 3rd October 1944, HQ Bomber Command, to Main HQ 84 Group; Hinsley, op.cit. pp.398-9.
20   TNA WO 291/873, Operational Research Group, Memo No.580.
21   TNA AIR 14/1427, OPERATION INFATUATE.
22   TNA AIR 14/1427, Message, Air Ministry to Main HQ AEAF, 22nd September 1944.
23   TNA AIR 14/911, Message, Air Ministry to HQ Bomber Command, 22nd September, Operations against WALCHEREN ISLAND.
24   TNA AIR 14/1427, Conference, 23rd September 1944, St. Omer; AIR 14/911, Conference at Main HQ, 1st Canadian Army, on 29th September 1944; AIR 14/1427, HQ 1st Canadian Army, INFATUATE Pre-D-Day Air Targets.
25   TNA AIR 14/1427, 1st Canadian Army/ 84 Group RAF, 22nd October, Pre-Planned Air Targets.

would be no assault until the softening –up was sufficient.[26] Throughout the planning process senior RAF officers consistently warned that bombing could not destroy
concrete defences. On 27th September Leigh-Mallory informed Eisenhower that
prolonged heavy bombing could not assist in the capture of heavily defended areas,
but that short and intense attacks could demoralise and neutralise the defenders, so
it would be best to make a concentrated attack for 48 hours on Walcheren immediately before the assault.[27] The Air Force officers at the conference on 23rd September
argued the same case. Oxland stated that '… Bomber Command could not undertake
to silence the guns…', but that attacks by heavy bombers could affect morale and
destroy communications, and this would be most effective if done just before D-day.[28]
On 26th October Simonds gave the impression that he had understood part of the
RAF view of the best use of heavy air power, because he remarked that the Pre-D-day
programme should be as short and late as possible; but he also remarked that due to
previous air action, 'the number of existing batteries has been decreased'.[29] In all,
Bomber Command made ten escorted daylight raids on Walcheren in October, using
1,339 Lancasters and 258 Halifaxes; four aircraft were lost.[30] The attacks on batteries
achieved a very high standard of accuracy, but knocked out only two of the twenty-six
guns targeted.[31]

The procedures for arranging attacks by Bomber Command caused great difficulty
in relations with the Canadian Army. At the conference on 23rd September, Oxland
stated that he, as an adviser on air operations, could not commit Bomber Command
to engage any target, because the power of decision rested with the C-in-C of Bomber
Command and the Supreme Allied Commander. There was a direct communications link between the Canadian 2nd Corps and Bomber Command, provided by
HQ 84 Group which was co-located with HQ 1st Canadian Army, which could be
used for the transmission of information and details of targets, and also for similar
communication with the US 8th Air Force. On 22nd September Canadian Army
believed that this link was to be used for direct communication between 2nd Corps
and Bomber Command, to include the list of targets to be attacked. On the 23rd,
when Oxland asked Brigadier Mann, CofS of Canadian Army, if his HQ had made
an official request for Bomber Command to start the desired programme of attacks,
Mann replied that he had not, because 21st Army Group had said that the Supreme
Commander had decided the heavy bombers should be used, so all that was necessary

26   TNA DEFE 2/311, 4th Special Service Brigade, Report.
27   TNA AIR 14/1427, Leigh-Mallory to Eisenhower, 27th September 1944.
28   TNA AIR 14/1427, Air Vice-Marshal Oxland, 26th September, Notes on the conference
     of 23rd September 1944.
29   TNA AIR 14/1427, Conference, 26th October 1944.
30   TNA AIR 22/345, AEAF War Room, Monthly Summary of Operations, October 1944.
31   TNA WO 291/873, ORG, Memo No. 580.

was to pass the requirements to HQ Bomber Command.[32] But on 29th September it was noted that the direct link was to be used solely for 84 Group to inform Bomber Command of the results of their attacks; and requests for more support from Bomber Command must be submitted through 'the normal channels'.[33] This requirement for the use of normal channels was emphasised on 8th October; when a request from 84 Group for attacks on batteries threatening Minesweepers clearing the way towards Antwerp was endorsed with a comment by the 'Senior Air Staff Officer' that the attacks had not been agreed, and no action should be taken without instructions.[34] On 30th October Bomber Command ordered that if the ground forces called for repeat attacks on individual targets in the last phase of INFATUATE, '...such requests are ONLY to be acted upon if they come from SHAEF.'[35] The deep concern for the use of 'usual channels' probably stemmed from the feeling that Bomber Command must not appear to be tasked by a mere Group HQ, and particularly not one from 2nd TAF, the reincarnation of the despised Army Co-operation Command.[36]

There was a particularly sharp clash over target, W260, a defensive position in the town of Vlissingen. The Canadian Army wanted this position to be hit by heavy bombers just before the assault across the Scheldt, and Eisenhower himself argued the case to win over Churchill, who had objections for humanitarian reasons.[37] The target had been requested by Canadian Army, on the 28th October, and queried by the Air Staff, and on the 30th the Air Ministry ordered that Vlissingen was not to be attacked.[38] 21st Army Group tried to trump the Air Staff by requesting authorisation of the attack from the Combined Chiefs of Staff. This caused outrage; senior RAF officers felt that whether or not the raid was an operational necessity was less important than the points of principle involved; any late 'political interference' with the plan must be rejected; earlier the Deputy Supreme Allied Commander (Tedder) had decided that heavy bombers must not be used to attack the town, and it was not for the Army to tell the RAF what aircraft and bombs to use in air operations. The conference concluded that there would be No Further Action.[39]

---

32 TNA AIR 14/911, HQ 1st Canadian Army to Main HQ 21st Army Group, INFATUATE, 26th September 1944; AIR 14/1427, Oxland, 'Notes on 23rd September', 26th September 1944.

33 TNA AIR 14/911, Conference, 29th September 1944.

34 TNA AIR 14/911, Message, 17:20, 8th October, HQ 84 Group to HQ 2nd TAF, info to HQ Bomber Command.

35 TNA AIR 14/911, Notes on Last Phase of OP. INFATUATE.

36 M.Powell, 'Army Co-operation Command and Tactical Airpower Development in Britain 1940-43', paper at BCMH 5th Annual Conference, New Research in Military History, University of Wolverhampton, 22nd November 2014.

37 Danchev, op.cit., p.615.

38 TNA AIR 14/911, SASO, Loose Minute to CinC, 30th October 1944.

39 TNA AIR 14/911, Air Commodore Dickens, Conference in Air Marshal Robb's Room, 10:30, 31st October 1944.

In contrast, 84 Group was dedicated to operations, '...to assist the Army to clear the approaches to Antwerp'.[40] The Air Plan for the assault recognised that because of the limited capabilities of the commandos, and the Naval forces and Artillery assigned to support them, the Group should play a major part in suppressing or destroying the defences on Walcheren. So the Group was to perform a series of co-ordinated operations to protect Force 'T' on approach by defensive cover, lay smoke to screen the assault force, and give close air support, both on pre-planned targets, and on call with a cab-rank system.[41]

There were also differences of opinion and of priorities between the Naval and Army commands. From 3rd September on Ramsay was concerned that the 21st Army Group showed insufficient interest in the need to free the approaches to Antwerp.[42] He was also very critical of the ground forces' general neglect of logistics in their strategy, their failure to appreciate the inherent difficulties of seizing Walcheren, and their lack of a sense of urgency as the weather deteriorated.[43] At the conference on 23rd September Captain Pugsley warned that in October the sea conditions would make a landing impossible on four days out of six, yet Crerar and Simonds were intent on taking Cap Gris Nez and the Channel Ports, and clearing the south bank of the Scheldt before any attempt on Walcheren.[44] On 21st October Ramsay warned Eisenhower that no assault on Walcheren would be possible after 14th November.[45] On 23rd October Montgomery accused Ramsay of breaching protocol by dealing directly with the Canadian Army rather than via 21st Army Group; Ramsay retorted that this was necessary due to Montgomery's lack of interest in the relevant operations.[46] Overall, Ramsay believed that Army formations were not giving sufficient consideration to INFATUATE, that because the Canadian Army acted 'unilaterally' without taking account of naval concerns, 'the army has decided to stage the landings at the worst possible spot from the naval point of view', and that the plan was an army one when the requirement was for, 'an agreed joint plan.'[47] On the other side, Simonds remarked that the time of day for the landing at Westkapelle, chosen for navigational reasons by the Navy was, '...from the Army point of view most unsuitable as the shore defences would then be at their greatest strength.'[48] In sum, the Navy disliked the place of the operation, and the Army the time.

The planning at operational and Tactical levels, in Force 'T' and 4th Special Service Brigade was done in a routine manner, no doubt facilitated by the prior experience of

40   TNA AIR 37/367, 84 Group, RAF, Summaries of Operations.
41   TNA AIR 14/1427, HQ 84 Group, OP. INFATUATE, Air Plan.
42   Hinsley, op.cit. p.378; Love, op.cit. pp.131,135-6,150.
43   Love, op.cit., pp.141-4, 151, 153, 159, 160.
44   TNA AIR 14/1427, Conference, 23rd September 1944.
45   Love, op.cit. p.160.
46   Love, op.cit., p.161.
47   Love, op.cit. pp.149-50.
48   TNA AIR 14/1427, Conference of 29th September, 30th September 1944.

both Captain Pugsley and Brigadier Leicester of NEPTUNE-OVERLORD. Both produced plans for joint and co-ordinated action and a rational division of command responsibilities. Force 'T' consisted of three basic elements; the Assault Squadron of LCIs and LCTs to carry troops to the beach; the Support Squadron to escort them and engage the shore defences; and the Bombardment Squadron of heavy ships, with their escorts. The Brigade Group comprised commandos, engineers, a squadron of tanks from 79th Division, and many detachments of support and administrative personnel. All was to be under control from the HQ ship, HMS Kingsmill, which had the gear for tri-service signals.[49]

Because there was no unified command co-ordination was arranged by liaison, in the British tradition. At the strategic level, this could cause uncertainty and friction, as illustrated in the planning process. But liaison was often conducted on an informal manner. One case concerned the way in which Bomber Command was induced to carry our repeat attacks on the sea dykes of Walcheren. On 6th October de Guingand, C of S of 21st Army Group met Oxland. He explained that the cutting of the dykes had been a great success, but that Simonds 'would like' four more; he was reluctant to ask, because he understood the importance of Bomber Command's work in Germany, but had to do so, because more flooding might lead to an enemy surrender, and so save many lives. Oxland remarked that the supply of 4,000 pound bombs had run out, and that the 10,000 pounders were destined for the KEMES dam, but agreed to give priority to Walcheren. The use of tact and diplomacy, as if in supplication, was outside 'normal channels', but succeeded.[50]

Officers from the strategic and operational levels of command met to make vital decisions at Ostend on the evening of 31st October. Ramsay, Simonds, Foulkes, Pugsley and Leicester conferred. Pugsley had reports that the weather off Westkapelle was improving, so was confident his Force could reach Westkapelle. But recce reports said that the enemy was alert, and he believed that the landing would be very difficult, on a narrow front, with proportionately less fire support than in Normandy in the face of 14 batteries and mined approaches. The RAF Liaison Officer reported that fog over England would probably prevent support from Fighter/Recce aircraft, and proposed a postponement. Ramsay advised that only the man on the spot could decide whether to proceed. The decision made was that Force 'T' would sail as planned, and on arrival off Westkapelle Pugsley would decide if the weather was good for a landing, Leicester must decide whether the strength of the resistance allowed an assault.[51] On 1st November at about 07:15 Force 'T' was off Westkapelle, and the enemy coastal artillery opened fire. Pugsley knew that without the planned support of Fighter/Recce

49   TNA DEFE 2/311, 4th Special Service Brigade Report; RiksArkiv, Oslo, KA2856 COHQ, Bulletin Y/47.
50   TNA AIR 14/1427, Oxland, Note of a meeting with C of S, 21st Army Group, 09:00, 6th October 1944.
51   Pugsley, op.cit., pp.187-90; Love, op.cit., p.166; TNA DEFE 2/308, 4th Special Service Brigade Group, Op. Order No.6, 24th October 1944.

aircraft spotting the fall of shot the heavy ships would not be able to deliver accurate fire. But Commander Sellars, CO of the Support Squadron, argued that his craft could distract the defending batteries and draw their fire so that the Assault Squadron would be able to land the commandos. Pugsley was influenced by the arrival overhead of aircraft from 84 Group, which were directed by the RAF LO to strike the shore defences at Westkapelle just before the Assault craft touched, and by the effects on one of the batteries of a salvo from *Erebus* which knocked out two guns in Battery W15 just north of the beaches. He also had in mind that other allied forces were attacking across the isthmus and over the Scheldt. During the approach and land-ings the Support Squadron suffered very heavy casualties, but the Assault Squadron delivered the commandos to shore and the operation proceeded roughly according to plan, if not to schedule.[52]

At tactical level LOs of various kinds were attached to HQs at Brigade and Commandos to co-ordinate support to the marine infantry. Their effectiveness depended to a great extent on the means of communication available. The RAF had Forward Air Controllers in *Kingsmill*, *Warspite*, and with the Main and Tactical HQs of the Commando Brigade. Their W/T sets worked, but because they were relatively distant from the locations of the actual Commandos it was usual to have a 30-minute minimum delay between a request for air support and its arrival.[53]

84 Group were certainly very willing to give support where and when possible. On 30th October the Group advised Pugsley and Leicester that the weather on the 1st November would most likely prevent air support, and on the morning the condi-tions were such that the Group should have stood down. But at 07:45 a signal from Kingsmill stated that the local conditions were suitable for close support, and so although the operations planned for H-40 to H-20were not flown, shortly after 'H' aircraft from 132Wng and 331Squadron hit the defences of Westkapelle.[54] Later, as the weather improved, and the Force 'T' Support Squadron was reduced '... a request was made to 84 Group for all available support. This simple expedient worked well ...' Fighter-Bombers and Typhoons gave Close Air Support. Information on targets and the locations of friendly troops was sent to the Group Control Centre by the FAC or to the Fighter Control Post via the Naval inter-ship link until the ASSU Tentacle was set up ashore to do the work. Aircraft in Cab Ranks attacked targets of opportunity as well as those indicated by the FCP.[55] During the following week air support was intermittent and patchy, mainly due to bad weather, but partly to other demands on

52   Pugsley, op.cit., pp.190-193; RiksArkiv, Oslo, KA2856, COHQ, Bulletin Y/47.
53   TNA DEFE 2/311, 4th Special Service Brigade Report; ADM 202/103, 41 (RM) Commando, War Diary; ADM202/111 48 (RM) Commando, War Diary.
54   TNA AIR 37/367, 84 Group, RAF, Summary, No.83; AIR 26/192, 132 Wing, RAF, Operations Record Book; RiksArkiv, Oslo, KA2856, COHQ, Bulletin Y/4.
55   RiksArkiv, Oslo, KA2856, COHQ, Bulletin Y/47; TNA AIR 26/210145, Wing, RAF, Operations Record Book; AIR 26/192, 132 Wing, RAF, Operations.

the Group.[56] The Commandos had expected much more than they got; for example the plan for the landing included 420 sorties; in fact attacks were made by 23 Spitfires and 28 Typhoons.[57] The response to calls for support could be long delayed; on 1st November at 13:00 41 Commando called for an attack on W17, but it was 16:00 when 24 Spitfires bombed and strafed the battery.[58]

Although less powerful than expected, the support from 84 Group was particularly valuable because the planned last attacks on Coastal Batteries by Bomber Command were cancelled on account of the weather.[59]

The Bombardment Squadron consisted of *Warspite*, plus the monitors *Erebus* and *Roberts*. They had targets to be shelled during the preliminary bombardment, with the fire corrected according to observations from Fighter/Recce aircraft. After the commandos had landed, these ships would be on call with Forward Officer Bombardment parties attached to each Commando HQ to direct their fire.[60] On the day, the spotter aircraft were grounded by mist at Hawkinge, and their absence handicapped the heavy ships in their bombardment as they were 14 miles out to sea, too far away for accurate direct observation.[61] *Warspite* and *Roberts* opened fire at 08:20; at 08:30 Artillery Air OP aircraft arrived overhead to assist them, but, unfortunately, 'Considerable difficulty was experienced by ships in establishing contact…', this being attributed to the aircraft having weak W/T sets. Despite the handicap, the heavy ships did temporarily suppress Battery W15, and actually knocked out two of its guns – as many as had Bomber Command in a month of raids.[62] Once the landing force was ashore the heavy ships were inhibited in their action by fear of hitting friendly troops; at 13:00 the FOB with 41 Commando called on *Warspite* to shell W15, but uncertainty about the location of the Commando stopped the shoot. The same concern led to the premature end to a bombardment of W13 in support of 48 Commando.[63] The situation in the 41 Commando sector improved in the afternoon; assisted by a Fighter/Recce aircraft and reports from the FOB, *Warspite* engaged W17 to such effect that a PoW said the garrison had been demoralised. The battery was taken with

56 TNA AIR 37/367, 84 Group, RAF, Summaries, 84-89.
57 TNA DEFE 2/311, 4th Special Service Brigade, Report; ADM 202/407, Major Sendall; WO 291/873, ORG, Memo No.580.
58 TNA ADM 202/103, 41 (RM) Commando, War Diary.
59 TNA DEFE 2/311, 4th Special Service Brigade, Report.
60 TNA DEFE 2/311, 4th Special Service Brigade, Report; TNA DEFE 2/308, 4th Special Service Brigade, Outline Plan No.3; TNA ADM 202/103 41(RM) Commando, Operation Order No.3.
61 Love, op. cit. p.167; TNA DEFE 2/311, 4th Special Service Brigade, Report; Pugsley, op.cit., p.190.
62 *The Story of 79th Armoured Division, October 1942-June 1945*; RiksArkiv, Oslo, KA2856, COHQ, Bulletin Y/47; TNA WO 291/873, ORG, Memo No.580.
63 RiksArkiv, Oslo, KA2856, COHQ, Bulletin Y/47.

minimal resistance.[64] South of Westkapelle events demonstrated the hazards of action applicable to FOBs; the party attached to 48 Commando found on landing that the W/T set was unserviceable; on finding another they went forward to direct fire from *Roberts* onto W13, but were killed by a mortar after two salvoes. Observation from seaward, whether from *Kingsmill* or vessels of the Support Squadron, was hindered by distance, smoke and poor light.[65]

The Support Squadron, in two groups, led the craft of the Assault Squadron to the beaches, and engaged enemy defences. Within the Squadron some errors of judgement and enemy action led to some of the rocket firing craft firing short; this disrupted and delayed the Assault Squadron, and temporarily blinded the HQ craft of the northern group. The other armed craft pressed on to very close range of the enemy, distracting them and drawing their fire.[66] The closest co-ordinated action was by the two LCG (M)s, which beached themselves adjacent to pillboxes north and south of the gap to engage them; one was soon ablaze and lost with all hands, the other sank shortly after kedging-off the beach.[67] Once the commandos were on land, the Support Squadron gave them direct and close fire support, directed by their FOBs or their own observation, closing to within 100 yards of their targets. Many were sunk or damaged; by 15:00 only six were fit for action, and they were withdrawn. Whilst these craft could inflict little material damage on the German defences, they had considerable psychological effect, and Pugsley believed their efforts were crucial to the success of the operation.[68]

The Artillery support, which was to include fire from two AGRAs, one British and one Canadian, was to be co-ordinated via a representative of the II Corps CRA, attached to 4th Brigade HQ, and directed by FOOs with each Commando HQ who could go forward when necessary. As the artillery positions were south of the Scheldt, only the heavy and super-heavy guns had the range to reach beyond Zoutelande. There was an elaborate and lavish fire plan for preliminary bombardment. After the landing, guns were to be on call. 41 Commando was to have three batteries of 155mm pieces in support, but they required a safety margin of 1,000 yards, too wide for support of

64 RiksArkiv, Oslo, KA2856, COHQ, Bulletin Y/47; TNA ADM 202/407, Major Sendall, The Royal Marine Landing at Westkapelle; TNA ADM 202/103, 41(RM) Commando, War Diary.

65 TNA ADM 202/111, 48 (RM) Commando, War Diary; TNA WO 291/873, ORG, Memo No.580.

66 TNA ADM 202/407, Gunnery Officer, SSEF, Diary of Events; Major Sendall, The Royal Marine landing at Westkapelle; TNA WO 171/858, RMO, 1st Lothians and Border Yeomanry, Report; RiksArkiv, Oslo, KA2856 COHQ, Bulletin Y/47.

67 ADM 202/407, Captain Peretz, Report on the use of LCG(M) 101 and 102 in OP. INFATUATE.

68 RiksArkiv, Oslo, KA2856, COHQ, Bulletin Y/47; Pugsley, op.cit., pp.197,201; TNA ADM 202/407, Gunnery Office.

an assault, and could not deliver smoke. The Brigade had a regiment of 155mm guns on call via an Air OP.[69]

Although the 350 guns were all surveyed –in and supposedly able to deliver accurate predicted fire up to a line just south of Domburg, during the preliminary bombardment the rounds generally fell 200 yards short, so,' little was seen or felt of the effect of these guns...' and they did not suppress W11 or W13.[70] After the landing it proved difficult to call up artillery support; the FOO with 48 Commando had a defective W/T set; the FOO for the 3rd Canadian Regiment could call via the CCRA representative on the Brigade 'B' link, but signals were 'difficult'; when 48 Commando was held up at W13, the CO had to go back to Brigade HQ on foot to contact the Canadian AGRA via the ASSU Tentacle and arrange a 15-minute concentration in support of his planned assault.[71] There was better support after the FOO found a working W/T set. During the afternoon of the 2nd November, three regiments put four stonks onto W11 and the dunes before it in support of the attack by 47 Commando, but some short rounds caused loss and confusion. On the 3rd the guns supported the advance along the dunes, but they took nine minutes to make a 200-yard adjustment. In addition, the Air OP ignored the yellow smoke used by the commandos to mark their forward locations, so they were also engaged by allied guns. Once the artillery had managed to bring up field guns, it was much easier to obtain accurate and timely concentrations.[72]

Within the Brigade Group, most of the units were well accustomed to working with each other, one of the exceptions being 'A' squadron of the Lothians from 79th Division, who had detachments from assault units of the Royal Engineers attached for the operation. They had LOs with each Commando HQ, and were equipped with Weasels for transport and W/T 19 sets for communication. The LOs were to act as FOO s for the tanks' fire support and assist with direct support to the Commandos as requested.[73] Few of the embarked armoured vehicles survived the landing, but those that did proved most valuable. One tank got onto the dyke and gave effective fire support to 41 Commando in storming the tower in Westkapelle.[74] The LO with 48 Commando experienced great difficulty because on landing he found his weasel and

69   TNA ADM 202/407, Major Sendall, The Royal Marine Landing at Westkapelle; TNA ADM 202/103, 41(RM) Commando, Operation Order No.3; TNA WO 171/858, 1st Lothians, War Diary; TNA DEFE 2/311, 4th Special Service Brigade, Report.

70   TNA WO 291/873, ORG, Memo No. 580; Riks Arkiv, Oslo, KA2856, COHQ, Bulletin Y/47.

71   TNA ADM 202/111, 48(RM) Commando, War Diary.

72   TNA DEFE 2/311, 4th Special Service Brigade, Report; TNA ADM 202/111, 48(RM) Commando, War Diary; TNA WO 291/873, ORG, Memo No. 580.

73   TNA DEFE 2/308, 4th Special Service Brigade, Outline Plan, INFATUATE; Operation Order No. 6; The Story of 79th Armoured Division..., p155; WO 171/858, 1st Lothians, War Diary.

74   TNA WO 171/858, LO to 41 Commando, Report, 1st Lothians, War Diary.; TNA DEFE 2/311, Notes on the Work of RE and 30th Armoured Brigade.

the 68 set were useless and his 19 set was too heavy to carry on foot; so he had to contact them by relay via the Regimental HQ using a lighter 38 set. In any case, the tanks were held up by debris in Westkapelle and could not move to a position from which they could fire in support of the commandos south of the gap.[75] The LO to 47 Commando was shipwrecked three times and left stranded north of the gap, so the LO to 48 stood in for him when 47 Commando took over the advance south. But by then the surviving four tanks had moved north, so he returned to Westkapelle.[76]

In the north the four remaining Lothians' AFVs arrived at 19:00 on the 2nd to support two troops of 10 Commando and two of 41 holding Domburg.[77] In operations on the 3rd and later days the tanks provided highly effective intimate support for the commandos as they assaulted and cleared the enemy defences. The LO was so entirely embedded that he went forward with the leading commandos, and maintained contact with the tanks by running back to them on foot. On occasion he went ahead of all, 'Captain McDowall ... was ... usually to be seen heading the charge with a rifle in one hand and a Sten in the other, uttering berserk Highland war cries whilst the commandos followed behind bewildered and shaken ...'[78] Direct personal face to face contact also led to close co-operation between the British of 41 Commando and the Norwegian and Belgians of 10 Commando.[79]

The Royal Engineers in the Brigade Group worked to clear beaches and routes of mines and other obstacles, and to create the logistic infrastructure, according to standard drills. When necessary they liaised directly with the commandos and Lothians. Each Commando had a platoon of GHQ Sappers attached, who made little use of their specialist skills and kit, but fought, fully integrated, as infantry.[80] Other sappers from the RE 1st Assault Brigade drove the LVTs which took most of the commandos from their LCTs to dry land.[81]

The necessary close co-operation was greatly facilitated by a period of realistic training conducted near De Haan over terrain similar to that on the Island, using abandoned German defence works to exercise assault tactics. Commandos, engineers and Lothians trained together, worked out operational procedures, and developed

75 TNA WO 171/858, LO to 48 Commando Report, 1st Lothians, War Diary.
76 TNA WO 171/858, LO to 47 Commando, Report; LO to 48 Commando, Report, 1st Lothians, War Diary.
77 TNA ADM 202/311, 41(RM) Commando, War Diary; TNA WO 171/858 LO to 41 Commando, Report, 1st Lothians, War Diary; TNA DEFE 3/311, 4th Special Service Brigade, Report.
78 TNA ADM 202/103, 41(RM) Commando, War Diary; TNA WO 171/858 LO to 41 Commando, Report, 1st Lothians, War Diary; WO 291/873 ORG, Memo No.580.
79 TNA ADM 202/103, 41(RM) Commando, War Diary; TNA DEFE 2/311, 4th Special Service Brigade, Report.
80 RiksArkiv, Oslo, KA2856, COHQ Bulletin Y/47; TNA DEFE 2/308, Notes on the Work of RE.
81 TNA WO 205/866, HQ 1st Assault Brigade RE, Report, INFATUATE I and II; TNA DEFE 2/308, COHQ Amphibians in OP. INFATUATE II.

mutual trust. The teams which trained together, fought together. 100 commandos were taught how to drive Weasels, and the LVT drivers knew their passengers.[82] Force 'T' consisted of units with relevant experience, but had to do much of their training in England because there was a lack of suitable ports on the Continent; they were unable to conduct a rehearsal exercise because there was a shortage of ammunition.[83] But the officers of the Support Squadron went to De Haan on 29th October to inspect the defences there, and hear a lecture from the CO of 48 Commando. They were impressed by the confidence of the commandos and gained an understanding of their needs.[84]

The aircrew and staffs of 84 Group were very experienced in giving Close Air Support to ground forces, having carried out such operations since June.

The quality of communications was extremely variable. Generally the Naval and RAF signals were reliable, although intercommunication could be difficult. The landing force did have equipment for line communication, but it was not much use in the fast and fluid operations. There were Despatch Riders in the Order of Battle, but no specific mention of them ashore. The main technical means was W/T. There were Naval Beach Signals Parties. The Commandos had a lavish provision of sets. 41 Commando had SCR60, 46, 38, 22 and 68 sets, all with specific functions. Each troop had two SCR536 sets. All the FOBs, FOOs and LOs had their own sets. Many spare batteries were carried, on men, Weasels, and LVTs. Security against enemy SIGINT was to be foiled by strict procedures and the use of SLIDEX code.[85] In the event the W/T sets were not always serviceable under the conditions; contacts with the Artillery in support had to be improvised; LOs often worked by moving on foot; and when 48 Commando landed it lost all its own sets.[86] This meant that much communication had to be done using runners or personal contact. In action at troop level and below the most ancient systems of all, shouting and hand signs were used.

Despite the many difficulties, failures of equipment and strong enemy action, Force 'T' landed the 4th Brigade in a condition fit to fight; the Commandos were able to achieve a sufficient level of co-ordinated combined arms action; in which regard the attacks on W13, W11, W18 and W19 were notable. The forces which carried out INFATUATE II suffered high casualties, but defeated an enemy superior in numbers holding strongly fortified positions and under strict orders not to surrender. Their conduct stands as an example to those at higher levels in the chain of command.

82   RiksArkiv, Oslo, KA2856, COHQ, Bulletin Y/47; TNA DEFE 2/311, 4th Special Service Brigade, Report; TNA ADM 202/103, 41(RM) Commando, War Diary.
83   TNA AIR 14/1427, Conference, 23rd September; RiksArkiv, Oslo, KA2856, COHQ, Bulletin Y/47; TNA DEFE 2/311, 4th Special Service Brigade, Report.
84   TNA ADM 202/407, Gunnery-Officer, Report.
85   TNA ADM 202/103, 41(RM) Commando, Signals instruction No. 3.
86   TNA ADM 202/111, 48 (RM) Commando, War Diary.

Bibliography

Archive
The National Archives (UK) ADM202/103; ADM202/111; ADM202/407; AIR14/911; AIR14/1427; AIR20/1595; AIR22/345; AIR26/192; AIR26/210; AIR37/367; AIR37/531; DEFE2/308; DEFE2/311; WO171/858; WO205/866; WO291/873
IWM, Documents; Miss E. Schuter, 05/62/1
Riks Arkiv – Norwegian State Archives: KA2856

Printed Sources
A.Danchev and D. Todman (eds), *Alanbrooke War Diaries 1939-1945*, Phoenix, 2001.
F.H.Hinsley, *British Intelligence in the Second World War, Vol.III, Pt. 2*, HMSO, 1988.
R.W.E. Love and J.Major (eds), *The Year of D-day, Diary of Admiral Sir Bertram Ramsay, 1944*, University of Hull, 1994.
A.F. Pugsley and D. MacIntyre, *Destroyer Man*, Weidenfeld, 1957.
The Story of 79th Armoured Division, October 1942-June 1945.

Conference Papers
M. Powell, 'Army Co-operation Command and Tactical Airpower Development in Britain 1940-43', given at BCMH conference, Wolverhampton, 22nd November 2014.

16

A Return to Static Warfare:
The New Brunswick Rangers and the Breskens Pocket

Matthew Douglass

Fourth Canadian Armoured Division's post-Normandy pursuit largely ended 15 September 1944 following an unsuccessful bid to bounce the Leopold Canal. Along this canal German defensive positions were established creating the Breskens Pocket in an effort to extract forces across the Scheldt Estuary. September and October 1944 was a period of static warfare for 4th Canadian Armoured Division's 10th Canadian Infantry Brigade. During this period the New Brunswick Rangers provided supporting fire for friendly infantry and occupied portions of the line. No. 2 mortar platoon of the New Brunswick Rangers became one of the most highly revered units within the brigade as heavy machine guns and heavy mortars became especially important once static warfare developed along the brigade's front.

Antwerp was captured by 11th British Armoured Division early 4 September 1944. This created a massive wedge between the German *Fifth Panzer Army* to the east and the *Fifteenth Army* to the west. Canadian Official Historian C.P. Stacey observes that the Germans acted too slowly to properly defend Antwerp, but the lack of Allied movement further north to Breda allowed the *Fifteenth Army* to continue retreating. Aware of the importance of Antwerp's deep water port for the Allies, the Germans began fortifying positions on Walcheren Island and a bridgehead on the south bank of the Scheldt Estuary (Breskens Pocket). So long as these positions held Allied shipping could not reach Antwerp. Despite their losses, the Germans were able to slowly regroup after Antwerp fell as other areas across the front were constantly changing.[1]

---

1   Mitcham, Samuel, Jr. *Retreat to the Reich: The German Defeat in France, 1944,* Westport CT: 2000, pp.202, 219; C.P. Stacey, *Official History of the Canadian Army in the Second World War, Volume III, The Victory Campaign: The Operations in North-West Europe, 1944-1945,* Ottawa: 1967, pp.298-303; Ellis, *Victory in the West, Volume II: The Defeat of Germany,* London: 1968, pp.11-12.

Two other significant problems existed for the Germans on the Canadian front. Along with preventing the use of Antwerp the Germans needed to rescue *Fifteenth Army* which was trapped between the coast and the Allied Armies. They also needed to maintain as many deep water ports along the English Channel as possible to deny the Allies the ability to alleviate their supply shortages. German garrisons at Boulogne, Calais, Dunkirk, and Le Havre were therefore ordered to fight to the last man and bullet to deny those facilities to First Canadian Army.[2] Similarly, Brest was besieged by the Americans, while some ports, such as Dunkirk and Lorient, held out until the end of the war.[3] As the Allied forces continued to advance beyond the limits of their supply lines, strategic opinions began to plague Allied command. Debates over strategy developed between Field Marshal Bernard L. Montgomery and General Dwight D. Eisenhower regarding a narrow or broad front strategy. The results of this forced First Canadian Army through September and October 1944 to wage the forming Battle of the Scheldt with limited resources. Mid-September 4th Canadian Armoured Division entered a static role as a result of supplies from their depots being used for Operation 'Market-Garden'.[4] This immobilization was also a further result of the logistical restraint. The Canadian infantry divisions coped via static operations until the end of September once supplies were able to reach the front via the Normandy Rear Maintenance Area and liberated Channel Ports.[5]

It was agreed that the Ruhr region, a large industrialized area of western Germany, must be captured. September supply shortages temporarily cancelled any notion of a broad advance as only enough supplies were available to launch a single thrust across either the Saar River in the south or the Ruhr River in the north.[6] While the strategic debate was being waged, 21st Army Group was tasked to clear the Pas de Calais, capture airfields in Belgium, and gain Antwerp as a base. These tasks were largely the responsibility of First Canadian Army.[7]

Montgomery believed that Antwerp was not required immediately and that his forces could be sustained through the use of Channel Ports and from airlifted supplies. This only allowed for supplies to reach the British Second Army.[8] In a directive dated 4 September from Eisenhower to Montgomery one of the tasks listed was to gain Antwerp, but there was no mention of the *use* of its port facilities.[9] Eisenhower desired

2   Terry Copp, *Cinderella Army: The Canadians in Northwest Europe, 1944-1945*, Toronto: 2006, pp.21, 38, 40.
3   Stacey, *Victory Campaign*, pp.301, 368.
4   Copp, *Cinderella Army*, p.124.
5   James F. Camsell, 'From Normandy to the Scheldt: Logistics and the First Canadian Army (June-September 1944)' MA Thesis, University of New Brunswick: 1995, pp.131-132
6   L.F. Ellis, *The Defeat of Germany*, p.9.
7   Stacey, *Victory Campaign*, pp.307-310.
8   Copp, *Cinderella Army*, p.59.
9   Ellis, *The Defeat of Germany*, p.10.

to have Antwerp available for its logistical support but allowed Montgomery to open the port at his discretion.[10] Rather than conduct operations to gain access to the port, Montgomery developed a joint air-ground operation, aimed at the western defences of Germany and the Ruhr. This operation, 'Market-Garden', was launched the night of 17/18 September and was over by 25 September.[11] 'Market-Garden' gains the vast majority of literary attention, while the 'more important' task of opening Antwerp became a sideshow in both action and writing.[12] Despite this, the Canadians still had to gain the Channel Ports and clear the Scheldt estuary to alleviate the logistical restraints.[13]

Following Operation 'Market-Garden', it was clear that the war in Europe would continue until 1945, making Antwerp's port facilities all the more essential. The trickle of supplies reaching the front line troops had become a crucial blow against defeating Germany from the west. As transport lines became further and further elongated from Normandy, the shortage of transport vehicles limited both the movement of supplies and reinforcements. 4th Canadian Armoured Division borrowed vehicles from 10th Canadian Infantry Brigade on 11 September to arrange for the transportation of reinforcements from Lisieux, some 250 miles from the front.[14] A policy of rationing petrol, oil, and artillery ammunition was enacted 9 September for First Canadian Army. The efforts to keep 4th Division's guns firing was noted by the headquarters of the Royal Canadian Artillery 14 September as the ammunition "figures for the past 24 hours reached an all time high – total expenditure 11,000 rounds. This in the light of the 300 mile trip to bring up the [ammunition] has been a first class Q[uatertermaster] effort."[15] Even when supplies and resources became available through the acquisition of ports, they were syphoned to other Allied ground forces.[16]

Clearing both the Channel Ports and opening Antwerp, Stacey explains that First Canadian Army was not properly equipped to perform both in close succession.[17] As an additional result of Operation 'Market-Garden', Stacey argues that Montgomery's 21st Army Group lost the initiative to destroy the German Fifteenth Army, and consequently had to clear the Scheldt estuary under increasingly difficult circumstances.[18] Following 10 days of operations surrounding Dunkirk 2nd Canadian Infantry

10   Stacey, *Victory Campaign*, pp.310-311.
11   Stacey, *Victory Campaign*, pp.311-312.
12   Copp, *Cinderella Army*, p.42.
13   Stacey, *Victory Campaign*, pp.317-322.
14   Library and Archives Canada, Record Group 24, Volume 13793, A and Q Branch, Headquarters 4th Canadian Armoured Division's War Diary, 11 September 1944.
15   Library and Archives Canada, Record Group 24, Volume 14332, Headquarters, Royal Canadian Artillery, 4th Canadian Armoured Division's War Diary, 14 September 1944.
16   Camsell, 'From Normandy to the Scheldt', pp.127-147.
17   Stacey, *Victory Campaign*, pp.329-331.
18   Stacey, *Victory Campaign*, p.356.

Division moved for Antwerp 16 September and was tasked with moving northwards with what resources were available and without sustaining heavy casualties. These largely began 22 September and lasted for close to a month, concluding with the division poised to enter South Beveland.[19] On 12 September General H.D.G. Crerar was told to take Boulogne, and that Antwerp needed to be opened as soon as possible. 3rd Canadian Infantry Division took the port city after 5 days when the German garrison surrendered the evening of 22 September.[20] It is likely that these endeavours were the cause of ammunition restrictions for 4th Division as the same day as operations began to liberate Boulogne, 4.2 – inch mortar and machine gun rounds were to only be used for defensive purposes.[21]

Montgomery ordered operations for capturing the Channel Ports and Antwerp to begin 13 September. The capture of Le Havre, though a sizeable port, could not aid the Canadian logistical issues as these were allocated to 12th US Army Group. As such, I British Corps was halted in order to replenish and augment its stores. Unfortunately First Canadian Army first had to solve its own logistics problems before those of 21st Army Group. Further requests for additional troops to accomplish their tasks were refused and divisions had to be shipped around or grounded in order for Operation 'Market-Garden' to be conducted, resulting in numerous occasions where the First Canadian Army was 'stealing from Peter to pay Paul' to accomplish troop movements over hundreds of miles.[22] All of this resulted in weeks of slow, and static warfare for 4th Division and 10th Brigade. The New Brunswick Rangers' specialized training with Vickers machine guns and 4.2 – inch mortars proved invaluable in those difficult days.

The New Brunswick Rangers were initially raised at the very outset of hostilities in 1939 to battalion strength. Hailing from the Atlantic province's south-eastern Westmorland, Albert, and Kings Counties, they spent time in various Eastern Canadian communities with a major stint in Newfoundland. Come September 1943 they embarked from Halifax, Nova Scotia for the United Kingdom. Once in the UK they were reduced in strength to form a 202 all ranks company and trained to serve as the forming 10th Brigade's heavy infantry weapons supporting unit.[23]

They familiarized themselves with the improved .303 Vickers medium machine guns which produced accurate, concentrated, and sustained fire at a larger range than rifles and the Bren light machine guns carried by regular infantry battalions. Their accurate fire derived from being mounted on a tripod with two legs that had 'shoes'

19   Copp, *Cinderella Army*, pp.55-56, 121-145; Stacey, *Victory Campaign*, pp.327, 365, 381-385.
20   Copp, *Cinderella Army*, pp.63-68.
21   A and Q Branch, Headquarters 4th Canadian Armoured Division's War Diary, 15 September 1944.
22   Camsell, 'From Normandy to the Scheldt', pp.153-157.
23   Library and Archives Canada, Record Group 24, Volumes 6623-6627, NB Rangers War Diary August 1939-July 1944.

which gripped the ground when firing. Dial sights and improved ammunition assisted in increasing the weapon's effectiveness in the Second World War. Machine gun sections employed a forward observer to record and correct the fall of shot. The weapon could deliver a concentrated 'beaten zone' at ranges close to 2000 yards. This is a long and narrow strike pattern that could be applied for enfilade fire or to engage targets deep in an enemy defensive zone. The gun was cooled by a water jacket surrounding the barrel connected to a 2 gallon water can connected by a 6 foot hose. The heat from continuous firing absorbed water through the hose into the jacket around the barrel keeping the barrel from overheating and warping to allow for sustained fire. This system enabled the Vickers to fire close to 500 rounds per minute per hour.[24] This is compared to air cooled machine guns must typically change barrels after each belt to prevent overheating and warping. Overall, a Vickers gun crew well supplied with ammunition could deliver drenching fire on critical points of the battlefield for long periods of time in an attack or defence.

While the Vickers guns engaged targets mostly with direct fire, the 4.2 – inch heavy mortar platoon could deliver bombs indirectly. The high angles of their trajectory allowed for fire from behind the cover of buildings and hills to strike enemy positions similarly protected. The mortar was operated by a 6 man crew and directed by a forward observer. The mortars could fire 12 rounds per minute, at a range of 4,100 yards and fired both high explosive rounds and smoke canisters.[25] When both heavy weapons systems were used in conjunction, they could isolate and contain an area about to be assaulted or recently captured by a regular infantry battalion. The 4.2 – inch mortars had a range of either 1,050 – 2,800 yards or 1,500 – 4,100 yards depending on the ammunition.[26]

In April 1944, the New Brunswick Rangers sub-units were organized in the manner that they would be for action; Company Headquarters with No. 1 platoon permanently attached, No. 2 mortar platoon, and three Vickers medium machine gun platoons, Nos. 3, 4, and 5. The teeth of the NB Rangers were the 64 men assigned to these platoons. Most of remaining men were employed to ensure that the unit remained mobile, with 68 men tasked to the vehicles in various capacities. The NB Rangers also had men working as carpenters, signallers, clerks, and cooks. To keep the

24   L.F. Ellis, *Victory in the West, Volume I: The Battle of Normandy*, London: 1962, pp.534, 539, 541; Chris Bishop, ed., *The Complete Encyclopedia of Weapons of World War II*, London: 1998, p.244; C.P. Stacey, *Official History of the Canadian Army in the Second World War, Volume I: Six Years of War; The Army in Canada, Britain and the Pacific*, Ottawa: 1967, p.544; *The Vickers Gun Simplified: Pocket Book and Illustrated Guide*, Melbourne: Circa 1942. Belts contained 250 rounds, and the gun weighed 40 pounds and the tripod 50.

25   Shelford Bidwell, ed., *Brassey's Artillery of the World: Guns howitzers, mortars, guided weapons, rockets and ancillary equipment in service with regular and reserve forces of all nations*, London: 1977, p.92.

26   The 4.2 – inch mortars had a range of either 1,050 – 2,800 yards or 1,500 – 4,100 yards depending on the ammunition. The chemical and smoke rounds had a shorter range, while the high explosive rounds had a longer range.

NB Rangers mobile, they utilized motorcycles, 15 cwt trucks and wheeled carriers, among others. The guns and their ammunition were carried by the vehicles.[27] The NB Rangers and 10th Canadian Infantry Brigade saw action in August 1944 in the major operations of that month being 'Totalize', 'Tractable', closing the Falaise Gap, and the pursuit northward.

With 3rd Division tasked with taking the Channel Ports and 2nd Canadian Infantry Division preparing to advance north from Antwerp towards the land approaches to the Walcheren peninsula, 4th Division was responsible for maintaining minimal pressure along their front.[28] This placed 4th Division in the polders of northern Belgium and southern Holland. Very few offensive operations were conducted as "polder warfare was an infantry-slogging job: armour would be of little effect."[29] A Belgian report described polder terrain as *"généralement impropre aux opérations militaires."*[30] This territory is noted by Dennis and Shelagh Whittaker as having been known to General Simonds as unsuitable to armour operations but that there was no alternative.[31] Mines and tree lines also provided means of delay.[32]

Stacey complains that the Canadian advance to the Scheldt was too slow, and had it been quicker, the battle would have been won earlier. Conversely, his British counterpart L.F. Ellis remarked that the "II Canadian Corps had embarked on a threefold advance which could hardly be completed in the short time which had been needed by Second Army to drive straight on to Brussels and Antwerp."[33] All the while the First Canadian Army struggled to maintain a steady stream of adequate supplies to front line units. Historian Terry Copp explains that criticisms directed towards the Canadian advance derive from comparisons made to the British advances to their east. He wrote that the "Canadians thought they had accomplished miracles with the limited forces and supplies at their disposal. Montgomery and his acolytes saw it differently."[34] Copp notes that as a result of the determined defence of the Germans and with a "low priority being given to 'an enemy who may be retreating' 4th Canadian Armoured Division was ordered to turn east, masking the Leopold Canal while the area between Terneuzen Canal and Savajaards Plaat was cleared. The division was delighted to hear that operations against the Breskens Pocket were more properly

---

27   The New Brunswick Rangers' War Diary, January 1944, 'Appendix P, Proposed War Effectiveness".
28   Copp, *Cinderella Army*, p.125; Whitakers, *Tug of War*, London: 1985, p.90
29   Whitakers, *Tug of War*, p.95.
30   Stacey, *Victory Campaign*, p.400. Translation; *"generally improper to military operations."*
31   Whitakers, *Tug of War*, p.96. Simonds commanded the First Canadian Army from 27 September to 7 November, while Crerar was hospitalized in England for medical treatment.
32   Library and Archives Canada, Record Group 24, Volume 14156, 10 Canadian Infantry Brigade's War Diary, 20 September 1944.
33   Ellis, *The Defeat of Germany*, p.6.
34   Copp, *Cinderella Army*, p.82.

work for an infantry division."[35] It was along this frontage that the New Brunswick Rangers demonstrated their value to their infantry counterparts.

As the division moved towards Terneuzen, resistance was met as the Fifteenth German Army evacuated through the city's port across the Scheldt. On 16 September, the NB Rangers were divided amongst 10th Canadian Infantry Brigade. No. 2 mortar and 4 machine gun platoons stayed with the Company's Headquarters, while No. 3 machine gun platoon went under the command of the Algonquin Regiment, and No. 5 machine gun platoon was placed with the Argyll and Sutherland Highlanders of Canada.[36] Often the NB Rangers were parcelled out to the command of the infantry battalions to provide better support with their weapons systems.

On 18 September, No. 3 machine gun platoon, along with a squadron of tanks and a troop from the 5th Anti-Tank Regiment were responsible for the defence of Ertvelde, while the Algonquins moved forward on to Assenede. For this movement, the Algonquins elected not to apply preparatory heavy mortar fire on the town. An operational brewery in the town was deemed too valuable to be destroyed, though some light counter mortar firing was conducted by the battalion's 2 – inch mortars.[37] Civilians were forced from their homes as a result of enemy shelling in No. 5 machine gun platoon's area. A quiet night ensued following civilian evacuations and some gave the keys to their homes to the men "and invited us to make ourselves comfortable."[38]

The following morning, No. 2 mortar and 4 machine gun platoons supported an Argyll attack on Sas van Gent with the mortars firing 120 bombs in ten minutes. The attack went forward at 0830, and by 1730, the Argylls moved into the town against weakening resistance. Two companies were sent with tanks from the 29th Reconnaissance Regiment (South Alberta Regiment) and encountered stiff opposition on the outskirts of the town, largely in the factory area. Once this industrial region was cleared, the rest of the city fell rather quickly.[39]

No. 3 machine gun platoon reconnected with the Algonquins in Assenede 19 September and took up positions near the railway tracks outside of the village to cover the left flank. An unusual task was carried out for Nos. 4 and 5 machine gun platoons on 20 September as they were tasked with protecting and patrolling the area occupied by 19th Field Artillery Regiment, though no hostile activity occurred. This service

35　Copp, *Cinderella Army*, p.55.
36　Library and Archives Canada, Record Group 24, Volume 6627, The New Brunswick Rangers' War Diary, 16 September, 1944
37　G.L. Cassidy, *Warpath: The Story of the Algonquin Regiment, 1939-1945*, Markham: 1990, p.155. Infantry battalions contained smaller, 2" mortars.
38　The New Brunswick Rangers' War Diary, 18 September, 1944,
39　The New Brunswick Rangers' War Diary, 19 September, 1944; H.M. Jackson, ed., *The Argyll and Sutherland Highlanders of Canada (Princess Louise's), 1928-1953*, Montreal: 1953, pp.121-122.

lasted for the better part of a day, until 19th Field Regiment moved off.[40] From that point on, 10th Brigade entered a prolonged period of static warfare.

The terrain became unsuitable for armour and 1st Polish and 4th Canadian Armoured Divisions were to be relieved by 3rd Canadian Infantry Division when it became available to clear north of the Leopold Canal. Geoffrey Hayes observes the Lincoln and Welland Regiment spent three weeks along the Leopold Canal, with the rifle companies switching every three days to return to Maldegem.[41] 4th Canadian Armoured Division spent the week of 22-28 September patrolling an area of resistance along the Leopold Canal from the Braakman inlet to Kersalaer. 1st Polish Division moved south east of Antwerp and was placed under the command of I British Corps 28 September leaving the area west of the Breskens Pocket to the responsibility of 4th Division along the Leopold Canal. The Germans were well suited geographically and began to dig in along the front.[42] 4th Division would need to cross the Leopold Canal as well as contend with polders in an attack. The land within these dykes fluctuates between plus and minus two metres of sea level.[43] Not only in an attack would the Canadians be facing the difficult terrain, they would also have to contend with fortifications built between Holland and Belgium that closely resembled the trenches of the First World War.[44]

The geographical limitations meant 10th Brigade spent the end of September conducting raids and patrols. The Algonquins were chiefly based out of the Isabella Polder, an area described as "a hamlet at a road, rail, dyke, and harbour junction... ".[45] The Argylls, along with the Lincs conducted patrols across the Leopold Canal. A typical patrol was led by a corporal and three riflemen with a section providing covering fire with artillery and mortars when available. The goal of such patrols was to nab prisoners for the Intelligence Officer to create a better understanding as to which formations manned the opposite lines.[46] The enemy 'proved elusive' which resulted in a large raid of a company strength that snagged fifteen prisoners at no cost. The information gathered from these patrols revealed the locations of enemy mortar pits which was used by 7 Canadian Infantry Brigade to clear the Breskens Pocket when it arrived in October.[47]

For their part, the NB Rangers continued in their supporting role. 22 September 54 mortar rounds were fired and knocked out a German gun position. The following day

40   The New Brunswick Rangers' War Diary, 19–20 September, 1944.
41   Geoffrey Hayes, *The Lincs: The Lincoln and Welland Regiment at War*, Alma: 1986, pp.53-54.
42   Library and Archives Canada, Record Group 24, Volume 15104, The Lincoln and Welland Regiment's War Diary, September 1944, Appendix 5, Sitrep 29, September 1944.
43   Stacey, *Victory Campaign*, pp.362-369.
44   R.A. Patterson, *A Short History of the Tenth Canadian Infantry Brigade*, Hilversum: 1945, p.40.
45   Patterson, *A Short History*, p.39.
46   Copp, *Cinderella Army*, p.89.
47   Copp, *Cinderella Army*, pp.89, 92; Hayes, *The Lincs*, p.54; Whitakers, *Tug of War*, p.104.

they delivered harassing and covering fire for the Algonquins west of Phillipine. No. 3 machine gun platoon fired 10,000 rounds, while No. 2 mortar platoon moved ahead of the Algonquin Regiment and in a 20 minute period of counter battery fire eliminated two guns of unrecorded size and a battery of mortars before returning behind the protection of the Algonquins. The Germans retaliated with a counterattack 24 September and the advance troops of the Algonquins requested supporting mortar fire. The fire of the NB Rangers was key in defeating this counter-attack. At 0400 the 4.2 – inch mortars fired 200 bombs in eight minutes in an area roughly 300 yards in front of friendly troops. By the end of ninety minutes of firing, 480 rounds had been spent. No. 3 machine gun platoon again had fired 10,000 rounds in the same time period to prevent any enemy from infiltrating through the Canadian lines. Between 1800 and 2000 hours, an additional 14,000 rounds were fired.[48]

If the Algonquins had not already recognized the worth of the mortar platoon, they did so the following day. After a direct hit on a German 20 mm gun with only four rounds fired, the War Diarist for the New Brunswick Rangers notes that, "The inf are beginning to show some appreciation for the job this pl can do and are unhesitantly calling upon the 4.2" Mor for more and more fire [sic]."[49] That day they called in 358 rounds.[50] At the end of 25 September the Algonquin Regiment handed over their region to the Argylls. No. 2 mortar platoon stayed in their positions with the Argylls as the Algonquins moved off to the east to assist the South Alberta Regiment in holding routes against any German movement.[51]

The skill of the mortar platoon was not lost on the Argylls who demonstrated the same appreciation as the Algonquins. No.2 Mortar platoon conducted 3 shoots from 1310 – 2100. At 2100 200 rounds were fired to support an Argyll patrol.[52] The Operations Log for 10th Brigade's headquarters contains an entry at 1340 hours the following day that states that the Argyll "Comdr wishes to keep 4.2" mortar in his fire plan as they are the backbone and are firing at extreme range."[53] No.2 platoon split its sections to better cover a section of the front with No. 3 machine gun platoon who was prepared to repel a counter-attack should one materialize.[54] This program of constant patrolling, harassing fire and counter mortar and battery fire suited the NB Rangers quite well. The flatness of the terrain enabled the machine gunners to have nearly unobstructed views, while the mortars were able to manoeuvre quickly into positions to engage German units in the manner of highly mobile howitzers.

---

48   The New Brunswick Rangers' War Diary, 22– 24 September, 1944.
49   The New Brunswick Rangers' War Diary, 25 September, 1944.
50   The New Brunswick Rangers' War Diary, 25 September, 1944.
51   Jackson, ed., *The Argyll and Sutherland Highlanders of Canada*, p.126.
52   New Brunswick Rangers' War Diary, 27 September, 1944.
53   The 10th Canadian Infantry Brigade's Headquarters' War Diary, September 1944, Appendix '4', 'Ops Log', 28 September, 1944.
54   New Brunswick Rangers' War Diary, 29 October, 1944.

1 October two companies of the Algonquins returned from their week-long period in Hulst and relieved the Argyll companies on the dikes.[55] Two Argyll companies in turn accompanied the South Alberta Regiment in Hulst, while the battalion's headquarters and the other two companies went west of the Bouchaute area where they patrolled an area with a 4000 yard frontage.[56] The Bouchaute area was then in turn manned by the New Brunswick Rangers, with the Algonquins on their right, and the Argylls on their left. For a week until 7 Brigade's Operation 'Switchback', the New Brunswick Rangers again acted in an infantry-like role with quiet patrols and a vigilant watch of the surrounding area. With knowledge of basic infantry skills and the unlikelihood of German aggression in their vicinity, the NB Rangers were ideal candidates for such a task. Besides, there was little the mortar platoon was able to do as they were again restricted to twenty rounds per mortar from 2 until 10 October with resources likely being diverted for use by 3rd Division.[57]

The New Brunswick Rangers were not alone in this. During the clearing of the Breskens Pocket the 3rd Anti-Tank Regiment was tasked to hold the western line of the Leopold Canal. 105th Battery, initially raised from St. George, New Brunswick was among those units drawn into temporary infantry roles. This was not the last instance where 3rd Anti-Tank gunners were used in such manner, nor was this type of reallocation isolated to just 3rd Anti-Tank.[58] Earlier in September during the crossing of the Ghent Canal by 10th Brigade; 8th Canadian Light Anti-Aircraft Regiment had its gunners act as infantry to relieve infantrymen from the Argyll and Sutherland Highlanders of Canada's defences on the immediate bridgehead of the Ghent Canal.[59]

6 October the Argylls made a feint near Kerselaer to bring German attention eastward while the real assault of 'Switchback' went in to the west delivered by 7 Brigade. To aid in this deception, smoke was to be laid out by artillery and mortar units while the Argylls crossed the canal near Kersalaer.[60] The Algonquins also made a diversionary attack out of the Isabella Polder to acquire the focus of the enemy in the early hours prior to the main effort. 7 Brigade was to attack across the killing ground of the pre-registered mortar and artillery fire and mutually supportive machine guns to obtain German attention in time for 9 Canadian Infantry Brigade[61] to cross the Braakman Inlet to strike the German rear. The Algonquins' feint used three companies and

55   Cassidy, *Warpath*, pp.161-162; Patterson, *A Short History*, p.40.
56   Library and Archives Canada, Record Group 24, Volume 15004, The Argyll and Sutherland Highlanders of Canada's War Diary, 1 October, 1944; Jackson, ed., *The Argyll and Sutherland Highlanders of Canada*, p.127.
57   The New Brunswick Rangers' War Diary, 1–10 October, 1944.
58   Marc Milner, "NB Gunners in NWE," narrative prepared for the "3rd Field Regiment History" by the Gregg Centre, University of New Brunswick.
59   Headquarters, Royal Canadian Artillery, 4th Canadian Armoured Division, 12 September, 1944
60   Jackson, ed., *The Argyll and Sutherland Highlanders of Canada*, p.128.
61   And with it the North Shore (New Brunswick) Regiment from the same province as the NB Rangers.

cost the battalion 28 casualties.[62] For both of these diversionary assaults, the New Brunswick Rangers did not take part, but from their positions the NB Rangers could hear the actions being conducted on either flank.[63]

The static period experiences varied for 10thBrigade's infantry formations. For 16 September to 20 October the New Brunswick Rangers were only short 11 other ranks at their worst and a surplus of men by 28 October. The Lincs are noted to have had a renewal and men found time to properly integrate reinforcements and train them with patrols and street fighting drills. The Lincs were able to rebuild their strength just shy of the war establishment of 812.[64] A stark comparison of the Algonquins who had a nightmarish three weeks along the dikes: "There was not even to be the illusion of victory or success – but simply the dismal succession of patrol after patrol. Patrols that didn't [sic] start off right, patrols that never came back, patrols that came back at half – strength, with not even a prisoner to show for the cost."[65] When the Algonquins learned the purpose of the 6 October assault, "many harsh words were recalled."[66] For their tenure on the dykes, the Algonquins sustained 134 all ranks casualties.[67]

Two divisions were transferred to Montgomery to expedite the opening of Antwerp on 9 October. Yet the clearing of the Scheldt remained a Canadian priority. The 104th U.S. (Timberwolf) Division and 52nd (Lowland) British Division, were given to the Canadians to reinforce their efforts, but were not available for a further ten days in time for the final operations to open the Scheldt.[68] In the meantime 3rd Canadian Infantry Division mopped up the Breskens Pocket with assistance on their flank from 10th Canadian Infantry Brigade.

10th Brigade continued to make probing assaults to assist 3rd Division with its task. The Algonquin Regiment was tasked with deducing the enemy strength on their front and should the series of road junctions that served as their objectives be taken, 8 Canadian Infantry Brigade was to push through their positions 24 hours later. Progress was slow and after casualties were taken, they withdrew under fire from light machine guns and grenades from mutually supportive strongpoints. The New Brunswick Rangers' No. 2 mortar platoon and No. 3 machine gun platoon had supported the Algonquin assault. At 0900 No.2 platoon delivered a 5 minute shoot and both platoons fired for a 20 minute period at 1030. For the day, No. 4 machine gun platoon had a section of the line situated in the event of a counter-attack. 12 October the Algonquins called for some harassing heavy mortar fire in the late afternoon and 80 rounds were fired. This was added to the weight of fire that had been delivered from Typhoon rockets and strafing along the enemy side of the canal. The

62   Copp, *Cinderella Army*, pp.94-95.
63   The New Brunswick Rangers' War Diary, 6–8 October, 1944.
64   Hayes, *The Lincs*, pp.52-53,
65   Cassidy, *Warpath*, p.190.
66   Copp, *Cinderella Army*, p.95. See also Cassidy, *Warpath*, pp.192-193.
67   Cassidy, *Warpath*, p.196.
68   Copp, *Cinderella Army*, p.138.

Argylls found that the Germans began to pull away from their defensive lines along the canal two days later. The Argylls concentrated in Watervliet so as to not be hit by friendly shells from 3rd Division's artillery programme.[69]

As 3rd Division mopped up the last of the Breskens Pocket, 10th Brigade headed eastward along the Eecloo-Ghent-Antwerp roadways and arrived in St. Antonius by 1600, 17 October. Here 10th Canadian Infantry Brigade prepared for its final phase of the Battle of the Scheldt with operation 'Suitcase'.[70] This operation forced the brigade into a series of muddy skirmishes through forests, hamlets, and cities where the terrain again favoured the defenders. Operating under I British Corps, 4th Division was to be the hammer against the Germans in front of 2nd Division freeing that formation's flank and rear as it reeled west for operations along the Walcheren Peninsula. 4th Division was to continue north and clear through Bergen-op-Zoom to the Maas River. It was expected to last from 20 October to 15 November, but was over by the night of 5/6 November.[71]

Literature regarding 10th Brigade during the Operation 'Market-Garden' phase of the Battle of the Scheldt is limited. This is the result of a few factors. 4th Canadian Armoured Division was unoccupied with the clearing of the Channel Ports and the offensives to reduce the Breskens Pocket. Academic attention is also devoted to the reinforcement issue that faced Canadian ground forces in Europe.[72] As well as the political and strategic controversy over opening Antwerp and Operation 'Market-Garden'. These undoubtedly play a factor in 4th Canadian Armoured Division's limited attention to their period of static warfare in a mobile war. Regardless, the employment of the NB Rangers during this period suited the company perfectly well.

The experience of 10th Canadian Infantry Brigade's infantry units differed during their time of static polder warfare. The New Brunswick Rangers were of continuous service and employ, the Lincoln and Welland Regiment pulled off a perfect raid; the Algonquin Regiment suffered; and the Argyll and Sutherland Highlanders of Canada were somewhere in the middle.[73] The Algonquin Regiment's regimental historian noted that morale was low and a victory was much needed to restore their spirits.[74] For their part the New Brunswick Rangers performed the tasks assigned to them with ease. These were not isolated to the conventions of their speciality, such as holding a stretch of the canal, but were successfully carried out. When called upon to

---

69   Library and Archive Canada, Record Group 24, Volume 15000, The Algonquin
      Regiment's War Diary, 10-12 October, 1944; The New Brunswick Rangers' War Diary,
      10-12 October, 1944; The Argyll and Sutherland Highlander's War Diary, 14 October,
      1944; Cassidy, pp.164-165; Jackson, ed., *The Argyll and Sutherland Highlanders of Canada*,
      pp.130, 133; Patterson, *A Short History*, p.41.
70   The New Brunswick Rangers' War Diary, 16-17 October, 1944.
71   Stacey, *Victory Campaign*, pp.387-390; Whitakers, *Tug of War*, pp.109-110
72   Another issue that is not discussed in great detail here.
73   Hayes, *The Lincs.*
74   Cassidy, *Warpath*, pp.164-165.

deliver heavy infantry support they were well recognized by members of the brigade and the hostility of the enemy who reacted long after they were gone. The mobility and efficiency of the New Brunswick Rangers greatly assisted 10th Canadian Infantry Brigade in this period.

The operations to make Antwerp a serviceable port reinvigorated First Canadian Army once it had become a priority for Montgomery.[75] The traditional narrative typically overlooks the role of 10th Canadian Infantry Brigade and the New Brunswick Rangers. Yet a closer examination of the New Brunswick Rangers reveals that during the latter period they were well suited for the static warfare of the Belgian polders. This is particularly true of No. 2 mortar platoon, as it was heavily relied upon as 10th Brigade's own force of indirect fire power on call.

Studying the New Brunswick Rangers during this period sheds new light on how the war was conducted in Belgium and Holland when most of the attention is given to 2nd and 3rd Canadian Infantry Divisions in liberating the Channel Ports, clearing the Breskens Pocket, taking Walcheren, and the larger Operation 'Market-Garden'. Like most of the First Canadian Army, 10th Canadian Infantry Brigade was conducting tasks beyond their capacity. As such, the harassing actions of the New Brunswick Rangers were important in masking the true size of their force along an elongated front; and even taking over sections of it for a time. The New Brunswick Rangers were able to hone their crafts, and when importance was finally given to the First Canadian Army in opening the approaches to Antwerp, were able to revert to their typical role to support the infantry battalions and armoured regiments in mobile actions.

75   Stacey, *The Victory Campaign*, pp.655-656.

17

Shadows of Arnhem:
British Airborne Forces and the Aftermath of Operation Market Garden

Dr John Greenacre

The shadows cast by the battle at Arnhem in September 1944 were long and deep and it was by no means certain how Britain's airborne forces would emerge after Operation MARKET GARDEN. The physical component of the capability had been badly damaged, perhaps irreparably in terms of the trained manpower that had been left dead, wounded and in captivity on the north bank of the Lower Rhine. As a result of those losses it was possible that the morale of the British airborne establishment may have been severely shaken if not broken. Furthermore, the failure of MARKET GARDEN to achieve its ultimate objective and the associated cost could have called into question or even threatened the very concept of airborne operations within the higher echelons of the British military hierarchy.

Similar circumstances in the late spring of 1941 had essentially curtailed the further development and employment of Germany's airborne forces. On 20 May 1941 Germany invaded Crete, initially with an almost exclusively airborne force. Gliders and paratroops landed at Maleme and assaulted the nearby airfield. Despite a high degree of air superiority it took the German airborne units thirty-six hours to capture the airfield and even then it was not fully secure. The operation cost 4,000 German casualties and 175 of the 530 transport aircraft employed were destroyed or damaged beyond immediate repair. Despite the losses British military intelligence assessed the results of the operation, from a German point of view, as 'disappointing' rather than catastrophic.[1] The invasion of Crete, despite its ultimate success stood in poor contrast to German airborne performance and accomplishments in Scandinavia and the Low Countries in the spring of 1940. In the intervening twelve months the operating environment in Europe had changed but Germany's *Fallschirmjäger* had failed to evolve to cope with the increased threat to their mode of operation. As a result, even though

---

1   The National Archives (TNA), Air Ministry (AIR) 23/6110, HQ RAF Middle East Intelligence Report, German Air-Borne Attack on Crete, 1 November 1941.

wider events were still favourable, the German high command lost faith with the airborne capability and it was generally relegated to conventional and minor operations for the remainder of the war.

In October 1944 Britain's airborne forces potentially faced a similar fate. At the end of 1944 the advantages within the operating environment were shifting inexorably in favour of the Allies. Offensive operations up to and beyond the border of the Reich were to continue through the winter of 1944/45 and airborne forces would certainly be required to contribute to a proportion of those being planned. Therefore it was critical to pay attention to the physical, moral and conceptual components of Britain's airborne capability in the wake of Arnhem to ensure it could continue to fulfil an effective combat role.

The most obvious damage had been done to the physical aspect of British airborne forces. Prior to MARKET GARDEN Britain boasted two capable and experienced airborne divisions operating in northwest Europe, an independent parachute brigade in the Mediterranean and a further airborne division of questionable capability and effectiveness in India. Figures compiled a few weeks after the operation showed Major General 'Roy' Urquhart's 1st Airborne Division deficient by 476 officers and 6,587 other ranks, more than fifty percent of the establishment. To all intents and purposes the division had been physically written off in the short to medium term. Soon after the battle General Dwight Eisenhower wrote to Urquhart with apparently disappointing news, 'The Chief of the Imperial General Staff has just informed me that, due to the great losses the First British Airborne Division suffered at Arnhem, it will probably not be possible to reconstitute it. This occasions me the same deep regret that I know you must feel...'[2] It would appear though that Eisenhower and Field Marshal Alanbrooke were premature in their assumptions. It was clear that elsewhere the War Office was not willing to permanently remove the division from the order of battle; 'I do not think 1st Airborne Division should be allowed to die now'.[3]

How the formation was to be reconstituted was subject to a degree of lateral and innovative thought. In order to bring the division back to fighting strength as rapidly as possible it was proposed to combine the remnants of 4th Parachute Brigade with the equally battered 1st Parachute Brigade. The plan foresaw 1st Parachute Battalion amalgamating with 156th Parachute Battalion, the 2nd with the 10th and the 3rd with the 11th. Even so, the merged battalions would still be understrength. The air-landing battalions and the divisional artillery and engineers would also be left at around half strength without special attention. It was further proposed that the then defunct 4th Parachute Brigade would be replaced by moving 2nd Independent Parachute Brigade from Italy to become the second parachute brigade within 1st Airborne Division. 2nd Independent Parachute Brigade had been an original constituent of the division up

---

2   R.E. Urquhart, *Arnhem*, p.201.
3   TNA, War Office (WO) 233/14, Untitled memorandum from Director Air (Major General K. Crawford) to Director Staff Duties, 16 October 1944.

until it was retained in Italy when the remainder returned to England in November 1943. Other suggested expedients to find reinforcements for the division included approaching the Canadian government to create a second Canadian parachute battalion, withdrawing parachute trained individuals from the SAS and even calling for volunteers from the approximately 6,000 deferred RAF aircrew trainees that were about to be transferred to the Army.[4]

What was clear was that 1st Airborne Division could expect no assistance, in terms of a transfer of trained manpower from its sister formation. 6th Airborne Division was now in the lead for future offensive operations. Having only returned from a protracted period of fighting in Normandy at the beginning of September 1944 the division was itself in need of reconstitution. Therefore 6th Airborne Division would be the priority for trained reinforcements emerging from the training pipeline. The War Office had agreed that two fully functioning airborne divisions could only be expected to execute one airborne operation each in 1945. To allow even that modest operational tempo 1st Airborne Division would need to be recuperated and rehabilitated as rapidly as possible.[5]

The question of how quickly 1st Airborne Division could be reconstituted and made available for airborne operations was not straight forward and had to be constantly amended taking into consideration the rate of inflow of new personnel, the speed at which individuals, units and formations could be trained and the evolving operational situation. Initial estimates were optimistic. Despite his assertion that the division was beyond reconstitution, Alanbrooke was informed by Field Marshal Bernard Montgomery that he was 'certain that the men should not be employed in battle again for two or three months. They require some leave and then a good period of training so that they can recover from the great strain they have been through…'[6] Whereas the CIGS's preliminary assessment of the future of 1st Airborne Division was excessively pessimistic, Montgomery's calculation of when the formation might be fit to fight again was overly optimistic.

Initial attempts to quantify the issue estimated that the physical reconstitution of the division, replacing the lost manpower by whatever means possible, could be completed by the end of 1944. There would then have to be a lengthy period of tactical and airborne training to bring the division to a state of readiness from which it could take part in operations again. A meeting convened in the War Office to consider 1st Airborne Division's reformation concluded there were two major actions required

4   TNA, WO 233/14, Strength State – 1st Airborne Division – as at 3 Oct '44. The figures for 1st Airborne Division's losses at Arnhem differ across primary and secondary accounts. See for example M. Middlebrook, *Arnhem 1944; The Airborne Battle*, pp. 438-441 and C. Ryan, *A Bridge Too Far*, p. 457.
5   TNA, WO 233/14, Minutes of a Meeting held on 9 Oct 44 to consider the reconstitution of 1st Airborne Div.
6   Letter from Montgomery to Alanbrooke 28 September 1944 quoted in Hamilton, *Monty: The Field Marshal 1944-1976*, pp.96-97.

to expedite the process. The first was that the division's constituent units had to be accommodated in a concentrated area within the United Kingdom so the reconstitution could be closely supervised. Urquhart personally insisted on this point. The second action concerned the subordination of 1st Airborne Division. It was agreed that the division would be removed from SHAEF's chain of command. It would then be subordinated directly to the War Office's Director of Organisation and Director of Military Training. This would allow the flow of reinforcements and the allocation of aircraft for training to be influenced by the highest authority. Day to day control would be exercised by HQ Airborne Troops on behalf of the War Office. Even with these measures in place the target for 1st Airborne Division to be returned to SHAEF for committal to operations was 1st April 1945.[7]

There was no disagreement with this estimate largely because there was no strong imperative to bring the division to a point where it could once again contribute to the campaign in Europe. The next major operation that was likely to require a major airborne component was the projected crossing of the Rhine. Outline plans had been drawn up for airborne formations to support Rhine crossings in the 21st and 12th Army Groups' areas in the north and centre of the Allied line (Operation PLUNDER) or to support 6th Army Group in the south (Operations TRIPOD and CHOKER).[8] The German counter offensive in the Ardennes in December 1944 delayed planning for the deliberate Rhine crossings but even so the very early spring 1945 target date meant that 1st Airborne Division was unlikely to be fit to take part. In any case there were another five airborne divisions available for operations in north-west Europe. The US 82nd and 101st Airborne Divisions had both been involved heavily in the fighting in the Ardennes during the Battle of the Bulge. British 6th and US 17th Airborne Divisions had also been involved in containing and defeating the German counter offensive but at a lower intensity. The US 13th Airborne Division only arrived in the European Theatre of Operations (ETO) in early February 1945 and was untried in combat. Operation PLUNDER, under Montgomery's command, was eventually scheduled for 24th March 1945 with Operation VARSITY being its airborne element. Two weeks before the operation the airborne order of battle was reduced from three to two divisions and US 13th Division was stood down leaving the US 17th and British 6th Airborne Divisions to take part under control of US XVIII Airborne Corps.[9] With this reduction in allocated formations any chance of British 1st Airborne Division being required was discarded.

7   TNA, WO 233/14, Minutes of a meeting held on 9 October 1944 to consider the reconstitution of 1 Airborne Div and Notes for meeting 11 December 1944 to discuss the problems of command and administration of 1 Airlanding Brigade.

8   TNA, WO 219/608, Airborne Operations: Operation Varsity and planning for future operations, November 1944.

9   TNA, WO 106/4437, Memorandum 'Operation 'Varsity'; Information obtained from H.Q. Airborne Corps, 9 March 1945.

On the eve of Operation VARSITY Alanbrooke wrote to Eisenhower on the subject of 1st Airborne Division's readiness. The 1st April 1945 estimate for the division to be operationally ready had been revised:

> I have been into the question as to whether the 1st British Airborne Division can be made available for operations before the beginning of June [1945]. I have issued instructions that the 1st Airborne Division should be prepared to undertake full operations by the middle of May... The Division could be made available in an airborne reinforcing role (as distinct from an assault role) by the 1st May if you should so require it.'[10]

The less taxing airborne reinforcing role certainly looked likely to be required. Operation ARENA was being planned immediately after VARSITY had been launched. ARENA envisaged airborne divisions being dropped on top of allied reconnaissance elements of 12th US Army Group in the area of Kassel as they advanced northeast from Frankfurt. The ARENA plan called for all six airborne divisions in Europe to take part, including 1st Airborne Division in a 'follow-up role if available in time.' The projected date for the operation, 15 May 1945 coincided neatly with Alanbrooke's estimate of readiness. In the event Operation ARENA was scratched as General Omar Bradley's 12th US Army Group made satisfactory progress without requiring airborne assistance.[11]

With the end of the war in Europe appearing inevitable in early 1945 immediate post-war plans were being refined. Operation ECLIPSE (formerly Operation RANKIN-C and then Operation TALISMAN) was designed to enable the most rapid occupation of strategic areas of Germany and German occupied areas in the case of an unconditional surrender. One effective of means of getting troops to key areas such as Berlin and Kiel was by airborne insertion. Such an operation would seize vital industrial and scientific objectives, such as those linked with V weapon and nascent atomic programmes, carry out disarmament of the *Wehrmacht* and preserve law and order and demonstrate the resolve of the Western allies to counter any Soviet violation of agreed boundaries.[12] With Operation ECLIPSE only to be launched in the case of Germany's unconditional surrender the full airborne assault role was unlikely to be required. As an airborne reinforcing task it was ideally suited to 1st Airborne Division's reduced capabilities.

10   TNA, WO 106/4437, Alanbrooke to Eisenhower, 23 March 1945.
11   TNA, WO 106/4437, Untitled memorandum from Air 2 to ACIGS, 28 March 1945.
12   TNA, WO 219/4989, Operation ECLIPSE: outline plan and requests for intelligence, 1 December 1944 – 30th April 1945. For an account of the evolution of Operations RANKIN-C, TALISMAN and ECLIPSE see K.O. McCreedy, *Planning the Peace: Operation Eclipse and the Occupation of Germany* (Fort Leavonworth: School of Advanced Military Studies, 1995).

Once it was clear Urquhart's division would not be required for VARSITY they were lined up to take part in ECLIPSE. The Commander 1st British Airborne Corps wrote to the Director of Air in the War Office to demand that 1st Airborne Division be prepared for operations by 1 April 1945. Although he was prepared to accept a lower standard of training across the division he did not consider there should be any lack of readiness in the forces earmarked for ECLIPSE.[13] Once again however, events on the ground and wider political considerations superseded the requirement for the airborne element of Operation ECLIPSE, although 1st Parachute Brigade, with only one battalion was flown into Denmark immediately after the German unconditional surrender.

Any preparations for Operation ECLIPSE were not wasted when, on 4 May 1945 1st Airborne Division was warned for immediate employment as part of Operation APOSTLE. As ECLIPSE was planned to allow a rapid occupation of strategic areas of Germany, the Netherlands and Denmark so Operation APOSTLE was designed to achieve similar objectives in Norway. Urquhart's division, without 1st Parachute Brigade (which had already been committed to operations in Denmark) had the Special Air Service (SAS) Brigade attached at short notice before taking part in Operation DOOMSDAY, the air-transported element of APOSTLE. Between 8 and 13 May 1945 the division flew into southern Norway to occupy Oslo, Stavanger and Kristiansand and for the next four months Urquhart's 6,000 airborne and SAS troops oversaw the disarmament and repatriation of 350,000 Germans.[14]

It was to be 1st Airborne Division's final operation. Once the war in the Far East was concluded the War Office decided that two British divisions in the airborne role were a luxury that was no longer required. Being the senior formation and having been designated the Imperial Strategic Reserve, on the surface 1st Airborne Division would have appeared the best candidate to survive. However, the division still had not fully emerged from the shadow of Arnhem. 6th Airborne Division was better manned, trained and equipped and more operationally ready. On 15th November 1945 1st Airborne Division was disbanded.[15]

Even before the disbandment decision the maintenance of morale was identified as a critical issue within 1st Airborne Division. The formation had gone through a horrifically tough battle at Arnhem, had lost well over fifty percent of its manpower killed, wounded or taken prisoner and ultimately had failed in its mission. Crucially, the command structure of the division had been all but destroyed. When the first roll call was taken after the battle two out of three brigade commanders and eight out of nine infantry battalion commanders had been left dead or wounded as prisoners and evaders on the north bank of the Lower Rhine. Within 4th Parachute Brigade two

---

13   TNA, WO 106/4437, Memorandum 'Operational Readiness of First Airborne Division', Commander 1st British Airborne Corps to Director Air, 9 March 1945.
14   Otway, *Airborne Forces*, pp. 324-328.
15   Ibid, pp. 329-330.

infantry battalion commanders were dead and the third was a prisoner of war. Only one out three battalion second-in-commands and the same proportion of adjutants returned. Approximately 100 officers of the brigade had jumped onto Drop Zone Y on Ginkel Heath; thirty-five were killed in action or died of wounds including most of the company commanders. Only one staff officer from the brigade's headquarters survived unwounded.[16]

That loss of commanders and staff made the process of recuperation and recon-stitution far more difficult for 1st Airborne Division in the weeks and months that followed. The huge influx of new personnel of all ranks to make up the losses incurred at Arnhem potentially threatened the effectiveness and even the very ethos of the division. The Glider Pilot Regiment provides one example of this fear. Of the 1,262 glider pilots that flew into Arnhem 219 were dead and 511 were missing after the battle.[17] This highly specialist regiment served both 1st and 6th Airborne Divisions and therefore the losses had to be made good as quickly as possible for future opera-tions. However, the glider pilot training pipeline was long and complicated and it could not suddenly produce over 700 new pilots. Therefore the regiment had to turn to the RAF and convert surplus air force pilots to the glider role. The commander of the Glider Pilot Regiment, Brigadier George Chatterton initially resisted this initia-tive on the grounds that all members of the regiment were trained to fight as infan-trymen and the RAF pilots would dilute that capability. Nevertheless, the policy was driven through and the RAF glider pilots' performance during Operation VARSITY demonstrated Chatterton's fears were unfounded.[18]

Together with the losses and the potential sense of failure, the lack of clear role after MARKET GARDEN, the threat of disbandment and the dwindling chance that the formation was going to be committed to full airborne operations before the end of the war all threatened the morale of 1st Airborne Division. The retrospective views of those that had fought at Arnhem varied, particularly among junior officers and soldiers. Many shared the opinion that the operation had been 'the biggest balls-up since Mons' but still 'wouldn't have missed this "adventure" for all the tea in China.' Others remained bitter about the experience for years.[19] Among more senior officers, as might be expected, the sentiment was more uniformly supportive of MARKET GARDEN. Brigadier 'Shan' Hackett, Commander 4th Parachute Brigade had been wounded at Arnhem and after the battle became an evader assisted by the Dutch

---

16   Hackett, *I Was a Stranger*, p.207.
17   For a comprehensive review of the Glider Pilot Regiment's casualties at Arnhem see Peters and Buist, *Glider Pilots at Arnhem*, pp. 334-345.
18   Chatterton, *The Wings of Pegasus*, pp. 208-212. In fact the decision to speed up the flow of trained glider pilots by recruiting surplus RAF pilots had been made before Operation MARKET GARDEN was launched. See Greenacre, *Churchill's Spearhead: The Development of Britain's Airborne Forces During World War II*, pp. 116-118.
19   See for example Middlebrook, *Arnhem 1944*, pp.451-453 and Blockwell, *Diary of a Red Devil*, p.182.

underground. When he eventually returned to England in February 1945 he wrote to Urquhart, 'Thank you for the party. It didn't go quite as we hoped and got a bit rougher than we expected. But speaking for myself, I'd take it on again any time and so, I'm sure, would everybody else.'[20] Urquhart himself was certain the potential outcome of the operation had been worth the losses incurred:

> The operation was not one hundred per cent successful and did not end quite as we intended. The losses were heavy but all ranks appreciate that the risks involved were reasonable. There is no doubt that all would willingly undertake another operation under similar conditions in the future. We have no regrets.[21]

Urquhart himself could have become a convenient scapegoat for the tactical failure at Arnhem but instead every effort was made to preserve his reputation. Hackett loyally defended Urquhart's performance during the battle on several occasions describing him as '...that great, brave, imperturbable fighting Scot, the best battlefield commander I fought under in all the war years...'[22] In fact it is difficult to find any Arnhem veteran willing to break ranks and criticise 1st Airborne Division's commander.[23] Having been a protégé of Montgomery it is unsurprising that the Field Marshal gave Urquhart his full backing, echoing Hackett's assessment immediately after the battle:

> Urquhart himself is perfectly all right; he is a completely imperturbable person and has not suffered in the least from the very trying experience he has had... I know him very well and he is quite first-class. He would command an infantry division excellently. He would also be very good for the job of Deputy Commander of the Airborne Army should Browning be required elsewhere.[24]

Montgomery remained MARKET GARDEN's principal cheerleader after the event. His advocacy took two forms. First he promoted the view that the operation had achieved valuable gains. His comment that 'The battle of Arnhem was ninety per cent successful...' has often been taken out of context. It was perhaps an overstatement but his wider point was valid.[25] The Waal bridgehead, sometimes known as the Nijmegen salient, became an important area from which to develop further operations

---

20   Anon, *By Air To Battle*, p. 145.
21   TNA, WO 219/5137, Operation 'MARKET' Lessons, 10 January 1945.
22   Baynes, *Urquhart of Arnhem*, p.165.
23   One of the rare examples of criticism of Urquhart at Arnhem was made by Tony Deane-Drummond, a signals officer who saw the divisional commander at close quarters in the headquarters during the battle. He described Urquhart's actions as being like a 'wet hen'. Tony Deane-Drummond letter to the author 18 May 2005.
24   Montgomery to Alanbrooke, 28 September 1944 quoted in Hamilton, *Monty: The Field Marshal*, pp.97-98.
25   Montgomery, *Normandy to the Baltic*, p.149.

through the winter of 1944/45. Montgomery was adamant that had Urquhart's men not held on as long as they did at Arnhem the Waal bridgehead would not have been secured. His views were supported to some extent by the senior German airborne commander of the war, *Generaloberst* Kurt Student during post war interrogation. He contended that MARKET GARDEN:

> [P]roved to be a great success. At one stroke it brought the British 2nd Army into the possession of vital bridges and valuable territory. The conquest of the Nijmegen area meant the creation of a good jumping board for the offensive which contributed to the end of the war.[26]

Montgomery's second approach to maintaining morale was to apply lavish public praise and appreciation on the men of 1st Airborne Division. On 27th September 1944, the day after he had skilfully handled the evacuation from Arnhem, Urquhart met Montgomery at his Tactical Headquarters. The two men discussed the operation frankly over dinner and Urquhart stayed the night. Before he departed the following morning Urquhart was given a hand written note by Montgomery, to be read to the survivors of 1st Airborne Division. The expression of the Field Marshal's appreciation and admiration has appeared in many accounts of MARKET GARDEN and does not require full reproduction here. The language was heroic:

> [T]here can be few episodes more glorious than the epic of ARNHEM, and those that follow after will find it hard to live up to the standards that you have set... In years to come it will be a great thing for a man to be able to say: 'I fought at ARNHEM.'[27]

Of course, all of this retrospective support could be interpreted as Montgomery attempting to conserve his own reputation through a cleverly manipulated media campaign. Certainly his letter to Urquhart and his division was simultaneously handed by the Field Marshal to his Public Relations Officer for onward transmission in the press but as Montgomery's biographer has pointed out, this cynical view is too simplistic. Hamilton suggests that Montgomery's purpose in praising those that had fought at Arnhem was a sign of his role as the '*paterfamilias* who looked upon all those who served under him as members of his family – members for whose welfare he felt responsible.'[28] In fact there was a more practical purpose to Montgomery's actions. He considered the morale of the soldier to be the biggest single factor in success in battle but that you could not raise morale through thanks, praise or flattery. Instead it

---

26 Hamilton, *Monty*, pp. 94-98
27 For the full transcript of Montgomery's letter of appreciation to 1st Airborne Division see Montgomery, *Memoirs*, pp. 273-274.
28 Hamilton, *Monty: The Field Marshal*, pp. 95-97.

was success in battle that led to high morale, hence he stressed the positive outcomes of the fight at Arnhem. In truth there was little to be gained in trying to raise 1st Airborne Division's morale for its own sake. As has been shown, it was unlikely that Urquhart's men would take any significant role in the campaign in the immediate future following Arnhem. Montgomery's words were more concerned with maintaining the morale of the wider airborne establishment so it remained fit and focused on impending airborne operations.

The Field Marshal need not have worried. The commander of 6th Airborne Division, Major General Richard 'Windy' Gale was of the opinion that no two airborne operations were alike, there was no set piece method of employment. Therefore failure at Arnhem did not necessarily herald failure in all future endeavours.[29] 6th Airborne Division was a more cerebral organisation than 1st Airborne Division. This was a result of the differing foundations of the two formations. Urquhart's command was a legacy of its all-volunteer inception, organic growth and development and had an almost overweening self-confidence born out of its experiences in early raids, unsupported operations in North Africa and hard-fought successes in Sicily. Its sister division had been deliberately created from extant infantry units with their own operational experiences. 6th Airborne Division's operational initiation would be in the critical role guarding the left flank of the D Day landings. Gale set about preparing his command for Normandy in a methodical, almost scientific manner in order to offset their lack of collective airborne experience. In the aftermath of MARKET GARDEN the conceptual element of British airborne warfare, the doctrine, tactics and procedures had to be called into question and forensically examined. With an airborne crossing of the Rhine imminent Gale once again began the methodical preparation of his division with a close eye on the conceptual lessons of Arnhem as a base on which to build future tactics and procedures.

The official British report on Operation MARKET GARDEN was produced under Urquhart's signature. The document as a whole was long on narrative, short on lessons and contained very few remedies to the shortcomings identified. The section dedicated to the lessons taken from 1st Airborne Division's experience stretched to just five pages and what might be considered the major lessons less than two pages. Furthermore the report was not published until January 1945, giving little time for 6th Airborne Division to absorb and act on its insights. Fortunately, the lessons from Arnhem were obvious to any reasonably well informed and critical observer and fell into three fundamental areas.

The first fundamental issue that required attention was the relationship of the drop zones and landing zones to the objectives during the planning process. The result of selecting areas for landing up to eight miles from the objectives, the bridges at Arnhem was evident to all as Urquhart made clear:

---

29   Gale, *Call To Arms*, p. 154.

It is considered that we must be prepared to take more risks during the initial stages of an Airborne operation. When the balance sheet of casualties at ARNHEM is made, it would appear a reasonable risk to have landed the Div. much closer to the objective chosen, even in the face of some enemy flak.[30]

Gale concurred and gave a reason why he thought the distance between drop and landing zones and the bridges had been so great:

Obsession with the dropping zones and their security, both on the part of the airmen and the troops, in my opinion tended to force them to land too far from their objectives. The casualties in a closer-in drop could scarcely have been greater than what these gallant men in the event suffered.[31]

The stretching of the planning distance between drop and landing zones and objectives had been a creeping process that began in the wake of Operation HUSKY. It had become embedded in the airborne psyche to the extent that, even in his post MARKET report, Urquhart considered five miles would have been an acceptable distance. Two brigade-sized British airborne operations were executed during HUSKY by 1st Airborne Division. 1st Air Landing Brigade deployed by glider during the night of 9 July 1943 to capture the Ponte Grande over the Anopo Canal by *coup de main*. Four days later, 1st Parachute Brigade dropped south of Catania to capture the Primasole Bridge over the River Simeto. In both cases the fly in to the objectives was severely disrupted and only much depleted forces made it to their respective bridges. However, both objectives were seized and held.[32]

Despite the relative success of both brigades the cost was generally viewed as excessive. 1st Air-Landing Brigade suffered more than fifty percent of its gliders ditching in the Mediterranean leading to a casualty rate of nearly 500 men killed, drowned, wounded or missing. 1st Parachute Brigade's insertion was severely disrupted by flak and in total the division suffered over 700 casualties. The high losses triggered a board of inquiry instigated by Allied Forces HQ.

The casualties sustained during 1st Air Landing Brigade's operation on Sicily were due almost entirely to the inexperience of the American aircrew that flew the Douglas C-47 Dakotas towing the gliders and a lack of collective training immediately prior to the operation. The British airborne formations achieved their objectives, despite the high attrition rate during the fly-in, in part due the tactic of using multiple, small drop zones and landing zones as close to the objectives as possible. The official report,

---

30   TNA, WO 219/5137, Operation 'MARKET' Lessons, 10 January 1945.
31   Gale, *Call To Arms*, p. 148.
32   Greenacre, "When Opportunity Arises: British Airborne Operations in the Mediterranean 1941-1944" in A. Hargreaves, P. Rose and M. Ford (ed), *Allied Fighting Effectiveness in North Africa and Italy 1942-1945*, pp. 76-77.

however, blamed this doctrine for the high casualty rate. It recommended that airborne troops should "not be landed in an area where they are immediately faced with opposition". Instead larger, mass landing zones and drop zones should be selected to simplify pilot navigation by concentrating troop carrier formations over a larger target. Those drop and landing zones were to be selected in areas free of anti-aircraft defences to allow the force to arrive unmolested and the aircraft to survive the operation.[33] The result of this flawed analysis, despite the relative success of the airborne operations on Sicily, was an implicit acceptance of a shift away from accepting risk to aircraft and men during the initial stages of an operation.

A year after HUSKY the idea of reducing risk at the front end of an operation had become implicit doctrine. When Urquhart stated '...we must be prepared to take more risks during the initial stages of an Airborne operation', it is fair to say that he actually meant the air forces had to be prepared to take more risk. Montgomery accepted the blame himself for the drops being so far from the objective and admitted he should have ordered Second Army and 1st Airborne Corps to arrange landings much closer to the main road bridge.[34] In truth even Montgomery would have had little influence over that area of the planning for MARKET GARDEN. The air forces held tight control over the air planning process and were able to select the drop and landing zones while fending off the objections of the airborne commanders due to the requirement to protect aircraft at all costs.

Avoiding aircraft losses essentially meant avoiding anti-aircraft defences. Arnhem proved this approach to be a false economy. Urquhart was forced to admit in retrospect that an additional two minutes flying into flak would have saved lives in the long run and greatly increased the chances of the objectives being achieved. An anonymous senior RAF officer neatly summarised and then debunked the issue.

> The impression which is uppermost in my mind, and which I am sure influenced the decision of the choice of actual D.Z.s, was that the R.A.F. would not accept the risk of dropping parachutists in mass, or landing a large number of gliders within a light flak radius... In point of fact there was very little accurate information as to the location of active flak; and in any case, light flak (which was the danger so far as the parachute and tug aircraft were concerned) is not static. The presence or otherwise of flak was incidental... there was no question of avoiding... flying in the face of enemy flak.[35]

The question of locating and then avoiding anti-aircraft defences, particularly light, mobile systems was a red herring but while the air forces maintained priority over the

---

33   TNA, WO 204/4220, Report on the Proceedings of a Board of Officers convened on 23 July 1943.
34   Montgomery, *Memoirs*, p. 275.
35   Otway, *Airborne Forces*, pp. 292-293.

planning process the potential dangers of flak would continue to feature disproportionately. A coordinating authority was required.

First Allied Airborne Army had only been established on 2 August 1944 and by the time MARKET GARDEN was being planned Lieutenant General Louis Brereton's new command was far from being an efficient or effective tool of control over its subordinate airborne and air force formations. By January 1945 it was in a more established position and better placed to coordinate the requirements of air forces and airborne forces, balance priorities and direct where necessary. The insertion plan for VARSITY far more closely resembled those for HUSKY than it did for MARKET GARDEN. 6th Air Landing Brigade landed gliders on three battalion sized landing zones almost on top of the bridges over the River Issel, which were its objectives. 3rd Parachute Brigade landed on a restrictively small drop zone immediately adjacent to the unlocated German gun positions it was expected to destroy. 5th Parachute Division landed directly onto the ground it was designated to defend against any potential counter-attack. All this was done with an acceptance that, despite a comprehensive anti-flak bombardment, anti-aircraft defences would inflict loses during the landings. Despite the inevitable losses that accompanied this approach the division landed in the optimal position to rapidly achieve its objectives.

The air forces' reluctance to risk any aircraft during the MARKET GARDEN fly in was a consequence of the second fundamental conceptual lesson to emerge from the operation. British airborne forces, since inception, had always lacked sufficient dedicated aircraft to lift a full division at once. Even with the vast resources of the American Troop Carrier Command available the scale of MARKET GARDEN would not allow all the troops committed to be carried into the operation as one.

With lifts for 1st Airborne Division being scheduled for three successive days it was critical that the maximum number of aircraft survived each successive sortie. Hence the drop and landing zones had to be selected well away from any potential flak areas and consequently far from the objective. Urquhart acquiesced in the RAF's selection of the drop and landing zones because he needed to be able to defend them over a three day period. The suitability of those chosen, in terms of defence, at least in part, offset the distance from the objectives in Urquhart's deliberations.

The staggered fly-in had a twofold effect on the amount of combat power 1st Airborne Division could generate to enable it to carry objective. First and most obviously Urquhart would not have his full division available until day three of the operation. With surprise and speed being critical to generate momentum, the attack would have to be launched with the units available on day one. Secondly, those units landing on the first day would be further denuded by the requirement to defend the drop and landing zones for days two and three. Urquhart's decision to use 1st Air-Landing Brigade in that defensive role exacerbated the problem. 1st Parachute Brigade, left to spearhead the advance into Arnhem alone was established for only nine rifle platoons whereas the air-landing brigade had sixteen. Admittedly Urquhart could justifiably expect his parachute battalions to cover the distance into Arnhem more quickly, thus increasing the chances of surprise. That was offset, however, by the parachute brigade only having one third of the three inch mortars and none of the six pounder anti-tank guns available to its air-landing partner. On the first day of MARKET GARDEN the combat power that 1st Airborne Division threw towards its objectives represented only a third of its infantry Battalion's, just over a quarter of its fighting infantry manpower and even less of its infantry support weapons, for what was recognised as a divisional task. In the aftermath it was agreed that the debilitating effect of a staged insertion had to be avoided at all costs in future operations.[36]

Despite having suffered far less than their British allies the American airborne establishment was in no doubt that this was a lesson from MARKET GARDEN that could not be ignored and had to be rectified before further major operations. The aircraft strength of IX Troop Carrier Command had increased to the point where any projected force could be:

> [D]ropped and landed complete within the time necessary to take full advantage of surprise and initial disorganization of the enemy and to avoid the risk of an incomplete airlift... To plan on any other basis is to invite disastrous consequences.[37]

Urquhart also stressed the fact that an airborne division was designed to fight as a whole and was weakened beyond the actual deficit of men and materiel if forced to land dislocated by time or distance.[38] With a rapid uplift in aircraft numbers unlikely to be achieved in the limited time available before VARSITY this strong cross-allied conviction probably led to the airborne strength allocated to the Rhine crossing being reduced from three to two divisions.

Oberst Friedrich von der Heydte, one of Germany's leading airborne exponents, had been captured by the Allies during the Battle of the Bulge. Under interrogation von der Heydte stated that he believed an operation to cross the Rhine in the Wesel area would require six airborne divisions in support, landed over successive drops over a twenty-four hour period.[39] Nevertheless, allied airborne conceptual thinking had advanced well beyond that of Germany by the beginning of 1945. First Allied Airborne Army was of the opinion that two divisions delivered rapidly in one lift would be more advantageous than six arriving over a protracted period. At 0950 on 24 March 1945 6th Airborne Division, alongside US 17th Airborne Division was dropped in a single lift on its drop and landing zones between the rivers Rhine and Issel. The entire force was on the ground within an hour and by 1100hrs the drop

---

36   Relative parachute brigade and air-landing brigade establishments based on TNA WO 205/751, Training of 6th Airborne Division: Planning Notes, undated 1944.

37   TNA WO 219/608, Memorandum from Commander First Allied Airborne Army to Adjutant General United States Army, 27th December 1944.

38   TNA, WO 219/5137, Operation 'MARKET' Lessons, 10th January 1945.

39   TNA, WO 219/2878B, Possibility of an Air Landing in Area Wesel, Opinions of PW CS/967 Obst von der HEYDTE, 23rd January 1945.

zones had been cleared. By 1345hrs all the division's objectives had been seized and were being secured.[40]

The third conceptual lesson from Arnhem had deeper foundations than the first two having been identified early in the development of Britain's airborne forces as a fundamental principle of employment. Military thinker Basil Liddell Hart had explained the issue by describing a concept that he called 'the interval'. This was the optimum temporal and geographic space in which to drop airborne troops. It had to be a balance between landing in a position where enemy positions could be threatened, where reserves could be blocked and, critically, where a link up with advancing friendly ground forces could be guaranteed.[41] Montgomery was ahead of most his peers in applying thought to the employment of airborne forces and he publicly expounded his views on the subject before Liddell Hart's contribution. These included the sacrosanct principle that an airborne force should not be dropped too deep into enemy territory but somewhere it stood a realistic chance of linking up with the ground force.[42]

Given his early thought on the subject and the inviolable principles he had defined, Montgomery's outline plan for MARKET GARDEN would appear paradoxical. Admittedly ego played a part but the chief motive behind the Field Marshal abandoning many of his cherished principles and taking an uncharacteristic risk was the potential prize; a secure route into the industrial heartland of Germany. In the event many of the risks were realised, the 'interval' had been stretched too far and 1st Airborne Division paid the price. Having violated the principle of a realistic link-up once, in order to maintain morale within the airborne establishment it would have to be rigorously reapplied during future operations, beginning with VARSITY.

The 'interval' that 6th Airborne Division dropped into, between the Rhine and the Issel, immediately and directly threatened the German positions, blocked the movement of enemy reserves and practically guaranteed a rapid link up with the ground force crossing the Rhine. This was achieved by the airborne landings taking place just four miles from the nearest assault river crossings and twelve hours after the first of those crossings had departed the western bank. These factors resulted in members of 3rd Parachute Brigade linking up with the leading elements of 15th (Scottish) Division just over five hours after landing. By 1500hrs on 24th March 1945 not only were 6th Airborne Division's objectives secure but so was its own position.[43]

Operation VARSITY was a success and represented the peak of British airborne achievement. It contributed significantly to the wider success of Operation PLUNDER. The Rhine, Germany's great psychological defensive barrier had been breached and victory for the Allies in Europe was inevitable. Nevertheless, it had not been without

---

40   Otway, *Airborne Forces*, p. 307.
41   Liddell Hart Centre for Military Archives, Liddell: 12/1941/5, Possibilities and Problems of Invasion, 19th November 1941.
42   Hamilton, *Monty: The Making of a General 1887-1942*, pp. 446-459.
43   Otway, *Airborne Forces*, p. 307.

cost. In the immediate aftermath of the operation 6th Airborne Division reported its casualties as 270 killed, 570 wounded and 690 missing.[44] However, these were a fraction of those sustained during 1st Airborne Division's protracted fight six months before and on this occasion all objectives had been secured and the link up made in less than six hours, something not achieved at Arnhem in nine days.

A degree of the success achieved on the east bank of the Rhine was a result of the attention paid to supporting lessons that had been raised by 1st Airborne Division after MARKET GARDEN. The issue of resupply was subject to examination and overhaul. The first resupply sorties by Eighth US Air Force B-24 Liberators dropped 145 tons of stores from low level onto the VARSITY troops just two and three-quarter hours after the initial drops.[45] Urquhart considered that directed close air support during the early stages of the battle at Arnhem 'might easily have turned the scale and allowed the whole of 1 Para Bde to have concentrated near the main ARNHEM Bridge.'[46] During VARSITY Forward Visual Control Points and RAF communication Tentacles were extended forward to 6th Airborne Division's constituent brigades. A cab rank of close support aircraft provided sustained and responsive ground attack, which proved invaluable to the forward troops of 6th Air-Landing Brigade astride the River Issel.[47]

However, the chief factor that brought success to VARSITY was the recognition of the three main doctrinal shortcomings identified at Arnhem and the work done by 6th Airborne Division to rectify the mistakes of MARKET GARDEN. The aversion to the risk from flak was overcome and drop zones and landing zones were selected as close as practically possible to the objectives. The airborne forces allocated to VARSITY were landed in a single, compact drop over a very short period of time. The 'interval' selected for the landings in terms of timing and geography practically guaranteed a swift link up. Although the physical component of 1st Airborne Division proved to be essentially irreparable after its battle at Arnhem the morale of the British airborne division did not appreciably deteriorate, thanks in no small part to the efforts of Montgomery and the stoicism of Urquhart and his officers and men. But it was the attention paid to the conceptual component by Gale and his successor Major General Eric Bols that laid the foundations for the success of VARSITY. As the paratroopers and gliders of 6th Airborne Division began landing on the east bank of the Rhine on the morning of 24 March 1945 the shadow of Arnhem was dispelled.

44 TNA, WO 106/4437, Notes for Director Military Operations – Operation VARSITY, 2nd April 1945.
45 Otway, *Airborne Forces*, p. 304.
46 TNA, WO 219/5137, Operation 'MARKET' Lessons, 10 January 1945.
47 TNA WO 205/947, 6th Airborne Division Report on Operation VARSITY, undated 1945.

Bibliography

Primary Sources (Unpublished)
The National Archives (TNA), Kew
Air Ministry Papers
AIR23, Air Ministry and Ministry of Defence: Royal Air Force Overseas Commands: Reports and Correspondence

War Office Papers
WO106, Directorate of Military Operations and Military Intelligence, and predecessors: Correspondence and Papers
WO204, Allied Forces, Mediterranean Theatre: Military Headquarters Papers, Second World War
WO205, 21 Army Group: Military Headquarters Papers, Second World War
WO219, Supreme Headquarters Allied Expeditionary Force: Military Headquarters Papers, Second World War
WO233, Directorate of Air: Papers

Liddell Hart Centre for Military Archives (LHCMA). King's College, London

Papers of Captain Sir B.H. Liddell Hart
Liddell: 12/1941/5, Can We Invade Europe?

Primary Sources (Published)
Official Publications
Anon, *By Air To Battle: The Official Account of the British Airborne Divisions*, London: HMSO, 1945.

Memoirs, etc.
Blockwell, Albert, *Diary of a Red Devil*, Solihull: Helion, 2005.
Chatterton, George, *The Wings of Pegasus*, London: MacDonald, 1962.
Gale, Richard Nelson, *Call To Arms*, London: Hutchinson, 1968.
Hackett, John, *I Was a Stranger*, London: Chatto & Windus, 1977.
Montgomery, Bernard Law, *Normandy to the Baltic*, London: Hutchinson, 1947.
Montgomery, Bernard Law, *Memoirs*, London: Companion, 1958.
Urquhart, Robert Elliott, *Arnhem*, London: Pan Books, 1958.

Secondary Sources (Published)

Books
Baynes, John, *Urquhart of Arnhem*, London: Brassey's, 1993.
Greenacre, John, *Churchill's Spearhead: The Development of Britain's Airborne Forces During World War II*, Barnsley: Pen & Sword, 2010.

Greenacre, John, "When Opportunity Arises: British Airborne Operations in the Mediterranean 1941-1944" in Hargreaves, Andrew, Rose, Patrick, and Ford, Matthew, (ed), *Allied Fighting Effectiveness in North Africa and Italy 1942-1945*, Leiden: Brill, 2014.

Hamilton, Nigel, *Monty: The Making of a General 1887-1942*, London: Hamish Hamilton, 1981.

Hamilton, Nigel, *Monty: The Field Marshal 1944-1976*, London: Hamish Hamilton, 1985.

McCreedy, Kenneth, *Planning the Peace: Operation Eclipse and the Occupation of Germany*, Fort Leavonworth: School of Advanced Military Studies, 1995.

Middlebrook, Martin, *Arnhem 1944; The Airborne Battle*, London: Penguin, 1944.

Otway, Terence, *Airborne Forces*, London: Imperial War Museum, 1990.

Peters, Mike, and Buist, Luke, *Glider Pilots at Arnhem*, Barnsley: Pen & Sword, 2009.

Ryan, Cornelius, *A Bridge Too Far*, Ware: Wordsworth, 1999.

Index

INDEX OF PEOPLE

Williams, Brigadier Edgar 'Bill' 30-31
Williams, Lt L. J. 164-165
Williams, Major-General Paul 24, 28, 41, 45-48, 51

Wimmer, *Hauptmann* Johann 90-91

Zgorzelski, Lieutenant Colonel Władysław 226, 230, 239

INDEX OF PLACES

INDEX OF ALLIED MILITARY UNITS & FORMATIONS

INDEX OF GERMAN MILITARY UNITS & FORMATIONS

INDEX OF GENERAL & MISCELLANEOUS TERMS

Wolverhampton Military Studies

www.helion.co.uk/wolverhamptonmilitarystudies

Editorial board

Submissions

The publishers would be pleased to receive submissions for this series. Please contact us via email (info@helion.co.uk), or in writing to Helion & Company Limited, 26 Willow Road, Solihull, West Midlands, B91 1UE.

Titles

No.1 *Stemming the Tide. Officers and Leadership in the British Expeditionary Force 1914* Edited by Spencer Jones (ISBN 978-1-909384-45-3)

No.2 *'Theirs Not To Reason Why'. Horsing the British Army 1875–1925* Graham Winton (ISBN 978-1-909384-48-4)

No.3 *A Military Transformed? Adaptation and Innovation in the British Military, 1792–1945* Edited by Michael LoCicero, Ross Mahoney and Stuart Mitchell (ISBN 978-1-909384-46-0)

No.4 *Get Tough Stay Tough. Shaping the Canadian Corps, 1914–1918* Kenneth Radley (ISBN 978-1-909982-86-4)

No.5 *A Moonlight Massacre: The Night Operation on the Passchendaele Ridge, 2 December 1917. The Forgotten Last Act of the Third Battle of Ypres* Michael LoCicero (ISBN 978-1-909982-92-5)

No.6 *Shellshocked Prophets. Former Anglican Army Chaplains in Interwar Britain* Linda Parker (ISBN 978-1-909982-25-3)

No.7 *Flight Plan Africa: Portuguese Airpower in Counterinsurgency, 1961–1974* John P. Cann (ISBN 978-1-909982-06-2)

No.8 *Mud, Blood and Determination. The History of the 46th (North Midland) Division in the Great War* Simon Peaple (ISBN 978 1 910294 66 6)

Lightning Source UK Ltd.
Milton Keynes UK
UKHW021646190619
344678UK00003B/300/P